Learning to Spe ...istian

Also by Stanley Hauerwas and published by SCM Press

Hannah's Child: A Theologian's Memoir
The Peaceable Kingdom
With the Grain of the Universe
Wilderness Wanderings
SCM Theological Commentary Matthew

Learning to Speak Christian

Stanley Hauerwas

scm press

This edition published in 2011 by SCM Press
Editorial office
13–17 Long Lane,
London, EC1A 9PN, UK

SCM Press is an imprint of Hymns Ancient & Modern Ltd
(a registered charity)
13A Hellesdon Park Road, Norwich,
Norfolk, NR6 5DR, UK

Published in the United States in 2011 as *Working with Words: On Learning to
Speak Christian* by Cascade Books, An Imprint of Wipf and Stock Publishers,
199 W. 8th Ave., Suite 3
Eugene, OR 9740

www.scmpress.co.uk

British Library Cataloguing in Publication data

A catalogue record for this book is available
from the British Library

978-0-334-04409-3
Kindle edition: 978-0-334-04451-2

To the Church of the Holy Family

and the Rector Search Committee:

Joe Bongiovi, Carl Fox, Adam Grobin, Bob Houghtlin, Verlene Kuoni, Cathy Leslie, Anne Liptzin, Martha Mundy, John Paul, J. R. Rigby, Susan Sunnarborg, Lisa Worster (Chair), and Sheryl Forbis (Clerk)

Contents

Contents

III. Habits of Speech Exemplified: Some Teachers

Preface

In *Hannah's Child: A Theologian's Memoir* I suggested—or is confessed the better description?—that I write because writing is the only way I know how to think.[1] That is not quite true. I am able to write, or I find I feel I have to write, because I read. Reading is also one of the ways I learn how to think. I am often asked how I have written so much. The only explanation, and it is not clear to me that it is an explanation, is that my writing is determined by my reading. Which means that I hope others will write about what I have written about because they have read what I have read.

I open with these remarks about the relation between my writing and reading to justify yet another book by Hauerwas. The world probably does not need another book by me. Yet I have generous readers who tell me they benefit not only from what I write about, but also from the way I write about it. In his memoir, *Little Did I Know: Excerpts from Memory*, Stanley Cavell, in reaction to those philosophers who find his work "unpalatable," asks, "What choice does one have over the way one writes?"[2] Cavell suggests that the way one writes "will have to create its own public," which he goes on to say, "may never be exactly public."

I have never written or tried to write with the studied style of a Cavell, but my work now has a "public." "My public" has a name. They are called Christians. Thank God that public does not depend on or

---

1. Hauerwas, *Hannah's Child*, 235. In a lovely blurb for the English edition of *Hannah's Child*, John Milbank observes that the book had to be written because "Hauerwas's work of writing and his work on himself are so clearly, as with Michel de Montaigne, one and the same." Though it is humbling to be compared with Montaigne I am sure Milbank is right.

2. Cavell, *Little Did I Know*, 442.

wait with baited breathe for the next installment of "my work." But I am aware that I now have many readers who are interested in what and how I think. That they exist is the only justification I have for putting this rag-tagged book of essays together.

Learning to Speak Christian is a "kitchen sink" book. These essays, sermons, and opinion pieces were not meant to, nor do I think they add up to, anything so grand as "an argument." I have the hope, however, that the reader will discover that I have only been able to preach this sermon because I had written that essay. In other words, I hope the reader will see how everything I write is interdependent. This collection of essays and sermons—and some may think all my books are but collections—makes no pretence that by being collected they are more than the sum of their parts. But I think the reader will also discover that they are not less than the sum of their parts.

What I offer the reader in this book is my explicit reflection and exhibition of what it means for theology to be work and, in particular, work with words. For it is my conviction that the work of the theologian is word work, or, as John Howard Yoder would have it, the task of theology is "working with words in the light of faith."[3] Accordingly, Yoder describes the approach he takes in *Preface to Theology* as inductive and historical—that is, he invites his students (and readers) to watch Christians at work doing theology to see what they can learn from those who have tried to do theology in the past.

"Tried" is a crucial word, because the theological task requires that we speak of God, but the God to whom and about whom we must speak defies the words we use. This defiance seems odd because the God about whom we must speak is, we believe, found decisively in Jesus of Nazareth, very God and very man. Yet it seems the closer God draws near to us the more we discover that we know not how to say "God." The same is true even when we invoke the Holy Spirit who draws us into God's very life.

According to Yoder, theology has a double function: (1) to transmit the heritage of the faith without deforming it; and (2) to speak to questions that arise in a new context.[4] There will always be a new

---

3. Yoder, *Preface to Theology*, 41.

4. Ibid., 228.

context, however, not only because the world cannot be kept still, but because the very character of God requires that those who worship God be witnesses. The missionary character of the church, therefore, means that the testing of the words we use as well as their grammar can never be finished. Rather the words we use, the relation between the words we use, and the character of the speaker who uses the words must be continually tested for their faithfulness to the Gospel.

Yoder observes that one of the characteristics of our times is the presumption that theology no longer has a dictionary adequate to its task. But Yoder argues, rightly I think, that an adequate dictionary has never existed. Yet some under the illusion that such a dictionary once existed lose confidence in our language because they are forced to recognize that there is no single correct grammar. Rather than despair about our linguistic limits, however, Yoder agues that we should take this as an opportunity to stop asking what we take to be a timeless philosophical question. Rather than ask, "How can we have perfect knowledge that would free us from finitude?" we should be inquiring as to how "God has chosen to use our human weakness, including the weakness of our linguistic and literary tools, for God's purposes." For whatever the philosophical inadequacy of language as a tool may be, "there still remains the historic usefulness and indispensability of language as a tool."[5]

When theology is done well the reader should be led to think, "This is true." Recognizing claims that are "true" enables readers to identify an honest expression of life's complexities. The trick is to show that the theological claims, the words that must be used to speak of God, are necessary if the theologian is to speak honestly of the complexities of life. The worst betrayal of the task of theology comes when the theologian fears that the words he or she must use are not necessary. The result too often is a desperate shouting. One of the reasons I so enjoy Barth is that there is nothing desperate about his theology; rather it is a joyful celebration of the unending task of theology.

5. Ibid., 370–71. As far as I know, Yoder did not read Wittgenstein, but these observations cannot help but remind me of Wittgenstein's remark that "philosophy is a struggle against the bewitchment of our understanding by the resources of language" (*Philosophical Investigations*, 109). This remark is often read to suggest that language is the tool in the struggle against bewitchment, but Wittgenstein seems also to suggest that it is language that bewitches us. Thus Yoder's suggestion that the only way to deal with our linguistic "weaknesses" is with language.

But is that what we really mean when we say, "This is true"? Did I not say that theology is speech about God? How can theology at once be about God and about the complexities of human life? Has it not been one of the besetting problems of modern theology to try to split the difference between speech about God and the complexities of human life, too often resulting in most theology being more about "us" than about God? Is not speech about God less about God but rather speech in praise of or prayer to God? How can it really be true that some words are necessary if we are to speak truthfully about ourselves and God? Does that not give the theologian unwarranted power in the life of the church?

These are all good questions making it difficult to know where to start. But it is a good place to begin, as I hope many of the essays in this book suggest, to remember that there is no place to start. We can only begin with what we have been given, and the "givens" come in all shapes and sizes. This does not mean we are at the mercy of the "givens" because the givens are too various, contradictory, and ambiguous to determine us without a fight. The word "God" is among the givens, but it is also true that God cannot be taken for granted, which requires us to rethink the givens.

"God" is a necessary word, but its necessity makes it subject to misuse. Those who believe in God and those who do not believe in God too often assume that they are using the same word. But if they happen to do so that would be a great achievement because as I try to show in a number of the essays and sermons learning to use the word "God" requires that one learn to use the words that surround the use of the word "God." For Christians, we learn to use the word through our worship and prayer to the one called God, and this requires a lifetime. Thus the process of learning entails a transformation so that we can hear rightly before speaking rightly; our pride must be humbled and our impatience tempered if we are to hear the storied words that enable us to speak of God.

Furthermore, the matter of rightly learning to speak of God becomes more complicated because "God" is not the first word Christians have to say when we pray. Rather Christians pray to the Father, the Son, and the Holy Spirit. "God" is the name we use to indicate the love that constitutes the relation Jesus and His Father share through the work of the Spirit. "God" is the word, the description, used to celebrate the

Father's sending of the Son and the Son's obedience to the Father's will so that the work of the Spirit might be fulfilled by judging the world in truth. We only know what it means to say "God" because we have been taught by Jesus to pray to the Father.

It is my hope that these essays and sermons exhibit the training necessary to say "God." Learning to say "God," as I suggested at the beginning, is hard but good work. It is good work because the training necessary to say "God" forces us to be honest with ourselves about the way things are. We are creatures destined to die. We fear ourselves and one another, sensing that we are more than willing to sacrifice the lives of others to sustain our fantasy that we can get out of life alive. The widespread confidence that medicine will someday free us of the necessity of death exemplifies what I mean by "fantasy." The attempt to create a medicine aimed to get us out of life alive, moreover, depends on the creation of wealth as an end in itself. A people constituted by such wealth are by definition unable to learn to use the word "God," because wealth cannot help but make us dull.

I need to be clear. I am not suggesting that the individual wealthy person is dull. Rather I am suggesting that a social order bent on producing wealth as an end in itself cannot avoid producing people whose souls are superficial and whose daily lives are captured by sentimentalities. They ask questions like, "Why does a good god let bad things happen to good people?" Such a people cannot imagine what kind of people would write and sing the Psalms.

Learning to say "God" requires that I learn to acknowledge that I am a "dependent rational animal."[6] It may be possible to acknowledge that we are rational dependent animals without learning to say "God," but to learn to say I am dependent without regret at least creates the space the practice of prayer can occupy. To be human is to be an animal that has learned to pray. Prayer often comes only when we have no alternatives left, but prayer may also be the joy that comes from the acknowledgment of the sheer beauty, the absolute contingency, of existence.

So this kitchen sink of a book hopefully provides examples of my writing, my work, and, in particular, my attempt to work on myself so that I might be a more adequate Christian speaker. I do not intend to

6. An obvious reference to MacIntyre's *Dependent Rational Animals*.

make a long book longer by "explaining" why I have included this or that essay or sermon. This is a collection, not a book, though I am not sure I know how to control that distinction. What is here is here because it is my work. I make no apologies.

I have followed the good suggestions of Father Nathaniel Lee about how the essays might be grouped, but I am sure many readers may think after they have read the book that they know better than me how I should have organized the book. If you do come to such a judgment all I ask is you let me know. God knows I need all the help I can get.

I do ask, however, that readers remember that this is a collection and that there is a rationale for the grouping of the essays. For example, the essays and sermons in the first section of the book try to address questions of learning to say "God." The essays and sermons in the middle section, "The Language of Love," can be characterized as those that deal with more "normative" matters. The last section of the book is about people and movements (Methodism and Roman Catholic Social Encyclicals) that have taught me how to do theology.

I have included the Appendix, "On Learning to See Red Wheel Barrows," because Carole Baker recently discovered a way to reclaim it from the misbegotten attempt to make the *Journal of the American Academy of Religion* an online journal. I have been asked so many times for a copy of the essay, a copy I did not have, I thought I would include it so that those determined to read what I write, a category of human beings for whom I am very grateful, would finally have it in an accessible form.

I confess that I have included a number of the essays in *Learning to Speak Christian* because I hope they might counter some of the mischaracterizations of my work. You would think by now that I would recognize that the more I publish, the more misunderstandings I encourage, but I am a stubborn person. It is my fondest hope that by making these essays and sermons available some may find by reading them that they have learned better how to speak Christian.

Acknowledgments

As usual I need to thank Carole Baker for all that she has done to make this book possible. She has not only worked with the individual essays but she's also made important suggestions for the overall book. I am also indebted to Nathaniel Jung-Chul Lee for his help in bringing together these essays. I would like to thank Charlie Collier and the wonderful people at Cascade Books for not only publishing this book but for the many fine books they publish in Christian theology. Timothy Kimbrough became dean of Christ Church Cathedral in Nashville, Tennessee, after having served Church of the Holy Family for twenty-one years. I was privileged to be asked by the vestry to serve on the search committee for a new rector for Holy Family. I've never been around a more remarkable group of people. They never asked who I liked, but rather prayed to be able to discern who God was sending Holy Family. I am convinced prayer makes all the difference in any search.

I. Learning Christian: To See and to Speak

1

Look at It and Live

A Sermon for Goodson Chapel
Duke Divinity School
March 26, 2009

Numbers 21:4–9
Psalm 107:1–3, 17–22
Ephesians 2:1–10
John 3:14–21

How odd of God to save this way. The people of Israel were very un-happy and so, as was their habit, they began complaining: "Why have you brought us up out of Egypt to die in the wilderness? For there is no food and no water, and we detest this miserable food." Things weren't good; the people of Israel discovered, however, that things could get worse. Miserable food is one thing, but how would they survive the threat of snake bites?

The Lord had sent the poisonous serpents because the people were complaining not only about Moses, but this time we are told they even "spoke against God." Not confident in their ability to intercede with God, they begged Moses to ask the Lord to take the serpents away. Moses did as he was asked, praying that God would save those he had led through the wilderness. We do not know the content of Moses' prayer, but one assumes he asked God to get rid of the serpents. But God did not take the serpents away. Instead he told Moses to make a replica of a poisonous serpent, set it on a pole, and if anyone bitten by a serpent looked upon Moses' snake they would live.

Moses did as he was told. He made a serpent of bronze, put it on a pole, and those who had been bitten by a serpent were saved by looking on Moses' creation. How odd of God to save this way. Surely it would have made more sense to do what the people of Israel asked, that is, just get rid of the serpents! God let Patrick drive the snakes out of Ireland, so it is possible to get rid of the snakes. I have never understood why God could not have seen fit to send a Patrick to Texas. But then, even Texans know that they are not God's promised people.

It remains a mystery, at least it remains a mystery for me, why God choose to save those who were bitten by the snakes by having them look at the bronze serpent. Even though it is usually not a good idea to second-guess God, I cannot help but wonder why God would save those bitten by the poisonous serpents this way. Why should the people of Israel look at this inanimate object for their salvation?

To look, to see, to *really* see, is never easy. In particular it is never easy to see death. You cannot help but be sympathetic with the people of Israel. They are being asked to look on, to see, that which threatens their very existence. To live they must look on death itself: "Look on death and live."

Philosophers have often reflected on the seeming paradox that we only come to life through the acknowledgment of death. Montaigne even entitled one of his essays, "To do philosophy is to learn to die." I suspect there is much to be learned from philosophers about the significance of death, as well as how to die, but I do not think God's command to Moses to make the serpent was meant to make the people of Israel more philosophical. Rather it was a reminder of what it means to be chosen by God.

To be called by God is serious business. To be God's people is a life-and-death matter. God would not have his people, his promised people, presume that by being his chosen they are free of danger. We are all individually and collectively going to die. "Dust you are and to dust you shall return." But the death Israel faces is not just any death; it is a death determined by her being God's beloved. The story of Israel is the story of her training to become a people whose survival depends on learning to trust God in a snake-infested world.

How odd of God to save this way. Jesus said to Nicodemus, "Just as Moses lifted up the serpent in the wilderness, so must the Son of Man be lifted up, that whoever believes in him may have eternal life." Jesus will be lifted up, but he is first lifted high on the cross. We are told he must die in this way because by being "lifted up from the earth" he will draw all people to him (John 12:32–33). Just as Israel had to look on the serpent to live, so now it seems we must look on this man's death if we are to have life.

Yet we cannot help but think that Jesus on the cross is surely of a different order than Moses' serpent. Jesus was lifted high on the cross, but the cross could not hold him. He will be raised from the dead to ascend to the Father. We know the cross could not hold him because we are, after all, Protestants. Our cross is empty. Our Jesus won. We do not need to look at him dying on the cross.

In fact, we are not sure we need to look on the cross at all. "God so loved the world that he gave his only Son, so that everyone who believes in him may not perish but have eternal life." Here we are not told to look but to believe. We believe, moreover, if we believe hard enough that we will not have to worry about the snakes. We assume God has done for us what God did not do for Israel. He got rid of the snakes.

That our cross is empty, therefore, tempts us to believe that we are a people no longer in danger. After all, when it is all said and done, as John 3:16 makes clear, it is all about love. God so loved the world that we might love one another. Accordingly we find it rather hard to understand the dramatic tension in the Gospel of John between those who choose to remain in the dark and those who love the light. Indeed we are told that those who love the darkness will hate those who are the light. Why should anyone hate a people who just want to be lovers?

It is all about love—and death. The light has come into the world, but the light that illumines from the cross does not rid the world of snakes. Eternal life does not mean that we escape death, but that even in death we will not be abandoned by Jesus. Like the people of Israel who had been bitten by the poisonous snakes, we must learn to trust God by looking on the cross of Christ. We are to look on the cross of Christ and see there the goodness of our God. He has taken into his life our love of the darkness so that we might live in the light of his cross.

To believe that God so loved the world he gave his only Son requires, therefore, that we look on the cross. To look and to believe are inseparable. We must see, moreover, that the cross is not empty. Jesus died on the cross. When we try to avoid that reality, when we believe without looking at our crucified God, I fear the ever-present temptation to Gnosticism is irresistible. Gnosticism, as Gillian Rose reminds us, is the normal spiritual condition, a condition almost unavoidable in modernity, for those who assume that salvation is to know without looking.

We must look, therefore, on the cross through which our salvation comes. But to look, to see, to *really* see, is never easy. We are tempted, particularly when we think we are no longer threatened by poisonous snakes, to stare at rather than to see Jesus on the cross. The empty cross has its own peculiar problems, but neither can a crucifix ensure we will avoid looking on the cross as a spectator; that is, even in looking at his crucified body we face the temptation to think the cross is God's attempt to resolve a problem peculiar to being God.

The temptation to become a spectator at the crucifixion is a particular problem around a divinity school. Here you learn that you need an atonement theory. Unable to decide which theory does justice to the scriptural witness or your experience, you will probably pick and choose depending on circumstance. Such theories may have their uses, but I fear too often they tempt us to stare rather than to look at the cross. Thus the presumption by some that our salvation demands we believe that the cross is the Father's infliction of violence upon the Son, who receives it on our behalf.

Such a view, I fear, leads many who say they believe "God so loved the world" to use that claim as a weapon against those they assume do not believe that God has so loved the world. They want the cross to be the sign through which their enemies are defeated rather than that which makes possible our love of the enemy. They refuse to acknowledge, as Augustine suggests, that on the cross Christ forgave those who reviled him "because he accepted the cross not as a test of power but as an example of patience. There he healed our wounds by bearing his own. There he healed us of an eternal death because he deigned to die a temporal death."

In his Letter to the Ephesians, Paul names the conditions necessary for us to see, to really see, the crucifixion. If we are to look on the cross and live we must recognize that we "were dead through the trespasses and sins in which [we] once lived." To look on the cross of Christ means we are able to see that we have been ruled by the power of sin making us "by nature children of wrath." Like the people of Israel we have been bitten by the snake, and it is not at all clear we will survive. When life itself is at stake we cannot be disinterested observers.

But notice Paul does not leave the matter there. To look on the cross is not an invitation to wallow in our sinfulness. Rather to look on the cross means the end of our fascination with sin. By grace we have been saved, made alive with Christ. And this means we have been raised up with him—even to being seated in heavenly places with Christ Jesus. Just as Moses lifted up the serpent in the wilderness so the Son of Man has been lifted up that we might also be for the world a light, a witness, of God's love for the world. To be raised with Christ means the end of any attempt to passively stare at the crucifixion. You cannot stare at that in which you participate.

An extraordinary claim to be sure but one I think to be true. For it turns out that in the process of learning to see, to *really* see, the life we are given through Jesus' death we become a people bronzed and lifted up by God so that the world may see there is an alternative to being captives of death. We are invited, therefore, not only to look on the cross and live, but to eat this bread and drink this wine which becomes for us Christ's body and blood. In this meal we are consumed by what we consume, and, therefore, we participate in the mystery of God's salvation of the world. How odd of God to save the world this way, that is, by making us his church. But then it is best not to second-guess God.

2

Seeing Darkness, Hearing Silence: Augustine's Account of Evil*

The question of why evil exists is not a theological question, for it assumes that it is possible to go behind the existence forced upon us as sinners. If we could answer it then *we* would not be sinners. We could make something else responsible. Therefore the "question of why" can always only be answered with the "that," which burdens man completely.

The theological question does not arise about the origin of evil but about the real overcoming of evil on the Cross; it asks for the forgiveness of guilt, for the reconciliation of the fallen world.[1]

—DIETRICH BONHOEFFER

The Attraction of Evil

"After one of my many presentations following my return from Rwanda, a Canadian Forces padre asked me how, after all I had seen and expe-

* This essay, like "God and Goodness: A Theological Exploration," was written because my good colleague in Political Science, Ruth Grant, organized interdisciplinary faculty seminars on evil and goodness.

1. Bonhoeffer, *Creation and Fall*, 78. I am indebted to Charles Mathewes for calling my attention to this passage in Bonhoeffer. See Mathewes, *Evil and the Augustinian Tradition*, 201.

rienced, I could still believe in God. I answered that I know there is a God because in Rwanda I shook hands with the devil. I have seen him, I have smelled him and I have touched him. I know that the devil exists, and therefore I know there is a God. *Peux ce que veux. Allons-y.*"[2] Lt. General Romeo Dallaire, a French-Canadian Catholic who was the force commander of the UN Assistance Mission for Rwanda, discovered the significance of his faith in Rwanda. Prior to Rwanda he was a conventional Catholic, but in Rwanda he found that without his Catholicism he could not comprehend the evil he saw there.

General Dallaire's story of his attempt to contain the genocide in Rwanda is a sad and tragic tale. That he thinks he "shook hands with the devil" in Rwanda is understandable, but theologically a mistake. Christians do not believe in God because we think God is necessary if we are to comprehend the reality of evil. Rather the Christian belief in God requires that we do not believe in the reality of evil or the devil.[3] Robert Jenson observes that Karl Barth, the theologian in modernity who is usually credited with restoring Christian "orthodoxy," puzzled

---

2. Dallaire, *Shake Hands with the Devil*, xviii. For an appreciative account of General Dallaire's attempt to prevent the genocide in Rwanda, see Power, "Hero of Our Time," 8–11.

3. In *Death of Satan*, Andrew Delbanco notes John Wesley's remark that because there is "no devil" there is "no God." Delbanco then observes that "we want satan back because God depends on him. This is because the essence of religious faith is the idea of transcendence, a concept that contains within itself the idea of its opposite—as in its two Latin elements (*trans-*beyond or over, and *scandere*, to climb or to scale): limitation, boundedness, the thing to be transcended. As an American evangelical put it a few decades after Wesley, 'in all . . . instances of God's permitting sin, he had a view to the manifestation of himself'" (228–29). I greatly admire Delbanco's book, but I think that he has allowed himself to be misled by bad Christian theology. Wesley (if he said what Delbanco attributes to him) was wrong, as is the evangelical Delbanco quotes who suggests God permits sin to manifest himself. To believe that sin can determine the character of God is to make sin more interesting than God—a problem Milton knew well. Just to the extent you let the devil become a major character in a play, the devil threatens to become the main character. The assumption that sin precedes salvation mimics the Protestant revival tradition that assumed that people would only "come to Christ" by first being convinced of their sin. As a result sin determined the character of grace resulting in quite distorted views of what the crucifixion is about. Sacrificial theories of the atonement often betray a quite crass understanding of the Trinity. That is why, moreover, it is very important not to let abstract notions of "transcendence" become an attribute of God in and of itself. You know you are on your way to deism when the most important thing you can say about God is that God is transcendent.

ordinary minds by saying the devil was a myth. Jenson notes that "Barth's point was that *not* believing in the devil is the appropriate relation to the devil's mode of existence. That the devil is a myth does not mean, in Barth's thinking, that the devil does not exist; it means that he exists in a particular way, as the ordained object of denial."[4]

That many, Christian and non-Christian alike, find the traditional Christian denial of the existence of evil unintelligible is but an indication of the pathos of Christianity in modernity. Many, like General Dallaire, think if Christianity is intelligible it is so because it helps us name what has gone wrong with our world. Christian and non-Christian now believe that even if we do not share a common belief in God we can at least agree about actions that are evil.[5] Accordingly modern accounts of morality are determined by agreements about what constitutes inhumanity.[6] But ironically just to the extent that Christians un-

4. Jenson, "Nihilism," 4. Barth's extended discussion of evil and the devil can be found in his *Church Dogmatics* III/3, 289–68. In answer to the question of "what is real nothingness?," Barth observes that only God and His creature really "are," and nothingness is neither God nor his creature. But Barth also thinks it would be foolhardy to conclude that evil is therefore nothing, i.e., that it does not exist. God strives against evil and overcomes it. "If God's reality and revelation are known in His presence and action in Jesus Christ, he is also known as the God who is confronted by nothingness, for whom it constitutes a problem, who takes it seriously, who does not deal with it incidentally but in the fullness of the glory of His deity, who is not engaged indirectly or mediately but which His whole being, involving Himself to the utmost. If we accept this, we cannot argue that because it (evil) has nothing in common with God and His creature nothingness is nothing, i.e., it does not exist. That which confronts God in this way, and is seriously treated by Him, is surely not nothing or non-existent. In the light of God's relationship to it we must accept the fact that in a third way of its own nothingness 'is.' All conceptions or doctrine which would deny or minimize this 'is' are untenable from the Christian standpoint. Nothingness is not nothing" (349). Though Barth's position may seem antithetical to Augustine's contention that evil does not exist, I hope to show there is little difference between Augustine's and Barth's accounts of evil.

5. No one has better described our inability in modernity to come to terms with evil than Delbanco in *Death of Satan*. Delbanco tells the story of what he calls "the advance of secular rationality in the United States," which he associates with the assumption that "no story about the intrinsic meaning of the world has universal validity" (221). As a result he believes "our culture is now in crisis because evil remains an inescapable experience for all of us, while we no longer have a symbolic language for describing it. Sontag herself expressed the crisis in the form of a question: 'How,' she asks, can we find our moral bearings 'when we have a sense of evil but no longer the religious or philosophical language to talk intelligently about evil'" (224).

6. Jonathan Glover is one of the best representatives of this way of thinking about

derwrite the high humanism that sustains the confidence that in spite of our differences we share common intuitions about evil makes the Christian faith in God unintelligible. One cannot help but be sympathetic to those like General Dallaire who have seen a violence beyond belief, but his very ability to be truthful about what he has seen is not because he has certainly seen the devil but because, as is clear from his book, he was sustained by the practice of morning prayer.

In a book entitled *Naming the Silences: God, Medicine, and the Problem of Suffering*, I argued that the question "Why does a good God allow bad things to happen to good people?" is not a question that those whose lives have been formed by the Psalms have any reason to ask.[7]

---

the nature of morality. He observes, "The prospects of reviving belief in a moral law are dim. Looking for an external validation of morality is less effective than building breakwaters. Morality could be abandoned, or it can be recreated. It may survive in a more defensible form when seen to be a human creation. We can shape it consciously to serve people's needs and interests, and to reflect the things we most care about. In trying to answer Nietzsche, I assume that a central part of morality should be concerned with avoiding repetition of man-made disasters of the kind the Nazis brought about" (*Humanity*, 41). I think Glover's use of "example" is exemplary as a way to do "ethics" after the end of "modernity." He is quite well aware that the humanism spawned by the Enlightenment too often resulted in the deepest inhumanity. See, for example, his account of modern utopias and, in particular, communism (310–27). However, Augustine's understanding of evil as privation would call into question Glover's assumption that atrocities could be named abstracted from assumptions about human flourishing. Augustine would think without an account of the good we would be more likely to fail to see or name atrocities. What was needed prior to the rise of National Socialism was more than an awareness that genocide was evil. What was needed was a way of life that could illumine the tiny steps, all the banal evils, that made genocide possible. I owe this way of criticizing Glover to Charlie Collier.

7. Hauerwas, *Naming the Silences*, 56–58. The book is still in print but the publishers thought *Naming the Silences* was too obscure and was hurting the sales of the book. So the book is now entitled with the subtitle.

The Psalms, for Jew and Christian, is the text for reflection on evil. For example, consider these words of the great Jewish theologian, Andre Chouraqui, in his Introduction to the Psalms: "It is not long before we meet the Prince of Darkness on the path of wickedness. The Psalter provides him with a frightful identity card that includes no less than a hundred and twelve names, surnames, titles, and qualities. He is essentially the Racha', the one who is unable to face God's judgment, the Reprobate. He is not a single or particular individual, but the very entity of evil under all its various visages. He is the opulent, the wealthy, the despoiler, the worker of sin, the man with the heart puffed up . . . as we know so well. He is the enemy of justice, the man oblivious to God; the oppressor, the adversary of peace. He wields the Scepter of Evil; he is the Accuser, so styled by his name in Hebrew; *Satan*. His name defines his works to good effect. The Psalter describes them to us in minute detail. The father of nothingness

Suffering, even the suffering occasioned by the death of a child, does not constitute for Christians a theodical problem. In *Theology and the Problem of Evil*, Ken Surin rightly argues that theodicy is a peculiar modern development that unfortunately shapes how many now read the Psalms as well as the book of Job.[8] The realism of the Psalms and the book of Job depends on the presumption that God is God and we are not. When Christians think theodical justifications are needed to justify the ways of God at the bar of a justice determined by us, you can be sure that the god Christians now worship is not the God of Israel and Jesus Christ.[9]

In *Naming the Silences* I suggested that the very presumption that a crisis of faith is created when "bad things happen to good people" indicates that the God whom Christians are alleged to believe has been confused with a god whose task is primarily to put us, that is, human beings, on the winning side of history. In sum, I argue that in modernity

> a mechanistic metaphysic is combined with a sentimental ac-
> count of God; in this way the pagan assumption that god or the
> gods are to be judged by how well it or they insure the success-
> ful outcome of human purposes is underwritten in the name of
> Christianity. It is assumed that the attributes of such a god or
> gods can be known and characterized abstractly. But the God of
> Abraham, Isaac, and Jacob is not the god that creates something

---

incarnates a radical inadequacy, and emptiness; and his works are the perfect likeness of the one who fathers them. His every word consummates a lie; his every action, a deed of violence." Chouraqui, "The Psalms," 119–20. I think it is not an accident that this "Introduction" written originally in 1956 is reprinted in a Cistercian journal. The lives of monks are formed by the Psalms. I am indebted to Ellen Davis for calling Chouraqui's work to my attention.

8. Surin, *Theology and the Problem of Evil.*

9. Tilley offers the most thorough critique of the Christian appropriations of theo-dicies in his *Evils of Theodicy*. Tilley argues that theodicies often assume a utopian view of the world in which all evils would be effaced. "The reason," according to Tilley, "that a monstrous generalization, or a staggering lie, can pass where a more restricted claim would be challenged is not only that it stabilizes an inherently unstable world by declaring it stable, but that it displays a world which we wished existed, a world in which evil was manageable, if not by us, at least by God. This is why the vast assertion, the mighty lie, overwhelms our faculties and puts our art of criticism out of action: it holds out the boon of stability and fulfills our wishes" (248–49). Jesus's words from the cross, "My God, my God, why have you forsaken me?" should be sufficient to render all attempts at theodicy jejune. For my reflections on the seven words from the cross, see *Cross-Shattered Christ.*

called the "problem of evil"; rather, that problem is created by a god about which the most important facts seem to be that it exists and is morally perfect as well as all-powerful—that is, the kind of god that emperors need to legitimate the "necessity" of their rule.[10]

In *The Evils of Theodicy*, Terrence Tilley suggests that those who engage in the theodical project "participate in the practice of legitimating the coercive and marginalizing ecclesio-political structure which is the heritage of Constantinian Christianity."[11] Once Christianity had become the established religion of the empire, Christians had a stake in justifying that the way things are is the way things are meant to be. But that project has now decisively come to an end. So it is not God that is the subject of theodicy, but the human. That is why the crucial theodical question today is not "Why does a good god allow bad things to happen to good people?" but rather "Why has medicine not cured cancer?" Medicine has become the institution in modernity dedicated to saving the appearances; that is, we look to medicine to create a world in which we can entertain the illusion that it may be possible to get out of life alive.[12] That is why one of the legitimating functions of modern states is to promise to provide the best medical care available.

If, as Tilley suggests, theodicy is a project of established orders, to turn to Augustine as the representative figure who taught Christians how to think about evil may seem strange. Augustine is often credited with providing the theological rationale for the development of Constantinian Christianity.[13] However, I hope to show that Augustine's understanding of the non-existence of evil not only is how Christians should think about evil, but also, in the world we currently inhabit, represents a challenge to those who would rule the world in the name of human "progress." Such a rule—that is, rule in the name of securing a future free from suffering in the name of humanity—is a secular

10. Hauerwas, *Naming the Silences*, 56–58.

11. Tilley, *Evils of Theodicy*, 136.

12. Ernest Becker argues that theodicy in modernity is not about the justification of God in the face of evil, but rather an attempt to explain why evil continues to exist in the absence of God. Becker names the latter effort "anthropodicy." See his *Structure of Evil*, 18.

13. See, for example, Alasdair MacIntyre's account of the relation of Augustine's theology to the papacy of Gregory VII in his *Whose Justice? Which Rationality?* 152–63.

version of what Constantinianism was for Christians.[14] Accordingly, Augustine's understanding of evil cannot help but be a political challenge to secular forms of Constantinianisms.

Augustine on Evil

In the *Enchiridion*, a text Augustine wrote around 423 at the request of a layman, Laurentius, for a handbook that would sum up essential Christian teachings, Augustine provides his most considered judgment on evil. According to Augustine, there can be no evil

> where there is no good. This leads us to the surprising conclusion: that since every being, in so far as it is a being, is good, if we then say that a defective thing is bad, it would seem to mean that we are saying that evil is good, that only what is good is ever evil and that there is no evil apart from something good. This is because every actual entity is good [*omnis natura bonum est*]. Nothing evil exists *in itself*, but only as an evil aspect of some actual entity. Therefore, there can be nothing evil except something is good. Absurd as this sounds, nevertheless the logical connections of the argument compel us to it as inevitable.[15]

In his *Confessions*, written soon after Augustine became a bishop (397), he anticipated this passage from the *Enchiridion* when he suggested that evil simply does not exist. He argues that:

> we must conclude that if things are deprived of all good, they cease altogether to be; and this means that as long as they are, they are good. Therefore, whatever is, is good; and evil, the origin of which I was trying to find, is not a substance, because if it were a substance, it would be good. For either it would be an

---

14. In *With the Grain of the Universe*, I argued that William James rightly understood that the implication of a Darwinian world is that our lives are but the reflection of chance. It was only after I read Louis Menand's *Metaphysical Club* that I began to understand the significance of the Civil War for why James (and Oliver Wendell Holmes) would find Darwin but a confirmation of what the war meant for them. In *Death of Satan*, Delbanco also calls attention to the significance of the Civil War for underwriting the conviction that our lives are constituted by "dumb luck" (144–53). Delbanco also thinks William James to be the American who quite clearly articulated the "pervasive pathology of modern life: the fear of annihilation" (163).

15. Augustine, *Confessions and Enchiridion*, 344, 4.4. My references to Augustine's work will first give the page number followed by chapter and paragraph numbers.

incorruptible substance of the supreme order of goodness, or it would be a corruptible substance which would not be corruptible unless it were good. So it became obvious to me that all that you have made is good, and that there are no substances whatsoever that were not made by you. And because you did not make them all equal, each single thing is good and collectively they are very good, for our God made his whole creation *very good.*[16]

I am convinced that Augustine has rightly said what any Christian should say about evil; that is, ontologically evil does not exist. Such a view, however, many find counter-intuitive. How can you say evil does not exist when, like General Dallaire, you have witnessed a genocide? I think Augustine has a very persuasive response to such a query, but to understand his response we need to appreciate how he came to his conclusion, a conclusion he says was forced on him by logic—that is, that evil is always parasitical on the good. I have no doubt that Augustine found himself driven to this conclusion by "logic," but Augustine's logic requires a narrative that takes the form of the story—namely, the "confession" of his sin. This means, I think, that you cannot understand Augustine's account of evil without following his account in the *Confessions* of how he came through his involvement with the Manichees as well as the Platonists to the conclusion that evil is nothing.

It is not accidental that the only way Augustine has to display how he came to understand that evil is nothing was by providing a narrative of how he arrived at that judgment.[17] That a narrative was required rightly suggests that to understand properly why evil does not exist requires a transformation of the self that takes the form of a story. Moreover, that a narrative is required for us rightly to understand the parasitical character of evil is not only true of our individual lives but is also required if we are to make sense of our collective existence as well as the cosmos. Christians believe the recognition of evil is possible because God never leaves us without hope. That is, hope makes possible the ability to take the next step necessary to discover that we are not

---

16. Augustine, *Confessions*, 148, 7.12.

17. Some years ago I wrote an article with David Burrell in which we used Augustine's *Confessions* as a paradigm for arguments concerning the traditioned character of rationality. That essay, "From System to Story," now appears in my book *Truthfulness and Tragedy*, 15–39.

condemned to live out our past. We discover that we are only able to name our sins on our way to being free from them. This means we are only able to give an account of our lives retrospectively.

By attending to Augustine's *Confessions* retrospectively, I hope to show that his account of evil as privation is keyed to his understanding of Scripture and, in particular, how Scripture is only rightly read as prayer (worship). In other words, Augustine's understanding of evil as privation is necessary to make sense of the Bible's story of creation, fall, and redemption. All that he says about evil is disciplined by that theological project, which means for Augustine there is no freestanding "problem of evil," but rather whatever Christians have to say about evil must reflect their convictions that we are creatures of a God who has created and redeemed.[18]

The *Confessions* is a complex prayer Augustine prays in an effort to discover how God has made his life possible. He unsparingly confesses his sins, his unwillingness to acknowledge the One who is his creator, because the *Confessions* are not about Augustine but rather about the God who makes Augustine Augustine. Moreover, he makes clear that it is his inability to understand God that makes it impossible for him to understand rightly the nature of evil. He confesses that his

> own specious reasoning induced me to give in to the sly arguments of fools who asked me what was the origin of evil, whether God was confined to the limits of a bodily shape, whether he had hair and nails, and whether men could be called just if they had more than one wife at the same time, or killed other men, or sacrificed living animals. My ignorance was so great that these questions troubled me, and while I thought I was approaching the truth, I was only departing the further from it. I did not know that evil is nothing but the removal of good until finally no good remains.[19]

The "fools" were the Manichees, a religious sect to which Augustine belonged for nine years, because he believed that they offered him a compelling account of the cosmos and, in particular, of evil. In her wonderful book *Augustine on Evil*, G. R. Evans suggests that what attracted Augustine to the Manichees was what he took to be the explana-

18. I am indebted to Prof. John Bowlin for helping me see how Augustine's account of privation is theologically determined.

19. Augustine, *Confessions*, 62–63, 3.7.

tory power of their position.[20] According to the Manichees the world is constituted by a god who is supremely good and by an evil principle that is identified with materiality, and in particular, the body. Therefore the Manichees did not try to avoid the problem of evil, but rather they "explained" evil by finding a place for evil in the ontological character of the universe.[21] Such an explanation appealed to Augustine because he had a passion to know the truth about his and the world's existence. In short, the Manichees seemed to offer Augustine a "scientific" account of the way things are. Such an explanation appealed to Augustine, he confesses, because when he was at that stage of his life he was readier to believe that the universe was out of joint than that there was anything wrong with himself.[22]

Evans also suggests that the Manichees might have been attractive to Augustine because their position seemed to share some aspects of what Augustine had learned from his mother about Christianity. Christians, like the Manichees, claimed God is completely good and the human task is to seek that good. Accordingly the *Manichean Psalm-Book* seemed to echo the Christian desire for illumination gained through being freed from bodily desire. Augustine, who certainly knew about bodily desire, was attracted to the spiritual discipline of the Manichees because they offered him a discipline by which he could join the spiritual elite.[23] No doubt one of the reasons the Manichees ap-

20. Evans, *Augustine on Evil*, 12–14. I am indebted to David Aers for calling Evans' book to my attention.

21. Ibid., 8.

22. Augustine, *Confessions*, 136, 7.3. Evans observes that Augustine was more inclined to believe "that God could be affected by evil, rather than admit that he himself was the agent of evil. He tried every way his wit could devise to avoid the conclusion that he himself might be the source of evil he was seeking, ensnarer of his own soul, gaoler of the prison" (Evans, *Augustine on Evil*, 13). If Becker is right about the development of "anthropodicy," then it is no surprise that we are ready to see evil "out there" in others rather than in ourselves.

23. Augustine is often described as a thinker who despised the body. Nothing could be further from the truth. The body is God's good creation and, therefore, cannot be despised. He is also interpreted as a Christian who thought sex is intrinsically evil. Again nothing could be further from the truth. He maintains, for example, that before the fall Adam and Eve would have had sexual intercourse that was free from lust. He notes that, just as we observe in craftsmen engaged in all kinds of physical tasks, where natural powers which lack strength and speed are developed by active training, then why should "we not believe that the sexual organs could have been the obedient servants of mankind, at the bidding of the will, in the same way as the other,

pealed to Augustine, a reason he suggests in the *Confessions*, is because they confirmed his high opinion of himself. The Manichees played to what Augustine was to learn was his deepest enemy—his pride—by providing him with knowledge befitting his intelligence. He was freed from the Manichees only when he was forced to conclude that "the very attempt to search for the cause of evil in the way he did was itself an evil thing."[24]

That the Manichees seemed to provide Augustine with the best account of the cosmos is crucial to understand his break with them. Augustine tells us he often asked questions the his fellow Manichees could not answer, but they assured him when the great Manichean scholar Faustus came he would be able to answer Augustine's worries. When Faustus came, however, though Augustine found him a man of "agreeable personality," Augustine also discovered that Faustus "was quite uninformed about the subjects in which I had expected him to be an expert."[25] In particular Augustine thought the Manichean books were full of "tedious fictions about the sky and the stars, the sun and the moon" and their mathematical calculations simply did not square with what he had studied in other books.[26]

---

if there had been no lust, which came as the retribution for the sin of disobedience?" (*City of God*, 585, 14.23). Augustine realizes that many cannot imagine that in paradise Adam and Eve might have had such control over their sexual organs so he gives some examples of people who can do extraordinary things with their body. For example, some people can move their ears, some can bring their scalp over their forehead, some can swallow an incredible number of articles and then bring them up from the diaphragm in perfect condition, some can imitate the cries of birds and beasts, and some can even "produce at will such musical sounds from their behind (without any stink) that they seem to be singing from that region" (*City of God*, 588, 14.23).

24. Evans, *Augustine on Evil*, 5.

25. Augustine, *Confessions*, 98, 5.7. Augustine's concern that what he believed should be tested by the best science of the day is often not appreciated. His early attraction to astrology, for example, ended because he rightly tested whether people born at the same moment had the same subsequent history. Platonist though he may have become, he always thought that what he thought should be tested by empirical methods. See, for example, his wonderful account of Firminus's birth in *Confessions*, 141, 7.6.

26. Augustine, *Confessions*, 98, 5.7. Evans observes that one of the attractions of Christianity for Augustine was that he was never able to exhaust, as he did after nine years with the Manichees, the intellectual depth of the Bible and Christian doctrine. Augustine, of course, would not have become a Christian if Ambrose had not introduced him to how the Bible should be read.

That the Manichean "science" proved to be false was one of the crucial reasons Augustine had for leaving the Manichees, but just as important was his discovery that his most fundamental mistake was assuming that God could be understood as part of the metaphysical furniture of the universe. Augustine confesses he "could not free himself from the thought that you (God) were some kind of bodily substance extended in space, either permeating the world or diffused in infinity beyond it."[27] It was by reading the Platonists that Augustine was freed of the presumption that metaphysically that which is a substance must have a body. Moreover it was the Platonists that helped him see that "all other things that are of a lower order than yourself, and I saw that they have not absolute being in themselves, nor are they entirely without being. They are real in so far as they have their being from you, but unreal in the sense that they are not what you are"[28]

It was from the Platonists, therefore, that Augustine began to imagine that evil is a privation, which means it is a mistake to try to understand how, as Evans puts it, "evil can have a bodily place in the universe".[29] For Augustine this meant that he was beginning to realize it is a mistake to ask from whence evil comes or where evil may be. Now Augustine understands for God

> evil does not exist, and not only for you for the whole of your creation as well, because there is nothing outside it which could invade it and break down the order which you have imposed on it. Yet in separate parts of your creation there are some things which we think of as evil because they are at variance with other things. But there are other things again with which they are in accord, and they are good. In themselves, too, they are good. And all these things which are at variance with one another are in accord with the lower part of creation which we call the earth. The sky, which is cloudy and windy, suits the earth to which it

27. Ibid., 133, 7.1.

28. Ibid., 147, 7.11.

29. Evans, *Augustine on Evil*, 35. Evans, however, calls attention to Augustine's *De Magistro*, in which Augustine, with his son, Adeodatus, explores the question of whether a sign can signify another sign by examining a line of Virgil word by word to see what each word signifies. In the process they "discover a special difficulty in the case of the word *nihil*, which, paradoxically, must signify something because all words signify something, while at the same time, it must signify 'nothing' because that is the meaning of the word *nihil*" (54). Barth, as I indicated above, struggles with the same problem.

belongs. So it would be wrong for me to wish that these earthly things did not exist, for even if I saw nothing but them, I might wish for something better, but still I ought to praise you for them alone. . . . And since this is so, I no longer wished for a better world, because I was thinking of the whole of creation and in the light of this clearer discernment I had come to see that though the higher things are better than the lower, the sum of all creation is better than the higher things alone.[30]

There can be no question of the significance of the Platonists for Augustine, but this passage in praise of God's creation indicates that for Augustine Platonism was a way station on the way for Augustine to become a Christian. Augustine never left his Platonism behind though I think the assumption that he remained more Platonist than Christian is clearly wrong. He understood that he could not remain a Platonist because to be a Christian requires that you believe that all that is is as it is because it has been created. Augustine tells us that "by reading these books of the Platonists I had been prompted to look for truth as something incorporeal, and I 'caught sight of your invisible nature, as it is known through your creatures,'"[31] but what he could not find in the Platonist books was "the mien of the true love of God. They make no mention of the tears of confession or of the sacrifice that you will never disdain, a broken spirit, a heart that is humbled and contrite (Psalm 50:19), nor do they speak of the salvation of your people, the city adorned like a bride (Revelation 21:2), the foretaste of your spirit (II Corinthians 1:22), or the chalice of your redemption."[32]

From Augustine's perspective the Platonists, as helpful as they had been, did nothing for his besetting problem, which he came to understand was his pride. Through his encounter with the stories of Victorinus and Anthony, and how those stories led him to face the humiliation of the cross of Christ, Augustine was finally able to confess that evil was "not out there," but rather resided in his will.[33] Augustine confesses "I

30. Augustine, *Confessions*, 148–49, 7.12. Augustine's understanding of the interrelation and hierarchy between God's creatures is extremely important for his account of what goes wrong in particular circumstances.

31. Ibid., 154, 7.21.

32. Ibid.

33. Augustine's discovery as well as understanding of the will is as important as it is oft times misunderstood. It would simply take me too far afield to try to "explain" what Augustine was about with the introduction of the will, but suffice it to say that I think

began to search for a means of gaining the strength I needed to enjoy you, but I could not find this means until I embraced the mediator between God and men, Jesus Christ, who is man, like them, (I Timothy 2:5) and also rules as God over all things, blessed for ever. (Romans 9:5) He it was who united with our flesh that food which I was too weak to take. For I was not humble enough to conceive of the humble Jesus Christ as my God, nor had I learnt what lesson his human weakness was meant to teach."[34] That lesson quite simply being that we are cured of our pride only through following the Word, the Truth, which surpasses even the highest parts of creation by becoming one of us.

The *Confessions* is Augustine's testimony to God and God's grace as necessary for the healing of his pride. We can only know our sin in the light of God's grace.[35] This means we cannot will our way out of our

---

James Wetzel is right to suggest Augustine was developing an alternative to "classical psychology's distinction between the rational decisions of the mind and the irrational impulses of the emotions of the appetites" (*Augustine and the Limits of Virtue*, 86). It is for theological reasons that Augustine discovered the necessity of the will, because without the will it might be thought that God was responsible for our waywardness. That is why the will for Augustine is not the source of our being "free," but rather names our unfreedom. Wetzel observes that "without a clearly delineated concept of the voluntary, the whole fabric of the moral order unravels. God cannot judge justly the disposition of souls who have no power of will, and when the foundations of divine judgment are undermined, there is a general undermining of moral evaluations of any sort" (90). Evans seems to me to get it right when she says for Augustine the truly free will is that which has through grace regained its freedom to choose the good and not evil. The free will of the elect is more free than the will of the unregenerate. For the secret of true freedom is "to give up the freedom to do evil which cannot be called a freedom, because it presents only one alternative. The good man regains his freedom to do good and at the same time loses the tendency to choose evil, with the aid of a truly liberating grace" (*Augustine on Evil*, 136).

34. Augustine, *Confessions*, 152, 7.18.

35. This point is often misunderstood particularly by conservative and liberal Christians. Both, for different reasons, assume that sin can be known independent of what God has done in Christ. As a result, salvation is determined by a prior understanding of sin that is not christologically disciplined. Sin then controls what God has done in a manner that makes God subject to human desires. Augustine knew better, so his account of his sinfulness is always dependent on grace. No theologian in modernity has done more than Karl Barth to challenge the presumption that sin is more intelligible than what God has done through Christ. In contrast to the view that our knowledge of sin is more or less self-evident, in contrast to our knowledge of God, Barth maintains that "only when we know Jesus Christ do we really know that man is the man of sin, and what sin is, and what it means for man" (*Church Dogmatics*, IV/1, 389). From Barth's perspective sin is simply a surd. We have no reason to sin but when

pride, but rather God's grace can only be appropriated through recollection.[36] Commentators on Augustine's *Confessions* often find his descriptions of being a sinner as a young child—that is, his greedy desire for his mother breast—to be exaggerated. Yet Augustine is not trying to make us think that even as a child he was the most sinful of sinners. To engage in that project would be another form of pride. Rather he is trying to help us see that the disorder that grips our most basic desires as well as our ability to reason, which is shaped by those desires, cannot help but lead to the destruction of ourselves and others. To appreciate a child's disordered desire is part and parcel of Augustine's rejection of the Manichees.

Augustine's famous account of the stealing of the pears is his paradigmatic example of what it means to discover that we do not so much choose to sin but rather that we are sin. Crucial for Augustine is that he stole that for which he had no need. He and his friends threw the pears to the pigs. To be sure Augustine joined in this petty crime because he desired the good opinion of his friends, but that he did so is not a sufficient explanation for his sin.[37] He did what he did for no purpose other

---

confronted by the Gospel we discover we are sinners—which means we can only know our sins on our way out of sin.

36. Wetzel wonderfully shows how it is only through recollection that "we are able to effect the gradual convergence of virtue and self-determination" (*Augustine and the Limits of Virtue*, 124).

37. In *City of God*, Augustine argues that "one should not try to find an efficient cause for a wrong choice. It is not a matter of efficiency, but of deficiency; the evil will itself is not effective but defective. For to defect from him who is the Supreme Existence, to something of less reality, this is to begin to have an evil will. To try to discover the causes of such defection—deficient, not efficient causes—is like trying to see darkness or to hear silence. Yet we are familiar with darkness and silence, and we can only be aware of them by means of eyes and ears, but this is not by perception but by absence of perception. No one therefore must try to get to know from me what I know, unless, it may be, in order to learn not to know what must be known to be incapable of being known" (480). Aquinas follows Augustine, arguing that "the cause of evil is good in the way in which evil can have a cause. For we should note that evil cannot have an intrinsic cause . . . so we see that no person does any evil except intending something that seems good to the person. For example, it seems good to the adulterer that he enjoy sense pleasure, and he commits adultery for that reason" (*On Evil*, 70). However, Gregory Reichberg argues that Aquinas did try to account for our sense that evil can have a positive reality by developing his understanding of malice in *De Malvo*. Reichberg suggests Aquinas maintained that evil cannot be directly intended, but agents can be said to do evil deliberately to the degree they accept the privation that is joined to their deed. See Reichberg's article "Beyond Privation," 751–84. I am

than his love of mischief. So acting, he sought to gain from the world what he learned he could only gain from loving the One alone worthy to be loved. In short he was trying to be more than he could be. Thus he confesses "all who desert you and set themselves up against you merely copy you in a perverse way: but by this very act of imitation they only show that you are the Creator of all nature and, consequently, that there is no place whatever where man may hide away from you."[38]

Evans notes that Augustine's observations about his early boyhood sins are meant to help us see that one of the distinguishing marks of an evil action is its unprofitableness.[39] That seems just right to me and helps us understand why Augustine thought we have no ability to will our way out of sin. That we cannot will our way out of sin is because we seldom pursue sin to sin, but rather our sins our done in the name of "great goods." We learn of the unprofitable character of sin only retrospectively. Indeed too often attempts to avoid sin rely on alternatives that are themselves sinful, but fail to be acknowledged as such only because they seem different than the sin we think we have clearly identified. For Augustine evil cannot be defeated by evil.[40] Rather our only

---

indebted to Reinhard Hütter for calling my attention to this article, as well as Jacques Maritain's superb study, *St. Thomas Aquinas and the Problem of Evil.*

38. Augustine, *Confessions*, 50, 2.6.

39. Evans, *Augustine on Evil*, 3. In a letter responding to this essay, Travis Kroeker suggested to me that "unprofitableness" fails to do justice to Augustine's sense of the sheer "gratuitousness" of sin. Kroeker observes that for Augustine sin is empty, that is, sin is a false parody of the gratuitousness of divine agency that is creative love.

40. Charles Mathewes rightly criticizes Reinhold Niebuhr—who is often credited with reclaiming the significance of Augustine's understanding of sin to illuminate modern political life—for "naturalizing" evil by positing evil "as a preexisting and primordial force which we meet in interpreting our world, and so undermines our confidence that God is wholly good" (*Evil and the Augustinian Tradition*, 8). Niebuhr made the mistake of thinking evil can be defeated, or at least the effects of evil, by being confronted by alternatives that are "less evil." Yet as Mathewes observes, "given the sheer negativity of evil, we cannot respond to it directly; we must respond to it through its manifestations as a perversion of our loves. But our loves are also the source of our every attempt at a response; that is, the problem is essentially with *us*, and not directly with anything 'external' to us. So our loves are simultaneously the root of the problem and the source of any possible response to the problem" (233). Niebuhr, like many Protestant liberals, wanted Augustine's account of sin without Augustine's Christology, but that is exactly what cannot be done, or at least cannot be done if we are trying to be faithful to Augustine. In *Death of Satan*, Delbanco takes Niebuhr (and Melville) to be one of the last representatives of an Augustinian understanding of the world, but such a view Delbanco judges, not happily I think, to be anachronistic

hope is that we are offered an alternative community and correlative way of life that make it possible for us to locate the extraordinary power of the evil we are and do in the name of the good. For all of its ambiguity, Augustine thought he had discovered that alternative community by being made a member of the church.[41]

Where Has This Gotten Us or Why I Am Not a Nazi

I do not pretend that I have provided an adequate account Augustine's understanding of evil, but hopefully my attempt to help us see how Augustine thought about these matters can help us gain some perspective on where we are today.[42] If Susan Neiman is right that "the prob-

---

having been lost through the development of a culture of irony (192–208). It is quite understandable that Delbanco so reads Niebuhr, but I think Niebuhr's reputation as a recovery of Augustine is belied by the fact that Niebuhr's work stands in the tradition of Protestant liberalism. For my understanding of Niebuhr, see *With the Grain of the Universe*, 87–140.

41. Much is made of Augustine's refusal to identify the church with the city of God. There can be no question that Augustine understood that the church, like his own life, was still under the power of sin. Yet the very ability of the church to confess its sinfulness meant for Augustine that the church was an alternative to the world. Rowan Williams argues that Augustine's politics presumes that the church has a distinctive character in his "Politics and the Soul," 55–72. This is the article on which John Milbank draws in his robust account of the significance of the church as an alternative *civitas* in his *Theology and Social Theory*, 380–438. For the best account of Augustine's political theology, see Dodaro, *Christ and the Just Society*.

42. In *Augustine on Evil*, Evans provides what I regard as the best account we have of Augustine's thinking on evil. For example, she gives an extremely interesting account of Augustine's understanding of lying as evil and how Augustine's commitment to truthfulness shaped his exegetical practice. Equally interesting is Augustine's controversy with the Pelagians and the Pelagian accusation that Augustine's denial of free will implied a return to the Manichean understanding of evil. On most matters I would certainly defer to Evans, but I do not think she is right to attribute to Augustine Plato's view that all natural evils, such as earthquakes, can be traced to a disordered will (97–98). She is certainly right that Augustine had little interest in our understanding of "natural evils," but I do not think that due to his Platonism. Augustine simply felt no need to "explain" such events. To be sure, such events were painful, but I suspect Augustine would have seen such events as opportunities to discover our sin. Thus Augustine confesses, "I broke all your lawful bounds and did not escape your lash. For what man can escape it? You were always present, angry and merciful at once, strewing the pangs of bitterness over all my lawless pleasures to lead me on to look for others unallied with pain. You meant me to find them nowhere but in yourself, O Lord, for you teach us by inflicting pain, you smite so that you may heal, and you kill us

lem of evil is the guiding force of modern thought" and that "nothing is easier than stating the problem of evil in nontheist terms" then we clearly have some indication that "modernity" names a development that stands at a great distance, and the distance is not best measured in centuries, from Augustine.[43] With all due respect to Neiman, I suspect she has no idea that Augustine's understanding of evil was not "theistic" but Trinitarian.[44] Yet I fear that Neiman represents the kind of misunderstanding of Christianity in modernity most determinatively found among Christians.

However, from Neiman's perspective, the Augustinian account of evil I have developed and hopefully defended in this paper cannot help but seem intellectually obscurantist if not dangerous. The problem quite simply is that the account I have provided is so Christian, so particularistic. Why should anyone who is not a Christian take it seriously? Moreover, appeals to particular traditions seem to reproduce the problem many assume is at the heart of the challenge facing us in modernity—that is, how to counter the violence perpetrated in the name of a god or tradition. In short, does not my vigorous defense of Augustine's understanding of evil play into the hands of the most destructive form of politics in our time? I fear that I cannot provide the kind of answer many desire to such a question because such answers undercut the contribution Christians have to make.

---

so that we may not die away from you" (*Confessions*, 44). Of course Augustine is here primarily referring to the unfortunate results occasioned by his sin, but I feel sure he would regard "natural evils" in the same light. It is extremely important, however, to understand that Augustine did not think we are punished for our sin but that our sin is our punishment. See, for example, my chapter "Salvation Even in Sin," in my book *Sanctify Them in the Truth*, 61–76.

43. Neiman, *Evil in Modern Thought*. The quotes are from pages 2 and 5. Kant's account of "radical evil" in *Religion within the Limits of Reason Alone* can be interpreted as fundamentally "Augustinian" just to the extent that radical evil names what should not be but is. For Kant, evil is radical because evil resides in the will which is also the source of our ability to live according to the moral law. See Kant, *Religion within the Limits of Reason Alone*, 15–39.

44. For the significance of Augustine's understanding of the Trinity, see Hanby, *Augustine and Modernity*. In particular Hanby's account of Augustine's *De Trinitate* emphasizes the importance of beauty and delight for understanding the relations of the three persons of the Trinity. Accordingly sin and evil are rightly understood as that which is profoundly ugly.

It has been the sad fate of Christianity in our time to be that form of life that tries to "bind up the wounds" of our existence. As a result Christians have tried to offer explanations of evil that do not implicate God. As I suggested at the beginning of this essay, you can be sure that when Christians attempt to justify the ways of God before the bar of human experience they no longer believe in the God that animates the work of Augustine.[45] Even worse, I suspect that Christians today do not know what it would mean to believe in Augustine's God precisely because we have no idea what practices are required to make our worship of the God of Abraham, Jacob, and Isaac, and Jesus Christ intelligible, not only to those who do not share our faith, but even to ourselves.

I need to be clear, however, that it would be a mistake to think the genocide in Rwanda is somehow better understood if we see what happened there as "sin." That would make "sin" exactly what Augustine suggests sin cannot be—an explanation. To say "sin" explains nothing.[46] Rather sin is a confession that holds out the hope that even in the face of a terror like Rwanda redemption is possible. To say that there is hope suggests that evil cannot overwhelm the good that is God's creation. Yet honesty demands that often we have nothing to say in the face of events like Rwanda. Nevertheless silence, at least the honest silence that can be a form of presence, can be a way not to let the darkness overwhelm us.[47] Indeed Christians believe that God would have his people be such a presence.

45. However, for a wonderful "defense" of God from the charge that God unjustly allows evil, see Herbert McCabe's chapter on "Evil" in *God Matters*, 25–38. McCabe argues that if you accept the principle that you are innocent until proven guilty, then any account of God's responsibility for evil will show he cannot be proved innocent, but "it will remain a mystery to you why God has done what he has done; but you will at least agree that what he has done does not prove his guilt" (26).

46. Terry Eagleton notes that this Wittgensteinian point is to know when justifications have come to an end—that is, that there is a point when we must simply say, "This is simply what I do." That does not mean that if what I do is defraud the elderly of life savings an account does not need to be given. But Wittgenstein, according to Eagleton, is "thinking of more fundamental matters than that. He has in mind the very cultural forms which allow us to think what we think and do what we do" (*After Theory*, 192).

47. *Naming the Silences* was my attempt to display how Christians should be present to one another in times as difficult as the death of a child without offering one another false sentimentalities. In his lovely book, *Love Almighty and Ills Unlimited*, Austin Farrer observes that "Evil commonly strikes us not as a problem, but as an outrage. Taken in the grip of misfortune, or appalled by the violence of malice, we

Silence, moreover, is required when the use of words like "sin" and "evil" are used, in Terry Eagleton's words, "to shut down thought."[48] Eagleton notes that the use of the word "evil" in the so-called war against terrorism really means:

> Don't look for a political explanation. It is a wonderfully time-saving device. If terrorists are simply Satanic, then you do not need to investigate what lies behind their atrocious acts of violence. You can ignore the plight of the Palestinian people, or of those Arabs who have suffered under squalid right-wing autocracies supported by the West for its own selfish, oil-hungry purposes. The word "evil" transfers the question from this mundane realm to a sinisterly metaphysical one. You cannot acknowledge that the terrible crimes which terrorists commit have a purpose behind them, since to ascribe purposes to such people is to recognize them as rational creatures, however desperately wrongheaded.[49]

---

cannot reason sanely about the balance of the world. Indeed, it is part of the problem of evil that its victim is rendered incapable of thought" (7). Farrer suggests that, so confronted, we face two problems: (1) a practical problem that is pastoral, medical, or psychological and that differs from case to case in a manner that does not allow any useful generalization; and (2) a theoretical problem that is not concerned with being comforting or tactful but to say what is true. He understands his book to be about the theoretical issues. I am, however, not convinced that the practical and theoretical can be so neatly distinguished, particularly in the light of the account I have given of Augustine.

48. Eagleton, *After Theory*, 223.

49. Ibid., 141. In his chapter "Revolution, Foundations, and Fundamentalists," Eagleton notes how modernity was the attempt to provide alternative candidates for God in such ideas as nature, reason, history, spirit, power, production, desire. Such candidates have come and gone, but in their different ways they were each different ways of making "Man" the new foundation. But he observes that this attempt was not satisfactory because "it seemed oddly circular to see Man as the foundation of Man. Man seemed a more promising candidate than God for foundational status because he was fleshly and palpable. The invisibility of God has always been a grave drawback to his career prospects as a foundation, leading many to the not unreasonable conclusion that it was not that he was there but hiding; it was simply that he was not there" (196). For my account of why it is a mistake to think God is the kind of foundation some think is needed if we are to avoid "relativism," see my "Connections Created and Continent: Aquinas, Preller, Wittgenstein, and Hopkins," in *Performing the Faith*, 111–34.

To describe enemies as evil ironically has the effect of creating the Manichean world that Augustine was intent on defeating.[50] If Augustine teaches us anything, it is that the Christian confession of sin is a first-person activity. Christians, of course, think it important to be able to name our sins as well as to confess our sins to one another.[51] We are obligated to reveal our sins so that we may have some hope of being freed from sin through the work of the Holy Spirit. Our ability to name our sins comes through our mutual responsibility we share with other Christians exemplified by lives such as Augustine's.[52] By attending to

50. Delbanco calls attention to Joseph Goebbels' "blood freezing candor" when he confessed, "Oh, I can hate, and I don't want to forget how. Oh, how wonderful it is to be able to hate." Delbanco observes, to listen to Goebbels is to realize again what Augustine and Melville knew: "that the crusader who construes evil as a malignant, external thing—a thing alien to himself—is by far the worst kind of barbarian. The struggle of the twentieth century was to keep this proficient hater from seizing the world" (*Death of Satan*, 183). Our problem may be even more complex because now those who express such hatred are assumed legitimate because they are representatives of "democratic" societies.

In his wonderful response to this essay, "Labored Knowledge," James Wetzel challenges Augustine's avowal that he has left Manicheanism behind. Wetzel does so by suggesting that Augustine's very depiction of the unintelligibility of his sin is connected to his sense of his self-created destructiveness. Wetzel argues that Augustine struggled, as we all must, to live acknowledging that God's forgiveness is ahead of our reactions, thus freeing us from "having to be the selves we imagine ourselves to be." As Wetzel recognizes, this is an Augustinian criticism of Augustine.

51. Some may wonder if sin and evil are equivalent expressions. Evil is often associated with events that seem to have no agency, which has led some to assume that evil is a more inclusive description than sin. However, the suggestion that evil is a broader category than sin can lead to the assumption that sin is intelligible because it is something we have done. Yet Augustine thinks sin and evil equally without explanation.

52. The first-person character of the confession of sin does not mean that the whole church cannot confess our sins as the church. So prayers of confession often use "we." For example, consider the prayer Christians pray at morning prayer (from *The Book of Common Prayer*):

> Most merciful God,
> we confess that we have sinned against you
> in thought, word, and deed,
> by what we have done,
> and by what we have left undone.
> We have not loved you with our whole heart;
> we have not loved our neighbors as ourselves.
> We are truly sorry and we humbly repent.
> For the sake of your Son Jesus Christ,
> have mercy on us and forgive us;

lives like Augustine's, Christians hope to be able to discover in what ways we are possessed by sin. If we attribute sin to another, we are able to do so because we have been enabled to recognize the power of sin in our own lives.[53]

But what could such a confession mean when faced by a Rwanda? I think if we are thinking with Augustine it might mean that to be a Christian requires us to believe that even a Rwanda someday might be a memory capable of being healed.[54] What it would mean for such a memory to be healed I think would mean that a story can be told about such senseless killing that offers those killed as well as those that killed reconciliation.[55] I confess I cannot imagine what such a reconciliation might mean, but that is why God is God and I am not.

Which finally brings me back to politics. In the "Preface" to her important book, *The Nazi Conscience*, Claudia Koonz observes that we may find it repugnant to think that mass murderers understood themselves to be acting morally. But according to Koonz that is exactly what they did. She observes:

> The popularizers of anti-semitism and the planners of genocide followed a coherent set of severe ethical maxims derived from broad philosophical concepts. As modern secularists, they de-

---

that we may delight in your will,
and walk in your ways,
to the glory of your Name.
Amen.

53. The language of the last two sentences in this paragraph is a reminder that the Christians confession of sin entails the presumption that sin is a power that possesses us. The New Testament understanding of the powers is particularly important to understand how sin effects the very character of existence. In Col 1:15–17 we are told that God created all things in heaven and on earth "whether thrones or dominions or principalities or powers; all were created through him and by him." Yet those same powers are fallen, though they were part of God's good creation providing the regularity and order we require. These structures that were to be our servants have become our masters holding us in servitude. (Col 2:20) Yet even in their fallen state the powers continue to exercise their ordering function. For the best account of this understanding of the powers see Yoder, *Politics of Jesus*, 134–61.

54. I owe this way of putting the matter to Charlie Collier. Mr. Collier wrote his dissertation on Augustine and John Howard Yoder. See Collier, "Nonviolent Augustianianism?"

55. I have tried to make a beginning to think through what it might mean to narrate a wrong so wrong there is nothing one can do to make it right in a chapter entitled "Why Time Cannot and Should Not Heal the Wounds of History," 139–54.

nied the existence of either a divinely inspired moral law or an innate ethical imperative. Because they believed that concepts of virtue and vice had evolved according to the needs of particular ethnic communities, they denied the existence of universal moral values and instead promoted moral maxims they saw as appropriate to their Aryan community. Unlike the early twentieth-century moral philosophers who saw cultural relativism as an argument for tolerance, Nazi theorists drew the opposite conclusion. Assuming that cultural diversity breeds antagonism, they asserted the superiority of their own communitarian values above all others.[56]

I suspect many will find my judgment that Augustine provides how Christians should think about evil far too close to what Koontz describes as the Nazi exaltation of their particular community's values. We, that is, we who are modern, think the only way to defeat the kind of evil we associate with the Nazis is to have at our disposal a universal ethic, that is, an ethic on which all agree. Christians are often thought to represent such an ethic. However, Augustine thought that virtue and vice were correlative to a particular community. According to Augustine, God's law is a law for anyone, but he also thought that law would differ from age to age and place to place. "What may be done at one time of day is not allowed at the next, and what may be done, or must be done, in one room is forbidden and punished in another. This does not mean that justice is erratic or variable, but that the times over which it presides are not always the same, for it is the nature of time to change."[57] The variable character of ethics does not mean justice is arbitrary, but Augustine argued that for justice to be rightly understood requires the right worship of the true God.[58] Absent that worship,

56. Koontz, *Nazi Conscience*, 1.

57. Augustine, *Confessions*, 64, 3.8.

58. In the *City of God* Augustine maintains "that justice is found where God, the one supreme God, rules an obedient city according to his grace, forbidding sacrifice to any being save himself alone; and where in consequence the soul rules the body in all men who belong to this city and obey God, and the reason faithfully rules the vices in a lawful system of subordination; so that just as he individual righteous man lives on the basis of faith which is active in love, so the association, or people, of righteous men lives on the same basis of faith, active in love, the love with which a man loves God as God ought to be loved, and loves his neighbor as himself. But where this justice does not exist, there is certainly no 'association of men united by a common sense of right and by a community of interest.' Therefore there is no commonwealth; for where

Augustine assumes that there can be no alternative to what we know as "relativism" or what James Edwards calls "normal nihilism."[59]

Does the loss of common worship mean, however, that there is no alternative, that there is no defense, against the "Nazi conscience"?[60] I do not think such a conclusion follows, but such an alternative will depend on whether communities exist capable of discerning their own propensities for the evil so often done in the name of good.[61] It would be tempting to put Christians on the side of those who advocate "universal moral values" as a bulwark against "relativism." That strategy, however, fails to see that "relativism" is the creation of the assumption that "universal values" can be known apart from formation in a community capable of recognizing the evil it does in the name of those same "values." Ironically, too often, as I suggested above, those who try to sustain accounts of morality in the language of universal rights or values are but secular versions of Constantinian Christians, pridefully assuming they know what is wrong with the world. That such is the case should not be surprising because the philosophical developments that gave original impetus to these now widespread political movements intended if possible to defeat or replace Christianity in the name of the human or, failing that, at least to render Christian convictions at best "private" having no role for the public discernment of evil or good.

But if we cannot rely on "universal values" does that not mean we live in a very dangerous world? That is exactly what it means. That world, moreover, has been made all the more dangerous by attempts to save the world from danger by appealing to "universal values" that result in justifications to coerce those who do not share what some consider

---

there is no 'people,' there is no weal of the people" (889–90, 19.23). It is not hard to see how Augustine's account of justice could lead to a Constantinian ethics, but such an alternative should be defeated by the Gospel. I, for example, can describe myself as a theocrat—the problem is that it is very hard to rule when you are committed to Christian nonviolence.

59. Edwards, *Plain Sense of Things*.

60. This way of putting the matter is misleading because "loss of common worship" suggests that at one time in the past Christians "got it right." On Augustine's grounds, Christian can never assume they ever get it right, but the past can serve as a spur for the imagination to save us from current alternatives.

61. For my attempt to begin to think through what it would mean for Christians to remember the Shoah, see my "Remembering as a Moral Task," in my *Against the Nations*, 61–90.

universal. If Christians have any contribution to make for helping us survive the world as we know it, it is because God has "brought us low," forcing humility on us by humiliation. Such humility hopefully might help Christians refrain from identifying or comforting themselves with the sentimentalities of reigning humanisms. Christians do not believe in the "human." Christians believe in a God who requires we be able to recognize as well as confess our sins. Exactly because Christians are in lifelong training necessary to be a sinner, it is our hope that we might be able to discern the evil that so often is expressed in idealistic terms. So what Christians have to offer is not an explanation of evil, but rather a story, and a community formed by that story, that we believe saves us from the idols of the world. That I think is what Augustine might say today.[62]

62. I am grateful to Charlie Collier, Greg Jones, and David Aers for their criticisms and suggestions.

3

Disciplined Seeing:
Forms of Christianity and Forms of Life*

with BRIAN GOLDSTONE

On How One Sees Things

"To work at seeing the world as though one were seeing it for the first time is to get rid of the conventional and routine vision we have of things, to discover a brute, naïve vision of reality, to take note of the splendor of the world, which habitually escapes us."[1] If Pierre Hadot's meticulous, often poignant reconstructions of the philosophical traditions of antiquity have taught us nothing else, it is that there was a time when what it meant to be a philosopher was to set oneself on the course of becoming a certain type of person. Beset with a kind of blindness, stemming above all from our unregulated desires and exaggerated fears, philosophy's charge was fundamentally that of a reeducation of the senses that would effect a "profound transformation of the individ-

* This essay was originally written for a special issue of the *South Atlantic Quarterly* 109:4 (Fall 2010), entitled *Global Christianity, Global Critique*, edited by Matthew Engelke and Joel Robbins. I have included this essay, though it was written primarily by Brian. We talked often about the argument, but Bryan did the heavy lifting. So I think of the essay as "Bryan's," but as one that represents what I think. I also included the essay to celebrate our friendship.

1. Hadot, *Present Alone*, 173. The title of our essay is adapted from Hadot's seminal lecture, "Forms of Life," 49–70.

ual's manner of seeing and being," a metamorphosis of personality and a thoroughgoing renovation of one's mode of existence. The ensemble of techniques deployed in this learning to live, the array of practices that unequivocally situated the philosophical act not merely on the terrain of theory and cognition but in the formation of a concrete attitude and a determinate lifestyle—these habits Hadot refers to as "spiritual exercises," and they show us, he asserts, that philosophy at its inception constituted more than a specific way of life; it constituted, necessarily, a *therapeutics* as well.

So it comes as little surprise that Hadot would discern in Ludwig Wittgenstein, whose writings he was among the earliest French intellectuals to discover (and in reference to whom, incidentally, he would first use the term spiritual exercises), a modern articulation of a decidedly premodern view of philosophy's curative function—even if, as Hadot rightly points out, Wittgenstein believed that "the true philosophy would consist in curing itself of philosophy, in making every philosophical problem completely and definitively disappear."[2] For like Hadot and the tradition he elucidates, Wittgenstein's therapeutics were directed at the recovery of a distinctive mode of looking—as in his famous injunction "To repeat: don't think, but look!"[3]—where *looking* at the world means to see it differently, that is, naturally, in all its "splendor . . . which habitually escapes us." Or in a note written on October 14, 1931: "Work on philosophy—like work in architecture in many respects—is really more work on oneself. On one's own conception. On how one sees things. (And what one expects of them.)"[4]

2. Hadot, "Wittgenstein, philosophe du langage," 973. As Arnold Davidson observes, it was likely Hadot's unique understanding of ancient philosophy that allowed him to perceive central, still-neglected dimensions of Wittgenstein's work. Interestingly enough, Hadot's writings would in turn prove to be a source of great inspiration for Michel Foucault, particularly in the latter's examination of the relation between ethics and *askesis* in his later lectures. For a brief but illuminating statement on Hadot's intellectual kinship with Wittgenstein and Foucault, see Davidson, "Spiritual Exercises," 475–82.

3. Wittgenstein, *Philosophical Investigations*, 27e. For Wittgenstein's equally well-known remarks on the therapeutic character of his philosophy, see especially section 133 of the *Investigations*: "For the clarity we are aiming at is indeed *complete* clarity. But this simply means that the philosophical problems should *completely* disappear. . . . There is not *a* philosophical method, though there are indeed methods, like different therapies."

4. Wittgenstein, *Culture and Value*, 24e. This remark comprises the point of depar-

Far from insinuating a retreat from the ordinary, Wittgenstein believed that the cultivation of a particular manner of seeing—here associated with the therapeutic "work" of a certain kind of philosophical training—might rather provide the conditions for our finally acknowledging the strangeness, the beauty, even the terror of it.

The wonder correlative of this acknowledgement is an experience that suffuses the whole of Wittgenstein's output.[5] But it is the shifting status or character of that wonder, as he moves from the *Tractatus* to his *Investigations*, that most clearly evinces the implications of its eclipse by our desire for explanation. Hence the loci of wonderment in his later philosophy are "small, local, various, and mundane" and reside in such commonplaces as *this* gesture or *that* flower blossoming—a wonder, in other words, not at the existence of the world as such but at the "amazingly intricate ways in which we are interwoven with it."[6] And yet, Wittgenstein seems to say, it is precisely this practice of seeing that becomes less and less tenable as we progressively, habitually, coast through the calculable currents of our modernity. Thus Wittgenstein writes in his journals from 1947, collected in *Culture and Value*, of a person who "might admire not only real trees, but also the shadows or reflections they cast, taking them too for trees. But once he has told himself that these are not really trees after all and has come to be puzzled at what they are, or at how they are related to trees, his admiration [*bewunderung*] will have suffered a rupture that will need healing."[7] Note that it is not puzzlement per se that is at issue here; rather, it is that *kind* of puzzlement whose incapacity to sustain awe in the face of, say, a tree's shadow betrays a style of "thinking" (or what Wittgenstein will

_____

ture for Fergus Kerr's, *"Work on Oneself."*

5. It would be worthwhile to explore the affinities and divergences between the philosophical therapeutics of Wittgenstein and Hadot and the "new thinking" advanced by Franz Rosenzweig, particularly as conceived in his *Understanding the Sick*. Thus Eric Santner notes that Rosenzweig's overriding concern in that book was to formulate a cure that might free us from what Rosenzweig often referred to as an acute *apoplexia philosophica*, or the attempt "to hold oneself at a distance from life and its temporal flow, to live life in the manner of [one] who tries to grasp the unity of life from a place outside of the temporally articulated 'language games' that constitute ordinary life." Santner, *On the Psychotheology of Everyday Life*, 20–21. See also Hillary Putnam's thoughtful discussion of Wittgenstein and Rosenzweig in his *Jewish Philosophy*.

6. Churchill, "Wonder and the End of Explanation."

7. Wittgenstein, *Culture and Value*, 57e.

otherwise refer to as a "scientific" or "causal" perspective) that searches for and invariably uncovers systematicity beneath the rough surface of things, and in whose characteristic pronouncement—"Of course, it had to happen like that"—lies the truth of its peculiar sickness.[8]

The political analogue of this will to mastery is to be found in the rationality and structuring order of modern bureaucratic states, such that the abnegation or at least domestication of contingency—the "taming of chance," as Ian Hacking would have it—becomes the critical precondition for a range of legal and administrative capabilities.[9] "Could there be," Wittgenstein queried, "human beings lacking in the capacity to see something *as something*—and what would that be like? What sort of consequences would it have?—Would this defect be comparable to color-blindness or to not having absolute pitch?—We will call it "aspect-blindness.""[10] Enabling human populations, their potentialities and pathologies alike, to be managed with unprecedented efficiency—and, when deemed unmanageable, to be efficiently discarded—aspect-blindness turns out to encompass more than a debased ethical disposition;[11] it turns out to name an indispensible modality of effective governance.

Seeing Christianity

It is no doubt strange that we should begin our contribution to a volume entitled "Global Christianity, Global Critique" by calling attention to the insights of Wittgenstein and Hadot. What, after all, might the awakening to wonder that their writings persistently beckon us to undergo, and the impediments they identify as recurrently preventing us

8. Ibid., 37e. "The insidious thing about the causal point of view is that it leads us to say: 'Of course, it had to happen like that.' Whereas we ought to think: it may have happened *like that*—and also in many other ways."

9. Hacking, *Taming of Chance*.

10. Wittgenstein, *Philosophical Investigations*, 213e.

11. An ethical disposition, moreover, that modern philosophy went some way toward establishing as the norm. Few thinkers have more powerfully articulated this condition than Stanley Cavell. "It is a recurrent cause of wonder to me that in philosophy's modern rebeginning, where philosophy finds the power to wipe clean the intellectual slate and ask for proof that we know anything exists—most poignantly expressed as wanting to know whether I am alone in the world—Descartes passes by, I have to say denies, the answer provided in the existence of the finite neighbor" (Cavell, "Forward," in Das, *Life and Words*, xiv).

from doing so, have possibly to do with the problematics with which the present volume is concerned? How might the ideas of two figures whose aim it was (and, in the case of Hadot, continues to be) to reorient philosophy toward the acquisition and enactment of a distinctive lifestyle and sensibility bear upon the intellectual developments we have been asked to address? Ours, admittedly, is an oblique way of approaching these concerns. Yet we want to suggest that the vocabularies by which the objects of our inquiries are conceived and apprehended are themselves manifestations of historically specific pedagogies connected, so Wittgenstein might say, to "how one sees things"—and, in seeing them, intuiting how properly to live with them.[12]

Of course, the "thing" in question here is Christianity: on the one side a Christianity whose rapid proliferation throughout the Southern Hemisphere has brought it under increasing scholarly as well as public scrutiny ("global Christianity"), and on the other a Christianity now taken by a heterogeneous grouping of philosophers and social theorists to contain within it resources that might revivify political projects once animated by avowedly non- or even anti-religious political desires and teleologies ("global critique").[13] Needless to say, given our own disci-

---

12. In an important passage in his *Sources of the Self*, situated amidst an assessment of post-Romantic remedies to the incapacity to any longer assert the basic goodness of nature and being, or what he refers to as the modern "crisis of affirmation," Charles Taylor writes of "a seeing which also helps effect what it sees," that is to say, one "conceived not simply as a *response* to what [the world] is, but as what *makes* it such." For Taylor such a seeing finds its original expression in the Judeo-Christian doctrine of creation, where "the goodness of the world is not something quite independent from God's seeing it as good" (Taylor, *Sources of the Self*, 449).

13. It is unclear, however, why the appellation "global" should be assigned to a style of theorizing as provincial as that which characterizes many of these thinkers—even when that provinciality is most clearly manifested in their respective versions of "universalism." Indeed, underpinning the intellectual projects with which this issue is preoccupied, we contend, is the presumption that the truth of Christianity cannot, as Daniel Boyarin put it in his review of the work of Alain Badiou ("Neither Greek nor Jew"), be a matter "of a particular time, place, or historical set of circumstances, conflicts, and possibilities." Hardly surprising, then, that Badiou's reclamation of Paul as the exemplary figure of a subjective militancy finds deep resonances with a long-standing Euro-Christian tradition of posing the "event" of Christianity in direct contradistinction to the putative "particularities" of Jewish norms and practices. "What does Paul want?" Badiou asks. "Probably to drag the Good News (the Gospels) out from the rigid enclosure within which its restriction to the Jewish community would confine it" (Badiou, *Saint Paul*, 13). Here the discovery of a political subjectivity up to the task of confronting the dual enemies of identitarian politics and consumer capital-

plinary itineraries we certainly have a stake in how such developments play out and are understood. Yet while it is indeed noteworthy that so many academics have thought it worthwhile to take Christianity as a topic of research—or even, as it were, a prototype of political militancy—we recall that the secular university, much like the secular state, has tended to be less concerned with *banishing* "religion" from its domain than with probing, circumscribing, recalibrating, and at times reactivating and mobilizing it (be it an abstract "religion" or specific "religions") to its various purposes.[14] So although it has become common among anthropologists, for instance, to narrate the emergence of an anthropology of Christianity in terms of a return of the repressed,[15] where Christianity—or a "fundamentalist" version of it—stands as the apotheosis of that "repugnant cultural other" through which the anthropologist's own sensibility has in no small measure come to be constituted,[16] it is not at all evident that such a repression ever took the form of any but the most superficial of absences. In fact, one might proffer a history of anthropology in which the discipline's energies were from the very beginning galvanized in an attempt not simply to distance itself from but to reflect on and, more significantly, *rearticulate* Christianity—and then "religion"—in ways commensurate with the moral and political determinants of a given moment.

Is positing the current preoccupation with Christianity as something new a means of evading that history? Perhaps not. But to the extent that scholars have failed to confront the myriad ways in which the Christianity they now seek to take seriously has itself been inscribed in, read through, and thereby refashioned as the result of such processes, there is no reason to suppose that these latest objectifications

---

ism finds itself drawing (obliviously or not) upon an archive in which Christianity is seen as the systematic undoing of Jewish election and Judaism as the antithesis of true—which is to say universal—religion. As Gil Anidjar has shown in his *Semites*, we might recognize in this impulse a specific formulation of Islam as well.

14. For a trenchant reassessment of secularism along these lines, see Mahmood, "Secularism, Hermeneutics, and Empire," 323–47.

15. See, e.g., Cannell, *Anthropology of Christianity*, 4. On the more general formulation of an "anthropology of Christianity," we are thinking especially of Robbins, "What Is a Christian?" 191–99; Bialecki, Haynes, and Robbins, "Anthropology of Christianity," 1139–58; Coleman, *Globalisation of Charismatic Christianity*; Engelke, *Problem of Presence*; and Howell, "Repugnant Cultural Other Speaks Back," 371–91.

16. The classic statement is Harding, "Representing Fundamentalism."

of Christianity will not similarly yield images of a religiosity made uncannily legible to the logics and circumscriptions of the disciplinary formations—and not only professional formations but political and economic ones as well—occupied by those who study it. Put somewhat differently, our worry is not (or not *only*) that this burgeoning interest across a range of scholarly orientations will inevitably engender explanations of Christianity foreign to the self-understandings of Christians themselves; it is that a long series of contingently linked intellectual, legal, and political developments have *already* rendered Christianity, as with everything else, translatable into a lexicon—what Alasdair MacIntyre once referred to as an "internationalized language"[17]—in which the conditions for explaining, repudiating, or, as the case may be, instrumentalizing it, have been firmly secured. (That some strands of Protestantism played no small part in shaping that lexicon is surely cause for further consideration.[18])

Thus, judging from the title of the present volume, it is not Christianity in and of itself that we are being asked to address. It is something called "global Christianity," which is to say, a purportedly historical-empirical phenomenon locatable in time and space (i.e., the time-space of a globalized world) that social scientists, religious-studies scholars, and others can identify and interpret as an object of theoretical analysis. So that Christianity, as we understand it, has already been converted into a particular idiom: the idiom of the global.[19] Whether and to what extent the notion of a "global Christianity" captures something real is beside the point, as are the panoply of questions—regarding the disparate archives from which this category emerges, its historical and

17. MacIntyre characterizes an internationalized language, or, specifically, a "late-twentieth century language of internationalized modernity," as one that "has been developed so as apparently to become potentially available to anyone and everyone, whatever their membership in any or no community" (MacIntyre, *Whose Justice? Which Rationality?* 373).

18. Ernst Troeltsch, the great liberal protestant theologian and philosopher, exemplifies this kind of development. See, for example, Troeltsch's *Absoluteness of Christianity*. The book was originally published in 1901.

19. Of course, some have argued that the idiom of the global already has a Christian history. Most recently (and compellingly), for example, Webb Keane has linked the concept of globalization to the much older idea of a Christian *ecumene*, which leads him to assert that "when it came to naming the global as a unity, until recently a capacity to imagine totality was inseparable from the expansive community, and perhaps the embracing ontology, of a given universalizing religion" (*Christian Moderns*, 42).

conceptual antecedents, its relation to a discourse on "world religions," and so forth—that one might easily pose of it. Likewise, although an explication of what exactly "global Christianity" *does* (or is taken to do) for those scholars who invoke it—the avenues of debate and research it occludes and opens up, the assumptions it fortifies and contests, the constraints it responds to and reproduces—would undoubtedly prove instructive, our intention here is to pursue something of a different route. We want to ask what it would mean to approach Christianity otherwise: to work, following Hadot, at seeing it, if not "as though one were seeing it for the first time," then at least in such a way that the questions we have grown accustomed to asking of it, and the words with which we have grown accustomed to answering those questions, might be subjected to the shock of other questions, different words, ones arising from the materiality of life-worlds not easily made available to the insatiable, ever appropriating curiosity typical of our regnant intellectual practices.[20] And so, in the spirit of unpredictable outcomes (and perhaps ill-advised beginnings), we have decided to make our entrée into this terrain via a confrontation with what Kavin Rowe, whose recent book we will be dependent upon in the following pages, refers to as "a highly charged and theologically sophisticated political document that aims at nothing less than the construction of an alternative total way of life": namely, that composed by Luke in his Acts of the Apostles, the first effort at depicting authoritatively the birth and character of the early community of Christians.[21]

Why Acts? Why, of all places, turn to a biblical text, and a notoriously contentious one at that? Our engagement with Acts may well

20. It worth remembering the long tradition within and beyond Christianity of conceiving curiosity as a potentially destructive vice. See, e.g., Augustine, *Confessions*, 10.14.54–55. Mary-Jane Rubenstein locates a similar suspicion of curiosity in Heidegger, for whom curiosity appears as "a persistent 'not-staying': a state of ontic dispersion resulting from the attempt to conquer all difficulties." Rather than dwell with the incalculable, Rubenstein writes, "curiosity at its most irresponsible skips from one marvelous phenomenon to the next, 'resolving' each puzzle as quickly as possible in order to possess it—materially or epistemologically—and move on to something newer or more bizarre" (Rubenstein, *Strange Wonder*, 27). Similarly, Paul Griffiths has recently characterized *curiositas*—as against the intellectual virtue of *studiositas*—as an "appetite for the ownership of new knowledge," its principle method being that of "enclosure by sequestration of particular creatures or ensembles as such" (*Intellectual Appetite*, 20–21).

21. Rowe, *World Upside Down*, 4

seem arbitrary and misguided, a cheap shot that, not unlike the philosophical aloofness that appears to have provided a tacit impetus for the present volume, willfully ignores the messiness and ambiguities of "real" (we ask again: "global?") Christianity in favor of a biased and idealized, even pristine account. Furthermore, we could rightly be accused of facilitating the collapse of the anthropological into the theological (here leaving aside the irony that it is only recently that theologians have begun to rediscover the value of Scripture), and thus of blurring the line between interpretation and assertion, dispassionate analysis and motivated confession.[22] It is our contention, however, that a descent into the rough texture of Luke's narrative, a narrative that has long instructed Christians as to what it looks like to be sent out into the world as witnesses to the reality called gospel, might at the same time provide a model of—or failing that, a way of exposing the limits to—what, on the one hand, is increasingly being taken up as an anthropology of Christianity, and, on the other, what has in recent years become an effort to envisage a novel political subjectivity derived from Christianity. As such, our purpose is less to dismantle than to interrogate and sharpen the prospects of taking Christianity as an object of study, be it as the site of ethnographic investigation or as the source of a critical register. But in doing so it is necessary to ask: What kind of Christianity are we dealing with? After all, it is one thing to study a Christianity whose theology tells us that it can be studied unproblematically, that is, by recourse to the same methods and conceptual discriminations that would be employed in the examination of any social fact. But it is, we imagine, quite another thing to study a Christianity whose theology asks us to consider the possibility that what we find in Acts might actually be true. It is a commonplace among anthropologists that taking the questions that concern their subjects "seriously" is a vital means of gaining access to the cultural-discursive milieus to which that subject belongs. What Acts shows us is that there may be questions that, in order to ask them, or to ask them *competently*, might well require a transformation of the agent of investigation. A disquieting thought: that attending the current "turn to Christianity" might be a problem involving not so much how

---

22. For a preliminary and quite provocative attempt to think through the potential resources theology might offer anthropology, see Joel, "Anthropology and Theology," 286–94.

we make our objects of inquiry, as how—and if so, in what ways—our objects of inquiry make us.

Involved, we want to suggest, in seeing Christianity otherwise, in "get[ting] rid of the conventional and routine vision we have of things," must be a willingness to submit ourselves to the training necessary to acquire the ability to read felicitously its defining texts; as his framing of Acts in the above paragraph attests to, Rowe's defamiliarizing study is as good a place as any to initiate such a training. For it is in Acts, according to Rowe, that the appearance of the church as the *novum* of God's apocalypse testifies to the contingent nature of all that is, thereby conferring upon the world, coterminous with the reality of resurrection, the possibility of a people in whose deeply specific language, "full to bursting with meaning," the world itself is both refracted and made afresh.[23] But it is also in Acts that the learning of such a language, and the seeing of such a world, is revealed to be indistinguishable from an ongoing habituation into the emplaced yet perpetually dislocated community of the radically dispossessed: dispossessed not simply of land and money, prestige and so forth, but of the requisite knowledges by which we could explain and thereby manage the world around us; what, for lack of a better term, we might call *epistemological dispossession*; or, better still, humility.[24] If Acts has anything to teach us it is that the world

23. We borrow this phrasing from an early text authored by Gershom Scholem. Spelling out the implications of what he took to be the transition, propelled by Zionism, of the Hebrew language from its status as a sacred tongue to its new function as the everyday language of politics and communication, Scholem writes: "That sacred language—is it not an abyss that must open up one day? The people certainly don't know what they are doing. They think they have secularized the Hebrew language, have done away with its apocalyptic point. But that, of course, is not true. . . . It is impossible to empty the words so bursting with meaning, unless one sacrifices the language itself. . . . The day will come when the language will turn against those who speak it. There are already moments in our own life when this happens, unforgettable, stigmatizing moments, when all the presumptuousness of our enterprise is suddenly revealed. . . . May the levity that has accompanied us on this apocalyptic path not lead us to our destruction." Quoted in Mosès, *Angel of History*, 168–70. Incidentally, it has often been noted that a defining characteristic of those Christians (i.e., Pentecostal-charismatics) most associated with "global Christianity" is their recovery of, and insistence on, the destructive and life-giving power of even casually spoken words, particularly that of the name of Jesus. Surely it is among the comforts of modern academic work that such things obtain only in the cultures we study and, therefore, need not affect the ways we write and theorize about them.

24. Daniel Barber's formulation of a "creativity of exilic deterritorialization," in-

to which such a condition gestures cannot be known, indeed does not exist, absent the lives of the people who enact it. The theological politics that emerges from Acts, therefore, is decidedly not one of a "plurality of viewpoints on the same world or object"; instead it is a matter of "each viewpoint . . . opening on to another world that itself contains yet others."[25] This is a world that must be believed in order to be seen; in the terminology of Acts, it is a world that must be *witnessed* to.[26]

Becoming Witness, or, Luke: Anthropologist of Christianity?

> All of us, even when we think we have noted every tiny detail, resort to set pieces which have already been staged often enough by others. We try to reproduce the reality, but the harder we try, the more we find the pictures that make up the stock-in-trade of the spectacle of history forcing themselves upon us. . . . Our concern with history, so Hilary's thesis ran, is a concern with preformed images already imprinted on our brains, images at which we keep staring while the truth lies elsewhere, away from it all, somewhere as yet undiscovered.[27]

To be sure, it was not the interpretation of Scripture that W. G. Sebald had in mind when he penned these remarks—the "Hilary" alluded to is André Hilary, a secondary school teacher in the Welsh countryside, and the impetus for his thesis is an inability to adequately recount a particularly gruesome battle in the Napoleonic Wars—but it may as well have been. They are, after all, literally set pieces that Alain Badiou resorts to when, taking a cue from Pier Pasolini's unfinished screenplay *Saint Paul*, he juxtaposes what he considers to be the radical temperament of the latter's epistles with "the pro-Roman benevolence harbored by the author of the Acts."[28] Apart from the sheer novelty of Pasolini's trans-

debted in equal measure to Gilles Deleuze and John Howard Yoder, nicely captures what we are trying to get at here. See, most recently, his "Epistemological Violence, Christianity, and the Secular," in Dula and Huebner, *New Yoder*, 19. According to Rowan Williams, it is through baptism, or what he refers to as "the process of self-forgetting that leads to the cross," that such a dispossession is displayed sacramentally. See R. Williams, *Resurrection*, 54.

25. Smith, "Life of Pure Immanence," in Deleuze, *Essays Critical and Clinical*, xxvii.

26. Hauerwas, "Believing Is Seeing," in *Cross-Shattered Church*, 27–32.

27. Sebald, *Austerlitz*, 71–72.

28. Badiou, *Saint Paul*, 30. For an interesting appraisal of what the author takes to

position of Paul into contemporary Europe, which finds the Pharisee-turned-apostle now portrayed as a leader in the antifascist Resistance, what is especially pertinent for Badiou's purposes is the fact that it is not the tyrannical dictator that is figured as the villain in Pasolini's script but instead the internal enemy who would write history in such a way as to eradicate from the Movement any trace of genuine revolutionary potential. Thus, against the militant "saintliness" exemplified by Paul and his comrades, Luke is exposed as a traitor, an agent of the devil, bent on domesticating the Resistance and therefore on making of Paul "a man of the institution," a "saint erased by the priest," or, closing the analogical gap entirely, "not so much a theoretician of the Christian event as the tireless creator of the Church."[29] To a large extent, it is this contrast effect—between Luke and Paul, accommodation and fidelity, sanctioned discourse and singular truth—that will supply the dramatic thrust of Badiou's own study. Indeed, one could suggest that Badiou's "startling reinterpretation" of Paul, and Pasoloni's as well, premised as they are on an explicit disavowal of what Badiou will elsewhere refer to as Luke's "retrospective construction whose intentions modern criticism has clearly brought to light," finally end up reproducing what, among New Testament scholars at least, has been a three-hundred-year-old habit of reading Acts as little more than an apologia for political quietism fashioned to appear as "uniform, organizational, and 'Roman' as possible."[30]

Such is the hermeneutical consensus that Kavin Rowe's *World Upside Down: Reading Acts in the Graeco-Roman Age* sets out to unsettle. And yet, as Rowe makes clear from the outset, the counter-reading he

---

be Pasolini's "impossible" screenplay, see Mariniello, "*St. Paul*: The Unmade Movie," 67–84.

29. Badiou, *Saint Paul*, 38–39. Badiou's assumption that the truth of the "Christian event" can so conveniently be distinguished from the contingent formation of the historical church is, in large part, exactly what we take Luke to be writing against in Acts. Here again, the "radical" impulse of Badiou's reading of Paul ends up looking remarkably managed and determinate. That his book has garnered the fawning attention that it has surely says more about the impoverished theological (not to say political) imagination of contemporary thought than about the power of Badiou's analysis.

30. Badiou, *Saint Paul*, 18, 26. That the editorial preface to Acts in *The New Oxford Annotated Bible*, 183–85 (New Testamnt), rehearses this perspective is no doubt further evidence of its now taken-for-granted status. Of course, critics have long held a similar view of Luke's Gospel. On such readings of Luke, see Yoder, *Politics of Jesus*, 53–54; Hays, *Moral Vision*, 125–28, 247–48.

undertakes to provide cannot proceed merely by way of a more precise exegetical style, but must concurrently take stock of the numerous, often inchoate ways in which the concepts and classifications endemic to modern life have imposed themselves on the social vocabularies of the ancient world—and that involves breaking not only with interpretations of Acts that view it as politically "conformist" but also from those that consider it "revolutionary" as well. Tempting though it may be to read Acts through the later vicissitudes of Constantinianism, Luke's portrait of the early church—he calls it "the Way"—is emphatically *not* that of a people whose desire it is to take the state.[31] Christians do not want to replace the Emperor, nor do they want a Christian to be the Emperor. That would be a far too conservative politics. Instead, recounted in Acts is the ceaseless, exuberant, often grueling dissemination of a "good news" that, resting as it does in the affirmation of a break between God and the pagan cosmos, the peace of Christ and the *Pax Romana* (the former constituting a "subversion and rearrangement of the very notion of peace"[32]), threatens to unravel the very fabric of the entire order of things—or so Rowe wants to suggest. Displaying a methodological acuity reminiscent of that advocated by R. G. Collingwood, whose "logic," as he called it, of "question and answer" held that a proposition can be properly grasped only when the question to which it forms an answer is first identified and articulated, Rowe begins with the basic observation that "Luke does not have a different *opinion* on the question of religion and politics from many modern thinkers, he has an entirely different question."[33] We need not go far in Acts to discover what that question is. After his crucifixion, we are told, Jesus ordered the disciples

> not to leave Jerusalem, but to wait there for the promise of the
> Father. "This," he said, "is what you have heard from me; for
> John baptized with water, but you will be baptized with the Holy
> Spirit not many days from now." So when they had come togeth-

31. By "Constantinianism" we mean the quite understandable attempt by Christians to find a permanent home in the world that promised safety. Less about the person of Constantine himself, the term rather refers to the shift by which "the church is no longer the obedient suffering line of the true prophets; she has a vested interest in the present order of things and uses the cultic means at her disposal to legitimize that order" (Yoder, *Original Revolution*, 65–66).

32. Rowe, *World Upside Down*, 35.

33. Ibid., 9, emphasis added. On Collingwood's question and answer method, see Collingwood, *An Autobiography*, 29–43.

er, they asked him, "Lord, is this the time when you will restore the kingdom to Israel?" He replied, "It is not for you to know the times or periods that the Father has set by his own authority. But you will receive power when the Holy Spirit has come upon you; and you will be my witnesses in Jerusalem, in all Judea and Samaria, and to the ends of the earth." When he had said this, as they were watching, he was lifted up, and a cloud took him out of their sight.[34]

What does it mean to be a living body of witnesses to the reality of the risen Christ? This, above all, is the question that animates Luke's account. Yet it is exactly this question that seems to have escaped several generations of New Testament scholars, whose uniformity of opinion as to (what Badiou calls) the "pro-Roman benevolence harbored by the author of Acts," and the non-threatening political imaginary thought to accompany it, can only be attributed to a profound misrecognition of the irreducibly particular question to which Luke's narrative was crafted as a response and in isolation from which the actions of its protagonists are divested of their original sense.

Which is not to say that the question is original to Acts. For inasmuch as the dominant motifs of that book are prefigured by an assortment of episodes depicted earlier in Luke's Gospel, as well as the Old Testament, what emerges is an intricate pattern of promise and fulfillment—a salvation history—that by necessity gestures beyond the confines of any single text.[35] Conceived fundamentally as a continuation of the biblical narrative, Luke arranges his literary project through a succession of echoes, allusions, and anticipations—some overt, others remarkably subtle—whose implications for the present take shape in their orientation to a past that is itself altered in the course of Luke's narrative redeployment.[36] It follows that the apprehendability of Acts must be built on a prior familiarity not only with the circumstances of Jesus' life and ministry, passion and resurrection, but with the larger yet startlingly parochial story that, then as now, enables Jesus to be called the Christ: that is, the story of God's enduring covenant with the Jews. It is no accident, for instance, that whereas Mark's Gospel places Jesus' appearance in his hometown synagogue at Nazareth well after

34. Acts 1:4–9, NRSV.
35. Hays, *Moral Vision*, 113–14.
36. L. T. Johnson, *Writings of the New Testament*, 219.

his public ministry has already commenced (Mark 6:1–6a), reporting only that Jesus "began to teach" and that "many who heard him were astounded," Luke moves the episode to the very beginning of Jesus' ministry and provides a detailed description of what transpires therein (4:16–21). According to Richard Hays, what Jesus' subsequent recitation from the prophet Isaiah amounts to is "nothing less than a public announcement of his messianic vocation," for by evoking these texts at the outset of his ministry, Hays writes, "Luke's Jesus declares himself as the Messiah who by the power of the Spirit will create a restored Israel in which justice and compassion for the poor will prevail." As the scene in the synagogue continues to unfold, as the crowd is "filled with rage" at Jesus' suggestion, made by way of a reference to the prophets Elijah and Elisha, that God's favor would extend to the Gentiles (4:25–30), we are at once clued into how the prophetic tradition has been recast in Jesus' inhabitation of it and at the same time offered a foretaste of issues that will persist into the final pages of Acts: specifically, those having to do with "the extension of God's grace beyond the boundaries of Israel and the hostility of many in Israel to this inclusive message of grace."[37]

If a key to understanding the signifying power of the inauguration of Jesus' public ministry lies in its embeddedness in and consummation of the deepest yearnings of Jewish law and prophecy, so, too, does Jesus' parting address at his ascension resonate with a promise that both presages and exceeds the advent of the apostolic commission. Indeed, it is a promise that spans the entirety of the biblical record: from God's pledge to make of Abraham the father of a nation that will be a blessing to all nations (Gen 17:1–27) to the angel's stunning proclamation in the final pages of Revelation ("He will dwell with them, and they will be his people"), the reality of a God who moves in history is consistently shown to be dependent upon the existence of a people whose lives bespeak the truth of his sovereignty and provision. It is, moreover, a promise that is made when, at the beginning of Luke's first volume and prior to the birth of Jesus, Gabriel appears to Zechariah and announces that his unborn son—John the Baptist—will have as his task to "make ready a people prepared for the Lord" (Luke 1:17).

But a promise, it ought to be stressed, is not a precedent; while it is not the case that "there never was a Jewish mission of any kind prior

---

37. Hays, *Moral Vision*, 115–16.

to Christianity," it is no less the case, Rowe argues, taking up the much-debated issue of whether precursors to Christian mission were extant in Jewish proselytizing practices, "that what we see in Acts—*taken as a whole*—finds no counterpart anywhere in the Jewish world prior to the end of the first century."[38] What may appear here to be mere historicist quibbling rather becomes a prelude to a crucial theological point: when Jesus says to his disciples that they will be his "witnesses in Jerusalem, in all Judea and Samaria, and to the ends of the earth" (Acts 1:8), he is describing for them a mode of being in the world that cannot arise naturally out of any "type" or "model." Instead, springing as it does from his death and resurrection, what Jesus enunciates at his ascension is the composition of a radically new creation, the very embodiment, socially and materially, of the fact that death no longer marks the boundary of human life, but that, to the contrary, as Rowan Williams suggests, it is through *this* death that "a new and potentially infinite network of relations is opened up."[39] The resurrection miracle, the miracle of miracles—not because a dead man has been resurrected but because Israel's messiah has been resurrected—soon gives way to the miracle of a church whose literally limitless mission, as Rowe puts it, "actively socializes the salvific reality that attends Jesus' universal Lordship."[40]

Luke, however, has little interest in "proving" the resurrection—or, better, the proof he offers, the only proof he *can* offer, is that of a people whose lives (and, in many cases, whose deaths) would be unintelligible had Jesus not in fact been raised from the dead. Put in slightly different terms, Luke is concerned to demonstrate that those who will follow Christ will be unable to "explain" his resurrection. The resurrection will explain them. And it is this impossibility of disentangling the event of the resurrection from the shape of the lives of the people who declare it that defines the *witness* announced in Acts. Of the apostles—that is, those who have been sent out to witness—depicted in Acts, it is Paul, the primary human protagonist in the book's second half (the book's principle actor, of course, is the Holy Spirit), who best exemplifies the necessary interconnection between the resurrection of Jesus and the subsequent biographies of the men and women who are to serve as

---

38. Rowe, *World Upside Down*, 119, original emphasis.

39. R. Williams, *Resurrection*, 53

40. Rowe, *World Upside Down*, 124

witnesses to it. Yet it seems strange that, of all people, Paul would be appointed a "witness to all the world of what [he] has seen and heard" (Acts 22:15), for, unlike many of his fellow apostles, he neither knew Jesus during the Messiah's lifetime nor was he present at Jesus' resurrection and ascension—nor, for that matter, and again unlike the other apostles, was he there for the arrival of the Holy Spirit on the day of Pentecost (Acts 2:1–4). In short, what he has actually "seen and heard" is, it would appear, far less impressive than we might have expected of this paragon of apostleship. To what, and in what particular manner, is Paul a witness?

Perhaps a brief detour into some prevailing conceptions of witnessing will allow us to better address this question. In his *Remnants of Auschwitz: The Witness and the Archive*, Giorgio Agamben observes that in Latin there are two words for "witness": "The first word, *testis*, from which our word 'testimony' derives, etymologically signifies the person who, in a trial or lawsuit between two rival parties, is in the position of a third party (*tersis*). The second word, *superstes*, designates a person who has lived through something, who has experienced an event from beginning to end and can therefore bear witness to it."[41] Commenting on this double meaning, anthropologist Didier Fassin explains:

> In the first case the witness was external to the scene, but observed it: to be more precise, he has no vested interest and it is this supposed neutrality that is the grounds for hearing and believing him, including in legal proceedings. In the second case, the witness lived through the ordeal, and suffered it: it is therefore because he was present, but as a victim of the event himself and hence a survivor, that his word is listened to. One testifies on the basis of his observation, the other on the basis of his experience. The truth of the *testis*, expressed in the third person, is deemed objective. The truth of the *superstes*, expressed in the first person, is deemed subjective. The latter has merit by virtue of the affects it involves, the former by virtue of those it eliminates.[42]

Fassin's purpose here is to trace the emergence within the domain of international humanitarianism and human rights discourse of what he calls "the key political figure of our time": namely, the humanitarian

41. Agamben, *Remnants of Auschwitz*, 17.
42. Fassin, "Humanitarian Politics of Testimony," 535.

worker-*cum*-"witness" whose aim it is to give voice to the unarticulated or unrepresented traumas visited upon those subjected to various forms of violence and catastrophe. While he does not mention it here (though he does so elsewhere[43]), the mounting efficacy of this figure correlates with the contemporaneous reimagining of the anthropologist's task as being fundamentally one of "bearing witness," such that one well-known anthropologist can suggest, in a formulation whose banality is offset only by its surprising parenthetical addendum, that "the work of witnessing is what lends our work its moral (at times its almost theological) character."[44] Less a matter of supplanting the discipline's signature method of "participant observation" than of imbuing it with an ethico-political mandate, a growing number of anthropologists have taken to conceiving of their work and, specifically, their writings as "powerful spaces in which to authorize and legitimate the painful and often devastating histories that we anthropologists are allowed to listen to and sometimes see with our own eyes."[45] Hence the salience, for Fassin, of the distinction between *testis* and *superstes*: the humanitarian worker, like the anthropologist, does not *live* the "painful and often devastating history" in question but rather *observes* (or otherwise hears about) it; both are witnesses exactly to the extent of their remove from the event to which they testify and, in an important sense, from those—as Fassin would say, those *superstes*—whose sufferings and resultant affects they seek to convey. The juridified world to which such testimonies are addressed, in other words, demands that the self of the witness be wholly separable from that which has, according to the aid worker or anthropologist, so indelibly left its mark on the psyche of the victim. And presumably, moreover, their identity qua aid worker or anthropologist, or whatever other name they may wish to assign themselves, will, barring some breach of professional conduct, endure inde-

43. Fassin and Rechtman, *Empire of Trauma*.

44. Scheper-Hughes, *Death without Weeping*, xxi. In a more searching, less affected way, Das writes: "This is how I see the public role of anthropology—acting on the double register in which we offer evidence that contests the official amnesia and downright acts of making evidence disappear—but also witnessing the descent into the everyday through which victims and survivors affirm the possibility of life by removing it from the circulation of words gone wild—leading words home, so to say" ("Trauma and Testimony," 304).

45. Angel-Ajane, "Expert Witness," in Sanford and Angel-Ajane, *Engaged Observers*, 79.

pendently of their work of bearing witness, for the latter task, though likely assumed in a moment of perceived necessity, was not after all essential to their capacity to go on.

The witness of Paul, on the other hand, derives not from observation, nor even—and here we need to challenge the usefulness of the *testis/superstes* opposition—from experience, but instead from *recognition*, an initial lack of which takes the form of Paul's remarkable bewilderment in the famous story of his conversion. "Now as he was going along and approaching Damascus," we are told in Acts 9:3–5, "suddenly a light from heaven flashed around him. He fell to the ground and heard a voice saying to him, 'Saul, Saul, why do you persecute me?' He asked, 'Who are you, Lord?' The incredulity of the question indicates that Paul must lose his vision before he will see, and that he will testify to what he has seen only when he has been able to identify the voice that summons him, and the light that blinds him, with the one who came to the people of Israel preaching peace, who healed the sick and fed the hungry, and who was later put to death on a tree. Against the Pauline event postulated by Badiou, the ostensible locus of which is the *ex nihilo*, "absolutely aleatory" moment of subjective "caesura," Paul is to become a witness not to the experience of a light blinding him on the road to Damascus but to the actuality of the resurrected Christ embodied in the corporeal existence of, among others, those who have fallen prey to Paul's repressive violence. The witnesses exhibited in Acts are not merely those who have observed or experienced something and then gone on to tell others about it. Paul is a witness because his very life, a life of rejection and persecution, has been made a testimony to the inauguration of a kingdom that, "against every Gnosticizing impulse," is not merely "spiritual" but is also practical and material—a kingdom, in short, "that takes up space in public."[46] Accordingly, in line with what Douglas Harink characterizes as the determinatively apocalyptic vision that runs throughout his writings, Paul "does not see in Christ one religious option among others. He sees in Christ nothing less than the whole of creation and all of humanity under God's final judgment and grace. . . . Paul is uncompromisingly focused on a single, incomparable, final, and exclusive theological reality which constitutes, includes, and determines all other reality: Jesus Christ."[47] And just as

46. Rowe, *World Upside Down*, 101.

47. Harink, *Paul among the Postliberals*, 81. Earlier (68) Harink writes that "in the

Paul's eyes have been opened to a new reality, so, too, has he been called to open the eyes of the gentiles "so that they may turn from darkness to light" (Acts 26:18, 23). Here, then, is apocalyptic at its most basic and comprehensive. "The resurrection of Jesus actually creates a new mode of seeing—'light.' To miss the resurrection of Jesus, therefore, is to forfeit the ability to see."[48]

Hardly a matter of brute facticity or abstract truth, the reality enunciated by the resurrection is one that is inseparable from—indeed, more often than not, is literally *written on the bodies of*—those who have assumed the task, however painful or demanding, of proclaiming and thereby participating in it. Now it may seem that this "reality enunciated by the resurrection" is by definition a happy one, a triumphalist one, a reality whose unending reenactment in the life of the visible church, far from necessitating "painful or demanding" practices of discipleship, might just as easily lend itself to assumptions such as those which, according to scholars of the Roman imperial Church, served to underwrite that institution's consolidation of power both within and beyond its borders: namely, the assumption that "the power of heaven and of the age to come had, in a sense, been domesticated and made available here and now."[49] In Acts, however, we discover that to partake of the body and blood of Christ is to be transformed into a community of crucifixion—with all of the uncertainties and discomforts (to put it blandly) that implies—even and at the same time as the resurrection remains its inescapable telos and condition of possibility. For what Acts shows us is that the resurrection can only be accessed and encountered once the believing community has learned to live not simply after but *through* the *experimentum crucis*, the experience of the cross. This is the case not only with the apostles and Paul, who, "captive to the Spirit,"

New Testament, in particular for Paul, all apocalyptic reflection and hope comes to this, that God has acted critically, decisively, and finally for Israel, all the peoples of the earth, and the entire cosmos, in the life, death, resurrection, and coming again of Jesus, in such a way that God's purpose for Israel, for all humanity, and all creation is critically, decisively, and finally disclosed and effected in the history of Jesus Christ."

48. Rowe, *World Upside Down*, 86.

49. Greer, *Fear of Freedom*, 5. Greer's study insightfully draws out what he takes to be the crucial place of the miraculous in legitimating the Constantinian church, such that a discourse on the resurrection—and the proliferation of miracles more generally—is increasingly mobilized in the service of securing the Church's this-worldly *auctoritas*.

is persistently led "to testify to the good news of God's grace" in cities where only "imprisonment and persecutions are awaiting" him (Acts 20:22–24), but also with Stephen, at whose lynching Paul makes his first appearance in the New Testament text.

Of course, it is with Stephen that another, maybe paradigmatic meaning of witness comes sharply into view: that of the martyr, whose faithfulness even to the point of death simply denotes the more acute form, the intensification, of what Luke suggests will be the typical Christian mode of acting and being in the world. The significance of Luke's conferral upon Stephen of the appellation "witness"—as in Paul's speech to the angry Jerusalem crowd in Acts 22, where he relates how he said to the risen Jesus that "while the blood of your witness Stephen was shed, I myself was standing by, approving and keeping the coats of those who killed him"—cannot, according to Rowe, be overestimated:

> Whether or not Luke was here consciously forging the first ex-
> plicitly verbal link between "witnessing" and becoming a "mar-
> tyr" in the later Christian sense of the term, the text doubtless
> draws clearly the line between the mission of witnessing to the
> risen Jesus and the reality of trial, suffering, and death. In so do-
> ing, it elevates for clear inspection what it means to be a witness
> in the missionary theology of Acts. It is, in fact, to reenact the
> life-pattern of the suffering Christ, to suffer for his Name, to be
> put on trial, to face the possibility of death, and to proclaim the
> resurrection. In short, it is to embody the cruciform pattern that
> culminates in resurrection.[50]

In marked contrast to the constellation of images that we tend to associate with martyrdom, images that have been filtered through entrenched ideologies of nationalism and warfare, masculinity and individualism, the violent deaths of Stephen and, soon thereafter, countless others are profoundly misconstrued when they are regarded as instances of courageous heroism or self-abnegating sacrifice. Such renderings threaten to extricate martyrs like Stephen from the narrative frame which alone makes their deaths intelligible, a narrative, Rowan Williams contends, in which the narcissistic drama of heroism has been eschewed in favor of freedom from the imperatives of violence.[51] Inhabiting this freedom means finding oneself most fully at home in a

---

50. Rowe, *World Upside Down*, 121.
51. See R. Williams, *Christ on Trial*, 107.

world that is no longer ruled by the specter of death—and yet, precisely to that extent, it also means finding oneself most fundamentally at odds with how the world runs itself. It is in this way that the remembrance of martyrs becomes a radical political act: in so remembering, we are reminded of the possibility of an alternative to the economies of fear and mastery that so unremittingly compel us.[52]

It is at this point that we may return to the accusation of accommodationism that has long inflected interpretations of Acts (among which, as we mentioned at the outset, characterizations like Badiou's are merely symptomatic). How can we continue to evoke an alternative politics in light of what appears to be such a seemingly insurmountable consensus? One of the foremost contributions of Rowe's book, it seems to us, flows from his assertion that the demarcations that populate our language—such as that of "religion" from "politics"—render it difficult to comprehend the far-reaching implications of the church's claim to be the social and material embodiment of the lordship of Christ. That modern readers would fail to recognize the nature of that claim is not the least bit surprising, for a great deal of Luke's account is given over to showing the multifarious ways in which the message of the early Christians could be misunderstood by their contemporaries, often violently so (although, as we have seen with Stephen, and as we shall see below, it is also when their message is *perfectly* comprehended that violence can ensue). Rowe's method of enumerating the distinctive contours of Christian mission, and hence its relation to the prevailing political structures of the period, is to unpack what he considers to be a profound, even constitutive tension at the heart of Acts. This tension (or "dialectic," as Rowe calls it) comprises not an accidental or inadvertent but a necessary dimension of Luke's theological and political vision, which means that the point is not so much to resolve it as to understand how exactly it is produced, and to exactly what ends. Here is the tension as Rowe presents it:

> On the one hand, Luke narrates the movement of the Christian
> mission into the gentile world as a collision with culture-

---

52. For an examination of martyrdom along these lines, see Whitfield, *Pilgrim Holiness*, esp. 115–28. Needless to say, the remembrance of martyrs has often given way to a politics of violence and subjugation. For accounts of martyrdom that situate it within the history of, respectively, the Crusades and post-Reformation religious conflict, see Mastnak, *Crusading Peace* and Kaplan, *Divided by Faith*.

constructing aspects of that world. From the perspective created by this angle of vision, Christianity and pagan culture are competing realities. Inasmuch as embracing the Christian call to repentance necessarily involves a different way of life, basic patterns of Graeco-Roman culture are dissolved. The pagans in Lystra, Philippi, Athens, and Ephesus are understandably riled: the Christians are a real threat.

On the other hand, Luke narrates the threat of the Christian mission in such a way as to eliminate the possibility of conceiving it as in direct competition with the Roman government. Of all forms of sedition and treason, Luke says, Christianity is innocent. Paul engenders considerable upheaval as a part of his mission, but time and again—in Corinth, Jerusalem, Caesarea, and Rome (so the reader understands)—the political authorities reject the accusations of his opponents: Paul is *dikaios* [righteous, or innocent]. The Christians are not out to establish Christendom, as it were. New culture, yes—coup, no.[53]

Nowhere, Rowe suggests, is this dynamic more visibly at play—and, consequently, the complex political disposition of Acts more explicitly elaborated—than in the manner in which Luke recounts the charges brought against Paul and Silas in Thessalonica (Acts 17:1–9); indeed, it is clear that an elucidation of what transpires in that city will be the fulcrum around which the thrust of Rowe's argument stands or falls. The scene opens with Paul in the Jewish synagogue at Thessalonica, trying to persuade his audience ("as was his custom"), composed of both Greeks and Jews, that "it was necessary for the Messiah to suffer and to rise from the dead" (17:2). Here again we are given a glimpse, one of countless such glimpses in Acts, not only of the fundamentally Jewish self-understanding of the community to which Paul belongs, but of the ways in which that community is seriously countercultural in relation to the prevailing forms of Judaism.[54] The rejection of messianic violence as a means of national liberation in favor of a suffering and servant Messiah, the expansion of the elect community to include uncircumcised Gentiles, and, most contentiously for some, the ascription of divine identity and lordship to the human Jesus—all this comes

---

53. Rowe, *World Upside Down*, 91.

54. Here and in what follows we are indebted to Hays, "Turning the World Upside Down."

together to constitute a minority people amongst a minority people, a subculture *within* Israel that hermeneutically *redefines* Israel.

However, it is not only in relation to Israel that Paul and his fellow Christians are deemed a subversive force; they must, crucially for Luke, defend themselves against allegations of sedition against the empire as well. Envious of their initial missionary success (Luke reports that some of the Jews "were persuaded and joined Paul and Silas, as did a great many of the devout Greeks and not a few of the leading women") and determined to rid Thessalonica of the Christian disturbers, a group of Jews organized a mob and attacked the house of Jason, presumably the local host of the Christians. When their search for Paul and Silas proved unsuccessful, they dragged Jason and some other believers before the city authorities, alleging, "these people who have turned the world upside down have come here also, and Jason has entertained them as guests. They are all acting against the decrees of Caesar, proclaiming that there is another king, Jesus" (17:6–8). The people and the magistrates were "disturbed," we are told, and the hearing rather abruptly concludes with Jason and the others being released on bail.

Much turns on how this scene is read, on where the narrative stress is seen to lie and on the sort of evidence that is brought to bear. Depending on one's orientation, the events in Thessalonica can be—and have been—taken to confirm the suspicion of a Lukan apologetic on behalf of a harmless church vis-à-vis the Roman order, or, alternately (and far less commonly), the view that Acts' political imagination announces an emphatic summons, not to direct revolt, but to a form of life that insinuates a thoroughgoing antagonism with regard to the present powers. Interestingly enough, exegetes from across the interpretive spectrum have long regarded these few verses as providing a window into the proper construal of Luke-Acts as a whole, with the central question being whether the accusation against the believers is to be understood as a false charge—thereby buttressing Luke's ostensible concern to demonstrate that Christians are innocent of the charges of stirring up trouble—or whether the hostile crowd, as Hays puts it, "rightly discerns something true about the impact of the gospel in the Roman world."[55] Conventionally, the critical reception of the episode in Thessalonica has tended to gravitate toward the former perspective; as has been maintained by New Testament scholars such as Hans

55. Hays, *Moral Vision*, 125.

Conzelmann—whom Badiou likely has in mind when he speaks of Acts as "a retrospective construction whose intentions modern criticism has clearly brought to light"[56]—Luke's project is to portray the Christians as docile subjects whose loyalty to the state is called into doubt only when the Jews manage to rouse the populace with baseless accusations against the church.[57] And, as a way of narratively preempting any further misgivings, it is argued, Luke places the most familiar, popular charge against the Christians—namely, that there is "another king" to whom they are subservient—onto the tongues of the Thessalonian mob, only to subsequently, unambiguously write this possibility out of the picture. Fortunately for the Christians, this dominant line of reasoning wants us to believe Luke is trying to suggest, the Roman authorities have the good sense to see through the jealousy-inspired tricks of the Jews and, therefore, to release Jason and his friends without further delay.

However Luke's vision of the church's mission, of becoming witness, and, ultimately, the social and political coordinates of the messianic community is finally to be understood, it must come down to this: Is Jesus a king who claims a definitive allegiance that supersedes the jurisdiction of all other kings? Based on what we have already related of Rowe's defamiliarizing account, it will come as little surprise that what he discovers in Luke's writings is a resounding, unmistakable "yes." What's more, and here against the more politically progressive readings of Christian witness, Jesus does not challenge Caesar's status as lord (*kyrios*)—as if, Rowe says, Jesus were somehow originally subordinate to Caesar in the order of being. Instead, because "of the nature of his claims, *it is Caesar who is the rival*; and what he rivals is the Lordship of God in the person of Jesus Christ."[58] It is Caesar, not Jesus, who bears the burden of proof—Caesar, not Jesus, who would attempt to pretentiously, idolatrously usurp the title of "king" for himself. Here we cannot wander into the dense thickets of Rowe's exegetical strategy, or, indeed, into each of the myriad references he mobilizes in order to make his case, so two particularly apt passages, both located within Luke's previous volume, will need to suffice. At the very beginning of his Gospel, Luke's readers are made aware that Jesus is destined to re-

---

56. Badiou, *Saint Paul*, 18.

57. See Conzelmann, *Acts of the Apostles*; *Theology of St. Luke*.

58. Rowe, *World Upside Down*, 112, our emphasis.

claim the sovereignty that the emperor has seized for himself when the angel Gabriel declares that "the Lord God will give to him the throne of his father David, and he will reign over the house of Jacob forever, and of his kingdom there will be no end" (Luke 1:32–33). With ascriptions such as these interspersed throughout each of Luke's texts, it is scarcely possible, Rowe avers, "that a Christian reader in the late first or early second century would not know that Christian claims about Jesus' identity as the Christ entailed royal claims as well, or that the advent and resurrection of Jesus was the coming of the Kingdom of God."[59]

The second example is even more striking. Luke's account of Jesus' post-baptismal temptation in the desert is in many respects similar to Matthew's, but there is one point at which Luke quite drastically goes beyond him. After showing Jesus all the kingdoms of the world, the devil says, "To you I will give their glory and all their authority, if you will worship me." The words are nearly identical to those spoken in Matthew 4:9; it is what the devil says next that is unparalleled in the Matthew's Gospel. "*For it has been given over to me, and I give it to anyone I please*" (Luke 4:6–7). The ramifications of Luke's political theology, as it were, could not be more conspicuously displayed: the emperor possesses authority because it has been given him by the devil.[60] The powers of this world, the world of the imperium, are said to emanate from Satan. So it is that when we move to Acts, we find the disciples portrayed, not as revolutionaries in any ordinary sense, but as emissaries of an emergent order in which Jesus has totally *reconfigured* kingship to reflect the inversion prophesied in Mary's song at the outset of the Gospel: "He has brought down the powerful from their thrones, and lifted up the lowly" (Luke 1:52).

To turn again, then, to the tension Rowe perceives to be running throughout the book of Acts and, thus also, to the fundamental question of whether the charges leveled against the Christians in Thessalonica—in contrast to the charges leveled against Luke by the New Testament scholars—are warranted: they are false, Rowe says, inasmuch as they attempt to place Jesus in competitive relation to Caesar, as well as to the forms, presuppositions, values, and sensibilities that "Caesar" represents. To posit such a relation would be an ontological mistake. The

59. Ibid., 100.

60. Hays, "Turning the World Upside Down"; see also Rowe, *World Upside Down*, 88.

accusations are true, however, "in that the Christian mission entails a call to another way of life, one that is—on virtually every page of the Acts of the Apostles—turning the world upside down."[61]

Church is the name of this form of life.

A Brief Concluding Postscript

"That's it?" some readers may ask. "You've taken us through all this only to conclude with 'Church is the name of this form of life'?" But we ask the reader, frustrated though you may be, to think again. Description is everything. And by calling attention to Luke's account of the birth and spread of what came to be referred to as "the church," we have tried to suggest that knowing how to describe that reality is anything but a straightforward process. Christianity did not spring from the head of Zeus readily identifiable. Indeed, as Luke makes clear, followers of Christ were first simply known as those who followed "the Way." It was their detractors who labeled them "Christians." The label turned out to be a useful description but, as we hope our brief rendering of Luke's account suggests, "the church" names an ongoing narrative which is itself a politics and a habit of sight. In an odd way the story Luke recounts allows us to see that Christians are a people who may never quite know who and where they are. That means descriptions are never settled. We hope, therefore, that our attempt to help readers see Christianity through Acts has made it apparent that any Christianity abstracted from flesh-and-blood manifestations of the lordship of Christ embodied in concrete communities of witness would, in fact, no longer be recognizable to those whose lives Luke sought to narrate—that is, to Christians.

It is our contention that, far exceeding the precision or plausibility of a specific argument, at stake in the current preoccupation with Christianity is a deeper, more intractable problematic having to do with how we perceive, name, appraise, possess—in short, *create*—that which we endeavor to know; and also with recognizing when the objects of such endeavors cannot (or perhaps should not) be known in quite the manner we wish to know them.[62] Here we have merely wanted to

61. Rowe, *World Upside Down*, 101–2.

62. In the course of his discussion of Wittgenstein's notions of grammar and

raise the question of what it might mean for those intellectual currents whose scholarly energies have been directed at enumerating the lineaments of various renderings of Christianity, "global" or otherwise, to grapple with the existence, so far as Luke has shown us in Acts, of a people whose attitudes and behaviors, passions and disputes signal the ineluctably specific after-effects of having been woven into a story not of their own design. In fact, what Acts shows us is that to "see something *as something*" is, in large measure, already to have been made by it—or, at the very least, to find oneself journeying down a path where the potentiality for such reordering is ubiquitous. Yet aspect-blindness might well be our normal condition.

This takes us to a final thought. Is it possible, or desirable, that an encounter with the life-worlds that comprise the focal points of our inquiries might make a claim not only on the certainties by which they are apprehended but on the life of the student who apprehends them? That retaining "what may be a discomforting—even scandalous—presence within our receiving languages" might reveal as slightly more tentative or provisional the assumptions that subtend them?[63] We cannot pretend to have avoided the tendencies that militate against such a possibility. We only hope that a semblance of what we have learned from Wittgenstein and Hadot has been made manifest in the preceding pages.

---

criteria, Stanley Cavell contrasts what he calls the "Austinian kind of object" with the "Wittgensteinian kind of object" by observing: "If you do not know the (nongrammatical) criteria of an Austinian object (can't identify it, name it) then you lack a piece of information, a bit of knowledge, and you can be told its name, told what it is, told what it is (officially) called. But if you do not know the grammatical criteria of Wittgensteinian objects, then you lack, as it were, not only a piece of information or knowledge, but the possibility of acquiring any information about such objects *überhaupt*; you cannot be told the name of that object, because there is as yet no *object* of that kind for you to attach a forthcoming name to: the possibility of finding out what it is officially called is not yet open to you" (*Claim of Reason*, 77). We take it for granted that a familiarity with the grammatical criteria of Christianity presupposes both a training in the exercises that comprise it *and* an awakening to the limits placed on our ability to know certain things (including ourselves) in anything like the way we might otherwise have sought to know them.

63. Asad, "Cultural Translation," in *Genealogies of Religion*, 199.

4

God and Goodness:
A Theological Exploration

Setting the Problem

> Then someone came to him and said, "Teacher, what good deed must I do to have eternal life?" And he said to him, "Why do you ask me about what is good? There is only one who is good. If you wish to enter into life, keep the commandments." He said to him, "Which ones?" And Jesus said, "You shall not murder; You shall not commit adultery; You shall not steal; You shall not bear false witness; Honor your father and mother; also, You shall love your neighbor as yourself." The young man said to him, "I have kept all these; what do I still lack?" Jesus said to him, "If you wish to be perfect, go, sell your possessions, and give the money to the poor, and you will have treasure in heaven; then come and follow me." When the young man heard this word, he went away grieving, for he had many possessions.
>
> Then Jesus said to his disciples, "Truly I tell you, it will be hard for a rich person to enter the kingdom of heaven. Again I tell you, it is easier for a camel to go through the eye of a needle than for someone who is rich to enter the kingdom of God." When the disciples heard this, they were greatly astounded and said, "Then who can be saved?" But Jesus looked at them and said. "For mortals it is impossible, but for God all things are possible." (Matt 19:16–26)

Jesus does not answer the question as posed. The young man asked him about what good deed he must do to gain eternal life. He seems to be asking a question we might identify as "ethical." Jesus, however, restates the question in a manner that suggests metaphysical issues are at stake, that is, "Why do you ask me about what is good?" Jesus' response to his own question, however, makes matters even more confusing because he suggests that the question is not about the "what" but "who."

I confess I find this exchange between Jesus and the young man, a young man who will turn out to have many possessions, puzzling. But that is probably the way it should be. Iris Murdoch's observation that "goodness appears to be both rare and hard to picture" certainly seems right.[1] Was Jesus trying to help the young man understand how difficult it is to "picture goodness"?[2] It is tempting to think Jesus was trying to make a philosophical point, but something more seems to be at stake. For Jesus tells the young man if he wishes to enter into life, which seems a more inclusive concept than the young man's question about "eternal life," he should keep the commandments. There must be some relationship between goodness and the keeping of the commandments, but it is not immediately clear what that relationship might be.

The young man reasonably responds by asking which commandments he should keep. Given Jesus' reframing of his question we might have expected Jesus to begin with the first commandment of the Decalogue. For surely God is "the only one who is good." But instead Jesus names the commandments of the Decalogue that deal with our relations with one another.[3] If the only one who is good is God, why

---

1. Murdoch, *Sovereignty of Good*, 53.

2. Hilary Putnam, I think rightly, argues that Wittgenstein's attacks on philosophers for being in the grip of a picture does not mean that Wittgenstein opposes or thinks pictorial thinking is always a mistake. Wittgenstein does not think we can or should avoid pictures, but a too steady diet of one picture can get in the way of thought. Thus Putnam argues that Wittgenstein's view is that religious people do employ pictures and draw certain consequences from them but they are not the same consequences we draw when we use similar pictures in other contexts. The trick is locating the differences. Putnam, *Renewing Philosophy*, 156–57.

3. I think it a mistake, however, to separate the so-called second table of the Decalogue from the commandments dealing with our relationship to God. Aquinas rightly argued that the commandments are inseparable, which means to honor father and mother depends on a people who have learned to have no other God than the one who delivered Israel from Egypt. For a more extensive account of the relation between the commandments, see Will Willimon's and my *Truth about God* and my

does Jesus not begin with the commandment that we should have no other God than the One who brought Israel out of Egypt?

Even more puzzling, Jesus adds to the list derived from the Decalogue that we are to love our neighbor as ourselves. Paul writes to the church in Rome (Rom 13:8–10) suggesting that the same commandments Jesus commends to the young man are summed up by "Love your neighbor as yourself," but that was Paul and this is Jesus. Later Jesus is asked by a Pharisee to identify the greatest commandment. Jesus answers with the commandment that we should love God with all our heart, soul, and mind and our neighbor as ourselves (Matt 22:34–40). And so it seems strange that he makes no such linkage in his reply to this young man. Even if such a linkage had been made one wonders what the connection is between loving God, keeping the commandments, and loving the neighbor.

Matters become even more complex with the young man's declaration that he has kept all the commandments Jesus enumerates, but he still thinks he must lack something. Jesus tells him to sell all he has, give the proceeds to the poor, and then come and follow him. Is this a condition for being good applicable only to this young man? Or is Jesus suggesting anyone who wants to be good must be dispossessed? Moreover what finally does following Jesus have to do with the one alone who is good? Jesus' declaration to the disciples concerning the status of the wealthy seems to suggest that goodness depends in some way on God, that is, "for God all things are possible." Is Jesus suggesting that he is the "who" that alone is good?

Christians are sure there is a relationship between God and goodness, but we have never been sure how to spell out that relation. Platonism has often seemed like an attractive way to display the relation between God and goodness. Christians have read Plato's account of the impossibility of "picturing" the good to be an anticipation of the Christian insistence that only God is good. Plato's account of the good, moreover, suggests that there is a mystery about how someone may ac-

---

book *Sanctify Them in the Truth*, 37–59. Jesus' naming of the commandments that deal with the neighbor is a nice confirmation of Herbert McCabe's contention in *Law, Love, and Language* that it is not that God reveals to us the ten commandments but that the ten commandments reveal God to us (57). McCabe's remark, I think, is where one must begin to think through the so-called Euthyphro question concerning the relation between the gods and piety.

tually be good that suggests something like the Christian understanding of grace.

One cannot help but hear, for example, the Platonic resonances in Augustine when he says in *The City of God*:

> Thus we say that there is only one unchanging Good; and that is the one, true, and blessed God. The things he made are good because they were made by him; but they are subject to change, because they were made not out of his being but out of nothing. Therefore although they are not supreme goods, since God is a greater good than they, still those mutable goods are of great value, because they can adhere to the immutable Good, and so attain happiness; and this is so truly their Good, that without it the creatures cannot but be wretched.[4]

Such a view can and has led some to think that Christians, and in particular Augustine, subordinate all earthly loves, including love of neighbor, to the love of God. However, as Eric Gregory has recently argued, Augustine's distinction between that which is to be enjoyed and that which is to be used is finally not determined by Augustine's Platonism, because Augustine's Platonism is christologically determined.[5] There can be no love of God, according to Augustine, apart from love of neighbor, but that is not to say, as Gregory observes, "that explicit love of God involves nothing more than love of neighbor."[6]

But what does it mean for goodness, even understood as love of the neighbor, to be christologically determined? How is the love of God, the love that determines how goodness is understood, inseparable from what it means to "follow me"? To follow Christ, moreover, has meant that Christians have at times found it necessary to sacrifice life itself, all

4. Augustine, *City of God*, 472, 12.1.

5. Gregory, *Politics and the Order of Love*, 319–62. For a particularly insightful account of Augustine's "Platonism," see Kenney, *Mysticism of Saint Augustine*. Kenny observes "Augustine understands divine transcendence according to his own logic, which owes its inspiration to the *libri Paltonicorum*, but which turns out, upon inspection to be a departure. He too is emphatic in asserting a level of intelligible reality beyond the sensible world. The intelligible/sensible distinction is fundamental to the theological narrative throughout the *Confessions*. Yet it is also, in the end, superseded by the distinction between the creator and the created" (124).

6. Gregory, *Politics and the Order of Love*, 322. Therefore in spite of Augustine's worries about how friendship can distract from the love of God, Gregory rightly I believe suggests Augustine never abandoned his view that particular friendships are the school of virtue where compassion and social trust are learned (356–57).

worldly goods including life itself, rather than betray what they took to be necessary to follow Christ. Whatever it may mean to be good from a Christian perspective cannot avoid the possibility of martyrdom.[7]

That there is some essential connection between death and goodness is not a thought peculiar to Christians. Raimond Gaita, a philosopher, who does not share my theological commitments, has argued that there is a necessary connection between how good people regard their deaths and how they understand how they should care for the neighbor. By directing attention to Socrates' contention that nothing can harm a good man, Gaita develops an account of goodness that challenges modern accounts of altruism that conflate harm and suffering. When harm and suffering are not properly distinguished, Gaita suggests, this leads to a condescending stance toward those whose suffering cannot be eliminated.

Before turning to Gaita, I need to make clear that I am not trying to argue that any satisfactory account of goodness requires belief in God. Such a project I take to be a theological mistake. It is a mistake often made by Christians faced by the loss of the status and intelligibility of Christian convictions in recent times: thus the attempt to show that, if you do not believe in God, the world will go to hell in a hand basket. I think we are long past the point that, as Troeltsch thought, the truth of what Christians believe should depend on Christianity being necessary to sustain the ethos of our "civilization."

By engaging Gaita, however, I hope it may be the case that the analysis of goodness I develop will be of interest to those who do not share my theological convictions. That I write for myself and Christians,

---

7. Chris Huebner provides an insightful account of martyrdom as a challenge to the modern account of identity in his *Precarious Peace*, 189–202. The martyr, from Huebner's perspective, is the paradigm of the Christian just to the extent they do not know who they are until God tells them who they are. A martyr cannot seek martyrdom not only because they rightly do not desire death but because they do not want those who would kill them to be murderers. Accordingly the church understands martyrdom to be a gift not an accomplishment. The martyr, therefore, is neither a hero nor a victim. They are martyrs. See also Hovey, *To Share in the Body*; and Whitfield, *Pilgrim Holiness*. Whitfield calls attention to an early Christian martyr named Sanctus whose body was so brutalized that it no longer was identifiable as a human body. Repeatedly questioned by his torturers about who he might be, he only would say, "I am a Christian." A reminder that whatever it might mean for Christians to be good their primary identity is determined by a narrative in which what most mean by "good" is rendered secondary.

however, is an attempt to respond to a problem identified by Charles Taylor. Taylor observes that Platonism and Christianity, in spite of their considerable differences, shared the view that the good was known through the self-mastery made possible by, in the case of Platonism, reason and, in Christianity, the transformation of the will by grace. Yet each tradition, according to Taylor, has been secularized primarily by being identified with the ideal of altruism.[8]

According to Taylor, most modern people assume that the highest form of ethical idealism is altruism. Because altruism is assumed to be the ideal, selfishness is then assumed to be the lowest form of morality. Such a high view of altruism means that those identified with dedication to others or the universal good are regarded with admiration and even awe. Such dedication has obvious roots, Taylor suggests, in "Christian spirituality," and no doubt is compatible with Christianity, but "the secular ethic of altruism has discarded something essential to the Christian outlook, once the love of God no longer plays a role."[9] Though Taylor does not explicitly draw the conclusion, I think his account of our lives makes clear that the current identification of Christianity with altruism hides from most Christians that they have learned to live as if God does not exist.[10]

That is a position I hope to render problematic. My strategy is not to argue that what it means to be good depends on belief in God, but rather to show how goodness and God cannot be distinguished in the life of Jean Vanier. "Showing" is the heart of the matter. Gaita argues that if we are to see what goodness looks like it will depend on the unanticipated ability of some to be present to the afflicted without regret. Without a people who have so learned to be with the afflicted, we are unable to see the humanity that their affliction threatens to hide. I

8. Taylor, *Sources of the Self*, 21–22.

9. Ibid., 22.

10. In a sermon on Matt 22:34–46 entitled, "Loving Yourself," Samuel Wells advises anyone who has been told they should always live for others as a way to avoid being selfish that when they hear the words "Love your neighbor as yourself" they should swap the words round and say, "Love yourself as your neighbor." They should do so because we ought to regard ourselves as the first among all the neighbors God calls us to love. Wells observes that the language of altruism never grasps this because it assumes we must choose between loving ourselves and loving others. "But God loves every one of us while still loving each of us as if we were the only one. We're able to love others because of the way God loves us. And to accept that love, we have to learn to love ourselves." Sermon Preached in Duke University Chapel on October 26, 2008.

hope to show how such a "seeing" is made possible by the work of Jean Vanier.

Raimond Gaita on Goodness

I am attracted to Raimond Gaita's account of goodness because his analysis betrays the influence of thinkers from whom I have also learned much, that is, Wittgenstein, Rush Rhees, and Iris Murdoch. As might be expected by one so influenced, Gaita develops his case slowly and with attention to what we say. He attends to what we say because there cannot be, according to Gaita, an independent metaphysical inquiry into the reality of good and evil that could underwrite or undermine our most serious ways of speaking.[11] So he begins his investigation of what we might mean by good by directing attention to Socrates' address to the jury in the *Apology*: "You too gentlemen of the jury, must look forward to death with confidence and fix your minds on this one truth—that nothing can harm a good man either in life or after death."

Gaita observes this passage is seldom discussed by Plato scholars because they assume that Socrates' claim about harm and what it means to be good is not relevant for understanding Plato's more developed metaphysics of the good. But Gaita lingers on Socrates' charge to the jury, arguing that Socrates did not mean that people who live virtuously could not suffer, but that Socrates thought, even in their suffering, people who see their life in the light of a certain kind of love, a love of philosophy, could not be harmed.

Socrates' understanding of goodness, Gaita suggests, astonished Aristotle, who thought Socrates' claim to be irresponsible. For Aristotle, who certainly thought a person of virtue could endure great suffering, recognized that there may come a time in the life of a person when their suffering is so great they could not help but think it would have been better never to have been born. Gaita characterizes Aristotle's reaction to Socrates as the "most serious in the history of philosophy."[12] Yet Aristotle understood that he could only react to Socrates because no argument in and of itself could count against Socrates' claim.

---

11. Gaita, *Good and Evil*, 192. Of course one of the problems with Gaita's "method" is who the "we" is.

12. Ibid., 193.

Aristotle objected to Socrates' view because he assumed that at stake was a certain kind of humanism. It is a humanism Gaita characterizes as a "non-reductive naturalism," which is committed to the view that what a person counts as harm depends on their ethical perspective. Aristotle, in contrast to Socrates, was attempting to defend what Gaita describes as an urbane humanism. From Aristotle's perspective, a Socratic point of view is but "highminded indecency" if it fails to acknowledge that there are some lives so steeped in appalling and ineradicable affliction that they are irredeemably ruined.

In order to explain why he thinks Aristotle represents such a view, Gaita raises the question of "whether we can see those who have no share in what gives our lives sense as our moral equals."[13] We would like to think we do so, but, drawing on Simone Weil, Gaita suggests that our reaction to those who we do not believe share our moral lives is one of condescension. Weil observes:

> We have the same carnal natures as animals. If a hen is hurt the others rush up to peck it. Our senses attach to affliction all the contempt, all the revulsion, all the hatred which our reason attaches to crime. Except for those whose soul is inhabited by Christ, everybody despises the afflicted to some extent, although practically no-one is conscious of it.[14]

Gaita is not questioning the fact that most of us do not believe that the afflicted should be despised or condescended to, but the question is whether we understand ourselves in believing it. He suspects we share with Aristotle the rejection of Socrates claim that a good man cannot be harmed because we do believe it is possible for misfortune irredeem-

---

13. Ibid., 195.

14. Quoted in Ibid., 195. I explored a similar observation made by Adam Smith about those who had gone mad in *Suffering Presence*, 174–75. Also relevant is the chapter, "To Love God, the Poor, and Learning" in my book, *State of the University*, 187–201. That chapter is my attempt to show the significance of Gregory's great oration on the significance of leprosy for constituting the Christian city. Gregory sees quite clearly that the sadness that constitutes the lives of lepers is their "sense that they are actually hated for their misfortune." They cannot help, moreover, identifying with such hate leading them to regret their own existence. Drawn to lie beside one another, Gregory describes, as "a wretched union born of disease, each contributing his own misfortune to the common fund of misery, thus heightening each other's distress; pitiful in their affliction, more so in the sharing of it" ("Letter 182" in *Fathers Speak*, 48).

ably to ruin a person's life even if they are virtuous. Such a view, according to Gaita, is based on the "sense of necessity which is internal to the judgment that there are lives such that it would have been better for those who suffer them if they had not been born."[15]

Gaita, however, argues that it is just at this point we see the profound difference between Socrates and Aristotle. For Aristotle did not see, as at least Plato seemed to gesture, that "there was goodness beyond virtue and evil beyond vice."[16] Such goodness Socrates not only possessed, but saw in others. In contrast to Aristotle, Socrates thought no amount of suffering could negate the good. Thus Socrates' claim that a good man cannot be harmed. Such a view of the good, Gaita observes, is essentially mysterious given our limited epistemic and logical powers. The task of philosophy is to provide conceptual space for the acknowledgement of such a mystery.

There are three requirements philosophy must meet, according to Gaita, if a space is to be left for an account of the good that respects this mystery. First, the concept of what is essentially mysterious must be connected to a certain conception of experience; secondly, the concept of experience must be connected with that of being bound in testimony; and, thirdly, "we must give a serious place to the concept of love, Goodness and purity."[17]

All Gaita can do, therefore, is to provide examples that display the pressure to claim as Socrates did that a good person cannot be harmed.[18]

---

15. Gaita, *Good and Evil*, 197. In *The Philosopher's Dog*, Gaita makes clearer the relation between how we regard our deaths and the deaths of others than he does in his earlier work. He says, "because animals have no reflective knowledge of death, they cannot dread it and if they could, they could not take comfort from the fact that they are not alone in their mortality. It is a fact utterly basic to human life that we are consoled by knowledge that others suffer as we do and must die as we must. At first sight that might seem like unsavory consolation, achieved by taking pleasure in the miseries of others. Really, it is not or, at any rate, mostly it is not. We are creatures who seek to make sense of our lives and the sense we make is never entirely private. What sense we make of our particular lives is always in large part sense we make of the human condition. The need to make sense of death is obviously driven not only by a response to one's own suffering, but also by a more general need to understand what it means to live a human life, and what death shows us about that meaning" (71–72).

16. Ibid., 202.

17. Ibid., 203.

18. Gaita has a quite interesting comment on Wittgenstein's remark as he was dying that his housekeeper was to "tell them (his friends) that it has been a wonderful

The example he provides is Mother Teresa of Calcutta. He does so because it is said of her that she showed to those who were appallingly afflicted "a compassion that was without a trace of condescension." That her compassion was without condescension means Mother Teresa was able to care for the afflicted "without a trace of the thought that it had been better if the person for who she felt compassion had never been born, even if they suffered affliction of the most protracted, severe and ineradicable sort."[19]

Her compassion was a denial that the affliction could, or even at a certain limit must, make a person's life worthless. Mother Teresa's love had a purity that can only be characterized as a gift. So it is not an achievement that on Aristotelian grounds might be found in a virtue such as courage, but rather her love is born of a humility that makes it a different order. We stand in awe of such a love, but our wonder is not determined by her achievements but by the light her love throws on the afflicted. "The wonder which is in response to her is not a wonder at her, but a wonder *that human life could be as her love reveals it.*"[20]

Gaita argues that it is a mistake, however, to try to retain the sense of what is revealed by the love Mother Teresa exhibits by constructing a metaphysics that would secure it.[21] He argues his account of her compassion requires no metaphysical underpinning and in particular the "metaphysical underpinning that is often associated with Christianity."[22]

---

life." Gaita observes that Wittgenstein was not expressing a judgment that might be reconsidered, but was rather an expression of gratitude for his life considered as a certain kind of whole. Gaita argues that Wittgenstein's remark rightly means "we cannot *flatly* say of any life, not even a life in which there had been much suffering, that it could have been better if only it had been blessed with more fortune. A human life can be seen under the aspect of that kind of unity which gives it a kind of completion, and indeed a kind of perfection, which resists any such appraisal. I think that is what Aristotle meant when he said a happy life was 'complete and lacking in nothing'" (*Good and Evil*, 198–99).

19. Ibid., 203.

20. Ibid., 206.

21. I suspect Gaita is reflecting the influence of Murdoch's claim that "the good has nothing to do with purpose indeed it excludes the idea of purpose. 'All is vanity' is the beginning and end of ethics.' The only genuine way to be good is to be good 'for nothing' in the midst of a scene where every 'natural' thing, including one's own mind, is subject to chance, that is, to necessity. That 'for nothing' is indeed the experienced correlate of the invisibility or non-representable blankness of the idea of Good itself" (*Sovereignty of Good*, 71).

22. Gaita, *Good and Evil*, 214.

He does not deny that Mother Teresa says she would not be able to do what she does were it not for the love of Jesus, but Gaita says he does not even have to ask what that means much less believe it. Rather we can retain a sense of what is revealed by her compassion by attention to like things which are absolutely good. "We know them only as they are revealed in the light of pure love."[23]

That is not, however, Gaita's last word on the matter. He returns to the question of goodness in his book *A Common Humanity: Thinking about Love and Truth and Justice*, first published in Australia in 1998.[24] He begins a chapter entitled "Goodness beyond Virtue" with a story of his work as a seventeen-year-old as a ward assistant in a psychiatric hospital.[25] It was in the early 1960s and the ward was more like a prison than a hospital. The patients were judged incurable so they were often subject to inhumane treatments such a being washed down with mops after they had soiled themselves. Friends and relatives had long ceased to visit them and they were often treated brutishly by those charged with their care.

There were some psychiatrists who worked to improve their condition in the name of the inalienable dignity of even patients. Gaita admired the psychiatrist's commitment to their patients, but, he observes, it probably did not help to appeal to the inalienable dignity of

23. Ibid., 214.

24. Gaita, *Common Humanity*. David Parker provides a fascinating reading of Gaita's work, and in particular his memoir, *Romulus, My Father*, to suggest that Gaita represents the exhaustion of the paradigm of autobiography that configures identity around ethnicity, gender, class, race, sexual preference, and natural language. Gaita is trying to react against the multiculturalist ethos by showing how goods that transcend boundaries of difference can shape lives. Parker treats Gaita's work as one illustration of his general contention, a contention shaped by Taylor's *Sources of the Self*, that "the good is an inescapable framework for understanding any human agent and therefore for any writer of life narrative" (*Self in Moral Space*, 6). Parker argues that Gaita's account of his father is the key to the philosophical position he develops just to the extent that Gaita depicts his father as one who would sooner suffer wrong than to do it (135). Parker argues, however, on the basis of Gaita's text that Gaita has not been able to escape the particularistic language that depends on difference.

25. Gaita's attraction to Mother Teresa and the nun he encounters in the psychiatric hospital is understandable, but I wonder why he did not also consider those whose "goodness seems beyond virtue" who have not led virtuous lives but have done extraordinary things. I am thinking of people like Oskar Schindler. That Gaita does not treat people like Schindler seems all the more surprising because Thomas Kineally, the author of *Schindler's List*, is like Gaita Australian. Graham Greene gave classic expression to "goodness beyond virtue" in *The Power and the Glory*.

the patients because such an appeal depends too much on appearances. The appeal to someone's "dignity" is too easily undermined by the complete loss of any "humanity."

However, Gaita reports, one day a nun came to the ward whose demeanor toward the patients—the way she spoke to them, her facial expressions, the inflexions of her body—was in marked contrast to even the psychiatrists Gaita admired. For like Mother Teresa she was without condescension.[26] She was able to interact with the people suffering from mental illness without any thought that it might be better that they had never been born.

Gaita says he does not know how important it might have been that she was a nun. Her behavior might have been a function of her religious belief but, because he argues beliefs can explain behavior independently of their truth or falsity, nothing follows from how her behavior was connected to her beliefs. More important is how her behavior was shaped by the reality which it revealed, that is, the full humanity of those whose afflictions had made their humanity invisible. Therefore no justification of her behavior is required because "the purity of her love proved the reality of what it revealed."[27]

Such love, according to Gaita, depends on the conviction that there exists goodness beyond virtue and evil beyond vice. True love requires that every human being, as Hannah Arendt argues, be regarded as "infinitely precious." To learn to love and regard others as infinitely precious, Gaita suggests, requires training exemplified in the lives of the saints.[28]

Gaita acknowledges that religious traditions have spoken most simply and deeply about such a view by declaring all human beings sacred. But he contends that the language of love nourished by the love of saints can stand independently of speculation about supernatural entities. What grew in one place can flourish elsewhere. He reports, however, that there is one question put to him by a theologian whose answer he is not sure of.[29] The theologian asked him whether the kind

26. Gaita, *Common Morality*, 17–18.

27. Ibid., 21.

28. Ibid., xix.

29. I was the theologian who asked Gaita the question Gaita is not sure how to answer. I do not remember when or where I asked him about from where such lives might come once such practices that shaped the nun are no longer in existence. Some

of love shown by the nun could exist in the prolonged absence of the kind of practices that were part of her religious vocation. In response Gaita says:

> Iris Murdoch said that attention to something absolutely pure is the essence of prayer and is a form of love. If she is right, then the answer to Hauerwas' question will depend on whether with the demise of religion, we can find objects of attention that can sustain that love, or whether they will always fail us. I don't know the answer.[30]

Nor do I know the answer. I certainly have no reason to suggest that Gaita's account of goodness as non-condescending love is unintelligible if God does not exist. But then the question has never been about God's existence—but ours. Gaita is quite right to think that if Mother Teresa and the nun he encountered at seventeen did not exist we quite literally would be less human. They did exist, however, and it at least makes sense to ask if and how they and the goodness they reveal makes sense if the God they worship does not exist.

That may well be a far too abstract way to put the question. For the God they worship is not some abstraction but rather a reality known though participation in a community across time and space. What I suspect Gaita misses is the role that friendship plays in lives like that of Mother Teresa and the nun he so admires. In particular, Mother Teresa and the nun Gaita admired were not afraid to be befriended by those they served. To suggest why friendship is so important for the development of such goodness I want to introduce another life that exhibits the kind of love Gaita thinks so defining of goodness.[31] The name of that life is Jean Vanier.

---

years ago we spoke at a conference in Australia but that was well before he had published *A Common Humanity*. When I asked the question matters little, but I think the form of the question is important. For note I did not ask him about "beliefs," but rather the practices that constitute belief.

30. Ibid., xx.

31. The role of examples for characterizing goodness is crucial yet a complex matter not easily analyzed. In the same passage I quote toward the beginning of this paper by Murdoch concerning how hard it is to picture goodness she comments further that goodness "is perhaps most convincingly met with in simple people—inarticulate, unselfish mothers of large families—but these cases are also the least illuminating" (*Sovereignty of Good*, 53). Such a comment may betray someone who lives in a world isolated from "simple people." Simple people often turn out, once you get to know

Jean Vanier on Being Befriended by the Disabled

Jean Vanier is the founder of the movement known as L'Arche. L'Arche is now a reality around the world in which people who are called mentally handicapped live with those who are not. A L'Arche home is first and foremost just that, a home. The core members of the home are the mentally handicapped. Those who are not mentally handicapped are called assistants. Assistants do not live in the home to care for the mentally handicapped. Rather they are there to learn to be with the core members in the hope that they can learn to be friends.

In a lecture at Harvard entitled "Through Their Wounds We Are Healed," Vanier told the story of how he, the son of a prominent family in Quebec, came to live with the mentally disabled. This is his story:

> I was thirteen when I joined the British navy during World War II. My adolescent years were taken up in the world of efficiency, controlling and commanding others. I was a technician of destruction. My last ship was the Canadian aircraft carrier, "The Magnificent." However, after a few years, I felt called by Jesus to take another path, the path of peace. I left the navy and did a doctorate in philosophy in Paris. I started teaching philosophy at the University of Toronto. Then through a priest-friend, I had the good fortune of meeting people with mental disabilities.
>
> In 1964 I took from an asylum two men, Raphael and Philip, and we began to live together. I did not know I was founding the first of many L'Arche communities. I simply felt called to live with these two men who had suffered rejection and a lot of inner pain and perhaps with a few others like them. When I had begun living with them, I soon started to discover the immense pain in their hearts. When we talk of the poor, or of announcing

them, as anything but "simple," but more important Murdoch does not explain why "such cases" are the "least illuminating." Is it because she thinks, in Charles Taylor's terms, that the kind of goodness they display is inarticulate? If so why is being articulate necessary for being good? I suspect goodness does require being articulate, but there are diverse ways to be articulate that Murdoch (and Taylor) may not have appreciated. In *Sources of the Self* Taylor contrasts an honor ethic with the ethic of Plato to show the former does not require the same kind of philosophical articulateness as Plato (20–21). Yet "I am a Christian" is probably closer to the "inarticulate warrior" than it is to Plato's philosophical account of the good. In *Self in Moral Space* Parker argues that Taylor rightly argues that we "are all almost necessarily living by many more forms of the good than we can be aware of," which makes it all the more important that we "bring to focus the suppressed structures of value that constitute the ethical lives that we moderns cannot avoid living" (175).

the good news to the poor, we should never idealize the poor.
Poor people are hurt; they are in pain. They can be very angry,
in revolt or in depression.[32]

Vanier wrote his dissertation at the Catholic Institute of Paris on
Aristotle. He would later write a quite favorable book on Aristotle's ethics but he was quite critical of Aristotle's understanding of his characterization that friendship was possible only between equals.[33] He was
critical of Aristotle's account of friendship because Aristotle failed to
provide the resources necessary to account for what Vanier felt living
with the mentally disabled had given him. Limited though they may
be, unable to read or write, moving slowly or clumsily, many unable to
speak, walk, or eat on their own, according to Vanier they have been
an incredible gift to him. For if you are open to them, if you welcome
them, "they give us life and lead us to Jesus and the good news."[34]

Vanier reports that when he began to live with Raphael and Philip
he discovered their deep cry for communion. From their loneliness and
pain they cried for love and friendship. Such a cry is often present when
we visit people in institutions. Through the look in their eyes the men
and women say to us, "Will you be my friend? Am I important to you?

32. Vanier, *From Brokenness to Community*, 11–12.

33. The dissertation was entitled "Happiness as Principle and End of Aristotelian
Ethics." The later book was entitled *Made for Happiness: Discovering the Meaning of
Life with Aristotle*.

34. Vanier, *From Brokenness to Community*, 9. Hans Reinders provides the best
account we have of how Vanier's work changes how we must think of friendship. In
particular Reinders argues that L'Arche requires that the prerequisite of friendship is
that we learn to receive the gift of unconditional love. That gift, the gift of unconditional love, Christians believe is bestowed on us by God. For we believe that the "final
end of our existence is to be reunited with God: friendship is the proper name of this
reunion. The theological warrant for this claim is that the Christian story of God is
about the promise that he will not abandon his creation, even when his creatures, for
one reason or another, do not know how to find him. To restore us to the possibility of
that reunion, God became one of us and gave himself to save us. This is, in essence, the
story of God with human beings as Christians understand it. We learn from this story
what living as human beings created in the divine image entails. Those who believe
that this story reveals the truth about their existence will live lives in the promise of a
gift that exceeds all other gifts: being one with God. Since they know that this promise
is grounded in God's self-giving and does not in any way depend on their own doing,
believers will know that living their lives in truth is possible only because of God's
unconditional love. Friendship with God is a gift that is only his to give" (*Receiving the
Gift of Friendship*, 351).

Do I have any value?" Some may be hiding away in a corner, hiding behind bars of self-hatred, still others banging their heads on the wall, but they are crying for love, friendship, and communion.[35]

According to Vanier, when these people are welcomed from their world of anguish, brokenness, and depression, when they gradually discover they are loved, they are transformed. Their tense and angry bodies become relaxed and peaceful. Such discoveries Vanier says have helped him understand what it means to live in communion with someone. "Communion means accepting people just as they are, with their limits and inner pain, but also with their gifts and their beauty and their capacity to grow: to see the beauty inside of all the pain. To love someone is not first of all to do things *for* them, but to reveal to them their beauty and value, to say to them through our attitude: 'You are beautiful. You are important. I trust you. You can trust yourself.'"[36]

Vanier confesses that communion did not come easily to him. Taught from an early age to be first, it is not easy to be asked by Jesus to share you life with those who have little culture. Only as he began to live with Raphael and Philip did he discover the hardness in his heart. They were crying out for friendship and Vanier did not know how to respond because of the forces in him that, as he put it, "would pull him up the ladder." Yet he tells us that over the years, the people with whom he lives in L'Arche have been teaching and healing him.

That he has been undergoing such training leads Vanier to observe that the people who come to L'Arche because they want to serve the poor are only able to stay once they discover that they are the poor. They must discover that Jesus came to bring good news to *the poor* not those who *serve* the poor. According to Vanier if you are called to live with wounded people you must discover that God is present in the poverty and wounds of their hearts. He continues:

> God is not present in their capacity to heal but rather in their need to be healed. We can only truly love people who are different, we can only discover that difference is a treasure and not a threat, if in some way our hearts are becoming enfolded in the heart of the Father, if somewhere God is putting into our broken hearts that love that is in God's own heart for each and every human being. For God is truly in love with people, and with

35. Vanier, *From Brokenness to Community*, 14–15.
36. Ibid., 16.

every individual human being. This healing power in us will not come from our capacities and our riches, but in and through our poverty. We are called to discover that God can bring peace, compassion and love through *our* wounds.[37]

Vanier reports that he is always moved when he reads the Gospels by how Jesus lives and acts, how he enters into relationships with each person he encounters. He asks, "Will you come with me? I love you. Will you enter into communion with me?" But his invitation to follow him is an invitation that forces us to make a choice. If you choose to follow him it means a refusal to go in a different direction. If you choose to follow Jesus you will receive the gift of love and communion, but at the same time you will discover you must say "no" to the ways of the world and accept loss.[38]

Gaita wonders at the compassion Mother Teresa displays because it is without a trace of condescension. He is quite right, moreover, that to be free of condescension is remarkable because as Weil insists we *do* despise the afflicted though we are seldom conscious we do so. We despise them I think because, as Vanier suggests, we fear them. We fear and hate them for revealing our own weaknesses, our powerlessness, to "make them strong." Some are even led to think in the face of our help-lessness it would be better that such people not exist. Compassion, par-ticularly when it takes the form of altruism, can become murderous.[39]

Showings

"The wonder," that is, the wonder Gaita suggests Mother Teresa should elicit in us, is not to be directed at her but rather is the "wonder that human life could be as her love reveals it."[40] Jean Vanier would not wish that we "wonder" or react with awe in response to his life. Any wonder would rightly be in response to the humanity revealed through those who have befriended him. He and his friends reveal our human-

---

37. Ibid., 20–21.

38. Ibid., 10.

39. See, for example, my chapter "Killing Compassion" in *Dispatches From the Front*, 164–76.

40. Gaita, *Good and Evil*, 206.

ity, a goodness, that we could not have known possible without their "showing."

Jesus did not answer the young man's question concerning what deed he must do to inherit eternal life. Instead he commanded him to sell his possessions, give the money to the poor, and follow him. To learn to follow Jesus is the training necessary to become a human being.[41] To be a human being is not a natural condition, but requires training. The kind of training required, moreover, has everything to do with death. To follow Jesus is to go with him to Jerusalem where he will be crucified. To follow Jesus, therefore, is to undergo a training that refuses to let death, even death at the hands of enemies, determine the shape of our living.

To learn to live without protection is to learn to live without possessions. To be dispossessed, however, cannot be willed. To try to be dispossessed is to be possessed by the will to be dispossessed. Rather, as Jean Vanier's life reveals, to be dispossessed comes by being made a friend of those who have no possessions. They have had to learn to live without possessions. Jean Vanier had to learn from them how to live without the protections we think possessions provide. To learn so to live is to learn that death is not the worst thing that can happen to us. The worst thing that can happen to us is to never have challenged our presumption that it would be better that Jean Vanier's friends should have never been born.

Iris Murdoch observes that the "notion that 'it all somehow must make sense'" seems necessary to preserve us from despair. The difficulty, according to Murdoch, is how to entertain such a consoling notion in a way that does not hide from us the pointlessness of our living. She argues, therefore, that "as soon as any idea is a consolation the tendency to falsify it becomes strong: hence the traditional problem of preventing the idea of God from degenerating in the believer's mind."[42] I do not think that belief in God somehow makes "it all make sense." I do believe that the life and work of Jean Vanier makes sense of believing in a God who alone is good.

41. I am indebted to Rom Coles for this way of putting the matter.
42. Murdoch, *Sovereignty of Good*, 56–57.

5

Naming God

A Sermon for the Church of the Incarnation
Dallas, Texas
March 6, 2010

Exodus 3:1–15
Psalm 103:1–11
1 Corinthians 10:1–13
Luke 13:1–9

"God is whoever raised Jesus from the dead, having before raised Israel from Egypt" is the hallmark sentence of Robert Jenson's *Systematic Theology*. This elegantly simple but dauntingly deep sentence took Jenson a lifetime of theological reflection to write. To write such a sentence requires that the grammar of our faith discipline our presumption that we know what we say when we say "God." For it turns out that we are most likely to take God's name in vain when we assume we can know what we say when we say "God."

One of the ironies of the recent spate of books defending atheism is the confidence the "new atheists" seem to have in knowing which God it is they are sure does not exist. They seem to have forgotten that one of the crimes Romans associated with Christians, a crime that often meant their death, was that Christians were atheist. The Romans were tolerant. All they wanted was for the Christians to acknowledge there were many gods, but Christians were determined atheist. Christians were atheist because they assumed the primary problem was not atheism but idolatry. Idolatry, moreover, has everything to do with knowing how to use God's name.

Augustine in *The City of God* even argues that the reason the Roman Empire has fallen on hard times is due to their worship of corrupt gods. He assumed rightly that there is a direct correlation between the worship of God, the character of our lives, and politics. According to Augustine, Rome fell because the people of Rome became corrupt by emulating the corruption of their gods. Needless to say, Augustine's account of idolatry was not well received by the Romans.

So depending on which god or gods the new atheists think they are denying they might discover that Christians are not unsympathetic with their atheism. For example, I suspect we should not be surprised in a culture that puts on its money "In God We Trust" atheists might be led to think it is interesting and perhaps even useful to deny such a god exists. It does not seem to occur to atheists, however, that the vague god that some seem to confuse with trust in our money cannot be the same God who raised Jesus from the dead having before raised Israel from Egypt.

Which is a reminder that the word "god" can be very misleading particularly for those that worship the One who raised Jesus from the dead and Israel from Egypt. For the word "god," and it is not clear that "god" is a name, can invite us to confuse the One who raised Jesus from the dead with the assumption by many that "god" is the designation many use to think something had to start it all and that must mean when all is said and done that there is "more" to life than this. Those who believe in such a "more" often agree with the new atheists that there is little evidence that such a "more" exists, but they nonetheless refuse to deny its possibility. Yet they assume that such a "more" has many names, for to think otherwise is to risk intolerance.

Our text for today makes clear, however, that naming God matters. God asks Moses to bring his people, the descendents of Abraham, Isaac, and Jacob, out of captivity in Egypt. God, who seems to have been reading Jenson's *Systematic Theology*, says that Moses should tell the Israelites that Moses has been sent to Israel by the God of their ancestors, that is, the God of Abraham, Isaac, and Jacob. But Moses, whose knowledge of Egypt means he senses that escaping from Egypt is going to be a risky business, knows that those who he is asked to rescue will want to know more. They will want to know God's name. God responds with the now classical identifying phrase, "I am who I am."

"I am who I am," or as some have translated, "I will be present to whom I will be present," has been a rich resource for Christian theologians and philosophers to reflect on the metaphysics of God's existence. For example, Aquinas argues that only in God are existence and essence inseparable. Put in more colloquial terms that means only God can act without loss. For Christians it is, therefore, never a question about God's existence, but rather what it means for all that is not God to exist.

"I am who I am," may be a helpful metaphysical response, but it is not a name. At best, as philosophers like to say, "I am who I am" is a grammatical remark that suggests that God is known by what God does. "I am who I am," therefore, is but another way to say you know all you need to know by knowing that God is the God of Abraham, Isaac, and Jacob. It is as if God is saying to Moses "Tell them not to worry. Just as I have been there for Abraham, Isaac, and Jacob so I will be there for you." In effect God is saying "trust me."

We, like the people of Israel, would like to think we get to name God. By naming God we think we can get the kind of God we need. We can make "the more" that must have started it all after our own image. But God refuses to let Israel or us assume that we can name the One who will raise Israel from Egypt. Only God can name God. That, moreover, is what God does. "God also said to Moses, Thus you shall say to the Israelites, 'The Lord, the God of your ancestors, the God of Abraham, the God of Isaac, the God of Jacob, has sent me to you': This is my name forever, and this my title for all generations." God's name is YHWH, but it is a name that Israel could not say.

The name it turns out is a holy reality sharing as it does in God's holiness. To know God's name is to know God. As Karl Barth observes, "'I am that I am' can scarcely mean anything else than just I am He whose name proper no one can repeat is significant enough; but the revealed name itself by its wording is to recall also and precisely the hiddenness of the reveled God."

The burning bush that is not consumed wonderfully displays God's unrelenting desire to have us know him, but to so know God requires the acknowledgment we cannot know God. Moses could not help but be drawn to the firry bush. How could the bush be on fire yet not consumed? He drew near, but the Lord called to Moses, named Moses, out of the burning bush telling him he was on holy ground. He was to remove his sandals and come no closer. Moses did as he was told hiding his face fearing to look on God.

For if God is God how could we hope to stand before God, how could we hope to see God face to face, and live? The burning bush was not consumed, but we cannot imagine that confronted by this God we could see God and live. Israel knew that there was no greater gift than to be given God's name, but that gift was a frightening reality that threatened to consume her. Israel, who would be tempted by the idolatrous presumption she possessed God's name, rightly never forgot she could not say God's name. Israel could not possess God because God possess Israel.

But we are Christians. We believe we have been given God's name. We believe we can say the name of God. Paul in his letter to the Philippians tells us:

> Let the same mind be in you that was in Christ Jesus,
>> Who, though he was in the form
>> of God,
>> did not regard equality of God
> as something to be exploited,
> but emptied himself,
> taking the form of a slave,
> being born in human likeness.
> And found in human form,
> He humbled himself
> And became obedient to the point of
> Death—
> Even death on a cross.
>
> Therefore God also highly exalted him
> and gave him the name
> that is above every name,
> so that at the name of Jesus
> every knee should bend,

in heaven and on earth and under
the earth,
and every tongue should confess
that Jesus Christ is Lord,
to the glory of God the Father. (Phil 2:5–11)

The fire that burned but did not consume the bush is Jesus Christ. Just as the fire did not consume the bush so our God has come to us by becoming one of us. Yet the humanity of the one he became was not replaced or destroyed. Rather our God is incarnate. Our God is the Father, Son, and Holy Spirit. There has never been a time that God has not been Trinity. The God that came to Moses in the burning bush, the God who called Moses to deliver his people, the God who game Moses his name, is Trinity. Only this God can be very God and very man.

The God we worship is not a vague, "the more." The God we worship is not "the biggest thing around." The God we worship is not "something had to start it." The God we worship is not a God that insures that we will somehow get out of life alive. The God we worship, as our passage from Luke makes clear, is not a God whose ways correspond to our presumptions about how God should be God. That God has come near to us in Christ does not mean that God is less than God. God is God and we are not.

Yet we believe that the God we worship has made his name known. We believe we have been given the happy task of making his name known. We believe we can make his name known because the God we worship is nearer to us than we are to ourselves—a frightening reality that gives us life. We believe that in this meal of bread and wine, just as Jesus is fully God and fully man, this bread and this wine will through the work of the Spirit become for us the body and blood of Christ.

To come to this meal is to stand before the burning bush. But we are not told to come no closer. Rather we are invited to eat this body and drink this blood and by so doing we are consumed by what we consume. So consumed we are made through the Holy Spirit God's witnesses that the world may know the fire that is Jesus Christ.

God is whoever raised Jesus from the dead, having before raised Israel from Egypt. There is no God but this God. Blessed be his name.

6

Speaking Christian

A Commencement Address
For Eastern Mennonite Seminary
May 1, 2010

God knows what possesses anyone to enter the ministry in our day. The lack of clarity about what makes Christians Christian, what makes the church the church, continuing ambiguity in our diverse denominations about ordination itself should surely make anyone think twice about becoming a minister. Moreover the lack of consensus about what it might mean for anyone to act with authority in our society and the church cannot help but make those of us who are not ministers wonder about the psychological health of those who tell us they are called to the ministry.

Too often I fear the ministry is understood by many Christians as well as many who become ministers to be but one expression of the more general category of something called a "helping profession." A minister is a social worker with "a difference." "The difference" is thought to have something to do with God, but it is not clear exactly what difference that difference is to make for the performance of your office.

As a result, many who enter the ministry discover after a few years of doing the best they can to meet the expectations of those they serve, expectations such as whatever else you may do you should always be nice, end up feeling as if they have been nibbled to death by ducks. They do so because it is assumed that, since pastors do not work for a living, those whom ministers serve, or at least those who pay them, can ask ministers to be or do just about anything. Though it is often not clear how what they are asked to do is required by their ordination vows, those in the ministry cannot say "no" because it is not clear what their "job" is in the first place.

Many in the ministry try to protect themselves from the unlimited demands and expectations of their congregations by taking refuge in their families, some alternative ministry such as counseling, or, God help us, a hobby. Such strategies may work for awhile, but often those who employ these strategies discover that no spouse can or should love another spouse that much, that even after you have done CPE you are still stuck with the life you had before you were trained in CPE, and a hobby turns out to be just that, namely, a hobby.

The failure of such strategies I think throws some light on clergy misconduct. I wish I could attribute the sexual misconduct character-istic of some Methodist clergy to lust, but I fear that most people in the Methodist ministry do not have that much energy. I think the problem is not lust, but loneliness. Isolated by the expectations of the congrega-tion, the challenge of developing friendships with some in the church without those friendships creating divisions in the church too often re-sults in a profound loneliness for those in the ministry. Unfortunately, the attempt to overcome that loneliness can take the form of inappro-priate behavior.

There is another alternative. You can become a scold urging the church to become more socially active in causes of peace and justice. This may earn you the title of being "prophetic," but such a strategy may contribute to the incoherence of the ministerial task. For it is not at all clear why you needed to be ordained to pursue causes of peace and justice. It is a great challenge for ministers who would lead their congregations to be more socially active to do so in a manner that does not result in the displacement of worship as the heart of the church.

By now you may well be trying to understand why someone thought it a good idea to ask Stanley Hauerwas to deliver your com-mencement address. This is a celebratory day. You have graduated from Eastern Mennonite Seminary. You are going into the ministry. It is not as if you are unaware of the challenges facing you. You do not need me to catalogue those challenges. That is certainly true, but I have taken the time to characterize some of those challenges, a characterization that no doubt is a caricature, because I want to suggest how the work you have done in seminary is crucial for the work you will do as a minister if you are to sustain the ministry for a lifetime.

For what you have learned to do in seminary is read. By learning to read you have learned to speak Christian. That you have learned to read and speak means you have been formed in a manner to avoid the pitfalls I have associated with the contemporary ministry. For I want to suggest to you that one of the essential tasks of those called to the ministry in our day is to be a teacher. In particular, you are called to be a teacher of language. I hope to convince you if you so understand your task you will discover that you have your work cut out for you. But that is very good news because now you clearly have something to do.

Yet in the book of James we are told

> not many of you should become teachers, my brothers and sisters, for you know that we who teach will be judged with greater strictness. For all of us make many mistakes. Anyone who makes no mistakes in speaking is perfect, able to keep the whole body in check with a bridle. If we put bits into the mouths of horses to make them obey us, we guide their whole bodies. Or look at ships: though they are so large that it takes strong winds to drive them, yet they are guided by a very small rudder wherever the will of the pilot directs. So also the tongue is a small member, yet it boasts of great exploits. (Jas 3:1–5)

The problem, according to James, is that no one has found a way to tame the tongue. Because the tongue cannot be tamed it becomes a "restless evil, full of deadly poison." The tongue is the source of discord because it at once makes it possible to bless the Lord and Father yet curse those who are made in the image of God. That we bless and we curse from the same mouth is but an indication of how dangerous the tongue is for those who have learned God will care for his world through patient suffering.

If James is right, and I certainly think he is, then how can I suggest to you that if you are to serve the church well in the ministry you must become a teacher and, in particular, a teacher of a language called Christian? I do so because I think the characterizations of the challenges facing those going into the ministry are the result of the loss of the ability of Christians to speak the language of our faith. The accommodated character of the church is at least partly due to the failure of the clergy to help those they serve know how to speak Christian. To learn to be a Christian, to learn the discipline of the faith, is not just similar to learning another language. It *is* learning another language.

But to learn another language, to even learn to speak well the language you do not remember learning, is a time-consuming task. You are graduating from seminary, which I assume means that you have begun to learn how to speak as well as teach others how to talk, as we say in Texas, "right." For as I suggested, there is an essential relation between reading and speaking; because it is through reading that we learn how to discipline our speech so that we say no more than needs to be said. I like to think that seminaries might be best understood as schools of rhetoric where, as James suggests, our bodies, and the tongue is flesh, are subject to disciplines necessary for the tongue to approach perfection.

That the tongue is flesh is a reminder that speech is, as James suggests, bodily. To speak well, to talk right, requires that our bodies be habituated by the language of the faith. To be so habituated requires constant repetition. Without repetition, and repetition is but another word for the worship of God, we are in danger of losing the grammar of the faith. At least part of your task as those called to the ministry is to help us, as good teachers do, acquire the habits of speech through the right worship of God.

You may have begun to suspect that my call for you to think of yourself as a teacher is an exercise in self-justification. I am not ordained, but I have spent a life, for better or for worse, as a teacher. No doubt I deserve to be judged, as James suggest, with greater strictness because I have surely made many mistakes. Indeed I am sure I still remain in the beginning stage of learning to speak and write Christian. But I am also sure that to the extent I have learned to speak Christian I have done so because I have had to teach others how Christians in the past have spoken.

In truth I have only come recently to understand that what I have been doing for many years has been teaching people how to talk. For example, I was startled by a remark a friend made to me recently. He is a graduate student in anthropology with whom I was writing a paper in which we tried to challenge the presumption that "global Christianity" was an adequate description of what it means for the church to be "catholic." He told me that when he is asked by his colleagues what it was like to write with me he has to say it is not easy because, in his words, "Hauerwas only knows how to write Christian."

I confess I found his response gratifying, though I am not sure I think him right that I know how to "write Christian." I am sure I did not know how to write Christian when I began to teach and write. If I have learned to write Christian it is only because I have learned through imitation. For I think what it means to write Christian is to have a vocabulary sufficient to order the words of that vocabulary into sentences, and the sentences become paragraphs that are meant to form readers to see that what is said cannot be said differently than how it is said. Put differently, the most important part of writing and speaking Christian is what is not said.

Scripture, of course, is the source as well as the paradigm of Christian speech. What we say must be said faithful to the language of Scripture. That is a complex task because it is by no means clear how the many ways of expression in Scripture are to be said coherently. The investigation of that process is called theology. But theologians are often tempted to say too much because the reticence of Scripture, the refusal of Scripture to tell us what we think we need to know, drives us crazy. I sometimes think that the work of historical criticism, essential work for helping us read the Scripture faithfully, is a rage against the silences of Scripture. Why do not the Gospels tell us what Jesus is "thinking?"

Reticence, however, is a hard discipline to learn not only for theologians but for those in the ministry. You also will be tempted to say too much as ministers of the gospel. For example, you will be tempted to use the simulacra of Christian speech in an effort to say more than can be said. Confronted by a sudden and unexpected death of a "loved one," it is natural to underwrite the phrase, "they have gone to a better place." It is hard to resist that language because you want to be of help; or put differently, because that language helps you not feel helpless. But it is not the language of the faith. God is not a "place." Moreover, such language can underwrite the pagan assumption that we possess a soul that is eternal and, thus, fail to gesture our conviction as Christians that our life with God on either side of death is a gift.

To speak Christian is an exacting discipline. It has taken the church centuries to develop habits of speech that help us say no more than needs to be said. But I fear too often those of us charged with responsibility to teach those habits fail to do so in a manner that those in the ministry can make their own. For example, a prominent figure in my church was asked how she understood the Christian faith in Jesus in relation to other religious traditions. She responded by saying that Christians believe that Jesus is our way to God but other traditions have their way to God. It seems to have never occurred to her that Jesus is not our way to God because he is the Son of God. A generous interpretation of what she said might think she was trying to indicate how, given the essential union of Christ's humanity and divinity, a union necessary for our salvation, Christ as the Incarnate Word is our way to God. But unfortunately she made no mention of the incarnation.

Her response, of course, was the response required by the speech regimes of a liberal culture that before all else demands that we be tolerant. The acknowledgement that others have other ways to God, even though it is not at all clear who the god to whom they have a way is, is a speech act necessarily learned by Christians to insure we are not identified as political reactionaries. Many Christians think being a Christian gives them all the problems they want. In particular, they fear being associated with the Christian Right. I am sympathetic with their desire not to be identified with the Christian Right not because the Christian Right is intolerant, but because the Christian Right has lost the ability to speak Christian just to the extent they identify Christian speech with what Americans call "freedom."

Yet that a prominent member of the clergy would seem not to know how to speak Christian I think raises profound questions about the kind of training she received in seminary. That she could say that Jesus is but one way to God suggests somehow that she must have missed the class on "Trinity." How can the second person of the Trinity be the way to God if Jesus is the second person of the Trinity? We not only follow Jesus. We worship Jesus. You can only worship God. So if Jesus is the way to God, he is so only because he is the second person of the Trinity.

This is Theology 101. It does not get more basic than this. But somehow one of the leaders of my church seems to have missed the lectures on the Trinity in her basic theology course. Or she may have heard the lectures, but somehow thinks the lectures to be information about "doctrine" that has little to do with answering the question about other faiths. But if that is the case, then I fear she was not adequately taught the politics of speech, which is crucial to understand if we are to speak Christian. In particular, I suspect she was seduced by the word "god" and how that word can be used to legitimate social formations that ironically tempt Christians to abandon the Christian vocabulary.

I am aware this last remark may strike you as strange, but I think it quite important. I can illustrate what I mean by relating a recent exchange in a class I taught this semester on peace. The class had read William Cavanaugh's *The Myth of Religious Violence*. Cavanaugh challenges the oft-made argument that after the Reformation the creation of the modern state became the necessary institution of peace just to the degree the state was able to stop Catholics and Protestants from killing one another. He argues that the very creation of the notion of religion as a transhistorical and transcultural concept is part of the legitimating myth that is now essential to the liberal nation-state. A correlative of such an understanding of religion is that "god" is a word acceptable for use in the public forums of the state because it is a word that does not entail the specificity of a particular tradition. So interestingly enough, just to the extent Christians think they can say "god" more easily than they can say "Jesus" they are underwriting the legitimating violence of the nation-state.

The politics of speech associated with the use of the word "god" that Cavanaugh exposes was wonderfully made concrete because one of the students in my class is a chaplain in the United States Army, who holds the rank of major. He has had a long career in the Army and has served in Iraq. He is a deeply committed Christian who is admirably forthright about the ambiguities of his position as a chaplain. He has been sent to Duke by the Army to study ethics because his next duty will be to teach ethics at one of the Army bases where soldiers are trained in artillery. During our discussion of Cavanaugh's argument, he reported that his reading of Yoder had put him in a real quandary because he cannot use the name of Jesus when he teaches ethics but he can talk about "god." One seldom has philosophical and theological arguments empirically confirmed, but that seems to have happened with his report of how "god" is used to confirm the status of the state as an instrument of peace. Such an account seems particularly persuasive when the state so conceived confronts an Islamic world that we do not think has learned the lessons allegedly associated with the Treaty of Westphalia.

I am not a Mennonite, so it would be inappropriate for me to comment on the decision at Goshen College to play the national anthem before sporting events, but I assume what I have said about how Christians should not say certain things has implications for singing the national anthem. Suffice it to say, in the very least, singing the National Anthem is not politically innocent. To speak Christian does not insure we will be faithful witnesses to Christ, but it may not be a bad place to begin rediscovering the radical implications of Christian orthodoxy.

If you are to minister to a church that is an alternative to a nation-state that has co-opted the word "god" as a means of legitimating the violence it calls peace, you should insist that it makes all the difference that when the church says "peace" the peace that is said requires that we also say "Jesus." I say this even though it may seem like bringing coals to Newcastle. After all, this is Eastern Mennonite Seminary, which at the very least means that John Howard Yoder is read here. Surely this is a place that has not forgotten that when you say "peace" the peace you say is unintelligible if Jesus has not been raised from the dead.

But you can never, or at least you should not ever, take for granted the locution that "Jesus is our peace." For learning to speak Christian means that what we say requires constant practice because the predominate speech habits that also shape our speech tempt us to not know what we say when we say Jesus. Take for example Yoder's comment on debates about effectiveness between William Miller and James Douglass in *Christian Attitudes to War, Peace, and Revolution*. In response to Douglass's claim that the promise of good effects is integral to nonviolent action's ethical basis, Yoder observes that such a claim is a mistake.[1] If Jesus is Lord, we betray the hope that makes our commitment to nonviolence intelligible if we try to prove it. For if we tried to prove our hope we would have to subject it to some other more fundamental standard. But that would mean giving our loyalty to another Lord. Such a move is analogous to trying to prove one religion is higher or purer than another by using standards external to the religions one is comparing. So our faith in the resurrection sustains a "hope that cannot

---

1. What follows is a close paraphrase of Yoder, *Christian Attitudes*, 360–61.

be destroyed by my failures or jeopardized by my inability to manipulate events."[2]

Such a faith, that is, a faith in the resurrection of Jesus, also means that to speak Christian does not mean such speech cannot be understood by others who do not speak Christian. It does mean, however, that like us they will need to undergo training to hear what is being said and hopefully thereby become more eloquent and confident speakers. Moreover, if we are confident Christian speakers we may well discover that there are other languages that have words and grammars we can use. After all, Christian speech has been and will continue to be forged from encounters that have resulted in Christian appropriation of other ways of speaking that help us be faithful to the gospel.

The hope that the resurrection makes possible, the hope that sustains the witness of peace in a world of war, the hope that Jesus names, is a hope that you must have if you are to sustain the slow and hard ministry of word work. To learn to speak Christian and to help others speak Christian means that many of the days you spend in the ministry will seem as if you have not done anything. When your spouse asks you at the end of the day, "How was your day?" you will discover you cannot remember anything you did. If you are looking for "results" to confirm you have lived a life worth living you probably are making a mistake by going into the ministry.

But then the ministry, like a commitment to nonviolence, does not promise success. For as Yoder reminds us, Jesus did not promise his followers they would conquer within time if they did things right. Rather the love that refuses to achieve the good through the disavowal of violence, the refusal to use mechanical models of cause and effect to force history to move in what is assumed the right direction, means the promise of victory can only be found in the resurrection. Victory, moreover, means for those in the ministry the willingness to do the same thing over and over again in the hope that by doing so the Christian people can speak truthfully to one another and the world.

So I hope that when you are asked about your day you might say, "Well I was reading Barth on the Trinity and I think I finally understand why 'Father' is in the first article of the Creed." I assume you will still be reading, and in particular reading Barth, because the reading hab-

2. Ibid., 361.

its you have developed during your studies here are habits crucial for sustaining your life in the ministry. I am sure you have read many good books in seminary, but that reading is meant to prepare you to spend a life reading. You must continue to read and study even though you may receive little reward for doing so. You must, moreover, help the people you serve recognize that their support of your study is a good the whole people of God have in common.

I hope occasionally when asked for a report of your day in the ministry you will be able to say "I think I wrote one good sentence in the sermon for Sunday." The sermon is at the heart of our ability to speak as well as sustain speaking Christian. The sermon is not your reflections on how to negotiate life. The sermon rather is our fundamental speech act as Christians through which we learn the grammar of the faith. As my colleague, Richard Lischer, puts it in his book *The End of Words*, "the preacher's job . . . is to do nothing less than shape the language of the sermon to a living reality among the people of God—to make it conform to Jesus. The sermon, in fact, is Jesus trying to speak once again in his own community."[3]

James may well be right that not many should be called to be teachers, but as one charged with the proclamation of the gospel I do not see how you can avoid being a teacher. For as Lischer observes, preachers are authorized to say things that, if they did not utter them, no one would ever hear the forms of language that require God as their final audience. One sentence may not seem like much, but our lives as Christians depend on your struggle to say Christ.

Finally, I hope, in response to the question about your how your day was, you might be able to say that you hope that you prayed with the dying the prayer that needed to be prayed. Prayer is the heart of Christian speech. Like all Christians you are called to live a life of prayer. As one called to the ministry of Jesus Christ you are called to help those like me learn to pray. That surely is the most important work in the world. I rejoice that you are graduating from seminary, but even more I am given hope that you are called to the ministry. There can be no higher calling.

---

3. Lischer, *End of Words*, 7.

7

Why "The Way the Words Run" Matters:
Reflections on Becoming a "Major Biblical Scholar"*

If we understand deeply enough the way in which the promise
of the Holy Spirit is linked to the church's gathering to bind and
loose (Matt. 18:19–20), this may provide us well with a more
wholesome understanding of the use and authority of Scripture.
One of the most enduring subjects of unfruitful controversy
over the centuries has been whether the words of Scripture,
when looked at purely as words, isolated from the context in
which certain people read them at a certain time and place, have
both clear meaning and the absolute authority of revelation.

To speak of the Bible apart from people reading it and
apart from the specific questions that those people reading need
to answer is to do violence to the very purpose for which we
have been given the Holy Scriptures. There is no such thing as
an isolated word of the Bible carrying meaning in itself. It has
meaning only when it is read by someone and then only when
that reader and society in which he or she lives can understand
the issue to which it speaks.[1]

---

* This essay was written for the festschrift for Richard B. Hays: *The Word Leaps the
Gap: Essays on Scripture and Theology in Honor of Richard B. Hays*, edited by J. Ross
Wagner, C. Kavin Rowe, and A. Katherine Grieb.

1. Yoder, "Binding and Loosing," in *Royal Priesthood*, 353. I am indebted to Chris
Huebner for calling attention to this quote from Yoder in his essay "Mennonites and
Narrative Theology," which appears in Huebner's book *Precarious Peace*, 61.

Hays's Challenge

In *The Moral Vision of the New Testament*, Richard Hays was kind enough to attend to my account of the status of the Bible for theological and ethical reflection.[2] Hays notes the diverse sources that shape how I read Scripture—that is, Barth, Aristotle, Aquinas, Yoder, Fish—but then observes it is not at all easy to see how I "can hold these different elements together in a coherent hermeneutical position; indeed given his [Hauerwas's] rather freewheeling approach to biblical interpretation it is not at all clear he has done so."[3]

I have never responded to Hays's criticism, but now that I am a "major biblical scholar"—that is, I have written a commentary on the Gospel of Matthew—I am in a position, or at least I owe Richard, a response to his challenge to my "freewheeling style" approach to the Bible.[4] I fear, however, that I will not be able to satisfy Richard's suggestion that I need to make articulate a "coherent hermeneutical position," yet I hope to make clear why I do not believe a "coherent hermeneutical position" is much help for helping us read the Bible.[5]

2. Hays, *Moral Vision*, 253–66. The very grammar of our speech often betrays us. For example I use the word "status" to avoid the word "use," but "status" sounds, well, too much like "a status." I also do not like to have to use the locution "theology and ethics" because I do not think they are two "things." But given the conventions I felt it necessary to refer to both.

3. Ibid., 254.

4. Hauerwas, *Matthew*. This book is dedicated to Ellen Davis, David Aers, and Richard Hays—close friends and close readers who have taught me much about how to read and, in particular, how to read Scripture. I continue to doubt, however, if the art of reading, particularly the art of reading the Bible, can be taught. Richard Hays is obviously a talented reader of Scripture, but I have always thought he is so not because of his training as a historian. Rather, his reading skills I suspect reflect his love of poetry. Of course it helps to know the Scripture as well as Richard knows Scripture. I only wish I had his familiarity with the text, because such familiarity is crucial for making the connections good readings exemplify.

5. My worries about hermeneutical theories derive from philosophical concerns about the "self" such theories too often presuppose. Paul DeHart rightly suggests that Hans Frei resisted the kind of hermeneutical theory represented by Gadamer and Ricouer because he was convinced they continued to reproduce romantic conceptions of the self. DeHart, *Trial of the Witnesses*, 200. In *Theology and Narrative*, Frei observes "In regard to understanding, I find myself influenced increasingly by Wittgenstein and J. L. Austin rather than by the Idealistic tradition that has dominated the field for so long, whether in its pure form (e.g. Dilthey), in existentialist form like that of Pannenberg, or in a more ontological form like that of Heidegger, Gadamer, and

However, I first need to say more about Hays's "bill of particulars" concerning my approach to the Bible. Hays quite rightly calls attention to my argument in *Unleashing the Scripture: Freeing the Bible from Captivity to America* that fundamentalism and historical criticism are but two sides of the same coin—that is, they are both developments of the Protestant stress on *sola scriptura* that was transformed into *sola text* by the printing press. These developments were then given ideological formation through the development of democratic social orders, which created something called the individual citizen that presumed the ability to read the Bible without spiritual formation and moral guidance. As a result, the Bible was separated from the community necessary for it to be read as the word of God—that is, the church.[6]

Hays quite rightly characterizes my position as entailing the view that the community already formed by the story of the Kingdom of God is prior to and necessary if the Bible is to be rightly read. Such a community is constituted by the liturgical practices and the lives of the saints that are necessary for the reading of Scripture. I, therefore, argue that it is a methodological mistake to ask how Scripture should be "used" in Christian ethics. Such a question assumes the ethicist has some epistemological privilege external to the Bible, a privilege often based on the "latest" historical reconstruction of the text, that allows them to determine the "meaning" of the text and then to ask how the text might be "used."

Hays worries that my emphasis on the church as the politics necessary for the reading of Scripture fails to do justice to "the clas-

---

among theologians Fuchs and Ebeling. There is it seems to me, a variety of descriptions for any given linguistic phenomenon, and hence, above all, no ontological superdescription or explanation for it. Furthermore, the 'grammar' (use according to rules of such a construct) is more readily exhibited or set forth than stated in the abstract" (33). In an odd way—odd because hermeneutical theories often claim to be political—hermeneutical theories of "meaning" involve an attempt to avoid making candid the politics of reading.

6. Hauerwas, *Unleashing the Scripture*. I am quite sympathetic with Kevin Vanhoozer's recent attempt to rehabilitate the notion of *sola scriptura* that views the Bible as an authoritative script not merely for intellectual assent but for live performance. Thus his claim "to practice *sola scriptura* means to participate in the canonical practices that form, inform, and transform our speaking, thinking, and living—practices that the Spirit uses to conform us to the image of God in Christ" (Vanhoozer, *Drama of Doctrine*, 237).

sic Protestant idea that Scripture can challenge and judge tradition."[7] Indeed, he even suggests that the logic of my position should require me to become a Roman Catholic, but that would mean that I would belong to a church that holds positions on major ethical issues such as war and the role of women that are at odds with my commitment to Christian nonviolence and my support of the ordination of women.[8] Hays concludes that finally in my hands the "New Testament falls mute, muzzled by the unfaithful church, and Hauerwas finds himself with no theoretical grounds for an appeal to Scripture against the church's practices."[9]

Hays acknowledges that I do provide "sermonic exhibits" that I claim to be evidence that I am not "muzzling" the text. However, Hays is not impressed by my sermons, observing that I am less inclined to exposit the text than to propose conditions that must be met if the text is to be rightly read. For example, in my sermon on the Sermon on the Mount, Hays notes that

> nowhere does Hauerwas engage in exegetical discussion of the structure and logic of the six antitheses in Matthew 5:21–48; nowhere does he explore the first-century historical background of such practices as turning the other cheek and going a second mile (Matt. 5:39–41); nowhere does he ask what source in Scripture or elsewhere might be said to instruct Jesus' hearers to hate their enemies (Matt. 5:43); nowhere does he investigate the meaning of the word *teleos* ("perfect"; Matt. 5:48). In short, he does not undertake any of the exegetical practices necessary

---

7. Hays, *Moral Vision*, 263. Of course, it was my contention that the development of historical criticism was also in service to a politics, namely, the developing nation-states of modernity. For example, Jon Levenson argues that "like the liberal state at its best, biblical studies in nonconfessional settings must facilitate rather than impede dialogue and debate among the primary communities, religious and secular, within its compass" (*Hebrew Bible, the Old Testament, and Historical Criticism*, 123). For substantiation of Levenson's argument that biblical criticism not only mirrored the liberal state but served as an ideology for its legitimation, see Howard, *Protestant Theology*, 207–11.

8. Hays, *Moral Vision*, 265.

9. Ibid., 265–67. Hays at one time thought it crucial to maintain the distinction between "what it meant" and "what it means" to insure that the Scripture can judge the church. I do not know if he still thinks such a distinction is necessary, but from my perspective such a distinction only insures that members of the Society of Biblical Literature can judge the church.

to demonstrate how the specific language of the text might or might not warrant an ethic of nonviolence.[10]

Finally, Hays argues that I fail to deal with texts that stand in tension with my synthetic construal of the New Testament message. According to Hays, I feel no necessity to show how the Pastoral Epistles or Revelation fits within my story of the Kingdom. Nor do I ever try to resolve the tensions within the canon. I use the category of story as an elixir to paper over discrepancies in the Gospels by stressing journey and cross as focal points around which everything in the Gospels can be organized.[11] From Hays's perspective, unlike John Howard Yoder, I ride roughshod over the Bible making it mean what I have predetermined it to mean. In short, I do not do what anyone that intends to be faithful to the Bible must do—that is, I do not do exegesis.

In My Own Defense

I cannot help but feel just a wee bit defensive in the face of Hays's criticisms of my "use" of Scripture. I should like to think my sermons are not as devoid of exegetical display as he suggests, but I do not think trying to show how I was reading the texts I used in the sermons will be much help for responding to Hays.[12] Moreover, given the develop-

10. Hays, *Moral Vision*, 259. Hays also notes that I have an overt hostility to historical criticism even though my account of Jesus in *The Peaceable Kingdom* draws on the work of such biblical scholars as Tinsley, Harvey, Riches, and Dahl.

11. "Focal images" is Hays's language, borrowed from David Kelsey, to provide shape to the diversity of the scriptural texts. See *Moral Vision*, 193–205. It is not language I use just to the extent the "image" threatens to become isolated from the way the words run. Hays's discussion of the images of community, cross, and new creation is subtle, but on the whole I worry that "cross" abstracted from Jesus' crucifixion, an abstraction Hays resists, too easily becomes a "symbol" to illumine the human condition.

12. I should like to think that the sermons Hays has included in *Art of Reading Scripture*, the book he edited with Ellen Davis, might suggest he would now find my sermons not quite as exegetically deficient as when he wrote *Moral Vision*. For example, in a wonderful sermon on Daniel he calls attention to the fourth figure that appears in the furnace, suggesting that this figure prefigures Christ. Hays acknowledges that prior to his participation in the Scripture Project he would not have been able to preach Daniel this way, but he now finds it impossible not to see Daniel as a prophecy of Christ. He is careful to avoid any suggestion that the author of Daniel intended to write a christological prophecy, but rather that the author wrote figuratively making such a reading possible (306–10). I, of course, do not disagree with his christological

ments in Hays's position exemplified in the book he edited with Ellen Davis, *The Art of Reading Scripture*, I think it may be the case that we increasingly share a fundamental outlook about how the Bible is to be read.[13] Yet the criticisms Hays made of my work in *The Moral Vision of the New Testament* are important, and I need to respond to them for no other reason than to get straight for myself what I really think about

---

reading, but I would not have worried at all about what the author of Daniel might have "intended." I assume even if the author was available he or she would have as much trouble saying what he or she intended as I would have trying to say what I intend by writing this paragraph. Moreover, Daniel is now Scripture, which means issues of "authorship" are more complex than questions about "intention."

I would contend, however—a contention well developed by John Wright in his book *Telling God's Story*—that preaching is the appropriate practice for biblical reading. Wright argues that contemporary preaching too often takes as its task to find "applications" for the text when its task should be to turn a congregation away from one narrative world into another. Wright's book is a brilliant analysis of how we got where we are as well as developing a constructive way forward.

13. In particular, see Hays's essay "Reading Scripture in the Light of the Resurrection," in *Art of Reading Scripture*, 216–38. The "Nine Theses on the Interpretation of Scripture" set out at the beginning of *Art of Reading Scripture* say better some of the points I was trying to make in *Unleashing the Scripture*. In particular, theses two ("Scripture is rightly understood in light of the church's rule of faith as a coherent dramatic narrative") and six ("Faithful interpretation of Scripture invites and presupposes participation in the community brought into being by God's redemptive action—the church") are expressions of the argument of *Unleashing the Scripture*. Hays, however, continues to try to have it both ways—that is, he wants a theological reading of the Scripture without calling into question the work of historical criticism. For example, he quite rightly argues that "the resurrection accounts teach us to read the Old Testament as Christian Scripture," but this does not mean "to deny its original historical sense, nor does it preclude responsible historical criticism. Christians have a stake in seeking the most historically careful readings of the Old Testament that we can attain. At the same time, however, in light of the New Testament witness, we cannot confine the meaning of the Old Testament to the literal sense understood by its original authors and readers, for these texts have been taken up into a new story that amplifies and illumines their meaning in unexpected ways" (233). I have quoted Hays at length because his wording continues to betray assumptions that, given his agreement with the "Nine Theses," he should leave behind. It is not the "accounts" of the resurrection that teach us to read the Old Testament as Christian Scripture. It is the resurrection testified to by the Holy Spirit. "Accounts" may indicate what we learn from walking with Jesus to Emmaus, but we are able to make that walk because of his resurrection. There is, moreover, no "original historical sense," and it is not at all clear why the "literal sense" should be identified as that which the "original" authors and readers understood. The very presumption of "original" needs to be left behind. I have no idea, moreover, what might count as "responsible historical criticism."

how the reading of Scripture matters for the up-building of the holiness of the church.[14]

I am very sympathetic with Hays's criticism that I am not sufficiently exegetical. I do not, however, think that was due to the argument I made in *Unleashing the Scripture* for why the church is the necessary politics for reading the Scripture. After all, the church insists that the words matter.[15] But when I wrote *Unleashing the Scripture* I did not know how to show that words matter because, as Rusty Reno observes, most theologians in modernity (including me) have lost competency in exegesis. As a result, according to Reno, "each decade finds new theories of preaching to cover the nakedness of seminary training that provides

14. The reader will note that I avoid using the language of "interpretation" because I think such language suggests that the text has "a meaning" which then must be interpreted. Such a view reproduces the habits of liberal Protestant theologians who assume the language of Scripture needs to be demythologized to meet the epistic standards of modernity. Such a view is nicely exemplified in a "Comment" in the *Journal of Religious Ethics* by William Schweiker in a response to an article by Michael O'Neil. O'Neil had criticized Schweiker for basing his critique of misuses of power on universal epistemic principles rather than on the practices and authority of the church. In his defense Schweiker noted that he employs a hermeneutical "method" because he assumes that the *moral meaning* of the Christian faith is different from the kind of knowing found in sensible experience or in logical truths. He observes, for example, that "the non-reducibility of understanding to empirical and/or logical knowledge claims is crucial to sustain. I may 'know,' for instance, that the sun is shining through my window, but that does not in itself determine its meaning for me or anyone else, or that I understand its possible range of meanings" (713). You know you are in the grip of a theory, a bad one at that, when you think the "sun is shining through my window" has a "meaning" or "meanings." As I will suggest below such a view of language continues to assume a dualism between language and world that is profoundly mistaken.

15. George Lindbeck puts the matter as well as it can be put noting that we do not and should not choose between the priority of church or Scripture. Rather, we best think of them as co-inhering because their mutually constitutive reciprocity. Lindbeck observes that the cannon is closed for those who believe in the eschatological decisiveness of Jesus Christ shifting the balance between church and Scripture. Originally the church formed Scripture, but now the church is formed by it. "Yet the Bible's community-forming role is not independent of community. It helps constitute the *ecclesia* only when interpreted communally in accordance with a community-constituting hermeneutics" (*Church in a Postliberal Age*, 204). "A community-constituting hermeneutics" may sound like a "general hermeneutic theory," but it is crucial not to overlook the definite article "a." Of course, the "a" means that different communities will produce different readings some of which may be in conflict. Attempts to develop a hermeneutical theory that can resolve such differences in advance are doomed to failure. The church did not develop a theory to resolve conflicting readings, but rather an office was given to the church to insure that one church's readings would be tested by other churches. The name of that office is "bishop."

theology without exegesis and exegesis without theology."[16] Indeed, that exegesis and theology are now thought to be two separate enterprises indicates a sea change in theology just to the extent that prior to recent times, to be sure in quite different ways, theology was exegesis.[17]

Put simply, I simply did not know how to go on to show what the arguments I had made about the ecclesial practices that should shape exegetical practice might look like.[18] The best I could do was to try to display how the words mattered through the sermonic exhibits. But Hays is quite right that given the character of sermons, or at least the form sermons usually take in our day, the sermons I used as exhibits did not exemplify the kind of close reading of texts he thinks crucial for responsible biblical interpretation.

I have now, however, at least tried to do the kind of work Hays think I needed to do by writing a theological commentary of the Gospel

16. Reno, "Series Preface" to my *Matthew*, 13. Commenting on the work of Karl Rahner, Lindbeck observes that while Rahner may have developed an authentically Christian idealistic-existential-evolutionary *Weltanschauung* "one can learn to think well in his categories while remaining biblically illiterate" (*Church in a Postliberal Age*, 212). Lindbeck's characterization of Rahner applies to most modern theologians. Our problem is that even if we want to make exegetical work constitutive of our theology, we do not know how. I suspect our loss of exegetical skill has everything to do with theology's role in the modern university. By making theology look like philosophy, theologians could claim academic respectability.

17. How and why theologians began to do theology as a systematic discipline that required no extensive readings of biblical texts is no doubt a story that needs telling. I have no special insight to account for this development, but surely it has something to do with theology finding its primary home in the universities of modernity. See, for example, my *State of the University*. I suspect theologians' loss of exegetical skill has to do with the diminishment of biblical authority and literacy among Christians in the mainline churches. How do you make an argument that turns on the exegesis of a particular passage when those to whom you are making the argument have little knowledge of the Scripture? As a result, the Bible cannot help but be a resource of "ideas" that become the primary focus of theology. In short, theology comes to look more and more like philosophy—bad philosophy I might add.

18. Of course, I did have the example of what such exegesis might look like in the work of John Howard Yoder and, in particular, in his book *Politics of Jesus*. For those interested, I need to report that I tried to convince John not to "update" the scholarship since the original printing of *Politics of Jesus* in the "Epilogues" to each chapter in the second edition. I thought such "updating" gave the impression that his readings of the texts depended on developments in historical scholarship. Yet he always thought, or at least said, that *Politics of Jesus* was nothing more than a report of where the scholarship had taken us. I have no doubt John thought that, but I do not think what he did in *Politics of Jesus* can be shown to be only a "report."

of Matthew.[19] By discussing some of the decisions I made in writing that commentary, I hope to provide at least a partial response to Hays's criticisms of my work. However before I do so I want to challenge some of the presumptions Hays seems to have held when he wrote *The Moral Vision of the New Testament*—presumptions that shaped some of his criticisms of me. For as the quote above concerning my sermon on the Sermon on the Mount suggests, Hays seems to have thought knowing more about the "historical background" was crucial for sustaining the "close readings" he found lacking in my work. Historians will do what historians will do and often we may learn something that may be of use, but I remain unconvinced that so-called historical knowledge trumps or is even necessary for how Scripture is to be read by the church.

For example, I simply do not believe that I will learn from word studies the "meaning" of the word *teleios*. I do not believe that I will learn the meaning of the word *teleios* because I think it is a philosophical mistake to think that *the* word has *a* meaning.[20] Such views about

19. I do not think I would have been able even to begin work on Matthew if I had not been asked to preach on the seven last words of Christ at Saint Thomas Church Fifth Avenue in New York City. I do not know what Hays might think about those meditations, but I know they forced me to attend to the words as witnesses to the Word in a manner I am not sure I had done in my previous work. See *Cross-Shattered Christ*.

20. Happily, the fourth thesis in Davis's and Hays's *Art of Reading Scripture* reads: "Texts of Scripture do not have a single meaning limited to the intent of the original author. In accord with Jewish and Christian traditions, we affirm that Scripture has multiple complex senses given by God, the author of the whole drama" (2). The very fact that Christians presume our Scriptures can be translated challenges the assumption that a word can be isolated for its "meaning." The necessity of translation I believe to be a faithful way to enact Matt 28:19. Of course, every translation is a new reading requiring each translation be tested by other translations. The words matter, but that the words are translations means that no "meaning" can be determined by a word isolated from the way the words run. Attempts to show what a word had "to mean" by the comparison with what the word may or may not have meant in other texts are not entirely without use, but such "word studies" cannot in themselves determine what the word "meant." For example, if I called Hays an "asshole" most would think I was making a very negative judgment about him. But where I come from, Texas, asshole is a term of endearment males use after they have scored a touchdown. Languages in use cannot be translated but rather we can, in Alasdair MacIntyre's way of stating it, learn a "second first language." The church has quite rightly asked some to learn Hebrew and Greek to test translation, but we must remember the Hebrew and Greek that is being learned is not the "original language." Ellen Davis and Richard Hays have an extraordinary "feel" for the respective languages of the texts over which they work, but the languages they know so well only come to life through the life they bring to it. "Life," of course, names the work of the Holy Spirit. For an example of how the study

the meaning of words reproduce presumptions that words depend on ostensive references that I simply do not think can be sustained after Wittgenstein. To try to isolate the "meaning" of a word from its use is to assume that language is one thing and that what the language depicts is something quite other. As a result language and the world are understood to be externally related to one another in a manner that language users are positioned as spectators rather than performers.[21] The presumption that a dualism exists between language and the world hides from us that "the world" is constituted by language and that there is no way to transcend language to speak about language.[22]

These are deep philosophical waters that require fuller development than I can provide for the purpose I want to achieve in this paper. The reason I cannot develop these philosophical issues is not simply a matter of space, but because the defense of claims concerning the practical force of language and the correlative theological reading of Scripture is best done indirectly and through example. I will try to provide some examples below, but before doing so I want to call attention to the argument Marcus Bockmuehl makes in his recent book, *Seeing the Word: Refocusing New Testament Studies*, because he helps us see,

---

of words should be done, see Rowe, *Early Narrative Christology*. George Lindbeck also calls attention to the significance of the Christian presumption that our Scripture can be translated in his *Church in a Postliberal Age*, 231–36.

21. My general rule is to avoid the grammar entailed in questions about "meaning." To ask the "meaning" of a word or sentence or paragraph is to tempt us to think the meaning is separable from what the words do—that is, it is to tempt us to think the "meaning" can be abstracted from description and/or depiction. Hans Frei's work stands as a challenge to the presumption that "meaning" can be isolated from how the story runs. For the best account of Frei's argument, see Dawson's *Christian Figural Reading*, 141–85.

22. It is tempting to footnote some remark by Wittgenstein to confirm this conclusion, but such a footnote would betray the character of the training Wittgenstein provides necessary to acknowledge the contingent character of ourselves as language users. For example, many allegedly influenced by Wittgenstein seem to think Wittgenstein put forward some theory about meaning as use, or that he provides a philosophy of ordinary language. Wittgenstein certainly does say in the *Philosophical Investigations*, "For a *large* class of cases—though not for all—in which we employ the word 'meaning' it can be defined thus: the meaning of a word is its use in the language" (43). But please note that he is not putting forward a theory of meaning, but rather some characteristics of the employment of the word "meaning." For those tempted to find a position in Wittgenstein, they should at least attend to his remark, "To understand a sentence means to understand a language. To understand a language means to be master of a technique" (199). For Wittgenstein, training is the heart of the matter.

and the very title of his book reminds us that we must learn to see, why theological readings are not an afterthought once one has done your historical homework.

Bockmuehl argues that Scripture requires "the wisdom of the implied exegete."[23] According to Bockmuehl, both Testaments of Scripture clearly presuppose such an interpreter, but the interpreter that is a reader of the Old and New Testaments is a disciple, that is, a witness to the Christ. Bockmuehl, therefore, argues

> the object of biblical interpretation is the interpreter as much as it is the text, and it is *performative* as much as it is hermeneutical. Taking a cue from John Webster, one might even say that this presumption of discipleship involves the interpreter in the kind of theological anthropology that the New Testament itself envisages: it presumes to engage an exegete whose very interpretation serves, is judged by, and is *converted* to the evangelical truth that inheres in Scripture's witness.[24]

Which means that the right reading of the gospel requires an ecclesial location. Thus Bockmuehl argues that "in spite of its foundational significance for Christianity, the New Testament does not *create* the church but rather *presupposes* and confirms it at every turn."[25] The very survival of what we know as the New Testament indicates that speculation about the origin of the texts of the New Testament will be inadequate to determine the meaning of the same texts. For the New Testament is not a ragtag collection of ill-conceived political agendas and diverse ecclesiologies, but the "New Testament as a whole and in parts *presupposes* an implied readership and a *Sitz im Leben* in which it functions as the abiding deposit of the apostolic witness to the gospel."[26] Accordingly, theological themes are not "added on" after exegetical work is done, but rather theological and ethical loci such as Trinity, sanctification, judg-

---

23. Bockmuehl, *Seeing the Word*, 75–99.

24. Ibid., 92.

25. Ibid., 113. I began this paper with the quote from Yoder, because in *Moral Vision* Hays, quite rightly, gave a very sympathetic account of Yoder's work that seemed to suggest Yoder focusing on the text was an alternative to my focus on the church. Yet Yoder was no less insistent that the kind of church mattered for the right reading of the text. I think it would be quite instructive to compare Bockmuehl's understanding of the implied reader with Yoder's understanding of discipleship.

26. Bockmuehl, *Seeing the Word*, 114.

ment, inspiration of Scripture, or the doctrine of heaven are the direct result of the New Testament text's continuing in the church.[27]

Such a view does not mean that the many-splendored thing called the historical-critical method must be abandoned, but no longer can such a method—and it is by no means clear what it means for it to be a "method"—claim that the work done in its name must precede a theological reading. Like Bockmuehl, I think the historical work that has helped us see the Jewish character of Jesus' life and ministry has been a singular contribution of recent historical scholarship.[28] But I remain unconvinced that the kind of theological reading Bockmuehl argues the New Testament demands of a reader is compatible with many of the readings that shape work done in the name of the historical reconstruction of the texts of the New Testament.

For example, from the perspective of what is claimed to be "history" we are taught to ask as well as answer:

> Why was Matthew written? He wanted to restate Mark to justify the existence of Jewish Christianity. Why did Luke write? To convince Rome that Christianity was not dangerous and so assure its existence. Or to establish his theology over and against Mark's. Why did the resurrection narratives arise? Because they needed a way to justify the continued existence of the Jesus community after his death. Why does Acts include the ascension? To justify the fact that Jesus was no longer with them. Why does Paul claim such a low status in II Corinthians? Because he's actually trying to regain control of the community. Why were early Christian communities attractive? Because they offered increased status. Why did Paul write anything? To get his congregations to do what he wanted. Why is Revelation written? To assure Christians that God will have his revenge on the

27. Ibid., 118.

28. Ibid., 200–201. Indeed, it is my view that historical criticism was a gift from God to counter the tendency in Protestantism to lose the life of Jesus because of the over-emphasis of justification by grace. So the liberal Protestant attempt to recover the lives of Jesus at least had the virtue of reminding us that Jesus had a life. I do not think that there is a necessary correlation between the emphasis on "doctrine" and the failure to account for the significance of Jesus' life, but they have often gone hand in hand. That historical critics will not let the church avoid the bits of Scripture that do not confirm our contemporary sensibilities is also a contribution we dare not ignore. Of course I do not believe that the historical criticism is necessary for the recovery of the significance of Jesus' life or for forcing us to attend to the unpleasant parts of Scripture. It just worked out that way.

beast. Why do the New Testament authors interpret the Old Testament out of context? To justify their own positions by what means possible.[29]

From my perspective, these questions and answers are simply not helpful for shaping the kind of readings Bockmuehl argues is required if we are to be the "implied exegete" Scripture demands we be if what we read is to be read for the up-building of the church. But that does not mean the words do not matter, but rather how the words matter is to be determined, as Davis and Hays suggest, "in light of the church's rule of faith as coherent dramatic narrative."[30] Our problem, quite simply, is that few of us know what such a reading of the Scripture disciplined by the rule of faith might look like. I tried to at least begin to work in that direction in my commentary on the Gospel of Matthew, but I have no illusions that I accomplished what I set out to do. However, I want to call attention to some of the ways I tried to work in the hope that others may learn from my mistakes.

Reading Matthew[31]

In his "Series Preface" to the volumes coming out in the Brazos Theological Commentary on the Bible, Rusty Reno declares that this commentary series is based on

29. I am indebted to Mr. Colin Miller for this paragraph, which is to be found in his paper, "Reading Scripture with Milbank and Saint Paul," written for my seminar in Philosophical Theology.

30. Davis and Hays, *Art of Reading Scripture*, 1.

31. As he comes close to the end of his chapter entitled "Scripture, Consensus, and Community" in his book *Church in a Postliberal Age*, George Lindbeck observes that he finds himself acutely aware that his essay is a counter-instance of what it recommends; that is to say, in making his argument he does not refer the reader to the biblical text (284). Desiring to avoid that result, a result I have often exemplified, I thought I would try to make candid some of the decisions I made in writing the commentary on Matthew. I was hesitant to do so, however, because I did not: (1) want to blow my own horn even though it is a very little horn, and (2) I did not think I could do justice to the details. One of the things I learned writing about Matthew is the inexhaustibility of the text, and I feared what I might say in this context might look like a "point" I was trying to make when I wrote the commentary. I wish I could have thought of an alternative, but I could not. I thank the reader for their patience with my attempt to "spell out" the way I approached the task of writing a commentary.

the assumption that the Nicene tradition, in all its diversity and controversy provides the proper basis for the interpretation of the Bible as Christian Scripture. God the Father Almighty, who sends his only begotten son to die for us and for our salvation and who raises the crucified Son in the power of the Holy Spirit so that the baptized may be joined in one body—faith in *this* God with *this* vocation of love for the world is the lens through which to view the heterogeneity and particularity of the biblical texts. Doctrine, then, is not a moldering scrim of antique prejudice obscuring the meaning of the Bible. It is a crucial aspect of the divine pedagogy, a clarifying agent for our minds fogged by self-deceptions, a challenge to our languid intellectual apathy that will too often rest in false truisms and the easy spiritual nostrums of the present age rather than search more deeply and widely for the dispersed keys to the many doors of Scripture.[32]

Reno contends that such an approach to Scripture does not mean that doctrine becomes a substitute for exegesis; rather, theological exegesis means Scripture is read as the living language of faith. "To put the matter in a formula, the more readily exegesis enters into the life and practice of the church, the more fully theological is the interpretation."[33] These were the conditions I assumed I was obligated to try to fulfill in the commentary I was to write on the Gospel of Matthew.

In order to force myself to write, and thus to think, differently I gave myself certain rules: (1) I would make no reference to the so-called Synoptic problem; (2) I would try to avoid all consciousness words in reference to Jesus or Matthew; (3) I would not write "about" Matthew, but would try to write "with" Matthew; and (4) I would try to respect the reticence of Matthew by avoiding all attempt to provide "explanations." Each of these rules in different ways was an attempt to avoid the temptation to "get behind" the text.[34]

32. Reno, "Series Preface," 12. Reno quite rightly and helpfully also insists that doctrine is a habit of mind rather than a list of propositions.

33. Reno, "Apostolic Legitimacy and Apostolic Vitality," 6.

34. Bockmuehl reads the temptation of Jesus, like the temptation of Eve, as an attempt to make Jesus assume the position of an autonomous reasoning subject isolated from the ecclesial context. Bockmuehl suggests that the tempter strategy is not unlike some of the rhetorical strategies surrounding Scripture just to the extent we are asked to assume a "more objective" stance than the "plain sense of the divine word." Thus the conditional: "'*If* you really are the Son of God . . .'" (Matt. 4:3). A divine Son surely is and does all that pleases him! Never mind that the baptismal heavenly voice in fact af-

To the extent I had or have a hermeneutic, I simply tried to display, in the words of Gene Rogers and Lewis Ayres, "the way the words run."[35] According to Ayres, "the way the words run" names the way a community has learned to read texts through training in the grammatical and figural reading habits necessary for the discovery of the plain sense of what is being read.[36] The "plain sense" is not a restrictive reading, but rather names the inexhaustible richness of the way the words run given that the words are inspired by God. To read the way the words run, therefore, is to let the words shape our imaginations in a manner that forces us to read the world scripturally rather than vice versa.[37]

---

firmed Jesus to be the Son who is and does all that pleases *the Father* (3:17). But unlike his foremother in the garden, this Son does *not* rise to the bait and does *not* produce the invited distortion of what God has 'really' said. Instead, the Word himself turns to find in Scripture the true representation, the textual icon, of God's life-giving and all-nourishing presence: 'Man . . . shall live by every word that proceeds from the mouth of God' (4:4)" (*Seeing the Word*, 94–95). Unfortunately, I did not have Bockmuehl's book prior to writing the commentary on Matthew, but I did read the temptation of Jesus as a "hermeneutical" lesson that teaches us to resist questions that would have us "go behind the text" in an effort to discover what God must have "really meant" (see Hauerwas, *Matthew*, 52–54).

35. Ayres's account of "the way the words run" is to be found in *Nicea and Its Legacy*, 32. Ayres borrowed the phrase from Gene Rogers's essay "How the Virtues of an Interpreter Presuppose," 64–81.

36. Ayres argues that this understanding of reading was not unique to Christians but rather reflected the Roman understanding of the relation between moral formation and reading. Ayres observes that "Roman educators wanted students to learn the right lessons from the right texts. Education in reading technique, therefore, became a contested cultural area and Christians eventually if slowly sought to adapt these teaching techniques by focusing them on Scripture. This feature of Roman education also helps to explain why Christians so naturally read scriptural texts as shaping a form of life, and it reminds modern readers to be clear about the distinction between figural practices—especially allegory—and moral readings" (*Nicaea and Its Legacy*, 36). The significance of training is crucial to understanding Wittgenstein. Thus his suggestion that "It disperses the fog to study the phenomenon of language in primitive kinds of applications in which one can command a clear view of the aim and functioning of the words. A child uses such primitive forms of language when it learns to talk. Here the teaching of language is not explanation, but training" (*Philosophical Investigations*, 5). For a good exposition of the *Investigations* that emphasizes the significance of training, see Lugg, *Wittgenstein's Investigations*.

37. I hope this claim exemplifies the argument Hays makes in *Conversion of the Imagination*. "Imagination" names for Hays the poetic character of Paul's reading of the Bible, which he associates with Paul's use of "images." But "images" are constructed by words, which means our imaginations depend on how the words run.

Accordingly, I begin my commentary on Matthew observing that Matthew's beginning, "The book of the genesis of Jesus Christ," is to indicate that the story he will tell, like Genesis, is a creation account. Is this an imposition on the text? If Matthew is beginning with creation why does he not, as Luke does, trace the genealogy back to Adam? Moreover, why does he identify Jesus the Messiah first as the son of David and then as the son of Abraham? If he were to follow chronology should he not have listed Abraham prior to David? Did he mention David first because Abraham provided a transition to the genealogy beginning with Isaac?

Rather than trying to "explain" the first verse of Matthew, I read the beginning in the light of Jesus' apocalyptic announcement that a new age was being inaugurated through his ministry, death, and resurrection. The beginning of Matthew's gospel is, therefore, read in light of Jesus' whole life, which is nothing less than the new creation. This is a king, the son of David, sitting in judgment on all the nations of the world (Matt 25:31–32). But unlike other kings this king will be sacrificed because he is also the son of Abraham. I do not, therefore, think it accidental that Jesus the Messiah is first identified as the son of David before he is also designated as the son of Abraham. The way the words run matters, making clear from the very beginning that we will only learn what it means for Jesus to be the Messiah by the hard and painful lesson of the cross. So it matters that Jesus is first identified as the son of David.

Some may object that I am making far too much out of what may have been nothing more than Matthew's attempt to assure a community that is in tension with a synagogue that they are inheritors through David of Israel's promises.[38] Thus David being mentioned before Abraham is of little significance. Yet given the way the words run, given the way the story is told by the way the words run, it is theologically significant that Jesus is first identified as the son of David before he is identified as the son of Abraham. This son of David, who is also the son of Abraham, will soon be identified as the very son of God (Matt

---

38. See Carter, *Matthew and the Margins*, 57. I footnote Carter because I deeply admire his readings of Matthew. He is, of course, an extremely skillful historian but like many skillful historians his reading of Matthew depends less on his historical reconstructions than his theological insights. He is quite simply a very fine Christian preacher.

3:17), transfiguring every presumption about what the rule of this king entails. For this is a king who will be sacrificial.

That is why Matthew helps us see that the "what" that is Jesus cannot be separated from how we come to know the what. It is, therefore, telling that Jesus' baptism and temptation are followed by his calling of the disciples. Matthew is a manual for discipleship requiring that the lives of those who would follow Jesus as king learn that this is a king that will rule from a cross. Therefore it is not accidental that after Jesus went up the mountain and sat down, "his disciples came to him" (Matt 5:1). The Sermon on the Mount is the constitution for the creation of a new people. These are not ideals impossible to live, but rather descriptions of a community Jesus has made possible.

But the descriptions and the life are inseparable. I, therefore, read the beatitudes christologically, which means I think it a mistake to speculate about what it might mean or who might exemplify what it means to be poor in spirit, or what it means to mourn, to be meek, to hunger and thirst for righteousness, to be merciful, pure in heart, a peacemaker, and persecuted. We only know what each of those descriptions entail by attending to the life of Jesus. No word studies can do what only a christological reading makes possible. For example, I suggest that Phil 2:5–8 is the text we best read to understand what it means to be poor in spirit. Of course, what it means to be "poor in spirit," even read through the incarnation, remains vague, but vagueness is required just to the extent that the absence of specificity means we will need many readings of this beatitude.[39]

In a similar fashion we learn what it means to be perfect only through participation in Christ's love of enemies. The assumption that we might know what "perfect" entails abstracted from the one who has loved us—and we must not forget that we are the enemy—results in turning the Sermon on the Mount into an "ethic" or a "law" about which we get to make up our minds. In contrast, I read the Sermon as the conditions for the possibility of a community being called into existence through the life and work of Jesus. Hays may well have found the argument I made in the "Sermon on the Sermon on the Mount" in *Unleashing the Scripture* not sufficiently exegetical, but the readings of the Sermon on the Mount in the commentary on Matthew I hope

---

39. For an account of the significance of the unavoidable character of vagueness, see Ochs, "Morning Prayer as Redemptive Thinking," 71–74.

reflect the sermon in *Unleashing the Scripture*. Of course, I do not assume that simply because my reading of Matthew 5 in the commentary is more detailed I have satisfied the suggestion that I need to be more exegetical—the good news is that the reading can never come to an end.

Lest it be thought that my theological exegesis means no reading is excluded, I do not think attempts to negotiate Jesus' underwriting of the law as well as the righteousness of the scribes and Pharisees by employing the distinction between the ceremonial, juridical, and moral do justice to the way the words run. I simply do not find in Scripture a basis for such a distinction. However, more important than whether the distinction is in Scripture is how the distinction creates a gulf between the Jews and Christians that results in a misreading of Paul.[40]

Marcus Bockmuehl entitles the last chapter of his book "Seeing the Son of David" in order to insist that "no theologically conscionable construal of Jesus' identity can finally bypass this vital and personified commitment to the salvation of Israel, centered on the city over which Jesus lamented."[41] Which at the very least means that Christians cannot protect themselves from questions about why Christians think they can pick and choose which parts of the law apply to their lives as Christians. How Christians answer such challenges, challenges as basic as the day set aside to worship God, will necessarily be christological. But that does not mean the current practice of Christians can be assumed to settle what we should say to Jews or ourselves when challenged about how we read the law.

---

40. Hays's refusal to "leave the Jews behind" in his exegetical practice I believe to be one of his great achievements. In particular, see his chapter "Christ Prays the Psalms," in *Conversion of the Imagination*.

Among other well known exegetical tactics I challenge in the commentary are those that try to deal with Matt 5:38–41 by invoking the distinction between private and public forms of retaliation. The distinction between the private and public simply cannot be sustained by the way the words run. That such a distinction has seemed to many a "natural" reading of the Sermon reflects a politics quite different from the church I think must exist if we are to avoid importing foreign categories to shape the reading of the Gospel.

41. Bockmuehl, *Seeing the Word*, 222. Elsewhere, Bockmuehl has shown that Jesus' and Paul's thinking on the law reflected modes of argumentation well without the presumptions of the practice of halakhah. See his *Jewish Law in Gentile Churches*. It may be objected that to use this earlier work of Bockmuehl seems to undercut my criticisms of historical analysis. But such a view presumes I have a stake in denying in principle that historical studies cannot be of use which is certainly not the case.

I conclude by calling attention to what is, perhaps, the most daring reading I offer in my commentary on Matthew, namely, that the desolating sacrilege Jesus tells the disciples they will see (Matt 24:15) is not the destruction of the temple but rather his crucifixion. I believe that is the way the words run once you begin, as Matthew begins, announcing that "this is the genesis of Jesus Christ." Jesus has already told his disciples that the temple will be torn down (Matt 24:1–2) so calling the destruction of the temple the "desolating sacrilege" adds nothing to what he has already said. There can be no sacrilege more desolating than the death of the Messiah, the Son of God. To be sure, such a reading is theological all the way down, but that does not mean it is any less "exegetical."[42]

I am aware that my reading of Matthew at best is only a beginning for what it might mean for some of us to learn to read Scripture theologically. We are dying—and I mean quite literally we are dying—for examples of what reading Scripture theologically might look like. Scripture, vivified by the Holy Spirit, is the heart of the church. Without a heart we cannot live. I suspect we are in a time of transition when some trained in historical criticism are attempting to work theologically and those trained theologically try to recover scriptural reasoning through exegetical practice.[43] Richard Hays has had the talent and courage to work both sides of that street and as a result has provided some of the examples, the heart, we so desperately need.[44]

42. I have not addressed Hays's criticism that I impose an order on the discordant texts that constitute the Christian Scriptures. I can do no better than to quote thesis two from the Nine Theses: "Though the Bible contains the voices of many different witnesses, the canon of Scripture finds its unity in the overarching story of the work of the triune God. While the Bible contains many tensions, digressions, and subplots, the biblical texts cohere because the one God acts in them and speaks through them: God is the author of Scripture's unity for the sake of the church's faithful proclamation and action" (*Art of Reading Scripture*, 1). I note that each of the theses is followed by a paragraph in which questions are posed for an ongoing discussion, indicating that the theses are not so much a conclusion as an agenda.

43. "Scriptural reasoning" is the name Peter Ochs has given to the work of a group of Jewish, Christian, and Islamic theologians commitment to reading Scripture together. For an introduction to their work, see Pecknold and Ford, "Promise of Scriptural Reasoning." Crucial is the word "reasoning" because I am sure one of the difficulties for theologians to argue exegetically is such "arguments" do not look like "reason." Peter Ochs, in an essay entitled "Philosophic Warrants for Scriptural Reasoning," provides a wonderful account of what such reasoning entails.

44. I am indebted to Ellen Davis and Kavin Rowe for critical comments on this paper.

II. The Language of Love: From Death to Life

8

Why Did Jesus Have to Die?
An Attempt to Cross the Barrier of Age*

On Being Young and Being Christian

I lecture and write often, but I am not sure how to write to those our society identifies as the young or adolescents. I do not know who you are, and I am a bit frightened by that unknown. The last band I knew was U2, and I only knew them because they were the last group introduced to me by my son before he "grew up." I do not know what you read or the movies you see. So, presumably, I do not know how to "connect" with you.

Moreover, I think it is disgusting for an older guy to try to show that he can be "with it." I do not want to be "with it." I quit teaching freshmen when I taught at the University of Notre Dame. I did so because I simply found it demeaning to try to convince eighteen-year-olds that they ought to take God seriously. Eighteen-year-old people in our society simply lack the resources to take God seriously—by resources I mean having noticed that before you know it you are going to be dead.

Alasdair MacIntyre, a philosopher, has suggested that one of the worst things our society does to the young is to tell them they ought to be happy. MacIntyre thinks if you are happy, particularly when you are young, you are probably deeply self-deceived. Your appropriate stance

* A lecture written for the Youth Academy at Duke Divinity School.

115

is to be miserable. What a terrible time to be young. Shorn of any clear account of what it means to grow up, you are forced to make up your own lives. But you know that any life you make up is not a life you will want to live.

I do not necessarily want this lecture to make you miserable, but I hope that at least some of what I say may help illumine why you are miserable. Indeed I do not want this lecture to be "memorable" for you, particularly if "memorable" means you will think the Duke Youth Academy was a "wonderful" experience. I went to church summer camp once when I was growing up in Texas. I remember the highlight of the camp was on the last night to watch the sun go down from a mountain—well, a hill (it was Texas)—while we sang "Kumbayah." This was an attempt to give us a "mountain top experience" that we could identify with being or becoming a Christian. About the last thing I would want is for you to have such an experience here. I do not want to make Christianity easy. I want to make it hard.

I assume most of you are here because you think you are Christians, but it is not at all clear to me that the Christianity that has made you Christians is Christianity. For example:

—How many of you worship in a church with an American flag?

I am sorry to tell you your salvation is in doubt.

—How many worship in a church in which the Fourth of July is celebrated?

I am sorry to tell you your salvation is in doubt.

—How many of you worship in a church that recognizes Thanksgiving?

I am sorry to tell you your salvation is in doubt.

—How many of you worship in a church that celebrates January 1st as the "New Year"?

I am sorry to tell you your salvation is in doubt.

—How many of you worship in a church that recognizes "Mother's Day"?

I am sorry to tell you your salvation is in doubt.

I am not making these claims because I want to shock you. I do not want you to leave the Youth Academy thinking that you have heard some really strange ideas here that have made you think. It is appropriate that you might believe you are here to make you think, because you have been told that is what universities are supposed to do—that is, to make you think. In other words, universities are places where you are educated to make up your own mind. That is not what I am trying to do. Indeed I do not think most of you have minds worth making up. You need to be trained before you can begin thinking. So I have not made the claims above to shock you, but rather to put you in a position to discover how odd being a Christian makes you.

One of the great difficulties with being a Christian in a country like America—allegedly a Christian country—is that our familiarity with "Christianity" has made it difficult for us to read or hear Scripture. For example, consider how "Mother's Day" makes it hard to comprehend the plain sense of some of the stories of Jesus. In Mark 3:31–35 we find Jesus surrounded by a crowd. His mother and brothers were having trouble getting through the crowd to be with Jesus. Somebody in the crowd tells him that his mom cannot get through the mass of people to be near him. Which elicits from Jesus the rhetorical question "Who are my mother and brothers?" which he answered, noting, "Here are my mother and my brothers! Whoever does the will of God is my brother and sister and mother." Even more forcefully Jesus says in Luke 14:26: "Whoever comes to me and does not hate father and mother, wife and children, brothers and sisters, yes, and even life itself, cannot be my disciple." When you celebrate "Mother's Day," the only thing to do with texts like these is "explain them," which usually means Jesus could not have meant what he plainly says.

Of course, the presumption that Christianity is a family-friendly faith is a small-change perversion of the gospel when compared to the use of faith in God to underwrite American pretensions that we are a Christian nation possessing righteousness other nations lack. Consider, for example, this report from *The Washington Times* on July 8, 2002:

> President Bush joined more than 100 parishioners at a seaside church yesterday in reciting the Pledge of Allegiance during services, a defiant dig at a recent San Francisco ruling on the pledge's "under God" phrase. In the middle of the morning service at St. Ann's Episcopal Church, Chaplain M. L. Agnew Jr. departed from the regular program and asked the congregation to stand and say the pledge to the U.S. flag. The pledge has

become a constant fixture of Mr. Bush's public appearances since a panel of the 9th U.S. Circuit Court of Appeals ruled that the phrase "under God" made public-school recitation of the Pledge unconstitutional. He (President Bush) led children in the Pledge during a Fourth of July stop in which the reciters all but shouted out "under God." Mr. Bush, who often talks of his faith in God and the role it plays in his stewardship of the country, has called the court's decision "ridiculous" and "out of step with the traditions and history of America." The Pledge of Allegiance is not a part of any Episcopal liturgy, nor is its recitation a common custom, a church theologian (Rev. Kendall Harmon) told *The Washington Times.*[1]

When you have the President of the United States claiming that the "God" of the Pledge of Allegiance is the God Christians worship, you know you have a problem. The Christian God is the Father, Son, and Holy Spirit. The Trinity is not some further specification of the generalized god affirmed in the Pledge, but the Trinity is the only God worthy of worship. The Christian pledge is not the Pledge of Allegiance, but rather is called the Apostles' Creed. That a church service, that a Priest in that service, would include the Pledge of Allegiance is a sure sign that Christians no longer know how to recognize idolatry. The "Christianity" represented by St. Ann's Episcopal Church in Maine is not in fact Christian.

A harsh judgment to be sure, but one that needs to be made if we are to recover faithful Christian practice. I am not calling into question President Bush's sincerity. I am convinced he is a very serious Christian. The problem is not his sincerity. The problem is that the Christianity about which he is sincere is not shaped by the gospel. Unfortunately, he is not unique, but rather is but one instance of the general failure of the church in America to be the church. That the church has failed to be faithful is, of course, why I suggested that your as well as my salvation is in doubt.

Why Love Is Not the Answer

One of the difficulties for anyone trying to figure out what it might mean to be a Christian in America is that our very familiarity with

1. See "Pledge follows Bush to Church."

Christianity has made it difficult to hear what is read to us Sunday after Sunday from the Bible. For example, I suspect many of you when you are talking with friends about what life might be about might say what makes you a Christian is a "personal relationship with Jesus." Such a relation you might suggest is about trying to be a loving person. You might even suggest that Christians are to love one another because our sins have been forgiven.

There is no question that love between the persons of the Trinity is at the very heart of the Christian faith, but I think nothing is more destructive to the Christian faith than the current identification of Christianity with love. If God wants us to be more loving, why do you need Jesus to tell us that? If Christianity is about the forgiveness of our sins, then why did Jesus have to die? If God is all about love, why go through the trouble of being this man, Jesus? Why did not God just tell us through an appropriate spokesman (it could have been Jesus) that God wants us to love one another? God, in such a faith, becomes that great OK who tells us we are OK and, therefore, we are taught we should tell one another we are OK. But if Jesus is the proclamation of the great "OK," why would anyone have bothered putting him to death? There must have been some terrible failure in communication.

One of the problems with the identification of Christianity with love is how such a view turns out to be anti-Semitic and anti-Catholic. The Jews and Catholics become identified with the law or dogma in contrast to Protestant Christians who are about love. Such a view assumes that any form of faith that creates divisions must be retrograde because such a faith is not about being loving. Of course, when love becomes what Christianity is all about, we can make no sense of Jesus' death and resurrection.

For example, consider how the temptation narrative of Jesus in the fourth chapter of Luke must be read if Jesus is all about love. It is as if we think Jesus went out to find himself. Of course, we are told that he "was driven out," to face the devil no less, but we know such language is "mythical." Such language was used to help us understand the spiritual struggle Jesus must have been going through—that is, he was confronting the existential nothingness of existence that was necessary for his ability to make an authentic choice about how he would live his life.

Returning from this desert, the disciples note he looks as if he has been through a very rough time. "Man, you look like you have been to hell and back," they might say. (No doubt they must have said something like this, for otherwise how do we explain the language of being tempted by the devil?) In response, Jesus can be imagined to say, "You are right, I have had a rough forty days, but I have come to recognize what God wants from us. So I feel compelled to lay this big insight on you. I have come to realize that God, or whatever we call that which we cannot explain, wants us to love one another. There, I have said it and I am glad I did."

Ask yourself, if that is what Jesus is all about—that is, getting us to love one another—then why did everyone reject him? They did so, I think, because when Jesus was told by the devil he would be given the power to turn stones to bread, he refused; when Jesus was offered authority over all the kingdoms of this world, he refused; when he was offered the possibility he would not die, he refused. Note that Jesus was offered the means to feed the hungry, the authority to end war between peoples, and even the defeat of death itself. But he refused these goods. He did so because Jesus knows that God's kingdom cannot be forced into existence using the means of the devil.

But note that Jesus' refusal to play the devil's game does not mean that the kingdom he proclaims is not political. Jesus' work is political, but the kingdom politics he represents is one that comes through the transformation of the world's understanding of how to achieve good results. Jesus refuses to use the violence of the world to achieve "peace." But that does not mean he is any less political or that he is not about the securing of peace. It is, therefore, not accidental that after the temptation narrative we seen Jesus in a synagogue on the Sabbath reading from the scroll of Isaiah. The passage he reads says,

> The Spirit of the Lord is upon me,
> because he has anointed me
> to bring good news to the poor.
> He has sent me to proclaim
> release to the captives
> and recovery of sight to the blind,
> to let the oppressed go free,
> to proclaim the year of the Lord's favor.
> After reading this Jesus sat down and said, "Today this scripture
> has been fulfilled in your hearing."

The offense is not that Jesus wanted his followers to be loving, but the offense is Jesus. Jesus is the politics of the new age; he is about the establishment of a kingdom; he is the one who has created a new time that gives us the time not only to care for the poor but to be poor. Jesus is the one who makes it possible to be nonviolent in a violent world. We should not be surprised that Jesus is the embodiment of such a politics. After all, Mary's song promised that the proud would have their imaginations "scattered," the powerful would be brought down from their thrones, the rich would be sent away empty, the lowly would be lifted up, and the hungry would be filled with good things. Is it any wonder that the world was not prepared to welcome this savior?

The Politics of Jesus

Jesus was put to death because he embodied a politics that threatened all worldly regimes based on the fear of death. It is quite instructive to read any of the crucifixion narratives from this point of view, but the account of Jesus' trial and crucifixion in the Gospel of John makes the political character of Jesus' work unavoidable. Consider, for example, how the arrest of Jesus makes clear the political character of Jesus' ministry. His arrest is often thought to represent the apolitical character of Jesus because he commands Peter to put away the sword Peter had used to cut off the ear of the priest's slave. To be sure, Jesus rebukes Peter, but he does so because that is not the "cup" the father has given him. But the cup from which Jesus must drink is no less political for being nonviolent. Indeed Jesus' command to Peter is one of the clearest indications that Jesus' challenge to the powers of this age is not only political but also a transformation of what most mean by "politics."

The character of Jesus' politics is manifest in his response to the high priest who questions Jesus about his teachings in John 18:19–24. That he is questioned by the high priest may suggest that his mission was "religious" rather than political, but such an account cannot be sustained for no other reason than Jesus' answer: "I have spoken openly to the world; I have always taught in the synagogues and in the temple, where all the Jews come together. I have said nothing in secret. Why do you ask me? Ask those who heard what I said to them; they know what I said." Politics is speech and Jesus is at once the speech, the Word of the

Father, and the speaker. Nothing is hidden because the kingdom Jesus brings in his person is open to all.

Frustrated by Jesus' response, the priests take Jesus to Pilate. There can be no ambiguity about the political challenge Jesus represents before Pilate. Pilate is Roman authority; he is an authority who has the power to determine whether those who appear before Roman governors live or die. Pilate obviously does not like the position in which he has been put by those who bring Jesus before him. Jesus' accusers, however, indicate Jesus is obviously guilty—otherwise why would they have Jesus appear before Pilate? But Pilate refuses to be bullied, so he examines Jesus.

He begins in an inquiring fashion, "They tell me that you are the King of Jews. Is that true?" Pilate's question is obviously meant to see if Jesus is "political." Jesus responds by asking if Pilate came up with such a view on his own or did others tell him such was the case. "I am not a Jew, am I?" replies Pilate. To which Jesus responds, "My kingdom is not from this world. If my kingdom were from this world, my followers would be fighting to keep me from being handed over to the Jews. But as it is, my kingdom is not from here." A response used often to deny that Jesus was political.

But note that Pilate understood what Jesus was saying. "So you are a king?" Pilate rightly saw that Jesus' denial that his kingship was not of this world is not the denial that Jesus is king. No, Jesus denied that his kingdom was just another form of Rome. Jesus' kingdom is not like other kingdoms of this world, but rather his kingdom is one that is an alternative to the kingdoms of this world. Jesus does not deny he is a king, but rather says, "You say that I am a king. For this I was born, and for this I came into the world, to testify to the truth. Everyone who belongs to the truth listens to my voice" (John 18:37). Pilate responds the way the world must respond when so confronted, that is, with worldly cynicism: "What is truth?"

The truth, of course, is that the Father has sent his Son so that we—that is, the church—might be an alternative politics, a politics of truth, to that of the world. The world's politics is based on violence: kill or be killed. That is the politics that has been overwhelmed in Christ's death and resurrection. A people have been created through the work of the Spirit to be an alternative politics to the politics of the lie—lies so blatant that we believe they must be true as otherwise they are so absurd. Lies that lead us to believe that peace can be achieved through war.

In *The Original Revolution*, John Howard Yoder helps us understand the political character of the salvation wrought in Christ.

> "The kingdom of God is at hand: repent and believe the good news!" To repent is not to feel bad but to think differently. Protestantism, and perhaps especially evangelical Protestantism, in its concern for helping every individual to make his own authentic choice in full awareness and sincerity, is in constant danger of confusing the kingdom itself with the benefits of the kingdom. If anyone repents, if anyone turns around to follow Jesus in his new way of life, this will do something for the aimlessness of his life. It will do something for his loneliness by giving him fellowship. It will do something for his anxiety and guilt by giving him a good conscience. So the Bultmanns and the Grahams whose "evangelism" is to proclaim the offer of restored selfhood, liberation from anxiety and guilt, are not wrong. If anyone repents, it will do something for his intellectual confusion by giving him doctrinal meat to digest, a heritage to appreciate, and conscience about telling it all as it is: So "evangelicalism" with its concern for hallowed truth and reasoned communication is not wrong; it is right. If a man repents it will do something for his moral weakness by giving him the focus for wholesome self-discipline, it will keep him from immorality and get him to work on time. So the Peales and the Robertses who promise that God cares about helping me squeeze through the tight spots of life are not wrong; they have their place. *But all this is not the Gospel.*[2]

The gospel is the proclamation of a new age begun through the life, death, and resurrection of Jesus Christ. That gospel, moreover, has a form, a political form. It is embodied in a church that is required to be always ready to give hospitality to the stranger. The gospel is a society in which difference is not denied but used for the discovery of goods in common. It is, as Yoder observes, a society called into being by Jesus who gave them a new way to live:

> He gave them a new way to deal with offenders—by forgiving them. He gave them a new way to deal with violence—by suffering. He gave them a new way to deal with money—by

---

2. Yoder, *Original Revolution*, 31–32.

sharing it. He gave them a new way to deal with problems of leadership—by drawing on the gift of every member, even the most humble. He gave them a new way to deal with a corrupt society—by building a new order, not smashing the old. He gave them a new pattern of relationships between man and woman, between parent and child, between master and slave, in which was made concrete a radical new vision of what it means to be a human person. He gave them a new attitude toward the state and toward the "enemy nation."[3]

That is the politics begun in Christ. That is the "good news"—we have been freed from the presumed necessities that we inflict on ourselves in the name of "peace." A peace that too often turns out to be an order established and continued through violence. Is it any wonder that Jesus was despised and rejected? Is it any wonder when the church is faithful to Christ that she finds herself persecuted and condemned? Yet if such a church does not exist, the world has no alternative to the violence hidden in our fear of one another.

Resurrection

Some may say that with all the talk above about death I seem to have forgotten the resurrection. The Father raised Jesus from the dead. Surely that is what Christianity is about—securing eternal life. All the talk about the "politics of Jesus" fails to recognize that the work Jesus did was to make it possible for us to enjoy God forever. I certainly have no reason to deny that we have an eternal destiny made possible by Jesus' good work, but too often I fear the stress on "eternal life" spiritualizes the work of Christ. As a result, the political character of Jesus' resurrection is lost.

Too often I think Christians think about the resurrection in terms of a story told by Søren Kierkegaard. Kierkegaard's story begins by telling us about a Prince who one day is riding through his fields. The Prince sees a peasant girl gathering the crops. She is beautiful and the Prince falls instantly in love with her. However, he is a noble prince and does not want to overwhelm her with his power and riches. So he dresses in peasant clothes and goes to work side by side with her.

3. Ibid., 29

Kierkegaard notes that what holds our attention as such a story is told is our curiosity about when the Prince will show his true identity. We know the Prince and the peasant girl will fall in love. After all, she is beautiful and he is noble, so we know they will love one another. But we want to know when and how the Prince will reveal to his beloved that she has fallen in love with the Prince himself.

We let our imaginations run. Perhaps one day they share a lunch during which he tells her of his love. She confesses she also loves him and suddenly he rips back the peasant clothes and reveals the purple. Or perhaps he will wait to the wedding itself. They exchange vows at the end of which he tears away his rough clothes to reveal that through this marriage she has become the queen of the land. If we are really letting our imaginations run, we might think he waits to the wedding night itself.

Kierkegaard uses this story to suggest that we think the resurrection must be like a prince who has been hiding the purple under his rough clothes. The resurrection reveals the purple. However, Kierkegaard notes that the only problem with so thinking of the resurrection is that Jesus has no purple under his flesh. Jesus is peasant clothes, flesh, all the way down. He is not playing at being a human. He is human all the way down. The resurrected Christ is the crucified Christ.

Only such a Christ, moreover, can save us. For Jesus is the Christ, being for us this particular man, making possible a particular way of life that is an alternative to the world's fear of one like Jesus. Christians have no fantasy that we may get out of life alive. Instead, we have a savior who was in every way like us yet also fully God. Jesus is not 50 percent God and 50 percent man. He is 100 percent God and 100 percent man; he is the incarnation, making possible a way to live that constitutes an alternative to all politics that are little less than conspiracies to deny death.

Such a savior does not promise that by being his follower we will be made safe. Rather, this savior offers to free us from our self-inflicted fears and anxieties. Jesus does so not by making our lives "more mean-ingful," though we may discover our lives have renewed purpose, but by making us members of his body and blood so that we can share in the goods of a community that is an alternative to the world. Do not, thereby, be surprised that, as followers of Christ, you may be hated and rejected; but you have been given such wonderful work I suspect you will hardly notice that you are so.

A Final Word to the Young

I have no way to know how you have heard or read what I have tried to say. I recognize that in some ways what you have heard is, as one of my graduate students once observed, a "completely different Christianity." I have no interest in being different to be different. Rather I hope this account of the gospel you will find compelling. People are dying to be part of an adventure that will give us a worthy task. I think the gospel is such an adventure. I hope what I have said at least gives you a glimpse of what a wonderful life you have been given through your baptism.

9

More
or, A Taxonomy of Greed*

Avarice is a timely topic. Our current economic downturn is often attributed to greed grown out of control. For many of us it is unclear how greed is causally related to our economic troubles, but we are usually ready to believe those who tell us there is a correlation between the unbridled pursuit of profits in the financial sector of our economy and the current recession. We are suffering because some became too greedy. We continue to be troubled, moreover, that some make millions in bonuses, without having any reason to assume that there is a connection between the bonus and the work they have done. Greed seems to have no limits or shame.

That we are able to make such judgments presumes that we know what we are talking about when we talk about greed. I think, however, that such a presumption may be just that—that is, presumptive. The desire for money may be an indication of greed, but I hope to show that greed is a much more subtle vice than simply the desire to be rich. It is interesting, however, that even if avarice is understood primarily as the desire for wealth we seldom hear sermons about greed. That we do not seems strange because at least as far as the New Testament is concerned

* This lecture was written for the University of Christ the King, which takes a week out of its coursework to concentrate on a theme. The theme for the week in which I lectured was "avarice."

greed is considered to be more of a threat for the ability to follow Christ than lust.[1]

In the Sermon on the Mount, Jesus says quite clearly "you cannot serve God and wealth" (Matt 6:24). Paul confesses in Romans 7 he would not have known sin, he would not have known the many forms of covetousness that possessed his life, if the law had not said, "You shall not covet." In 1 Tim 6:10, Paul even suggests that the love of money is the root of all kinds of evil, leading some to wander away from the faith because of the self-inflected pains they have suffered due to their desire for money. At least one of those pains greed produces is identified with idolatry in Col 3:5.[2]

In the book of James, Christians are unrelentingly chastised for thinking they can delay doing God's will in order that they can go to this town or that town to do business and make money. Such people simply fail to realize that their wealth will not save them from miseries or death (Jas 4:13—5:5). James is very blunt. "You want something and you do not have it; so you commit murder. And you covet something and cannot obtain it; so you engage in disputes and conflicts" (Jas 4:2).

Scripture is clear. If you are a Christian who is wealthy or desires to have wealth, you have a problem. Yet in our day greed is seldom identified as a major problem for Christians. Lust, which is usually associated with sexual misconduct, seems to have become the sin that Christians worry about. I confess it is not clear to me why that is the case, but it may be that we think we know what it looks like when we are under the power of lust. For all the changes alleged to be characteristic of our sexual ethics, it is still assumed that we can spot promiscuity or adultery. We assume, moreover, that such behavior can be attributed to lust understood as out-of-control sexual desire.

---

1. Aviad Kleinberg observes that though Jesus was neither a glutton nor a libertine he seems to have viewed gluttony and lust with a compassion that was distinctively different from his condemnation of greed. He, in particular, calls attention to the rich man and Lazarus as an indication that Jesus regarded wealth itself as an obstacle to salvation. *Seven Deadly Sins*, 101.

2. Brian Rosner provides a very useful background that helps us understand the connection between greed and idolatry in his *Greed and Idolatry*. He concludes that the claim that greed is idolatry presumes that "to have a strong desire to acquire and keep for yourself more and more money and material things is an attack on God's exclusive rights to human love and devotion, trust and confidence, and service and obedience" (173).

Yet I suspect that greed grips our lives more than lust. But we fail to focus on greed because we are not sure we know how to identify what greed looks like. Indeed I am of the opinion that what is often identified as lust may actually be a form of greed. The very fact that the lust that grips so many lives is never satiated suggests that lust has become a form of greed. For if any one characteristic is to be associated with greed it is the presumption that no matter how much we may have we need "more." We need more because we cannot be sure that what we have is secure. So the more we have the more we must have in order to secure what we have.

Bill May observes that the vices in traditional catalogues of sins were often associated with various body parts—lying with the tongue, lust with the genitals, gluttony with the throat, pride with the chest, conceit with the turned head, and avarice with the arms and legs. The person possessed by avarice reaches and grasps for the goods of another. Things come into the possession of the greedy by reaching and holding. Mastery and possession are the marks of a person who is determined by avarice.[3]

That greed names the felt necessity to have more may help explain the seeming paradox that greed seems to become a particularly prominent challenge in economies of plenty. It is quite interesting, for example, that with the rise of money economies in Western Europe in the eleventh and twelfth centuries there is a distinct increase in references to the sin of greed by theologians and bishops.[4] Money, it seems, allowed more people to manifest signs of wealth, which meant that the more wealth they had the more wealth they needed to sustain the wealth they had. For the rich, there is never "enough."

I do not mean to suggest that avarice only became a named vice with the development of moneyed economies. The rise of monasticism clearly was the crucial development necessary for the articulation of the seven deadly sins.[5] Augustine would identify pride as the cardinal or

---

3. May, *Catalogue of Sins*, 51–52.

4. Newhauser, "Avaritia and Paupertas," 330–31.

5. Newhauser, *Early History of Greed*. According to Newhauser, Basil the Great drew on the developing monastic tradition to identify avarice as the failure to care for one's neighbors needs because of a concern for our material well-being. Basil applied this to monk and laity alike demanding that both "purify themselves from avarice and the desire for excessive ornamentation. By concentrating their attention on God alone,

original sin, but the monks who inhabited the Egyptian desert thought greed to be the sin that birthed the other sins. "They observed a deep human fear of dependence on God that manifested itself in a perennial desire to accumulate some small margin of protective, sustaining property."[6]

That monasticism preceded the identification of avarice as the primal sin is a nice confirmation that our very ability to name our sins is a theological achievement. In other words, the very presumption that we can name our sins and declare that we are sinners prior to God's grace is an indication that we are possessed by sin. For we are only able to confess that we are possessed by sin on our way out of sin. Accordingly a community must exist that makes possible the identification of the subtly of sin. That is particularly true when you are dealing with a sin as subtle as greed.

I think, for example, it is not accidental that you needed a Saint Francis for the discovery by Christians that we had lost the ability to recognize how greed possessed our lives. The subsequent development of the Franciscan order was crucial for the acknowledgment by the church that the church itself was possessed by possessions. Yet the very Order that had at its center the discipline of begging was soon able to make holiness a commodity subject to greed.[7] William Langland in *Piers Plowman* depicts the friars' ability to turn their alleged sanctity into a means to acquire money. Langland characterized the friars, in the words of Kelly Johnson, as "hawkers of holiness," who are "all the more prone to simony because of their practices of poverty and begging."[8] Thus in the "Prologue" to *Piers Plowman* the dreamer says,

---

they would avoid giving serious thought to a superfluous amount of life's necessities or possessions meant only for themselves" (25–26).

6. Reno, *Genesis*, 87. I have never been able to decide if it is helpful to identify one sin as *the* primal sin. Augustine, and much of Christian tradition, identified pride as the primal sin. The monks, however, often focused on avarice as even more basic than pride. Given the complexity of our lives, I suspect that our sins are interrelated in a manner that defies easy identification of one sin as the source of all other sins.

7. Kleinberg argues that the failure of the Franciscan order was more than an episode in internal ecclesiastical politics, but rather that in the struggle between God and Mammon it was clear that Mammon had won. That Mammon had won, moreover, was an indication that the attempt to reinvigorate the Christian world had failed. *Seven Deadly Sins*, 108.

8. K. Johnson, *Fear of Beggars*, 64.

I found there friars from all four orders,

Preaching to people to profit their gut,

And glossing the gospel to their own good liking;

Coveting fine copes, some of these doctors contradicted authorities.

Many of these masterful mendicant friars

Bend their love of money to their proper business.

And since charity's become a broker and chief agent for lords'
    Confessions

Many strange things have happened these last years;

Unless Holy church and charity clear away such confessors

The world's worst misfortune mounts up fast.[9]

Langland's suggestion that the "worst misfortune mounts up fast" might well be a description of our situation. That a poem like *Piers Plowman* could be written suggests that the poet could still draw on the tradition to show what greed looks like and why it is such a threat to Christians. But it is unclear if that is the case with us. For greed has become the necessary engine to sustain economic growth.[10] We are obligated to want more because if we do not want more then we will put someone out of a job.

For example, in his book *Rediscovering Values: On Wall Street, Main Street, and Your Street,* Jim Wallis calls attention to the adulation of greed by the Wall Street tycoon Gordon Gekko in the movie *Wall Street.* In the midst of the hostile takeover of the fictional company Teldar Paper, Gekko declares, "Greed, for lack of a better word, is good. Greed is right. Greed works. Greed clarifies, cuts through, and captures the essence of the evolutionary spirit. Greed in all its forms, greed for life, money, love, knowledge has marked the upward surge of mankind, and greed will not only save Teldar Paper but that other malfunctioning corporation called the USA."[11]

9. Langland, *Piers Plowman*, 56–65. Not to be missed is the characterization of covetousness in Passus VI of the poem.

10. Kleinberg calls attention to Adam Smith for transforming the providential hand of God into an ensemble of individual egotisms working by some mysterious ways to produce the good of the collectivity. He quotes Smith: "By pursuing his own interests, he frequently promotes that of society more effectually than when he really intends to promote it" (*Seven Deadly Sins*, 110–11).

11. Wallis, *Rediscovering Values*, 45.

Gekko's praise of greed, of course, found its most original, elegant, and persuasive form in Bernard Mandeville's *The Fable of the Bees*:

> Vast Number throng'd the fruitful Hive;
>
> Yet those vast Numbers made 'em thrive;
>
> Million endeavouring to supply
>
> Each other's Lust and Vanity
>
> Thus every Part was full of Vice,
>
> Yet the whole Mass a Paradise.[12]

From Mandeville's perspective, "frugality is like honesty, a mean starving virtue, that is only fit for small societies of good peaceable men, who are contented to be poor so that they may be easy; but in a large stirring nation you may soon have enough of it."[13] Deirdre McCloskey has tried to qualify Mandeville's account of the necessity of avarice for economic growth by arguing that markets live in communities of virtue for which economists often fail to account.[14] William Schweiker suggests that "property" being a cultural construction entangled with arrangements for human identity and worth may mean that what we call "greed" should be better understood as an appropriate desire necessary to sustain market-driven economies.[15]

---

12. Mandeville, *Fable of the Bees*, 24. According to Mandeville, avarice may be the "occasion" of many evils, but it is most necessary for a society to flourish. He argues that if you would "render a society of men strong and powerful, you must touch their passions. Divide the land, though there be never so much to spare, and their possessions will make them covetous. Rouse them though but in jest, from their idleness with praises, and pride will set them to work in earnest. Teach them trades and handicrafts, and you'll bring envy and emulation among them. . . . Would you have them bold and warlike, turn to military discipline, make good use of their fear, and flatter their vanity with art and assiduity. . . . Great wealth and foreign treasure will ever scorn to come among men, unless youll admit their inseparable companions, avarice and luxury" (95–96).

13. Mandeville, *Fable of the Bees*, 64.

14. McCloskey, "Avarice, Prudence, and the Bourgeois Virtues," 324.

15. Schweiker, "Reconsidering Greed," 259. Schweiker does not mean to suggest that greed is unproblematic but rather to suggest that we need to appreciate how greed inscribes selves into a culture's values but at the same time threatens the bonds that sustain trust in a society. Thus "the paradox is that a commercial culture, through the power of its sign values, can and does foster excessive consumption and thus greed, but in the act of doing so threatens social stability and flourishing. Is it any wonder, then, that in advanced commercial cultures we see the breakdown of concern for the common good both among the wealthy, who consume at an alarming rate, and the

I am not convinced, however, that McCloskey's and Schweiker's language-transforming proposals to understand greed even in a limited way as a good is a good idea. For example, Alasdair MacIntyre observes that for those shaped by the habits of modern societies it is assumed as a fundamental good that acquisitiveness is a character trait indispensable to continuous and limitless economic growth. From such a standpoint, it is inconceivable that a systematically lower standard of living can be conceived as an alternative to the economics and politics of peculiarly modern societies. For such societies prices and wages have to be understood to be unrelated so that desert in terms of labor, notions of just price and just wage, makes no sense. Yet a community shaped by the virtues that would make greed a vice "would have to set strict limits to growth insofar as that is necessary to preserve or enhance a distribution of goods according to desert."[16]

That we find it hard to conceive of an alternative to limitless economic growth is an indication of our spiritual condition. It is a condition well understood by the monks who thought the desire for honor and power to be an expression of the felt need to control the world around us so that we might be more godlike. Thus Cassian saw anger as one of the forms greed takes in those who no longer cling to the One alone who can provide stability. Deprived of God, we become self-absorbed, seeking in external goods a satisfaction for our inner emptiness.[17] When those goods fail we turn on others as well as ourselves as a way to hide the emptiness of our lives.[18]

In *The City of God*, Augustine suggests that the Roman elites indulged in various forms of luxury and illicit pleasures to distract them from the inevitability of death. He observes that "the essential context for ambition is a people corrupted by greed and sensuality. And greed

poor, who desire that level of consumption ? Traditional Christian thought was simply right on this point: greed is a capital vice because it gathers around it other forms of viciousness that undercut the possibility of sustainable social existence" (268).

16. MacIntyre, *Whose Justice? Which Rationality?* 112. MacIntyre's suggestion makes clear that a focus on the virtues can have profound social implications. It is often alleged that an ethics of the virtues is at a disadvantage for issues associated with social and political questions, but MacIntyre's observations about the significance of temperance makes clear that is not the case.

17. Straw, "Gregory, Cassian and the Cardinal Vices," 51.

18. I suspect that there is a close connection between avarice and envy. The latter becomes almost unavoidable in social orders that depend on greed to fuel the engines of "progress."

and sensuality in a people is the result of that prosperity which the great Nasica in his wisdom maintained should be guarded against, when he opposed the removal of a great and strong and wealthy enemy state. His intention was that lust should be restrained by fear, and should not issue in debauchery, and that the check on debauchery should stop greed from running riot."[19]

Augustine, according to Robert Dodaro, argued that the fear of death, the fear that their lives would not be remembered, meant the Roman elites lived in fear of the loss of status and comfort. They were greedy for glory hoping by glory their lives might have significance. Empire was the means of sustaining status and well-being, but empire also produced an ever-increasing social anxiety about annihilation. As a result, the Romans became over-dependent on military force. Dedaro observes that from Augustine's perspective the Romans were caught in a vicious circle that "linked the threat of annihilation with an ever-growing political and military response to foreign threats, disseminating anxiety throughout the Empire to such an extent that even the inhabitants of Roman Africa are alarmed by the Visigothic assault on Rome."[20]

Of course, we may think that the Romans are Romans and we are not. We assume, therefore, we are not subject to the same death-denying greed that characterized the lives of the Roman pagans. Henry Fairlie, however, has given an account of how greed grips our lives—an account that echoes the suggestion in the book of James that there is a connection between greed and war—that sounds very much like Augustine's characterization of the Romans. Fairlie suggests that we are a people harassed by greed just to the extent our greed leads us to engage in unsatisfying modes of work so that we may buy things that we have been harassed into believing will satisfy us. We complain of the increased tempo of our life, but that is a reflection of the economic system we have created. We know, moreover, no other way to keep the system going other than the threat of war. We tolerate the world shaped by our avarice because that world in return temptingly and cunningly makes us believe that there are no alternatives to a world so constituted.[21]

19. Augustine, *City of God*, 42, 1.31.

20. Dodaro, *Christ and the Just Society*, 42.

21. Fairlie, *Seven Deadly Sins Today*, 142. Fairlie also observes that avarice is a form of solitude because we are walled off from our neighbors by our possessions.

I do not mean to suggest that it is only with the development of capitalist economic systems that we have lost the ability to recognize greed or, even if we are able to recognize it, think it a moral liability. For example in a sermon on Luke 16:19–31, Luther observed that the rich and arrogant people of his day no longer heed the warning contained in the story of the rich man and Lazarus. They do not because the rich think of themselves as pious and without greed. They are able to do so because vice has been turned into virtue. Greed has come to be viewed as being talented, smart, and a careful steward. Therefore "neither prince nor peasant, nobleman nor average citizen is any longer considered greedy, but only upstanding, the common consensus being that the man who prudently provides for himself is a resourceful person who knows how to take care of himself."[22]

I am sure many of you do not think of yourselves as greedy. After all, you are students. You have not yet become actors in the world of wealth in a manner that might tempt you to be greedy. You are still without possessions so you cannot be greedy. Of course such a view may fail to recognize that to be poor, or at least "not rich," is no guarantee that our lives will not be possessed by greed. However, I want to call your attention to a celebrated virtue often commended for students that I think exhibits Luther's suggestion that, subtle creatures that we are, we can turn greed into a virtue.

In his important book, *Intellectual Appetite: A Theological Grammar*, Paul Griffiths provides a telling account of curiosity.[23] Curiosity has had an interesting history. We may not be able to imagine a world without avarice, but we still think avarice is a vice. According

---

Greed cannot help but produce loneliness. Thomas Dumm observes, "What is it that we want? Perhaps it is only the acquisition of more of what we have. In our culture—a civilization of consumption if ever there has been one—the lonely self seeks to possess something to call its own, and ends up by confusing that something with itself. The great drive of capital is to turn everything into a commodity, including the self. In this sense, capitalism may be thought of as a symptom of the lonely self. I do not think we can separate the two—they are conjoined in our epoch. But if the lonely self is in an important sense shaped by the creation of a desire for more, and if this desire in turn gives rise to an anxiety that accompanies the experience of buying and selling, then the anxiety of the lonely self when facing the world of others leads to the deep risk of our selves being bought and sold" (*Loneliness as a Way of Life*, 52–53).

22. Luther, *Faith and Freedom*, 169.

23. Griffiths, *Intellectual Appetite*.

to Griffiths, however, though we think curiosity to be a commendable virtue that scholar and student should try to develop, that has not always been the case. According to Griffiths, prior to modernity curiosity was universally thought to be a vice. It was so because curiosity was an ordering of the affections, a form of love, by which the knower sought to make that which they knew unique to themselves. The curious desired to create new knowledge in an effort to give them control over that which they knew. By dominating that which they came to know they could make what they know a private possession. "Curiosity is, then, in brief, *appetite for the ownership of new knowledge*."[24]

The curious seek to know what they do not yet know. As a result, that which they come to know ravishes them by enacting what Griffiths characterizes as a "sequestered intimacy." Griffiths uses the language of "sequestering" to suggest that the curious think that what they have come to know is for their exclusive use. The curious assume they are masters of what they have come to know. Because they claim what they know is peculiar to them they seek as well as create envy in those who do not know what they know.

In a way not unlike Augustine's understanding of the place of the spectacle for the Romans, Griffiths suggests that the curious seek spectacles to distract them from the loneliness that is the necessary result of their desire to possess what they have come to know. The desire for novelty, the desire to have knowledge that I alone can possess, produces a restlessness that "is inflamed rather than assuaged by the spectacles it constructs."[25] Curiosity so understood is the intellectual expression of the greed correlative to an economic system built on the need to have those that make up the system always want "more."

The alternative to curiosity, according to Griffiths, is studiousness. Studiousness, like curiosity, entails an ordering of the affections and is, therefore, a form of love. But the studious do not seek to "sequester, own, possess, or dominate what they hope to know; they want to participate lovingly in it, to respond to it knowingly as gift rather than as potential possession, to treat it as icon rather than as spectacle."[26] For the studious what they know can be loved and contemplated, but not

24. Ibid., 20.
25. Ibid., 201–2.
26. Ibid., 21.

dominated by sequestration. The studious, therefore, accept as a gift what they have come to know which means they assume that which they know is known in a common making possible a shared life.

The contrast between the curious and the studious will be determined, according to Griffiths, by their willingness or unwillingness to share what they know with others. Whether we are or not possessed by our possessions can only be determined to the extent we are ready to give away that which we have. Griffiths associates such a willingness to share our knowledge of Christ just to the extent that the degree to which any of us know Christ and what the gospel is, and demands, is the "degree to which we must share that knowledge by giving it away."[27]

The studious Christian, therefore, seeks in Griffiths' words, a "participatory intimacy driven by wonder and riven by lament," which makes it impossible for them to seek ownership of what they have been given.[28] For Christians believe that all creatures have been brought into being by God out of nothing.[29] Accordingly, the studious recognize that only God possesses or owns any creature. Only God, therefore, has the power to sequester any being into privacy or to grant it public display. Alms, and the sharing of what we know is a form of alms giving, is rightly understood not as our giving away what is ours, but rather is making available to others what was God's before we had a use for it.[30]

Greed is rightly called a deadly sin because it kills the possibility of a proper human relation to the Creator. Greed presumes and perpetuates a world of scarcity and want—a world where there is never

27. Ibid., 160.

28. Griffiths identifies three kinds of wonder: (1) the metaphysical wonder of astonished delight that there is anything at all; (2) the wonder that comes from the recognition that we exist and we can be aware of ourselves as existing, and; (3) wonder directed at particular creatures such as ladybugs and heavenly bodies. *Intellectual Appetite*, 127–28. The role of wonder is crucial for Griffiths' account of studiousness because through wonder an intimacy is possible between the knower and the known otherwise impossible. That such an intimacy is possible, that is, that in the dual good of our knowing something we can know and something's being known as it is by the knower there is "the vestigial trace of God's knowing act of *creation ex nihilo*" (132).

29. Lance Webb stresses the significance of creation to provide an account of joy, which he takes to be the alternative to avarice. "To glorify God and to enjoy him forever" comes from the recognition that nothing belongs to me, but I belong to Christ. "This is our Sin: that we have upended the order of our Creator and gone out to glorify ourselves and to enjoy things forever." *Conquering the Seven Deadly Sins*, 150.

30. Griffiths, *Intellectual Appetite*, 154.

"enough." But, as Sam Wells argues, a world shaped by scarcity is a world that cannot trust that God has given all that we need; greed prohibits faith. But the contrary is true. Wells reminds us that the problem is not that there is too little in God but that there is too much. Overwhelmed by "God's inexhaustible creation, limitless grace, relentless mercy, enduring purpose, fathomless love," we turn away, finding such a God "too much to contemplate, assimilate, understand."[31]

And so Wells reminds us that it is in the Eucharist that we have the prismatic act that makes possible our recognition that God has given us everything we need. The Eucharist is not only the proclamation of abundance, but also the enactment of abundance. In the Eucharist we discover that we cannot use Christ up. In the Eucharist we discover that the more the body and blood of Christ are shared, the more there is to be shared. The Eucharist, therefore, is the way the church learns to understand why generosity rather than greed must and can shape our economic relations.[32]

The good news is that we have been given all we need in order not to be possessed by greed. The good news is that we worship a God who, through our worship of Him, makes it possible for us to recognize that although we may be possessed by greed, through confession and repentance we can be forgiven. Forgiveness, moreover, is the gift of grace that turns our lives of entitlement into lives of humility and gratitude. To learn to be forgiven, to be able to accept the gift of forgiveness without regret, is the condition that makes possible the recognition that all that we have we have through sharing. There is an alternative to a world based on greed. The alternative to the world of greed is a people capable of participating through worship in the love of the Father for the Son through the Spirit.

31. Sam Wells, *God's Companions*, 7.
32. Wells, *God's Companions*, 211.

10

Love

A Sermon for the Marriage of
Sheryl Overmyer and Andy Grubb
October 2, 2009

Jeremiah 31:31–33
Psalm 33:12, 18, 20–22
1 Corinthians 12:31—13:13
Matthew 5:1–2

Christians are required to love one another—even if they are married. That may be a cruel and even heartless demand, but it is nonetheless the way things are if you are a Christian. From Paul's perspective marriage is not necessarily the context that determines the character of love or our ability to love and be loved by another. Rather, Paul seems to think we need to learn to be loved by God and so to love God, and then possibly ourselves, and if we have gotten that far we may even discover we can love our neighbor, who may be our enemy, which often turns out to be the necessary condition for those who are married to love one another.

But if that is true, why is 1 Corinthians 13 read so often at weddings? Is it because the people being married think 1 Corinthians 13 describes their love for one another? No doubt it is true that the characteristics of love described in 1 Corinthians 13 seem like good advice for making a marriage work. If your marriage is to be livable you will need to be patient, kind, free of jealousy and snobbishness, non-possessive, and, most of all, you cannot brood over past wrongs.

That seems like good advice. The problem, however, is that to turn 1 Corinthians 13 into advice for a successful marriage too easily underwrites the sentimentalities associated with romantic conceptions of marriage in our culture. Such a view of love assumes that we naturally know what love is and how to do it. But that does not seem to be what Paul thinks. Paul thinks love is a gift—one that comes through the training of the whole church by the Holy Spirit.

Interestingly enough, when Paul's descriptions of the character of love are abstracted from their ecclesial home and turned into general recommendations for those to be married, the result is a legalization of the gift of love. As a result, love is transformed into a form of works righteousness. We assume it is up to us to give content to Paul's vague recommendations about the character of love and then we have to make what we have said love must be, work. So understood, love is anything but good news. Even worse, the recommendations divorced from their theological home are not particularly helpful.

Think, for example, about Paul's claim that the love he commends does not rejoice in wrongdoing, but rejoices in truth. A love that rejoices in truth is not an everyday affair precisely because the everyday tempts us to love half-truths. We never lie more readily, I suspect, than to those whom we love. For our loves are often constituted by misperceptions of one another that we later learn are just that—that is, misperceptions. Yet we fear an acknowledgement of the illusions constitutive of our loves because such an acknowledgement would prompt the recognition that they are not, nor are we, who we thought we were when we said, "I love you."

So thank God the love Paul commends is not meant first of all to describe the love between those about to be married. Rather, just as the beatitudes are exemplified by Jesus, so the love Paul commends names Jesus. Faith, hope, and love abide, but love never ends. Only Jesus, the second person of the Trinity, is without a beginning and end. Thus Karl Barth's suggestion that we substitute the name Jesus every time 1 Corinthians 13 says love: "Jesus is patient, Jesus is kind, Jesus is not envious or boastful or arrogant or rude. Jesus does not insist on his own way; he is not irritable or resentful, he does not rejoice in wrongdoing, but rejoices in the truth. Jesus bears all things, believes all things, hopes all things, and endures all things."

Paul's great hymn of and to love is, therefore, not first about us. Rather the love about which he speaks is that which characterizes God's very life. Thus Barth's remark: "to say 'God is' is to say 'God loves.'" We can say God loves because the Father would have the Holy Spirit rest on the Son so that we might participate in the very life of God. The love that is the Trinity was before we were, yet it is the same love that called us into existence. It is the love that assumed our flesh, even to be crucified by our sin, so that sin might be crucified by love. Love prevailed, overwhelming our sin, making possible our ability to love one another as Christ has loved us. Through love we have been made participants in God's very life.

It is good, therefore, to remember that Paul's hymn to love comes in the midst of his account of spiritual gifts. The Corinthian church is blessed by and torn apart by a variety of gifts. Some have the gift of healing, others the gift of miracles, another of prophecy, to others the gifts of discernment, and to others is given the gift of tongues, and still to others is given the gift to interpret what is said by those who have the gift of tongues. All are gifts of the same Spirit constituting a body that makes possible the recognition that we desperately need one another, just as the eye needs the hand and the head needs the feet.

That we need one another may, moreover, be why 1 Corinthians 13 is rightly read so often at weddings. It is certainly rightly read at weddings if Benedict XVI is right about the character of love. In the first encyclical letter of his papacy, *Deus Caritas Est*, Benedict XVI reminded us that to be a Christian is to be among those who have come to believe in God's love. According to Benedict, to be a Christian is not to believe in some lofty idea, but rather to encounter a person, to encounter Jesus, and thus to believe that "God so loved the world that he gave his only Son, that whoever believes in him should have eternal life."

Benedict acknowledges that we do have a problem of language about love that leads to many misuses of the word. We speak of love of country, love between friends, love of work, love of parents and children, love of neighbor and of God. That love can be used to describe quite different relations according to Benedict makes it hard to think that love might name a single reality. Yet Benedict says amid this multiplicity of meanings one particular love stands out: love between man and woman. The love between a man and a woman is crucial for our understanding of love, according to Benedict, because of its bodily character. That body, the Corinthian body, is the source of ecstasy, that through renunciation and purification, we are put on a path towards the Divine.

Love is an ecstasy, but not in the sense of intoxication; rather, love names the journey from a self curved in on itself to the recognition of another. Such a love Benedict boldly suggests is a dim prefigurement of the mystery of the cross. For God's love for us is an erotic self-giving revealed by his passionate love for the people of Israel, but most deter-minatively found in the embrace we call the incarnation. The embrace of very God and very Man has made it possible for us to share in the love that is Trinity. God is a bold bodily lover possessing our bodies so that we too might be love.

Benedict observes, therefore, that we are rightly commanded to love one another. "Love can be 'commanded' because it has first been given" (§14). So we rightly command Sheryl and Andy to love one an-other. For today they are for us 1 Corinthians 13. Today they are for us the gospel. The vows they make to one another, the exclusive love they promise to give to one another, is a love in time that binds time. Through such love they will lose their lives, but in the process they will be redeemed. What a happy thing, therefore, they do for us. For the promise they make to love one another makes us all more than we otherwise could be, because through their love the body of Christ, the church, is built up. Let the people say, Amen.

11

Love's Work—Discerning the Body

A Sermon for the Church of the Holy Family

February 1, 2009

Deuteronomy 18:15–20
Psalm 111
1 Corinthians 8:1–13
Mark 1:21–28

What a mess. The Episcopal Church in North America is being torn apart by questions surrounding the status of homosexuality. The Church of England not only has that issue to confront, but the ordination of women as bishops is no less divisive. As a world church we are facing division we do not know how to heal. Perhaps even more troubling is that many may not want to have our alienation from one another healed. Good people are on every side, and there are many sides of every division. What a mess.

Compared to the church in Corinth, however, our presumption that we know enough to know that we are in a mess is just that—presumption. You think we have got troubles. Try Corinth—a church divided into factions, a church wracked by sexual immorality, a church in which many members are but a short step out of paganism, a church beset by class and economic divisions, a church in which some speak in tongues no one can understand. If you are ever tempted to think the early church got it right and it has been downhill ever since, I urge you to read Paul's letters to the church in Corinth. We have never gotten it right.

We are, of course, polite people. We know there are divisions among us but we refrain from calling one another names. Paul, however, is not at all hesitant to describe some in the church at Corinth as "the weak" in contrast to those we can only assume must be "the strong." The strong it seems are the knowledgeable class of the Corinthian church. They know, for example, that "no idol in the world really exists" and that "there is no God but one." Accordingly, they have no problem eating meals in the temples of idols because they know that idols and gods do not exist.

The strong, moreover, are able to provide philosophical reasons for their behavior. The monotheistic god of the strong cannot be captured in human form. Their god transcends all attempts to worship a god—or gods—through sacrifice. They know, therefore, that "food will not bring us closer to God." So it makes no difference whether you eat or do not eat the food in pagan temples. The strong are rationalists. The strong are enlightened. They have degrees from UNC and Duke.

By contrast the weak are those still possessed by the everyday habits of a pagan culture. After all, they live in a city with a temple on every corner making it hard to deny that in fact there are many gods and many lords. The normality of paganism makes it hard to remember, moreover, that Christians believe, in Paul's words, that there is one God, "from whom are all things and for whom we exist, and one Lord, Jesus Christ, through whom are all things and through whom we exist."

Paul's way of putting the matter—that is, that there is one God in whom all things exist and one Lord, Jesus Christ, in whom all things exist—has got to have been confusing for the weak. Paul acknowledges the contention of the strong that there is one God, but it turns out that the oneness of God is manifest in and through the Lordship of Jesus Christ. For a people who live in a world with many lords, it is quite understandable that they might have trouble distinguishing the worship of Jesus and the worship of other lords. Therefore they might well worry that eating food sacrificed to idols would defile their conscience.

I confess, however, I have little patience with the weak. Given the divisions in Corinth, I find it almost impossible not to identify with the strong. After all, our linguistic habits make it hard to resist the presumption that Paul's contrast between "the strong" and "the weak" is evaluative. To be strong is good. To be weak is not good. But Paul does not seem to use these descriptions to separate the good from the bad. To be either strong or weak, from Paul's perspective, is a problem. At least it is a problem for the church. Paul is not taking sides. Too much is at stake.

What seems to be at stake, from Paul's perspective, is a contrast between knowledge and love. The problem with the strong is the knowledge they have; knowledge such as "no idol in the world really exists," they assume, gives them status and power. Paul's lovely description is that such knowledge "puffs up." The sure sign that such knowledge is driven by pride is that the strong do not take into consideration how their behavior affects the weak. They, therefore, lack love.

As much as I would like to apply Paul's division between the strong and the weak to the current divisions in the Episcopal Church, I confess I am not sure how that might be done. Are the strong those who know what we should or should not think about homosexuality? Are the weak those who just wish the issue would go away because all we need to do is love one another? I am not sure how to draw up the sides, but I am sure it is a mistake to think we must choose between love and knowledge.

For Paul, love does not call into question all forms of knowledge, but only those forms of knowledge that make it impossible to discern the body. Paul acknowledges that "all of us possess knowledge," but the knowledge we possess does us no good if it is not determined by love. It may be true that "no idol in the world really exists," but such knowledge does not serve for the up-building of the body. At least it does not serve to build up the body of Christ.

The knowledge love produces Paul calls "necessary knowledge." Notice after the remark that "knowledge puffs up but love builds up," Paul makes the following observation: "Anyone who claims to know something does not yet have the necessary knowledge; but anyone who loves God is known by him." "Necessary knowledge" is first and foremost not our knowing God but our being known by God.

We may well find this an odd way to put the matter. We tend to think we first need to be monotheists, which means we believe in God's existence, and then we might consider loving God. But that is not the way Paul's grammar works. For Paul we are able to love God because we have been known by God through the Son. Such a love is possible because God is not an abstract idea we associate with monotheism, but rather God is, as we say in Morning Prayer, the One in whom "we live and move and have our being."

It is, therefore, not unimportant that Paul describes the knowledge born of love with the striking claim that "there is one God, the Father, from whom are all things and for whom we all exist, and one Lord, Jesus Christ, through whom are all things and through whom we exist." This is the knowledge our love of God produces. We were created by the love of God, the undivided Trinity, in order to be known by the loving God without whom we would not exist. Knowledge, as it turns out, is learning to love God because he loved us first.

How extraordinary: God desires that we know him by participating in the very life of the Trinity. We had not expected such intimacy from God. We would prefer more distance. Knowledge not born of love turns out to be one of the ways we try to maintain our independence from God. "Food will not bring us close to God" sounds right and true, but such knowledge, exactly because it is not a knowledge born of the love of God, turns out to be false. Thus Paul's decisive judgment on the questions about eating food offered to idols:

> Therefore, my dear friends, flee from the worship of idols. I speak as to sensible people; judge for yourselves what I say. The cup of blessing that we bless, is it not a sharing in the blood of Christ? The bread we break, is it not a sharing in the body of Christ? Because there is one bread, we who are many are one body, for we all partake of the one bread. Consider the people of Israel; are not those who eat the sacrifices partners in the altar? What do I imply then? That food sacrificed to idols is anything, or that an idol is anything? No, I imply that what pagans sacrifice, they sacrifice to demons and not to God. I do not want you to be partners with demons. You cannot drink the cup of the Lord and the cup of demons. You cannot partake of the table of the Lord and the table of demons. (1 Cor 10:14–21)

Food does draw us closer to God when that food is the bread and the wine that will become for us the body and blood of Christ. And only by drinking his cup do we know that there are other cups from which we cannot drink. The love extended to us through the body and blood of Christ is the necessary knowledge to discern what does and does not build up the body of Christ.

Love has work to do. The work love has to do is a "knowing," a discernment, of the body. Love's work is often difficult, slow, and sometimes painful. It requires a passionate patience. But we do not wait alone; we are gifted with sustenance for the work of love each time we gather to share this meal. In this meal the body we received in baptism is enacted. For through this meal we are reminded that the gift of Christ is offered regardless of what we think we know or do not know.

We are a divided church. We do ourselves and the world no justice by denying our divisions. Some of us are strong and some weak. Many of us are both. Yet through sharing this meal we learn, as Paul observes, "the members of the body that seem to be weaker are indispensable." Indeed, through the sharing of this meal we discover that we learn our strengths and our weaknesses by being shown who we are by those who have learned who they are by loving God.

Our inability to deal with the divisions that threaten our church, I think, has everything to do with our inability to discern the body. Our inability to discern the body, moreover, involves the presumption that some of us have knowledge that makes us the strong and others weak. Unlike Paul, moreover, we assume that the division between the strong and the weak is one between the good and the bad. We are divided by what we think we know, but it is not clear how what we think we know is the necessary knowledge that Paul describes as that born from the love of God, who knows us better than we know ourselves.

What does that mean? Interestingly enough, I think it has to do with idolatry. We assume we no longer have a problem with idolatry. Pagan temples have been destroyed. We are not tempted to eat food sacrificed to idols because we believe, I suspect mistakenly, that such a description no longer applies to any food. We may live polytheistic lives, but few of us think of ourselves as committed polytheists. Even atheists now assume there is only one god worth denying. But the one god who is denied is not the God that would have us love him. Believers

and atheists alike too often fail to see that idolatry hides in any knowledge not determined by a God who loves us so that we might love him.

The challenge is discovering the idolatries—the loves not born
of the love of God—that possess us so completely we are unable to
discern the body of Christ. Idolatry is first and foremost a matter of
desire. What we know is determined by what we desire. What we most
desperately want will usually indicate the idolatries that shape our lives.
We were created by the love of God to love God, but we end up loving
what we think will make us strong. The good news is, however, that by
being members of the body of Christ we have the means to discover our
misshapen desires and loves.

We live in a city like Corinth where there are many gods and many
lords. We live in a time that is confused and confusing. We should not
be surprised that our church is in a state of confusion. But let us not
despair. We have been given everything we need to discern the body.
We have Christ himself. This is the God who knows us even before we
know ourselves. This is the God who would be loved by us. To know
him and to be known by him is the work, the knowledge, of love. Praise
God.

12

Body Matters

A Sermon for the Divinity School
Duke University
September 24, 2009

2 Kings 9:1–16
Psalm 146
1 Corinthians 6:12–20
Matthew 6:1–6, 16–18

"It has been reported to me by Chloe's people that there are quarrels among you." So Paul observes early in his letter to the Corinthians. That Paul learned about the problem from Chloe's people—that is, from one of the factions—means he has a problem that is not going to go away. Those in the church in Corinth seem to think they "belong" to the person who had baptized them and, of course, that seems to have led to ideological divisions. In contrast to the Corinthians, we believe we belong to no one, which, I hope to convince you, makes us quite similar to the Corinthians.

We need to begin, however, by asking why and how the Corinthians ended up in such a mess. I think it was Paul's fault. Through his preaching, they had become Christians. They had probably been pretty normal before Paul came along, but because of Paul their everyday worlds became unstuck. They had become Christians, people of a new age, so they were no longer subject to what most people assumed was "normality." They possessed new knowledge expressed in slogans, slogans they may well have learned from Paul, such as "All things are lawful for me" or "Food is meant for the stomach and the stomach for food." It turns out, of course, that a little knowledge is a very dangerous thing.

But then a little Christianity is a very dangerous business. To be a Christian does turn the world upside down. That the Corinthians quickly divided into factions is quite understandable. When your world has been turned up side down you need assurance that what you think others may also think. Divisions in the church may be the result, but that is the price you pay when you are in the business of trying to figure out this "new thing" being a Christian entails. It was, after all, whether you were a Jew or a pagan, no easy thing to figure out what you were getting yourself into when you became a Christian. We have been at it for over two thousand years, and we are still not all that sure what we have gotten ourselves into.

In some ways we face more difficulty than the Corinthians, who were trying to figure out what it meant to be a Christian at an early stage when there were no clear examples. We have more examples than we can use, but we are not sure we trust any of them. The world has taught us to be skeptical of others and to trust only ourselves. As a result, we are now shaped by forms of life that make it nearly impossible even to begin to understand a way of life that could produce a question such as, "Should I therefore take the members of Christ and make them members of a prostitute?"

We find it hard to comprehend the presumptions that would make such a rhetorical question intelligible. We may not be Chloe's people, Apollos's people, or Cephas's people, but we may share some of their presumptions that Paul means to challenge because we are John Stuart Mill's people. In his *Principles of Political Economy*, Mill argued that freedom from social interference is the best way to encourage the growth of strong individuals who turn out to be necessary for creating societies in which the greatest good for the greatest number can be made a reality. This is the basis for what Mill calls the principle of liberty—that is, we should be free to do as we like without impediment from our fellow creatures "so long as what we do does not harm them, even though they should think our conduct foolish, perverse, or wrong."

Mill, of course, was trying to articulate a political philosophy to shape a liberal culture and the corresponding liberal state. He was not trying to tell Christians how they should shape their lives in the church. But Mill's "principle of liberty" is hard to resist. You can hear it at work in slogans we use as Christians. "Who am I to judge another Christian? After all when it is all said and done we are all sinners." "It is up to each of us to do the best we can by loving one another. What I eat and with whom I sleep, therefore, is my business as long as I do not hurt anyone." "To be a Christian is not to get hung up on moralistic judgments but to care about those who have less than we have."

Paul, however, has no use for the slogans the Corinthians use, nor do I think he would care for our slogans. He thinks what we do with our bodies is more indicative of who we are than what we say we believe. "Do you not know that whoever is united to a prostitute becomes one body with her? For it is said, 'The two shall be one flesh.'" Paul seems to think that our bodies have been united with Christ's body in a manner that is even more determinative than the union enacted in marriage. It does not get more physical than that.

We are a culture that prides ourselves on our frank awareness of the body. In such a culture, Christians are often depicted as those who have no use for the pleasures of the body. But from the perspective of Paul, our culture, the slogans that our culture produces, is fundamentally body denying. For example, consider the ready explanation often offered to excuse promiscuity or adultery—"What we did meant nothing to me personally. It was just sex." From Paul's perspective, you could not wish for a better expression of a Gnostic denial of the significance of the body.

Our grammar often betrays us. We say we have a body. That seems to suggest I am something distinguishable from my body. In good capitalist fashion, the body becomes another possession I can use as I see fit. But Paul does not think there is an "I" that *has* a body. We are our bodies. And the body we are together is one that has been bought with a price. Our bodies are, therefore, not our own to do with as we please. Rather our bodies are a resting place for the Holy Spirit. Paul even seems to think that what our bodies do and do not do makes a difference for our ability to be a holy people.

For it turns out that none of this makes sense if we are not called to a life of holiness. It is too easily forgotten that Anglicanism is a holiness movement. If you doubt that, read through the anthology, *Love's Redeeming Work: The Anglican Quest for Holiness*, and you will discover that Anglicans have, amid that ambiguity of being an established church, sought to be a church that is a witness to the holiness of God as made known in Jesus.

It is true, of course, that Anglicans distrust any simplistic formulas that suggest holiness is a matter of trying harder. Anglicans rather like texts that tell us to pray and give alms in secret, because it is just such bad taste to make too much about being a Christian. There is, moreover, as the editors of *Love's Redeeming Work* observe, an appropriate skepticism about our ability to live as Christ's holy people. We know we are fallen beings who are ready to live lives of deception made all the more resistant to discovery by our presumed righteousness. Such skepticism is altogether appropriate, but secrecy also has its dangers just to the extent secrecy can be a strategy to avoid having our fantasies about who we really are challenged.

If you want to know who you really are, according to Paul, attend to where your body is and what your body is doing. In truth we do not find this particularly good news. We are, after all, John Stuart Mill's people. We may think using prostitutes is not a good idea, but we are more likely to be concerned, with good reason, about what prostitution does to the prostitute than the implications it may have for the up-building of the body of Christ. The idea that the whole church is present in an act of prostitution simply is a thought we have trouble comprehending. We may say piously that the body is a temple of the Holy Spirit, but I suspect few of us have any idea what we have said when we say this.

But you are people preparing for the ministry. I am and you are John Stuart Mill's people, and you will be serving churches made up of his people. How will you even begin to help yourself and those you serve discover that your body and their bodies have been bought with a price? I quite frankly have no sure answer, but I do think I know where you need to begin. Expose the half-truths contained in the slogans we use. Follow Paul's example. "'All things may be lawful,' but not all things are beneficial." Paul is not underwriting Mill's principle of liberty. Rather he is reminding the Corinthians that what they do with their bodies makes a difference for the unity of the body of Christ. "All things are lawful,' but I will not be dominated by anything" is Paul's way to suggest that hell is where we have to do what we want to do.

To challenge such slogans is not an invitation to self-righteousness or to play the prophet. Never forget, behind the Mill-like slogans there lies a terrible loneliness. It is a desperate loneliness fueled by the presumption that we are our own creator. It is a loneliness that tempts us to think, as bodies destined to die, that somehow we are more than our bodies. It is a loneliness that results from the denial that we have been bought with a price. It is a loneliness that leads us momentarily to try to forget ourselves by using the body of another. There is nothing quite as lonely as sex used as a substitute for intimacy.

The good news is that we have been bought with a price, making it possible for us not to have to do what we want to do. We do not have to be dominated by a world shaped by John Stuart Mill. We can rejoice in our bodies because our bodies are now members of Christ. Timothy will soon tell us we are to receive and feed on these gifts of the body and blood of Christ and by so doing we will become living members of our Savior. Because Christ has given his body to us we are not alone. Because we receive these gifts of the body and blood of Christ we belong to him. That is surely the good news the world is dying to hear.

13

Finite Care in a World of Infinite Need*

I often ask lay audiences—that is, people who are not associated with medicine—"How do you want to die?" The answers are almost always the same. They want to die quickly, in their sleep, painlessly, and without being "a burden." They do not want to be a burden because they do not trust their children. They want to die quickly, in their sleep, and painlessly because when they die they do not want to have to know they are dying. As a result, we now expect doctors to keep us alive to the point that when we die we will not know we are dying, and then we get to blame doctors for keeping us alive.

It is quite interesting to compare this way of dying with death in the middle ages. People in the middle ages wanted what modern people fear, that is, they wanted a lingering death. They feared a sudden death. They did so because they feared dying without having the time to be reconciled with their enemies, who were often their family, the church, and God. Today we fear death. They feared God.

Those different fears have everything to do with many of the dilemmas we face when confronted by modern medicine. Many assume that the development of medical ethics, a phenomenon begun in America some years ago, was an attempt to respond to the increasing technical power of modern medicine. That may account for the creation of such a field, but I think it far more likely that medical ethics was an attempt

* "A lecture delivered at Sanford University on "Theology and Medicine."

to think through how to practice medicine in a morally fragmented culture.

Put more strongly, I think the development of medical ethics was an attempt to understand how medicine could be practiced in a world in which there are no longer any perceived limits—including the limit of death. Accordingly, modern medicine, and the ethics developed to legitimate such a medicine, took as its task to serve the desire of modern people who want to get out of life alive. To care for the ill when you cannot cure their illness is no longer the aim of medicine. Patients now demand to be cured.

Let me try to illustrate these observations by calling attention to a discussion I became aware of when I joined the faculty of the Divinity School at Duke University in 1984. There was a debate at Duke Medical Center that centered on questions of organ transplants. The medical center was to begin liver transplants that were projected to cost $140,000 an operation. Dr. Harvey Estes, chair of Duke's Department of Community and Family Medicine, questioned whether the money spent on organ transplants could not be better spent in other ways. In response, Clark Havighurst, a professor in Duke's Law School, observed, "It is very hard for society to face the death of someone who could be saved, but we will have to face this more and more."[1]

I call attention to this brief scrimmage at Duke in 1984 because I think the issues remain with us, but contrary to Havighurst, we still have not faced them. Indeed, if anything the problems have gotten worse. Every center dedicated to high-tech medicine knows it must compete with other centers if it is to command research funds requiring the development of more exotic forms of care. Just as anyone who is facing surgery wants to believe that they have the best surgeon available, so it seems every medical school and center must give the impression that they represent the "cutting edge" of research medicine.

The result, as Estes suggested, creates a bizarre world. Why should we develop extraordinary forms of therapy when we are increasingly unable to give even the most minimal medical care to the poor? The result is a multi-tiered system for the delivery of medical care—one for people with health insurance and the other for those without such insurance. Faced by this kind of discrepancy we assume someone must be

---

1. *Durham Herald Sun* (November 11, 1984) 11D.

at fault. I do not want to exclude that possibility, but I want first to try to understand why we seem caught in this unhappy dilemma.

Paul Ramsey, I think, put the issue about as well as it can be put in 1970 in his book *The Patient as Person.*[2] Ramsey observed:

> With sufficient resources of money and personnel, any one or more remedy could be extended to all in need. But not all remedies can together be effectively extended in the social practice of medicine in this day of extraordinary treatments. Since health needs are almost by definition unlimited in any given society, and since the health needs of the world as a whole are infinite, choices must somehow be made among them. How shall sparse medical resources be allocated? Which needs should be given priority in medical practice and medical institutions generally? Beyond this, there is the question of the priority that should be given to medical needs among the many social causes having valid claims upon a nation's resources. Ideally, any one of these could be satisfied, but not all at the same time or in no order of priority. The needs of men (of which health is only one) are certainly unlimited; and, by comparison to the felt-needs or demand, the supply of resources of any society are irremediably sparse. There is no avoiding this question of choosing societal priorities. We must choose how we shall go about choosing and ordering our medical and societal goals.[3]

Ramsey argues that these questions are even more intractable than the challenge of how to choose who is to live and die when, for example, there are a limited number of dialysis machines for people with kidney failure. Faced by such a choice we can argue whether a lottery or some other selection procedure is appropriate. But Ramsey argues that we have no way to determine whether we ought or ought not to develop dialysis technology in the first place. Faced with such a question Ramsey notes that "the larger questions of medical and social priorities are almost, if not altogether, incorrigible to moral reasoning."[4]

Ramsey illustrates this dilemma by discussing Dr. Warren Warwick's satirical article on organ transplants, which bore the subtitle: "A Modest Proposal." The subtitle is meant to suggest Swift's famous article that recommended that inhabitants of Ireland might increase their

2. Ramsey, *Patient as Person.*

3. Ibid., 239–40.

4. Ibid., 240.

food supply by eating their children. In the same spirit, Dr. Warwick suggests that "accident watching clubs" should be formed to supply helicopters able to reach scenes of accidents quickly to secure organs of the victims of the accident. Such clubs also ought to lobby to prohibit the use of seat belts and other safety devises. If anyone objects that such a policy is deliberately designed to kill people, let them reflect on how modern medical know-how can respond by mastering the logistics of using several of the organs of a single victim for the good of five or six needing the resulting organs. Such a procedure can be justified by basic utilitarian calculus.

Ramsey reports that Warwick argues that we not only need a new definition of death to harvest organs more efficiently, but a new philosophy of the body. "Society should have the right to tax a man's body by claiming its organs, since social resources have maintained his health—just as we tax his estate on the grounds that the common prosperity had something to do with the wealth a man earns."[5] If necessary, this understanding of the body might be extended to encourage, for example, women seeking abortions to allow the fetus to develop to the stage they could be used to supply organs.

Ramsey reports that Dr. Warwick concludes his article with the plea that, since organ transplantation has clearly won the hearts of the American people, physicians must not back "proved losers," such as the archaic notion that preventive medicine is better than later treatment. Funds to learn more about how we should live to prevent heart and kidney disease are not going to be forthcoming, but research funding for transplanting those organs will be supported by modern people. Medical students should learn quickly that the action is not in preventive care but crisis intervention.

Ramsey acknowledges he could not refrain from calling attention to Warwick's article for the "sheer fun of it," but he thinks the article raises the central issues. For the article rightly raises the question of how the ordering of our medical priorities might be subject to some rational scheme. Ramsey asks, "who shall say or how do we go about deciding what sorts of medical services should be given priority over

5. Ibid., 266–67.

others, and how much of a nation's resources should be spent on medical care in comparison to other claims and needs?"[6]

Ramsey argues that once such questions are raised there are no good reasons to avoid them by indecision, but that is the way it seems we have chosen to proceed. That is, we choose to order our priorities by not ordering them—or perhaps more accurately, we do not make explicit or acknowledge the forces that are ordering our priorities. We tell ourselves that we want nothing other than the best medical care for every patient—"you cannot put a dollar value on human life"—but in fact we know we participate in, as well as support, social institutions that put a dollar amount on human life. Physicians learn to organize their practice in a manner they do not have to acknowledge that certain patient populations are hidden from them—you cannot neglect patients you never see.

Of course, there is a conception of justice that determines the distribution of health care in most industrial societies like America. It is assumed that justice is achieved by satisfying the needs and wants of individuals in an open market of supply and demand. Justice is determined by our ability to pay. Accordingly, there is no general right to health care. The professional skill a physician possesses is a property they can sell to whom they please. Attempts to respond to the inequities this system creates only reinforce its character because they are in fact public subsidies for private markets.

Yet many argue that market justice is inappropriate to determine the distribution of medical care. For when we are ill we are in no position to bargain. For the market to work fairly, it is assumed that everyone is a free and rational agent able to barter and choose intelligently the service offered. But when we are sick our capacity to judge is compromised and our choices are severely limited. Moreover, in matters of medical care assumptions about supply and demand presupposed on the market model simply do not apply. The general presumption that doctors are experts who decide what constitutes an illness needing intervention, as well as the recipients of the rewards for such an intervention, means there is no incentive for control of costs. For example, when and who thought baldness is a disease needing medical intervention?

6. Ibid., 268.

That justice produced by the market, particularly a market in which people are encouraged to believe that whatever they want is legitimate, results in inequity for those needing basic care I think is beyond dispute. But I think the problem is deeper, involving how such an account of justice may distort the very character of medicine itself. For as I suggested above, such a view encourages physicians to look on their skills as their property; but a physician does not own their craft—they are their craft. To be a physician is not to have a job, but to be engaged in a practice that constitutes the common good of a community. The trust a physician enjoys is based on the presumption that the physician is committed to the care of a patient in a manner that trumps all other considerations. Such trust constitutes a good to be commonly shared.

The good that is at the moral heart of medicine, the good that shapes all a physician is and does, I take to be the commitment of a physician to care for a patient in a manner that any judgments about the patient are moot other than what needs to be done to care for that patient. A patient may be someone who mistreats children, but if they have a bad gall bladder they are to be cared for. A person who has a heart attack because they are seriously overweight is still to receive medical care. I call attention to these common commitments we expect from medicine because if we fail to make them articulate we risk losing their significance.

That we treat those whom we may well think do not deserve to be treated is why issues of distribution of health care, in Ramsey's terms, are so intractable. The commitment of those in medical care to care for the patient without attending to their individual worth creates an almost interminable need. For in an attempt to help one individual patient—for example, with leukemia—modalities of care are discovered to help a wide range of patients who in the past could not have been helped or even recognized as needing to be helped. In other words, the commitment to the care of the individual patient creates possibilities that encourage us to have needs that we otherwise would not have. As a result, medicine creates the bizarre world in which some will receive heart transplants while others die of pneumonia.

Thus the argument by many that need should determine the character of justice in regard to the distribution of health care. Ill health is unevenly distributed and we can exercise only moderate control over what makes us healthy or ill. Illness is not just one burden among others, but rather to be ill is a condition of compromised human agency. The sick live on the dark side of the human condition and to deny them medical care is to write off their existence. That is why our care of one another through the agency of those trained in medicine is foundational if we are to recognize the goods we share in common.

But even if this argument for a need-based account of justice is right, it does not settle or resolve the incorrigible questions raised by Ramsey. We still do not know if we rightly spend so much of our resources on those who are in their last year of life. Of course, we often do not know they are in their last year of life. Indeed one of the problems with the celebration of the power of modern medicine is patients are encouraged to believe they have the right to any procedure that may help keep them alive. As a result, we corrupt ourselves as well as the character of medicine by trying to make it do more than it is capable of doing.

So I suspect questions of how medical care should be distributed cannot be settled by developing more sophisticated accounts of justice. Indeed, I suspect one of the problems with such accounts is that justice is separated from other virtues that are crucial for recognizing what is and is not just. In particular, justice must draw on the virtue of courage if we are to know how we are to face our deaths as well as the deaths of those we love. The ill distribution of our healthcare resources I think reflects the general inability of people that make up modern societies to come to terms with death. For if we share anything as a people, it is that death ought to be avoided in the hope that we can finally get out of life alive. As a result, those with the economic and social power are able to command resources to keep their deaths at bay to the detriment of those who are not facing death.

For example, Ramsey points out that when the first heart transplant was done in Britain a dozen operations had to be postponed due to the limited facilities at the National Heart Hospital. We may well think: that is England and other societies are not subject to such limits. Ramsey, however, argues that this example is a prism through which we can comprehend the realism of the situation, namely, that measured against the human need of any nation, we possess at best sparse medical resources. Moreover, the truth is that the human condition is made worse in modern times when the fear of death appears to have become ubiquitous with secularism.[7]

Ramsey argues, therefore, that before we get to questions involving who will live and who will die, there are more fundamental questions to be raised about the medical priority to be given to the development of increasingly exotic medical procedures. Behind these questions, moreover, is the even more challenging question of how the medical profession and society in general decide such questions and the immorality of leaving such questions to professional and social indecision.

But I suspect such "professional and social indecision" will rule the day as the inequity that results will appear to be no one's fault. That those who are poor fail to get even minimal medical care can be interpreted as a matter of bad luck—not social policy. The assumption that there is nothing we can do about such matters works to the advantage of those who have the economic and social power to serve their feverish desire to get out of life alive. Perhaps the poor's only consolation is the biblical insight that often those who would command the powers to do their will end up subject to those very powers. That is, it may well be that sinners no longer fear falling into the hands of an angry god. Instead, we now fall into the hands of a seemingly benevolent medical establishment whose self-interest is underwritten by our fear of death.

But surely such a perspective is not all that can be said. Those who argue that the development of modern medicine may be a danger for our moral health may be right, but that does little to help children who need basic medical care. What can be done to insure adequate medical care for the poor? I have no concrete proposals, but I hope calling attention to Ramsey's analysis may at least suggest where we might begin. For if he is right, our problems are theological. The problem is quite simply that medicine has been put at the service of cheating death by a people who no longer believe our deaths have any meaning.

I do not make this point in order to suggest that a recovery of belief in God is necessary to secure a more nearly just distribution of medical care. One should only believe in God if you think such a belief is true. Moreover I do not believe, even if there were some robust return to belief in God, that our problems would be over. That is especially not the case given the expectations that are now in place.

---

7. Ibid., 269

However I do not think this means nothing can be done, particularly by people who call themselves Christians. For I assume that they are a community of people who have learned that their deaths are not an unmitigated disaster. Even more importantly, they are, or should be, a people who have learned that service to one another is more important than life itself. As a result, they can envision forms of care in which the poor are not excluded. We need to remember that the great imaginative invention we now call the hospital was the result of a people, monks, who thought that even amidst the injustices of the world you could take time to be with the dying. They cared for the dying by being present even when they could not cure—a reminder that medicine is not justified by the power to heal, but by the refusal to abandon those who are sick even when there is little we can do other than to be present.

If I am right about this, then I think that hospitals that are sponsored by as well as serve people called Christian may well be called on to take a more distinctive stand than they currently can imagine. The attempt to get more resources to serve the poor is to be welcomed. But more important is the possibility Christians may have to learn to deny themselves forms of extraordinary care that medicine seems determined to develop. In other words, I suspect that we may well have to imagine as Christians that there may actually be something like a Christian practice of medicine.

I am well aware that such a suggestion may seem outrageous. For if unbelief is our problem, then it seems we face an intractable problem. Christians have long pursued social strategies, not only in medical care, that assume belief in God makes or should make no difference for how we think about justice. In the name of charity or justice we seek social policies that we hope will be good for the poor. In no way do I mean to disparage the good that has resulted from these endeavors, but I worry that such strategies are no longer sufficient for the care we offer one another through the good office of medicine.

For the problem with abstract conceptions of justice, whether they be market, merit, social worth, or need, is they are just that—abstractions. No account of justice can be intelligible without drawing on the profoundest convictions and practices of a community and its traditions. Indeed the very attempt to develop conceptions of justice abstracted from such communities but manifests in conceptions of community that assume we are individuals free of such traditions. In contrast, I am suggesting that Christians must recover our sense of care and concern for one another as a resource for helping us better know why everything we can do to prevent our own death may not be done if such a project makes it impossible to care for the weakest member of our community. Only when we recover a sense of ourselves as death-determined creatures will we know what we are about when we call for a society to employ the scarce resources of medical care in service to one another.

14

Sent: The Church Is Mission

A Sermon for the Church of the Holy Family

July 4, 2010

2 Kings 5:1–14
Psalm 30
Galatians 6: (1–6) 7–16
Luke 10: 1–11, 16–20

In June 1910, twelve hundred representatives of one hundred and sixty Protestant mission societies gathered in Edinburgh, Scotland. The World Missionary Conference, as it came to be called, marked the high point of European Christianity by celebrating the spread of the gospel, a gospel to be sure that reflected the habits of Europe and America, throughout the world. In 2010, the centennial year of that great gathering, there are numerous conferences to celebrate, as well as evaluate, this remarkable event and the missionary enterprise it represented.

The delegates in 1910 were largely white males. They were, however, men of extraordinary energy and imagination. They thought, moreover, that at Edinburgh they saw a new possibility for the church. Edinburgh was the beginning of what we now call the ecumenical movement. At Edinburgh the delegates thought they caught a glimpse of a worldwide Christian unity that they took to be the fruit of their shared passion to spread the gospel in the name of Jesus Christ. That glimpse of unity was shattered by an event called World War I.

We, that is, Christians in a church of declining membership and with little enthusiasm for what was once described as "foreign missions," are not quite sure what to make of Edinburgh, 1910. In general we have accepted the critique of the nineteenth-century missionary movement as being an expression of Western military and cultural imperialism that we do not want to repeat. The delegates at Edinburgh, such as V. S. Azariah from India, who spoke eloquently against the colonialist attitude of superiority, often go unnoticed. Azariah praised the sacrifices of the missionaries who had brought Christianity to India, but he asked that they now think of themselves as partners in the development of the indigenous church in India. Such a partnership became the rule of the day through most of the twentieth century, climaxing in the astonishing growth of indigenous churches throughout the world for which the adjective "indigenous" no longer makes sense. They are simply "the church" in India, Africa, and Asia.

In truth, many of us are not sure we know what we think about the growth of Christianity among those peoples who received the gospel from people who were shaped by a colonialist mindset. Like some of the delegates at Edinburgh who, under the influence of theological developments in eighteenth- and nineteenth-century German universities, wished to place a moratorium on missions because they had increasing doubts about the uniqueness of Christ, we are not at all sure we want missionaries who think they need to act in the name of Jesus. We think it good to build schools and hospitals, but we are quite hesitant to ask people to believe in Jesus. We now confront the paradoxical situation in which Christians who then received Christ from missionaries, whom we now call Western colonialists, do not share our hesitancy to ask others to let Jesus change their life. And these Christians have begun to send their missionaries to Europe and America.

These brothers and sisters are now reminding us that to be Christian is to be someone who is "sent." Luke is the great theologian and historian of what it means for the church not to *have* a mission but to *be* mission. Luke thinks Christianity is not just a missionary faith because it had to be given its beginnings, but Luke assumes that the church is mission. Just as Jesus in the Gospel of Luke is always on the go, so the church—particularly as it is personified by Paul in the book of Acts—is on the move. To be sure, Paul is constantly on the go because everywhere he goes he gets in trouble and has to leave. But Luke does not think rejection is a defeat, but rather through rejection Paul is forced by the Holy Spirit to go to people and places he had not anticipated having to go in order to witness to the gospel of Jesus Christ.

Christians are missionaries by necessity because all that we are and do only makes sense if what we are and do is done in the name of Jesus. Thus the seventy return joyfully, reporting: "Lord, in your name even the demons submit to us." The demons submit to the name, "Jesus," for the one that bears that name is also rightly called, "Lord." The seventy have not been sent out to do what can be done whether you know or do not know the name of Jesus. They have been sent out to do what only can be done in the name of Jesus.

That they are to act in the name of Jesus is a crucial clue if we are to understand why the church does not have a mission but why the church is mission. Jesus is a name—a definite name for a distinct history. You only learn that name, the name of Jesus, the way you learn other names, that is, by the willingness of the name bearer—or someone who knows them—to make their name known. We have to tell one another our names, because names name singulars, that is, a particular that defies generalization. A name not only represents but constitutes a history that requires "a telling."

You may well think that may be true about "Stanley," but is it true about Jesus? Jesus is the name above every name. Stanley is not that kind of name. It takes time for you to get to know me because to get to know someone, to know their name, entails a complex process of learning the history that bears the name "Stanley." But surely Jesus is different. He is, after all, the Son of God. You do not call just anyone, "Lord." When the seventy call Jesus "Lord" they do so because they have discovered that even the demons submit to the name of Jesus. Yet to know this man is Lord depends on his being this very particular man, this very particular Jew, named Jesus. That is what it means to say he is the One who is God's incarnate.

Given our hesitancy about missions in the name of Jesus, we would prefer that what we call the gospel to be a set of generalizations—we ought to love one another, we should work for the dignity of every human being, we are a people of justice seeking a world of greater equality, etc. But the gospel is the proclamation that "the kingdom of God has come near to us" and that kingdom has a name, Jesus. Origen called Jesus "the Autobasileia," that is, the kingdom in a person. To be sure, Jesus is unlike any of us for he is the very Son of God. But it remains true that he is only known through witnesses who act in his name through the power of the Holy Spirit. Just as Jesus sent the seventy to every place he intended to go, so he would have you and me go to where his name is not known, places like Durham and Chapel Hill, North Carolina, to be witnesses to his name.

We find this a very uncomfortable demand. We are, after all, Episcopalians. Episcopalians just do not do that kind of thing. Baptists, and in particular, Billy Graham, do that kind of thing. But we Episcopalians more or less have the view that suggesting the name of Jesus matters might prompt some to think we did not graduate from the University of North Carolina or Duke. After all, you do not have to be a Christian to be a good person. At best we might ask someone to come to church because everyone needs a bit of community, but we find it quite awkward to ask someone to believe in Jesus as the Son of God. I have only done it once.

But Jesus appointed seventy to go ahead of him to every town and place where he intended to go. He assured them that although they were but a few, he is the Lord and the harvest is plentiful. He was, however, quite blunt about their status. He is sending them out as lambs in the midst of wolves. They will be in danger, but the mission on which they are sent means they must do their work without protection. They are to carry no money, no food, or any other provision for their journey. Even worse, he sends them in pairs, which means they are going to have to be at peace with one another to survive. Moreover they must learn to depend on the good will of those to whom they have been sent. They must learn to receive hospitality from those who would have them in their homes. For the gospel is not the gospel until those who have been witnesses hear from those to whom they have witnessed what God has said through them. To be in mission is a profoundly humbling practice.

I cannot help but think these missionaries provide essential insights to help us recover the missionary character of the gospel: the witness required by the name of Jesus. We are a church that has been burdened by the success of Christianity in the West. This is the fourth of July. That success has made it difficult to distinguish the gospel, the

name of Jesus, from what many associate with being American. Like
Naaman we find it hard to believe that an Elisha and not the king of
Israel, that the river Jordan and not the rivers of Damascus, have the
power to heal.

But God, it seems, is determined to make us listen to the prophet.
God is whittling us down. We are a church that is quickly losing its
power and status in the world as we know it. Those losses may well
mean that whatever witness we are capable of making will be a witness
without protection. The witness of those who have come before us must
serve as a reminder that to be without protection is the condition necessary to learn how to live in peace with one another. For if we fail to live
peacefully with one another the witness we bring will not be a witness
to the gospel of Jesus Christ.

But the church's present dispossession is not an occasion for self-
pity. Rather it is an occasion for attending to the demons we have allowed
to possess us—i.e., greed, arrogance, sloth, and pride. We are being humiliated, which turns out to be necessary discipline for being a people
of humility capable of recognizing that Jesus is Lord. For only under
the Lordship of Christ can the powerlessness of the demonic powers,
powers that feed off our fears of not being in control, be exposed.

For this is the good news—not that we need to be saved, but that
we have been saved! "I saw Satan fall from heaven" means the good
news we have been given to proclaim in the name of Jesus, the news we
become through proclamation, is about a salvation that is cosmic. We
do not make him Lord, he *is* Lord! That is the good news—that is the
peace—we cannot help but want to share.

When the church is not in mission, when we are embarrassed to
witness in the name of Jesus, we are not the church. We have rightly
worried that too often those who preach that salvation comes only in
the name of Jesus do so in a voice so strident that the peace that is
offered in that name is lost. There is a story told by Drury, a friend of
arguably the most important philosopher of the last century, Ludwig
Wittgenstein, about a walk he was taking with Wittgenstein that I think
nicely suggests what it might mean to recover the missionary character of the church. Wittgenstein, who more than any other philosopher
helped us recover the essential relation between what we say and how
we live, on the walk with Drury passed a street evangelist preaching to

all who passed by. Drury reports Wittgenstein remarked, "If he really meant what he was shouting he would not use that tone of voice."

What we seek as God forces us to rediscover the missionary character of our lives as Christians is the right tone of voice. Karl Barth exemplified what I take to be that tone when he responded to an American evangelical query about when he was saved with the straightforward answer, "33 AD." Barth's answer, the witness of Barth's life and work, is one that defies the desperate attempt by some Christians to reassure themselves that what they believe cannot be true unless they force others to believe what they believe. The witness shaped by the name of Jesus cannot be desperate, but rather must be one of joy made possible by the recognition that we have been sent into the world that the world might know the truth. For finally that is what makes missions possible, namely, we want to share with others the joy that comes with the recognition that Jesus is Lord; he is the truthful love that moves the sun and the stars; he is the one who makes it possible to live in peace with one another.

In June 1910 in Edinburgh, Scotland, those gathered there caught a brief glimpse of the unity of the church. A unity soon shattered by WWI. It turned out that was but the beginning. We have just lived through a century—a century some thought might bear the name, "The Christian Century"—that saw an atomic weapon explode directly over the cathedral in Nagasaki. That century, and the church that identified with what it took to be the most progressive forces of that century, has come to an end. We have learned that a church that is willing to kill in the name of histories that are not determined by the name of Jesus, our humiliated Lord, is rightly not often trusted when she says, "Peace to this house!" But the good news is that God is forcing the churches to need one another so that the world can see that peace is not an ideal but a reality present in this, the very body and blood of Jesus. What unbelievably good news. It makes you want to share it.

III. Habits of Speech Exemplified: Some Teachers

15

"Long Live the Weeds and the Wilderness Yet": Reflections on *A Secular Age*

with ROMAND COLES

And of course, this incapacity of language is a crucial facet of an incapacity of being, that our lives are reduced, flattened. "All is seared with trade; bleared, seared with toil . . . "

"What would the world be, once bereft
Of Wet and wildness? Let them be left,
O let them be left, wildness and wet;
Long live the weeds and the wilderness yet."
—GERHARD MANLEY HOPKINS*

We begin where the man reaches his height with the wings of a friend whose stirred flight is the spirit of the book: Charles Taylor, with Gerard Manley Hopkins. We begin here so that we might linger at this apex and reflect upon "incapacities of being" as well as possibilities for living less badly—and sometimes even well—for a world of "the weeds and the wilderness yet." And the "we" of our own words in this essay is very much the fledgling practice of one such possibility, where incarnations of what Taylor calls "transcendence," on the one hand, and

* Cited by Taylor, *Secular Age*, 761.

173

the transcendence of immanence, on the other, cross paths and engage cross-pressures in ways that we hope enrich and complicate Taylor's account in *A Secular Age*.[1] Enrich and complicate: for in practiced accents more akin to the likes of Wendell Berry and Jean Vanier we think our words in this context may be of use to the extent that we speak less of immanence and transcendence and more of specific liturgies from which our incapacities and capacities for being receive, give, and take lives. With and beyond Taylor we would call theory and theology to the complex textures of tending to ordinary life as the most hopeful locus for radical renewal beyond the closures and flattening of Constantinian articulations of transcendence and neo-Constantinian articulations of immanence.

"Tending to ordinary life" is a phrase that gestures to the heart of the case we tried to make in *Christianity, Democracy, and the Radical Ordinary: Conversations between a Radical Democrat and a Christian*.[2] We should like to think that the argument we make in that book shares much in common with Taylor's *A Secular Age*, but we will try to suggest how our directing attention to the "radical ordinary" may offer a more variegated account of the possibilities in our "age," our time, than do Taylor's depictions of the irruptions of transcendence the immanent frame cannot control.

We admire Taylor's unapologetic acknowledgment of his Christian convictions (637). We think he is right, moreover, to disavow Christendom (514). We think it is a good thing that Christians now live in a world in which it is no longer impossible not to believe in God (3). We are also convinced that many aspects of modernity are the result of a corrupt or corrupted Christianity (740). We share Taylor's judgment that when the Christian faith is identified with a civilizational order Christians lose sight of the full transformation to which Christians should be committed (743).

Taylor is surely right, moreover, that the hold of Christendom on the imaginations of Christian and non-Christian alike is hard to break. As a result, the "dominant immanentist orders" remain defined by Christendom models often now expressed primarily in secular terms[3]

1. All further references to Taylor, *A Secular Age* will be given parenthetically in the text.

2. Hauerwas and Coles, *Christianity, Democracy, and the Radical Ordinary*.

3. In his important but largely ignored delineation of various forms of

(734–35). We worry, however, that Taylor's use of the immanent/transcedence duality may reproduce the habits of a Christianity that still longs to be a civilizational order. It does so just to the extent such a scheme can tempt us, Christian and non-Christian alike, to think our primary concern is maintaining a place for transcendence.

But that is to make immanence and transcendence freestanding concepts lacking christological discipline.[4] For Christians, immanence first and foremost names that God became man that we might participate in the very life of God. So nothing can be more immanent than God with us. Transcendence, moreover, is not simply the name for James's "more," but rather the other side of God's immanence. For Christians, transcendence first and foremost is the acknowledgement that death could not hold him. When immanence and transcendence are so understood we can begin to see what is missing, or at least plays no decisive role, in Taylor's account, namely, the existence of a people—call such a people if you will, "church"—who are able to discern possibilities in the immanent frame that could not be seen if such a people did not exist.

We suspect Taylor may well be sympathetic with our attempt to complicate his account of "the secular." Late in his book he acknowledges that the transcendence/immanence distinction is unsatisfactory. He observes that when the bar of "normal behavior" is high "immanence" may not seem to be the right term. The notion of transcendence may fail to show how very demanding forms of exclusive humanism generate a counter-reaction from within unbelief itself (632). However he thinks for purposes of his principle thesis it important to maintain the distinction. We hope to convince him that may not be the case.

~

Constantinianism, Yoder identified neo-neo-neo-Constantinianism as the "preoccupation of the church to be allied even with post-religious secularism as long as this is popular" (*Original Revolution*, 144–45).

4. It also abstracts these concepts from the complexities and disciplines of radical democratic practices such as early SNCC, Industrial Areas Foundations, etc. We do not find that their liturgical engagement in political practices (across so many differences) such as one-on-one meetings, house meetings, neighborhood walks, assemblies, and so forth, is illuminated well by this frame.

A secular age, in Taylor's sense, refers to those tendencies in the present that seek and claim the hegemony of an uncomplicated world picture. At the level of practice, much in Taylor's analysis of the secular could be articulated in relation to Talal Asad's argument in *Formations of the Secular* concerning the pressures in modernity toward nation-state and market simplifications of time and space. Premodern space, as Asad describes it, was a more "complex space" of "intersecting boundaries and heterogeneous activities of individuals as well as of groups related to traditions"; and premodern time was "heterogeneous time" in the sense that it recognized "simultaneous temporalities" "of embodied practices rooted in multiple traditions, of differences between horizons of expectation and spaces of experience—differences that continually dislocate the present from the past, the world experienced from the world anticipated, and call for their revision and reconnection." In contrast, secular modernity seeks to translate everything into the homogeneous time of national politics devoted to the game of corporate exchange, and it would deny all that will not fit within this frame.[5]

Taylor's book provides a magisterial narrative of many of the philosophical moves implicated in efforts to establish an uncontested hegemony of the secular—a world in which all that resists the closures of what Taylor calls the "immanent frame" are dismissed as weakness, immaturity, lack of courage, being out of touch with the self-evident truths of our material age. Both Taylor and Asad seek to open the closures of the secular to the deep, uncertain, and repeatedly renegotiated pluralism of complex spaces and times that slip beyond the grasp of any sovereign that would, in John Howard Yoder's terms, lay claim to the "handles of history."[6] Such a deep pluralism should not be confused

---

5. Asad, *Formations of the Secular*, 179–80. For an exploration of the significance of Asad's understanding of time, see Hauerwas, *State of the University*, 165–86.

6. In *Politics of Jesus*, Yoder observes that one of the characteristics of the way Christians have thought about social ethics in recent times is the obsession with trying to discern the meaning and direction of history. So the task of social ethics is thought to be the attempt to move history in the right direction. "Thus, part if not all of social concern has to do with looking for the right 'handle' by which one can 'get a hold on' the course of history" (228). One way to put our worries about Taylor's account in *A Secular Age* is how the immanence/transcendence scheme may tempt us to think we know how to get a handle on our time. The various forms of Constantinianism Yoder identifies in *Original Revolution* represent the attempt to get a handle on history. For what it means to think without handles, see Chris Huebner's *Precarious Peace*.

with the flat pluralism of practical-philosophical orders governed by closed renderings of reason, nation, and exchange value—leaving other traditions and the "transcendent" nothing more to do than arrange the furniture.[7]

In this sense Asad's and Taylor's efforts converge. And it is from the vantage point of this convergence—the intersection of "incapacities of language" and "incapacities of being"—that we find it most interesting to read and reflect upon Taylor's project. Yet convergence is only part of the story. Asad himself suggests as much (several years before the publication of *A Secular Age*) when he writes, in response to the problematic defined above: "Our attention needs to be directed not so much at how identities are negotiated and recognized (for example through exploratory and constructive dialogue, as Charles Taylor has advocated). Rather the focus should be on what it takes to live particular ways of life continuously, co-operatively, and unselfconsciously."[8] We will try to show ways in which Taylor's most recent book offers more insight in relation to the later focus than do many of his earlier works. Nevertheless, Asad's divergence from Taylor remains illuminating to us and we seek below to illustrate how we ultimately find ourselves closer to Asad's project, and thus drawn to explore paths beyond certain limits in Taylor's—even if Asad overstates the difference.

With Asad, our engagement with Taylor accents the question of "what it takes to live particular ways of life" that refuse totalizing closures. While (in)capacities of language are absolutely crucial to this question, we think a focus on incapacities and capacities of being that are engendered in the liturgies of everyday life is of greater significance: both because it is difficult to imagine how people thoroughly engaged in the liturgical work of shopping malls, television, exploitative labor, and the studied movements of gated geographies would cultivate capacities for richer languages, and because the sense, textures, and intensity of

7. "Flat pluralism" is the kind of "diversity" capitalism celebrates. We find it odd in that respect that Taylor has so little to say about capitalism in *A Secular Age*.

8. Asad, *Formations of the Secular*, 178. We understand Asad's remark here not to be a affirmation of tradition as nostalgic return to uncomplicated life, but rather as a call to modes of traditioning that escape the stances of being self-consciously defensive, subordinate, and subservient to the baseline imperatives of secular modernity that homogenize by relentlessly disrupting human efforts to develop continuities and often conflictive cooperation in a politics that seeks to discern, protect, and create common goods among different people(s).

such languages will only be learned in relation to our engagement in a set of counter-practices through which our bodies acquire the vitality of better possibilities. By such counter-practices, we have in mind what we have, in *Christianity, Democracy, and the Radical Ordinary,* called radical ecclesia and radical democracy.

~

With a keen eye, Taylor situates the emergence and force of the immanent frame in a genealogy of "disenchantment," according to which the porous self (understood in a web of enchanted relations) is gradually displaced by a "buffered self" whose interior is grasped as something radically distinct from the world outside it. The development of this rich interiority is co-implicated in the development of disciplinary practices; and while Foucault is important here, it is Norbert Elias's work on the development of "fastidiousness," the waning of earlier forms of bodily promiscuousness, and the insistence on practices of privacy (co-constituted in intimate spaces with other interiorized individuals), that are most accented in Taylor's account. These changes are accompanied by more interior forms of Christianity and a growing distance from interpretations tied to collective ritual. As our lived relationship to an enchanted cosmic order wanes (aided by post-Galilean science), the buffered self intensifies its instrumental relation to the world (articulated by post-Baconian science), and "our sense of being comprehensively in secular time is very much reinforced by the very thick environment of measured time which we have woven around ourselves in our civilization . . . instrumental rationality in our world, and the pervasiveness of secular time go together" (542).

While the sharp distinction between natural and supernatural originated in a nominalist rejection of Scholasticism that aimed to assert the radical sovereignty of God beyond all entanglements with the world, as instrumentality and secular time increasingly come to govern this world, the distinction comes to align with assertions of the self-sufficiency of the natural from the supernatural.[9] The divorce of the im-

9. In the "Epilogue" to *A Secular Age* Taylor suggests his narrative might have some relation to that developed by John Milbank concerning the implications of the "univocal" understanding of being. Perhaps even more interesting would be Taylor's engagement with Milbank's defense of de Lubac's account of nature/grace in *Suspended Middle*. The nature/grace distinction, particularly when "nature" is thought identifiable

manent from the transcendent is further intensified when the natural and the social are themselves understood primarily as a construction of human being, reason, productivity, civilization, etc. This assertion of independence becomes aggressive when all claims that transcend this immanent order are viewed as impediments to the secular arrangements that "deliver the goods"—whether they be the political order of sovereign nations (obstructed by "fanatics") or the productivity of "free" markets (obstructed by "values" or modes of life recalcitrant to commodification). At its most stark, Taylor writes: "This movement can go farther. It is not just that the good is allegedly threatened by the supposedly better, higher. It may also come to be identified with the rejection of the higher" (546).

On Taylor's reading, this political-economic pressure to close the immanent frame is supplemented by a series of *moral* narratives that generate "spin" that adds "unjustified force" to "the illusion of the rational 'obviousness' of the closed perspective" of much secularization (551, 556). He argues that rather than being the (self-professed) logical conclusion of neutral assessments of the "facts," the closed world structure is driven by (highly questionable) moralistic motifs that accompany a hubristic rendering of the secular self. In this latter story, the self who can acknowledge the death of God is manifesting "honesty," whereas those who remain in some way religious evince a "childish lack of courage" to do so that inflicts tremendous suffering upon self and others (561). The mature unbeliever "knows human beings are on their own. But this doesn't cause him just to cave in. . . . he determines to affirm human worth, and the human good, and to work for it, without false illusion or consolations. And that means that in his moral beliefs he is also counter-mortification. Moreover he has no reason to exclude anyone as heretic; so his philanthropy is universal. Unbelief goes together with modern (exclusive) humanism" (562). Free from the perversities of faith, humans can now dictate the ultimate values by which they will

---

as "pure nature," can be used ideologically to legitimate social and political formations that are not open to criticism on theological grounds. As Milbank observes, "If grace now no longer fulfills the deepest longings of our nature, of our ethical, contemplative, and (even) naturally mystical impulses, then it resembles a politics proclaiming that it is puristically 'about the political' and not about education, welfare, transport, the environment, and defense, etc. If grace does not elevate nature in such a way that it further develops the natural (as not sufficient unto itself), then just what is grace after all?" (21–22).

live, and in this there is a heroic nobility and honor in the face of a universe recognized to be devoid of intrinsic value. Camus is the humanistic face of this "revolt against absurdity" that fights for "ordinary human happiness": he knows that human projects will be crushed but heroically refuses to resign himself in the face of this knowledge with a dazzlingly compelling pride. Of course, Nietzsche's darkest moments of will to power are another direction this move can take, and, Taylor claims, it is difficult to make a strong case for one or the other within the immanent frame.

Taylor has little difficulty showing the contingency, over-reaching, and looming emptiness that is concealed by these moral-affective-practical closures of the immanent frame. Such closures are less a thing of logic and undeniable facticity and more like Wittgenstein's "picture that held us captive"—a frame that we "have trouble often thinking ourselves outside of, even as an imaginative exercise" (549). The brunt of Taylor's account is not to deliver a knock-out punch to purveyors of various accounts of immanence (reason, Romanticism, postmodernism, he says) in order to re-establish the hegemony of transcendent pictures. Indeed, he sees much that is providential in modernity—including favorable reevaluations of ordinary life. Rather he seeks two more modest interventions. The first is to reveal our age—beyond the spin and the "default option" for immanence (14)—as one in which each of us finds ourselves questionable in the sense that *all* positions ought to recognize their inability to suture shut the uncertainties from which none in modernity are rightly released. A hero, for Taylor, in this regard is William James, who lived with unsurpassably exposed honesty and lucidity in that cross-pressured realm between immanence and transcendence: "that open space where you can feel the winds pulling you, now to belief, now to unbelief . . . [which] requires that you . . . can actually feel some of the force of each opposing position" (549).[10]

10. For Taylor's extended reflections on James, see his *Varieties of Religion Today*. Taylor characterizes James as "our great philosopher of the cusp. He tells us more than anyone else about what it's like to stand in the open space and feel the winds pulling you now here, and now there" (59). Hauerwas shares Taylor's admiration for James. See his *With the Grain of the Universe*. In *Varieties of Religion Today*, Taylor criticizes James for his inability to accommodate the phenomenon of collective religious life and, in particular, his deaf ear for the Catholic understanding of the church as a sacramental communion (24). We are sympathetic with Taylor's critique of James but worry that such an understanding of the church plays so little role in shaping the narrative

The second of Taylor's interventions is to show that the question of transcendence endlessly reasserts itself not because transcendence is somehow self-evident, but because claims for closed immanence are at once so uncompelling, so contestable, so unsatisfying, so hubristic, and in a sense so *uninteresting* when shed of unwarranted pretense. What many proponents of immanence view as a coming to adulthood, Taylor reads as childish bravado; where there are assertions of heroic generosity beyond return, Taylor sees an impoverished view of human relationships lacking a rich account of mutuality; where the immanentist sees a path beyond mortification, Taylor sees a host of disciplinary pressures and fewer sources to resist them. The heroes of immanent closure—it turns out—are in cowardly denial of the fragility of their own positions.[11]

Taylor is, of course, fluent with the violence that has been wrought across the ages by many articulations and lived expressions of transcendent faith, and his intention is not to call us back to a time when all was well. Proponents of Christian transcendence have often wrought and justified violence against those identified as beyond the "external boundary of God's people" (669)—thus perversely transforming Christ's incarnation of love into horrifying form of closed immanence-justified-in-the-name-of-transcendence.

Taylor says his point is rather to show that proponents on all sides are throwing "huger rocks . . . than are safe for dwellers in glass houses" (635), and "both sides need a good dose of humility" concerning how "fragile" their positions are and how deeply each is implicated in histories of violence (675). Rather than seeking a final word (a violent quest, at any rate) the question ought to be, "who can respond most

---

of *A Secular Age*. You need transcendence when you do not have a people who are an alternative immanence to the immanence of the world.

11. Steven Weinberg ends his a lovely essay, "Without God," explaining why he cannot believe in God with the confession, "Living without God isn't easy. But its very difficulty offers one other consolation—that there is a certain honor, or perhaps just a grim satisfaction, in facing up to our condition without despair and without wishful thinking—with good humor, but without God." "Without God," 76. We have no reason to question Weinberg's sentiment that he finds it hard to live without God, but it never seems to occur to those who express such a difficulty that it is by no means easy to live with God. The idea that somehow believing in God makes it all make sense cannot be had by anyone that has been shaped by the Psalms. One of the great virtues of Taylor's book is how he helps us see that atheism may not be all that interesting.

profoundly and convincingly to what are ultimately commonly felt dilemmas?" (675). The most compelling path, for Taylor, is to work to "tikkun olam," or "heal the world," bit by small bit—and to free such efforts from the exclusionary moves that so often insinuate themselves into both Christian and humanist responses to the world's suffering. Key to such efforts—pointing beyond the politics of horizontal territorial scarcity—is the virtue of forgiveness and the ever-renewed pursuit of reconciliation beyond "fairness" envisioned in a vertical dimension: "The vertical space opens the possibility that by rising higher you'll accede to a new horizontal space where the resolution will be less painful/damaging for both parties. . . . Christian faith can never be decanted into a fixed code. Because it always places our actions in two dimensions, one of right action, and also an eschatological dimension."

The eschatological dimension calls us to pursue hitherto unacknowledged abundance in the face of scarcity: "Christ is constantly doing that in the Gospel" (707). And Taylor's twentieth-century exemplar is Ivan Illich, who always called Christians to search beyond whatever codes (even universalistic codes) encapsulated their reading of the gospel, and toward a sense that the vital core of Jesus' parable of the Good Samaritan is the *movement*, the *response* called for by the other, that moves the self in "friendship/love/charity" beyond the bounds of the "we" that had defined and circumscribed the right, the good, the holy. It is this *moving healing* that surpasses the unnecessary scarcities embedded in any code and "creates links across boundaries, on the basis of a mutual fittingness which is not based on kinship but on the kind of love which God has for us, which we call agape" (739). To cultivate this movement of the agape network—in resistance to protective demonizing stances, on the one hand, and the lazy idolatrous relationship to rules, on the other—is the call that animates a creative and charitable relation to plurality. In a conversation across the differences of Christian tradition—the Communion of Saints—Taylor sees the possibility of a generative abundance that is not only compelling on its own terms, but is also likely to become more and more attractive in comparative terms if his prediction is right: "this heavy concentration of the atmosphere of immanence will intensify a sense of living in a 'waste land' for subsequent generations . . ." (770). One of the tasks for all of us to be sure, but especially poets, is to use language "as an event with a performative force, words which open up contact, make something manifest for the first time."

> [This] has an objective side: something language-transcendent is manifested, set free. But it also has an inescapably subjective aspect. This reality is made manifest to us, who speak this language, have this sensibility, have been prepared by previous speech or experience. So this new word resonates in/for us: that the word reveals what it does is ALSO a fact about us, even though it is more than this. It *could* in principle eventually resonate for everyone, but only because they will have been inducted into the language and human meanings within which it can resonate. . . . [M]odern poetry doesn't rely on already recognized structures. It opens new paths, "sets free" new realities, but only for those for whom it resonates. (758)

This resonance, in turn, requires that the poet works with constellations of meanings, contexts, and inter-textual historical legacies of meaning. No one, on Taylor's reading, does this more powerfully than Hopkins. And with this point we are inclined to agree.

Hopkins however—to whom we now return in order to evoke resonances that tilt our inquiry in directions that begin to diverge from Taylor's at this juncture—was a profoundly *liturgical* human being—both as priest and as a practiced witness of the natural world. He conscientiously forged a *body politics* that made possible and enhanced the resonances he thought were highest. We are moved both by the heights he set free in poems like "Windhover" and the "Wreck of the Deutschland," as well as by the heights he reaches in the homoerotic love he penned about Dolben, about which Hopkins himself was profoundly uneasy—at best.[12]

As Taylor notes, Hopkins's poetry was deeply infused with a sense of what he called "instress," "the inner tension by which a thing maintains its proper form"—its "inscape" or particular "thisness." Instress and inscape both *are* in a being's relation to God, as are we, and "this means that we discern the particularity that God has chosen for us, and ratify it, choose it in our turn" (763–64). At the heart of human particularities that seek their proper relationship with God is the desire and practice of participating in God's love. And as Taylor puts it most

---

12. Ron Hansen's recent novel, *Exiles*, is a loving portrayal of Hopkins and the significance of "The Wreck of the Deutschland" for his returning to poetry.

profoundly: "What is striking is the way Hopkins brings to the fore once again the deep connection between this *telos* of communion and a recognition of the particular in all its specificity" (764). This is not easy, for as Hopkins puts it, "Each in his own imagining; sets up a shadow in thy seat" (765). He spent no small part of his life sensing not only the proximity of God in specificities, but also his painful distance in the shadows of imagining, crying out: "Mine, O thou Lord of life, send my roots rain" (764).

We note that Jesus too cries out, "I am thirsty" (John 19:28b), and he does so as a constitutive expression of his most radical liturgy: bearing his cross. In thirst we seek communion in the radically specific situations of our lives that exceed even our most penetrating anticipations. Which is to say that the Holy is so *incarnate*, so *immanent*, that it *is* only in becoming—only as *incarnating, thirsting. This is God's love.*

Taylor would not disagree, but let us venture some differences signaled in the intonational deviance of our italics. "Send my roots rain" suggests to us two things: *First*, thirst is not simply privative but also constitutive of communion. This means that radical *incarnating* is the essence of God such that we should not only italicize Taylor's acknowledgment, concerning "how problematic are the distinctions between . . . transcendence/immanence" (632), but infuse it more deeply, thoroughly, and persistently into the construction of patterns of resistance and alternative to the closed frames of *both* immanence *and* transcendence that Taylor identifies. Even as Taylor illuminates, we think as, we suggested above, that he reifies and overplays these terms and their distinctions in the way he deploys the "immanent frame."

What this means concretely is that the daily liturgical work of the likes of Jean Vanier, Ella Baker, Robert Moses, Martin Luther King Jr., Rowan Williams, John Howard Yoder, and Ernesto Cortés deserves to be at the heart of our search for paths beyond the impasses and closures of this secular age. With Hopkins, their sense is for the daily practices and rituals that are the lifeblood of incarnating *caritas* and *agape*. It is in the dense and difficult practices of learning to tend to the radical complexities of the ordinary that we become bodies that can express and perhaps more importantly *resonate* such that we can receive a higher glory than the flattened world of Constantinism and neo-Constantinianism would allow us to hear and engage.

It is in the seriousness of the difficult yet joyous good work of incarnating that happens in L'Arche communities and Beloved Communities of radical democratic struggle, that the secure handles of "transcendence" and "immanence" might give way and allow us—beyond the detrimental closures of each as well as the insidious collusions of both together—to open in vulnerable ways to the unwonted lessons we need to learn in order to love our neighbors. We suspect that much of the most important learning we must do at this historical juncture will happen precisely in relations where "immanence" and "transcendence" become intertwined and confused in ways that allow us to hear, discern, and become communities beyond the legacies of damage that tend to adhere to each. Our texts must increasingly call us to and prepare us for these intertwinements and—we think—helpful confusions. Even the words of a Hopkins will fall flat as they enter the bodies of those not thus engaged. Beyond the buffered selves and communities too often produced by attachments to the abstractions of "immanence" and "transcendence," we need traditions of body practices *thirsting for the unimaginable*. Cross and resurrection.

Second, if thirst is constitutive of our capacity to engage in the liturgical work through which we might learn to receive and give friendship and love, then it is crucial to re-read the parable of the Good Samaritan in ways that exceed the work Taylor does when he reads with Ivan Illich. Illich, recall, evokes the "incarnation extending outward" toward the Good Samaritan, as evidence of the expanding network of *agape* and the search for abundant possibilities beyond the horizontal planes of contestation. Yet we see something deeper in this parable that is a too-often overlooked condition of this vital possibility. When the legal scholar asks Jesus "and who is my neighbor?" Jesus isn't just responding "the outsider, too." Rather he teaches that Jews and Christians might well often *learn* the very meaning of the word and practice of neighborliness *from the outsider*. It is the Samaritan in Luke 10 who informs not just love beyond the law, but the very meaning and practice of love. Thus, the movement of love is not just a giving but a receiving in which love discovers what it is to become from the other—it always becomes at the vulnerable border—in the strange and difficult twists of thirsting when and where we may be least ready to do so.

From this we might draw a few important insights. First, this theme is not absent in Taylor's story, but it is underplayed in ways that perhaps contribute to ways in which he is insufficiently attentive and receptive to the "Good Samaritans" who surround him. Hence, we would suggest that Taylor's critical analytical framework—"the immanent frame"—itself conceals the more fruitful possibilities and lessons that are at work in some theoretical and practical articulations of what Taylor lumps together as "immanence." While many of his critiques are illuminating, they systematically conceal or avoid altogether the richer articulations in theorists like Merleau-Ponty, Foucault, Adorno, Derrida, and many others from which he might learn not only a greater appreciation of that which lies beyond the pressures of his own buffered closures (including the strong line between immanence and transcendence), but also, perhaps, more about the movement of love and neighborliness.[13]

Second, the richest articulations of Christian practice have themselves sought to give an account of God, Christ, and church in ways that exemplify precisely the vulnerable receptivity that is at the heart of the gospel in ways that are consonant with but significantly extend Taylor's Illich-inspired readings. We find it quite odd in this respect that Taylor does not engage the lives and work of Karl Barth or Dietrich Bonhoeffer. Barth and Bonhoeffer, the most christological theologians of modernity, saw earlier and more clearly than most how the eruption of transcendence exemplified by the Nazis was idolatry. They were able to do so not because they thought maintaining some account of transcendence was at stake, but because they saw that the "immanent one," Jesus of Nazareth, was being denied by the refusal to let him be preached to those to whom he had been sent.

Third, nevertheless most of human history is teeming with articulations and practices of those who are far from what we take to be the richest. And this is certainly true of much Christianity and much radical democracy in America, where many dominant articulations of each are both blind and reinforce the closures of the other. Christianity in America has too often taken accommodationist and Constantinian forms; as secular democracy has accommodated itself to the neo-Constantinian rule of exchange value and corporate markets. The recent work of Sheldon Wolin and William Connolly shows ways in which Constantinianism and neo-Constantinian neoliberalism—or "transcendence" and "immanence"—work together in ways that multiply the

---

13. There is not space to defend this assertion here. Coles has sought to explore such possibilities in 1992, 1997, 2005, and 2007.

forces and violence of each. In a world in which we are, as Yoder says, not just "fallible" but "peccable in fact," it may paradoxically be the case that cultivating some of the most important wealth of each tradition hinges precisely on each's capacity to vulnerably and imaginatively engage the other. It may be at the complexity of this border between radical ecclesia and radical democracy that each might renew and radically reform itself beyond the abstractions that are making each go blind and deaf.

At a recent conference hosted by the Interfaith Educational Network (an organization that regularly gathers hundreds of grassroots organizers and leaders to discuss with scholars works that the organizers find interesting) we had the privilege to discuss *Christianity, Democracy, and the Radical Ordinary* with people trying to engage in radical democracy and radical ecclesia in dozens of communities in the United States. One of the things that was particularly striking in these conversations was the extent to which, in radical organizing efforts, Christianity (and Judaism, Islam, etc.) and radical democracy seem repeatedly to prod and provoke each other beyond the failings of each. In this largely faith-based network, people from a variety of faith traditions have—in the context of anemic democracy—inspired, informed, and engaged the work of rebuilding daily practices of forming radical democratic communities struggling to tend to common goods across treacherous divides. This work is consonant with and inspired by many grassroots movements and organizing efforts that throughout U.S. history have often been led by people whose visions and practices were deeply churched or templed. Yet at the same time we heard many people express a disillusionment with their institutions of faith: people saying, "I leaned far more about church in IAF democratic organizing than I ever did in my own church" and "This democratic organizing is now helping the church be the church." These strange relations of indebtedness are, too, consonant with the history of many grassroots movements and organizing efforts throughout U.S. history—from Wendell Phillips who was thrown out of churches in which he tried to discuss abolitionist ideals, to organizers in the civil rights movement in the early 1960s who were frustrated by the timidity and complacency of many churches and pastors in towns throughout Mississippi. It thus appears that agonistic—and even *antagonistic*—indebtedness has been an integral aspect of many of the reformations in which radical ecclesia and radical democracy have in the past couple centuries renewed what we take to be most promising about each. At this level of practiced engagement, a transcendence that is not "transcendence" and an immanence that is not "immanence" might provoke the ethical-political work in the vertical dimension that Taylor rightly calls us to pursue. Yet this is more likely if we recognize how confused these categories have become at the richest moments of our recent history—if we retrospectively story and acknowledge this intertwinement in ways that cultivate a greater readiness for such in the future, and if we rework our philosophical performances in ways that encourage us to do so as well.

Failure in this regard will likely perpetuate the current course of things—in which Constantinian Christainity (transcendence) and neo-Constantinian democracy (immanence) are collaborating in ways that are propelling the world toward certain hell. Yet there is the possibility of a ladder—or ladders—that might ascend in better directions if the traditions of radical ecclesia and radical democracy each dispossess themselves of the idea that they must be the sole author of each and every rung. This is not an easy or a comfortable ladder to climb. For beneath every rung there is a long way to fall and a tragic history of falling. Reliance on a ladder where some of the rungs have been built significantly by others is dangerous to be sure. Yet there are also these strange histories of ascent. And the ethical and political question at each moment, as Foucault said, is "where are the greatest dangers?" In our views, the radical reformations that are likely to discern paths that avoid the greatest dangers, and perhaps articulate some of the greatest possibilities, are most likely to be found in traditions that discern within their own radicality sources for the vulnerable and receptive work with strange others that is at the heart of any relationships worthy of the name "political friendship." Taylor has advanced our understanding of some of the closures that stand in the way of the good work of such relationships. Beyond the categories of his text we seek to continue to pursue paths—and other rungs—that disclose hopeful alternatives to this secular age. Resonating at the heart of any such endeavors we suspect we will hear something akin to Hopkins's cry: 'O let them be left, wildness and wet; Long live the weeds and the wilderness yet."

16

H. Richard Niebuhr

Introduction

H. Richard Niebuhr's fate is to be known as the "not as well known" brother of Reinhold Niebuhr. H. Richard Niebuhr often stressed the fated character of our lives, that is, that whatever religious or ethical convictions may shape our lives we cannot escape the history in which we find ourselves.[1] Even though Reinhold remains the better known of the brothers, I think it fair to say that H. Richard's influence on recent theology has been deeper and more widespread than that of his brother. For example, the current theological developments associated with the so-called "Yale school" of theology is better understood against the background of H. Richard Niebuhr's work. H. Richard no doubt would have thought Hans Frei's work too influenced by Karl Barth, but the influence of Barth on Frei was at least partly the result of what Frei had learned from H. Richard Niebuhr.[2] Niebuhr's analysis of the "responsible self," moreover, provided the background necessary for the recovery of the importance of the virtues for any account of the moral

---

1. Niebuhr, *Responsible Self*, 112.

2. Hans Frei wrote two very important articles on Niebuhr. The first article was for Niebuhr's festschrift, but was therefore early in Frei's academic work. The second article was the last thing Frei wrote before he died. Indeed he died before he was able to read the paper at a conference on Niebuhr at Harvard. See Frei, "Niebuhr's Theological Background," 9–118; and "H. Richard Niebuhr on History," 1–23.

life. Niebuhr also anticipated the focus on "narrative" and the correlative understanding of the storied character of the church in Christian theology and ethics.

H. Richard Niebuhr was born in Wright City, Missouri, in 1884 two years after Reinhold had been born.[3] Their father, Gustav Niebuhr, was a pastor in the German Evangelical Synod. Not only was German the first language Reinhold and H. Richard learned, but they were also introduced to their father's critical reception of German theological figures such as Harnack. H. Richard followed Reinhold's educational path, going to Elmhurst College (1908–1912) and then on to Eden Theological Seminary (1912–1915) in Saint Louis. These were the denominational schools of the Evangelical Synod whose primary purpose was to train young men for the ministry. H. Richard Niebuhr was accordingly ordained in 1916 to be the minister of Walnut Park Evangelical Church in Saint Louis.

In contrast to the frantic pace of Reinhold's life, H. Richard's life was that of a teacher. He was called back to teach at Eden in 1919, but in 1922 he left to do graduate work at Yale Divinity School. However before going to Yale he completed an M.A. at Washington University in Saint Louis in German writing on the German poet, Richard Dehmel. He also took courses at Union Theological Seminary as well as the University of Chicago. His work at Chicago with G. H. Mead, the pragmatist philosopher and social psychologist, was particularly important as Mead's influence on Niebuhr is apparent from the beginning to the end of Niebuhr's work. He went to Yale Divinity School in 1922 where he received both his B.D. and Ph.D. in 1924. After finishing his degrees at Yale, he became president of Elmhurst College until 1927 when he became the academic dean at Eden Seminary. Returning from a sabbatical to Germany in 1930, he received an invitation to teach at Yale Divinity School where he taught until his retirement and death in 1962.

During his life H. Richard Niebuhr published "only" six books, but his influence on American theology was immense. He became the teacher of teachers who would determine the main directions in theology and ethics in the second half of the twentieth century. Waldo Beach, Paul Ramsey, and James Gustafson were his students in Christian ethics, but Niebuhr also had a lasting influence on Gordon Kaufman, Van

---

3. Diefenthaler's *H. Richard Niebuhr* provides the best overview of Niebuhr's life we have.

Harvey, as well as his son, Richard Reinhold Niebuhr. A continuing theme in Niebuhr's work is his criticism of what he called the ethics of defense or survival, which attempts to protect ourselves against the threat of the other by defending the status quo. His teaching reflected his determination not to protect himself, his students, the church, or theology from criticism. As a result students, whether those he actually taught or those he taught through his writing, seemed to sense that here was a man and his work that could be trusted to think hard and honestly about God and our relationship to God. Whatever the questions one may have about Niebuhr's "orthodoxy," and I shall certainly raise questions about Niebuhr's understanding of the Trinity, it is undeniable that in his person as well as in his work Niebuhr was a God-intoxicated man.

Background and Development

Niebuhr wrote his dissertation on the philosophical theology of Ernst Troeltsch.[4] To understand Niebuhr's project, it is important to note that Niebuhr was primarily interested in Troeltsch's attempt to provide a response to historicism. In the "Acknowledgments" that prefaced Niebuhr's most famous book, *Christ and Culture*, Niebuhr observes his book attempts to do no more than supplement and correct Troeltsch's *The Social Teachings of the Christian Churches*. Yet Niebuhr is not really interested in correcting *The Social Teachings*, other than providing a more supple typology. Rather, Niebuhr observes Troeltsch taught him to respect "the multiformity and individuality of men and movements in Christian history, to be loath to force this rich variety into prefashioned, conceptual molds, and yet to seek *logos* in *mythos*, reason in history, essence in existence."[5] According to Niebuhr, Troeltsch helped him to accept the relativity not only of historical objects but, even more importantly, the relativity of the historical subject, the observer, and interpreter. Niebuhr notes if he does "correct" Troeltsch it is only because he tries to understand "historical relativism in the light of theological and theo-centric relativism." He does so because all attempts to absolu-

4. Niebuhr, *Ernst Troeltsch's Philosophy of Religion*.
5. Niebuhr, *Christ and Culture*, xii.

tize the finite is an aberration of faith as well as reason and a denial of the governance of the absolute God.[6]

This claim for God's absolute sovereignty is the heart of Niebuhr's life and work. His rejection of any ethic that tempts us to live and think defensively is but a correlative of his insistence that "radical monotheism" is the determinative characteristic of the Christian faith. When Christians fail to acknowledge God's absolute sovereignty they sinfully accommodate the church to the world. Such an accommodation was the subject of Niebuhr's biting critique in his first book, *The Social Sources of Denominationalism*. In fact Niebuhr's critique of how the church in America was determined by economic class and nationalism in many ways provided the necessary background for his discovery of the significance of God's sovereignty. *The Social Sources of Denominationalism*, however, was a book shaped by categories that reflected the influence of the Social Gospel movement. For example, Niebuhr asserted in *The Social Sources of Denominationalism* that the purpose of Christianity is not the establishment of an ecclesiastical institution or the proclamation of a metaphysical creed, but its "purpose is the revelation to men of their potential childhood to the Father and their possible brotherhood with each other."[7]

Just prior to the publication of *The Social Sources of Denominationalism*, Niebuhr had published an article in *The Christian Century* entitled "Back to Benedict?" There he argued that Protestantism had grown so sick with its bargain with nationalism and the failure to apply Christian principles to business that the only alternative was to recover the virtues of monasticism.[8] Niebuhr certainly developed a more mature theological position, but his emphasis on God's sovereignty did not mean he became less concerned about the accommodation of the church to the world. Indeed in the famous exchange between H. Richard and Reinhold concerning how the United States should respond to the Japanese invasion of Manchuria in 1931, H. Richard argued that the "nothing" Christians should do in the face of such aggression is not quietism. Rather Christians "can build cells of those

6. Ibid., xii.

7. Niebuhr, *Social Sources of Denominationalism*, 278. The original publishing date was 1927. Niebuhr does say in the same passage that Christianity does seek "the formation of a divine society and presupposes the metaphysics of a Christlike God."

8. Niebuhr, "Back to Benedict?," 860–61.

within each nation who, divorcing themselves from the program of nationalism and of capitalism, unite in a higher loyalty which transcends national and class lines of division and prepare for the future. There is no such Christian international today because radical Christianity has not yet arrived as yet at a program and a philosophy of history, but such cells are forming."[9]

The book that not only established H. Richard Niebuhr as a force in American theology as well as reflecting his mature position was *The Kingdom of God in America*.[10] Niebuhr, drawing on what he had learned from Troeltsch, argues that there can be no easy separation of theology from history particularly if we are to understand American culture. Accordingly, Niebuhr argues that America represents the experiment in constructive Protestantism originating with the Puritan acknowledgment of God's sovereignty, which was, through developments in the eighteenth century, transformed into the belief that Christ's kingdom could be realized on earth. The Social Gospel became the exemplification of the domestication of God's sovereignty that finally resulted in the secularization of Christianity. Niebuhr characterized this development with the observation that the final result was "a God without wrath brought men without sin into a kingdom without judgment through the ministrations of a Christ without a cross."[11]

Niebuhr's stress on God's sovereignty as well as his criticism of liberal Christianity in *The Kingdom of God in America* seemed to put him on the side of the ill-defined "neo-orthodox" developments in theology. This impression was only strengthened by his claim in the "Preface" to his book *The Meaning of Revelation* that he was attempting to combine the critical thought of Troeltsch with the constructive work of Karl Barth.[12] In *The Meaning of Revelation*, Niebuhr argued that "revelation cannot mean history, if it also means God."[13] Yet Christian theology

---

9. Niebuhr, "The Grace of Doing Nothing," 10, in *War in the Twentieth Century*, edited by Richard Miller. Miller's book also includes Reinhold's response to his brother as well as H. Richard's reply.

10. Niebuhr, *Kingdom of God in America*. The book was originally published in 1937.

11. Ibid., 193.

12. H. Richard Niebuhr, *Meaning of Revelation*, xi. The book was originally published in 1941.

13. Ibid., 40.

has no way to think about God other than through our existence as historic and communal beings. At best, therefore, Christian theology cannot aspire to be anything more than confessional, that is, the self-critical exercise by which faith seeks to understand itself. According to Niebuhr, therefore, revelation names the special occasion by which images or symbols are provided that make it possible for communities and individuals to tell an intelligible story about their lives. Such a unity is the "inner history" that faith and repentance—that is, the confession of sin—makes possible.

The tensions entailed by Niebuhr's attempt to combine Troeltsch and Barth make *The Meaning of Revelation* an extraordinarily interesting and suggestive book. However, Niebuhr became increasingly critical of what he characterized, no doubt with Barth in mind, as Christomonism. In the final chapter of *The Meaning of Revelation*, Niebuhr draws out the implication of his claim that revelation cannot mean history if it means God with the declaration that revelation must point to that which is more certain than Jesus.[14] In the collection of his essays, *Radical Monotheism and Western Culture*, Niebuhr clearly draws out the implications of his understanding of radical monotheism, observing, "we may use the theological word 'incarnation' in speaking of the coming of radically monotheistic faith into our history, meaning by it the concrete expression in a total human life of radical trust in the One and of universal loyalty to the realm of being."[15] Therefore from Niebuhr's perspective Christians do not so much place their faith in Jesus Christ, but rather they model their faith on the radical monotheistic faith of Christ. Accordingly, he criticizes liberal theologies that make love the primary attribute of Jesus' life, noting that "it was not love but God that filled his soul."[16]

H. Richard Niebuhr's "Ethics"

H. Richard Niebuhr is usually regarded as one of—if not the—most important Christian ethicists of the second half of the twentieth cen-

---

14. Ibid., 111.

15. Niebuhr, *Radical Monotheism*, 40. The book was originally published in 1943.

16. Niebuhr, *Christ and Culture*, 19.

tury.[17] Niebuhr's work, however, defies any strong distinction between theology and ethics. His theology shaped how he thought about the moral life and how he thought about the moral life was reflected in his theology. That his theology so determined his work is not always obvious. For example, most readers of his book *Christ and Culture* accept Niebuhr's claim in the last chapter of the book, "A 'Concluding Unscientific Postscript,'" that it would be a mistake to regard any one of the "types"—Christ against culture, Christ of culture, Christ above culture, Christ and culture in paradox, Christ the transformer of culture—as the "Christian answer."[18] To do so would, as James Gustafson insists, mistakenly turn the typological method Niebuhr had learned from Weber and Troeltsch into normative recommendation.[19] Yet as John Howard Yoder has argued, the very way Niebuhr describes the alleged "Enduring Problem" between Christ and culture presupposes Niebuhr's understanding of Christ as the embodiment of radical monotheistic faith that relativizes all cultural achievements.[20]

There is no question, however, that *Christ and Culture* became the framework by which various ethical alternatives were evaluated. Niebuhr may have genuinely believed that the five types were each authentic expressions of the social implications of the gospel, but "Christ the transformer of culture" was assumed by most readers of the book to be the most attractive position. That Niebuhr did not end his chapter on "Christ the Transformer" by criticizing it, as he had in his discussion of the other types, provides some warrant for the assumption by many that Niebuhr was in fact recommending the "transforming" type.

Niebuhr's criticisms of the other types is extremely interesting because his criticisms expose his understanding of the Trinity. Niebuhr often made reference to the Trinity, but he seldom used the language of Father, Son, and Holy Spirit. For Niebuhr, the Trinity is used to refer to God as creator, governor, and redeemer. Accordingly, he criticized representatives of the "Christ against culture" type (Tertullian, Tolstoy, and Mennonites) for failing to acknowledge that God is not only the redeemer, but God also is the creator. Niebuhr, therefore, argued rep-

17. For an extremely informative account of Niebuhr's influence for the development of Christian theology and ethics, see Werpehowski, *American Protestant Ethics*.

18. Niebuhr, *Christ and Culture*, 232.

19. Gustafson, "Preface," xiii–xxxv.

20. Yoder, "How H. Richard Niebuhr Reasoned," 31–89.

resentatives of the "against culture" type fail to give an account of the social and political institutions that make life possible.[21]

Although *Christ and Culture* obviously focuses on "Christ," Niebuhr maintained throughout his life and work a strong emphasis on the significance of the church. He assumed, with Troeltsch, that the sociological character of the church is the crucial indicator for understanding the content and shape of theological convictions. Accordingly, in stark contrast with Reinhold Niebuhr, H. Richard Niebuhr often directed his attention to what the church should be and do if it was to be faithful to its calling. In 1954 Niebuhr directed, along with Daniel Day Williams and James Gustafson, a major study of theological education in North America. His book *The Purpose of the Church and Its Ministry* is the outgrowth of that study. According to Niebuhr, the church's task is nothing less than the "increase among men of the love of God and neighbor."[22] Niebuhr elaborates that purpose in one of the great passages on love in contemporary theology, noting that by "love" he means the ability to rejoice in the sheer presence of the beloved, to give thanks for the presence of the beloved without seeking equality, to revere the beloved by keeping our distance even as we draw near, and in a loyalty that may well let the self be destroyed rather than for the beloved to cease to be.[23]

Niebuhr's most important book, *The Responsible Self: An Essay in Christian Moral Philosophy*, was published posthumously.[24] We can have confidence, however, that the book reflects Niebuhr's most developed position because it not only comprises the lectures he gave in the first part of his Christian ethics course he taught for many years at Yale, but also is comprised of the Robertson Lectures he gave at Glasgow in 1960 and the Earl Lectures at the Pacific School of Religion in 1962. The dominant motifs of his previous work, moreover, not only continue to be present in *The Responsible Self*, but their systematic development in this book makes clear how Niebuhr understood how "it all fits together."

Niebuhr describes *The Responsible Self* as a work in Christian moral philosophy. By that he means no more than the book should

21. Ibid., 76–82.

22. Niebuhr, *Purpose of the Church*, 31.

23. Ibid., 35. Josiah Royce, and in particular Royce's account of loyalty, was a decisive influence on Niebuhr.

24. Niebuhr, *Responsible Self*.

be read as one written by a Christian who seeks "to understand the mode of his existence and that of his fellow human beings as human agents."[25] Accordingly Niebuhr's primary purpose in *The Responsible Self* is to provide a phenomenology of our moral experience that not only does justice to the character of our lives but also to the character of our relationship with God. He argues that the image of "man the responder" more adequately reflects who we are as human beings as well as Christians than the images of man the citizen or man the maker. Those who consistently think of man the maker subordinate the giving of laws to that of goals in the future whereas those who think of our existence with the aid of the image of the citizen subordinate the good to the right.[26] Each of these images have corresponding accounts of God as the giver of the law or the One good to which all other goods are to be judged.

In contrast, the image of responsibility focuses our attention not by asking, "What does the law require?" or "What is the good to be done?" but rather asks, "What is going on?" Niebuhr argues as a result the image of man the responder more adequately helps comprehend that we are more than what happens to us, what we suffer, than what we do. From such a perspective ethics is not so much about helping us to discern what should and should not be done, as it is an exercise in understanding. To understand our lives as responders is to see ourselves as agents who exist in response to other agents in accordance with our interpretation of their actions in anticipation of their response to our response and all of this as part of a continuing community of agents.[27] The narrative character of our existence is unavoidable once we understand our lives from the perspective of responsibility. For to be responsible we do not ask what is the good or the right, but rather what is the fitting. The fitting is determined by the ongoing narratives that shape the patterns of interpretation in which we find ourselves.

Having developed the typology of man the citizen, maker, and responder, Niebuhr then tests the adequacy of each in relation to the

25. Ibid., 42.

26. Ibid., 55.

27. Ibid., 65. Niebuhr credits G. H. Mead's continuing influence for shaping this understanding of responsibility, but he also credits Adam Smith's understanding of the "impartial spectator" for helping him understand that moral reflection necessarily pulls us toward a universal point of view.

self in society, in time and history, in absolute dependence, and finally in relation to sin and salvation. The first two images, Niebuhr suggests, fail to do justice to the social character of our existence, nor can the images of man the citizen or maker account for our being in time or, more importantly, how time is in us. Moreover ethics shaped by the images of citizen and maker tempt us to deny our dependency in an effort to be our own creation. As a result we find ourselves unable to trust our existence, forcing us to live defensively, fearing the chaos that seems to make it impossible to live coherent lives.

The image of responsibility, however, does not make our attempts to live morally coherent lives easier, but rather once we understand the responsive character of our lives we can see clearly why living responsibly is so difficult. Niebuhr asks: "How is it possible to be *one* self in the multiplicity of events and of one's interpretations of them? How does the self as such become responsible instead of remaining a concatenation of responsive systems, fitting their actions now into this, now into that series of events?"[28] What ties all these responsibilities together so that there is a responsible *self* amid the many roles we may inhabit? Niebuhr answers these questions by returning to his claim in *The Meaning of Revelation*, that is, "To be a self is to have a god; to have a god is to have a history, that is, events connected in a meaningful pattern; to have one god is to have one history. God and the history of selves in community belong together in inseparable union."[29] To be responsible, therefore, requires that we affirm: "God is acting in all actions upon you. So respond to all actions upon you as to respond to his actions."[30]

Niebuhr was well aware that to respond to all actions on us as God's action is as frightening as it is necessary. It should never be forgotten that the Niebuhr who wrote *The Responsible Self* is the same Niebuhr who wrote essays entitled "War as the Judgment of God" and "War as Crucifixion" during WWII.[31] For Niebuhr, therefore, the great moral challenge is how to live, particularly in the face of death, in a manner that we will be delivered from the deep distrust of the One in the many that tempts us to interpret all that happens to us as issuing from

28. Ibid., 121.

29. Niebuhr, *Meaning of Revelation*, 59.

30. Ibid., 126.

31. Both essays can be found in *War and the Twentieth Century*, 47–55 and 63–70.

animosity willing little else than our destruction. Christians believe that in the figure of Jesus Christ they have found the assurance that makes possible "the reinterpretation of all our interpretations of life and death. Death no less than life appears to us as an act of mercy, not of mercy to us only, but in the great vicariousness of responsive and responsible existence, as mercy to those in whom, with whom, and for whom we live."[32]

Niebuhr's "ethics" is bound to leave dissatisfied any who think ethics should provide guidance about what they should do in this or that circumstance. According to James Gustafson, Niebuhr's favorite way of describing his work, a description borrowed from F. D. Maurice, was that of "digging."[33] Niebuhr did not seek to provide a comprehensive account of Christian ethics, but rather to provide a rich phenomenological account of human existence in order to spell out the implications of a radical monotheistic faith. At the end of *The Responsible Self*, Niebuhr observes he does not know whether to call the self-interpretation he thinks required if we are to live responsibly "Christian" or simply "human." Yet he is sure that, though Christians believe that the reinterpretation of existence has come into the world, it is equally the case that such a reinterpretation "is not confined to those who say, 'Lord, Lord,' nor even necessarily best represented by them."[34]

Coming to Terms with H. Richard Niebuhr

Niebuhr was not a polemical thinker, which makes those who criticize him appear less than charitable. He commended J. S. Mill's view that men were generally right in what they affirmed and wrong in what they denied.[35] However, I believe that John Howard Yoder is right in the criticism he makes of *Christ and Culture*. Indeed, I think Yoder's criticism are not only right about *Christ and Culture*, but apply to Niebuhr's overall position. For example, Yoder observes that the intention of the post-Nicene accounts of the Trinity was to deny what Niebuhr seems to want—that is, to deny that we receive different revelations from each

32. Ibid., 143–44.

33. Gustafson, "Introduction" to *Responsible Self*, 14.

34. Niebuhr, *Responsible Self*, 144.

35. Niebuhr, *Christ and Culture*, 238.

person of the Trinity.[36] Of course, Niebuhr can rightly respond that he feels under no obligation to adhere to Nicene orthodoxy, but then he needs to say why he thinks he can use and exploit Christian language without acknowledging any responsibility to the Christian tradition.

Yoder also criticizes Niebuhr for assuming a monolithic concept of culture, but Yoder observes that his account of culture is but the reflection of his account of Jesus as the exemplification of a radically monotheistic faith. Jesus, so understood, simply becomes an empty cipher to remind us never to place our faith in anything other than the One that makes the finite finite. Because Niebuhr assumes a monolithic account of culture, his criticism of the "Christ against culture" for allegedly denying the goodness of God's creation is but a truism. Yet as Yoder argues, the representatives Niebuhr names as exemplifications of the "Christ against culture" type never argued that culture must be accepted or rejected as a whole.[37] Yoder observes that Niebuhr seems to have forgotten in his early work he thought the church should be a sociological unit distinguishable from the rest of the society as well as constituting an option to the culture in which it finds itself.[38]

Though Yoder's criticism are directed to *Christ and Culture*, they are but an indication of the theological difficulty created by Niebuhr's account of "radical monotheism." For a position that centers on the absolute transcendence of God, Niebuhr's theology seems oddly enough to be primarily an anthropocentric account of why some understanding of faith is unavoidable.[39] To be sure, his phenomenological account of human existence can be quite suggestive, but it is by no means clear on what basis Niebuhr can provide a response to darker, alternative accounts of the human situation. Niebuhr often provided insightful assessments of other theological alternatives as well as of the work of theology in the modern university, but his account of divine transcen-

36. Yoder, "How H. Richard Niebuhr Reasoned," 62.

37. Ibid., 52–61.

38. Ibid., 75. In 1935, Niebuhr, along with Wilhelm Pauck and Francis Miller, wrote a book entitled *Church against the World*. The last chapter of the book was written by Niebuhr and entitled "Toward the Independence of the Church."

39. Niebuhr translated as well as wrote an appreciative "Introduction" to Paul Tillich's *Religious Situation*. Niebuhr's most extensive account of faith is to be found in a manuscripts found after his death by his son, Richard Reinhold Niebuhr. They are now published as *Faith on Earth*.

dence worked to qualify truth claims made on behalf of other alternatives with the effect of validating his own account of why all is relative.[40]

Yet I believe it would be a profound mistake for H. Richard
Niebuhr to be ignored or dismissed because he fits so uneasily in categories used to type theologians as liberal or conservative. Niebuhr
struggled to find the theological expression that could help Christian
and non-Christian alike not to be determined by the temptation to live
defensively. Niebuhr was convinced that we should lives of trust and
openness and he struggled mightily to help us see how we could so live.
We still have much to learn from his "digging."

40. Yoder, "How H. Richard Niebuhr Reasoned," 82. Some of Niebuhr's important
occasional essays on other theologians as well as American democracy have been published in *Theology, History, and Culture.*

17

The Virtues of Alasdair MacIntyre

Few dispute that Alasdair MacIntyre is one of the most important philosophers of our time. That reputation, however, does him little good. It is as though, quite apart from the man, there exists a figure called *Alasdair MacIntyre* whose position you know whether or not you have read him—and whose name has become a specter that haunts all attempts to provide constructive moral and political responses to the challenge of modernity.

The curious result is that MacIntyre's work is often dismissed as too extreme to be taken seriously. In fact, MacIntyre's work *is* extreme, but we live in extreme times. And though he is certainly critical of some of the developments associated with modernity, MacIntyre is also a constructive thinker who has sought to help us repair our lives by locating those forms of life that make possible moral excellence.

Born in Scotland in 1929, MacIntyre began teaching at Manchester University in 1951. He came to the United States in 1969 to teach at Brandeis University, and he has held in the years since a large number of academic appointments, including stints at Boston University, Wellesley, Vanderbilt, Yale, Duke, and Notre Dame. His books began with *Marxism: An Interpretation* in 1953 and have continued in a steady flow, including *The Unconscious: A Conceptual Analysis* in 1958, *A Short History of Ethics* in 1966, *Herbert Marcuse: An Exposition and a Polemic* in 1970, *After Virtue* in 1981, *Whose Justice? Which Rationality?*

in 1988, *Three Rival Versions of Moral Enquiry* in 1990, *Dependent Rational Animals* in 1999, and *Edith Stein* in 2005.

After Virtue remains MacIntyre's most widely discussed book, and a third edition has just been published in celebration of its twenty-fifth anniversary. We are also fortunate recently to have two volumes of his selected articles published by Cambridge University Press: *The Tasks of Philosophy* and *Ethics and Politics*. These essays are crucial for any assessment of MacIntyre's position: arguments and observations he makes in his books were often first developed in articles and defended later in other articles, not widely assessable.

The constructive character of MacIntyre's work is apparent in his understanding of the philosophical task. A philosopher, he insists, should try to express the concepts embedded in the practices of our lives in order to help us live morally worthy lives. The professionalization of philosophy into a technical field—what might be called the academic captivity of philosophy—reflects (and serves to legitimate) the compartmentalization of the advanced capitalistic social orders that produce our culture of experts, those strange creatures of authority in modernity.

General dismissals of MacIntyre too often rest on a fundamental failure to understand the interconnected character of his work. His criticisms of modernity are often thought to reflect a nostalgic and unjustified preference for the Middle Ages. MacIntyre sometimes cannot resist wickedly confirming his critics' mistaken views, but those who refuse to take MacIntyre seriously because they think him anti-modern fail to understand the fundamental philosophical arguments that shape his position. A focus on his accounts of action and practical reason reveals that his fundamental perspective has been remarkably consistent.

I am not a disinterested spectator when it comes to disputes surrounding MacIntyre, for I have been deeply influenced by him. Most commentators point to MacIntyre's influence on my work concerning the recovery of the virtues and corresponding criticism of modern moral philosophy, and it is true that I have learned much from MacIntyre's account of the virtues. But far more important for me is his work on the philosophy of action. I was fortunate to stumble on his early work on the philosophy of social science when I was writing my dissertation (subsequently published as *Character and the Christian Life*). As a result, I have always thought that the center of MacIntyre's work was his development of key arguments from Wittgenstein concerning the conditions necessary for our actions to be intelligible to others as well as ourselves.

To understand MacIntyre takes work. Indeed, he *intends* for it to be a daunting and challenging task to understand him. I suspect he assumes most of his readers, possessed as they must be by the reading habits of modernity, cannot help but refuse to do the work necessary to understand him. Which is but another way to say, as he makes explicit in the last chapter of *Whose Justice? Which Rationality?*, that those who think they must think for themselves will need to undergo a transformation amounting to a conversion if they are to understand "that it is only by participation in a rational practice-based community that one becomes rational."[1] MacIntyre provides a rich account of such a conversion in *Edith Stein* by a close analysis not only of Stein's conversion but also Rosenzweig's and Lukacs's conversions.

Moreover, the sheer range of MacIntyre's work is a challenge to anyone who would understand him. He is able not only to write in a scholarly and intelligent manner about Aristotle, Abelard, and Aquinas, but he is equally adept when he treats Freud, Lukacs, Weber, and Wittgenstein. I sometimes have the impression he has never forgotten anything he has read. Few know what MacIntyre knows, but to know MacIntyre it is often necessary to have to read what he has read. He seldom discusses a figure for no reason, but each philosopher, artist, and historical figure he examines becomes integral to the argument he is making.

He is equally at home in technical philosophy dealing with brain and mind questions as he is in political and social theory. That he is so adept is not just an indication of his mental power, but is integral to his understanding of philosophy he attributes to the influence of R. G. Collingwood. It was from Collingwood, as he indicates in the prologue to the third edition of *After Virtue*, that he came to recognize that "what historical enquiry discloses is the situatedness of all enquiry, the extent to which what are taken to be the standards of truth and of rational justification in the contexts of practice vary from one time to another."

MacIntyre has always been driven by a desire to repair our lives morally. Nowhere is his moral project more apparent than in a short essay in *Against the Self-Images of the Age*, originally published in 1971.

1. MacIntyre, *Whose Justice? Which Rationality?* 396.

There he identifies two groups of questions requiring further investigation after his analysis of the inadequacies of Marxism. The first involves the nature of moral judgment and the meaning of such key evaluative words as good, right, virtue, justice, duty, and happiness. He notes that Marxists share with conservative philosophers a disdain for concerns about the meaning of language, but he observes that it is exactly at the level of language that the moral inadequacies and corruptions of our age are evident.

The second group of questions he raises in the essay concern the explanation of human action: whether we can find reasons for actions in the modern world that would not only enable us to act effectively but also move us to act in a manner that who we are and what we do are of a piece. The pursuit of answers to these interrelated questions—answers, as he makes clear, that continue to be indebted to the Marxist analysis of the distorting effect of the economic, social, and cultural order of capitalism—is the animating heart of MacIntyre's subsequent work, including his illuminating account of Edith Stein. (In his *Aristotelian Philosophy: Ethics and Politics from Aristotle to MacIntyre*, Kelvin Knight provides the best account we have of MacIntyre's work and in particular the continuity between his early Marxism and later position.)

MacIntyre's work after *Against the Self-Images of the Age* forms the ongoing attempt to help us understand how it is that we now live lives we do not understand. He pursues that investigation by analysis of philosophical alternatives, because, as he says in *After Virtue*, key episodes in the history of philosophy were what fragmented and largely transformed morality. MacIntyre's respect for such philosophers as Kant and Mill reflect this understanding of the philosophical task. Their attempt to develop accounts of morality in the name of some impersonal standard was an understandable response to the loss of shared practices necessary for the discovery of goods in common. Such a project was doomed to failure, however, exactly because no such standards can be sustained when they are abstracted from the practices and descriptions that render our lives intelligible. Modern moral philosophy becomes part of the problem, for its stress on autonomy, like its corresponding attempt to free ethics from history, produces people incapable of living lives that have narrative coherence.

His 1966 book, *A Short History of Ethics*, was the first installment of MacIntyre's attempt to diagnose what had happened that makes our lives unintelligible to ourselves. But the 1981 *After Virtue* was the book in which his mature position received its most compelling presentation. In the preface to the second edition, MacIntyre says he will be able to overcome the mistakes he made in *A Short History of Ethics* only when he writes something called *A Very Long History of Ethics*. Yet many of his friends and colleagues suggest that is exactly what the bulk of his work comprises: *A Short History*, which led him to write *After Virtue*, only to retell the story again in *Whose Justice? Which Rationality?*, climaxing in *Three Rival Versions of Moral Inquiry*.

Each of these books contains wonderful new material, of course. I do not think, for example, the chapters on Plato and Aristotle in *Whose Justice? Which Rationality?* have been sufficiently appreciated. Yet there is some truth to the contention that the story the books tell remains similar. Like a great novelist, MacIntyre often goes over the same ground. But through the development of subplots and the introduction of new characters, the story he tells is thickened and made more complex.

If I am right about the trajectory of MacIntyre's work, the central contention in *After Virtue* is his remark that the "the concept of an intelligible action is a more fundamental concept than that of an action." This may seem a small philosophical point. But much revolves around it—his understanding of the centrality of practical reason, the significance of the body for agency, why the teleological character of our lives must be displayed through narrative, the traditioned character of rationality, the nature of the virtues, why training in a craft is paradigmatic of learning to think as well as live, his understanding of why the Enlightenment project had to fail, his particular way of being a historicist, and why the plain person is the necessary subject of philosophy.

The importance of MacIntyre's argument about intelligible action is suggested by the problems he must confront in order to sustain his case. For example, he has had to deal often and critically with issues surrounding the mind-body distinction, as well as those that assume a strong distinction must be drawn between facts and values (the assumed impossibility to move logically from an is to an ought). Though clearly separable these philosophical problems are interrelated to the extent they each served to set modern philosophy and ethics on a mistaken path.

In an article first published in 1982, wonderfully titled, "How Moral Agents became Ghosts, or, Why the History of Ethics Diverged from that of the Philosophy of Mind," MacIntyre writes, "At the beginning of modern moral philosophy—which I date in the 1780s—the moral agent as traditionally understood almost, if not quite, disappeared from view. The moral agent's character, the structure of his desires and dispositions, became at best a peripheral rather than a central topic for moral philosophy, thus losing the place assigned to it by the vast majority of moral philosophers from Plato to Hume."[2] Choice—conceived by Kant and Reid as deciding between desire and the requirements of morality and later by Sartre as the condition of an individual's authenticity—replaced character as crucial for moral agency. And the rest, as the story goes, is history.

In a recent study, *Tradition, Rationality, and Virtue: The Thought of Alasdair MacIntyre*, Thomas D. D'Andrea provides a helpful overview, just prior to his treatment of *After Virtue*, that rightly directs attention to MacIntyre's engagement with psychoanalysis and the philosophy of social science. It was, in D'Andrea's view, the preparatory work MacIntyre needed to do in order to write the crucial chapters in *After Virtue* on "'Fact, Explanation, and Expertise" and the "Character of Generalization in the Social Sciences." Those chapters reflect the arguments MacIntyre had been developing against behaviorist and deterministic accounts of action, as well as his development of Wittgenstein's distinction between description and explanation—all of which is crucial for the constructive account *After Virtue* gives of practical reason and the virtues.

MacIntyre's most concentrated statement of his understanding of action is in "The Intelligibility of Action," an article written in 1986. Here he argues that essential to our learning to act is that we learn to behave in a way that others can construe our actions as intelligible. In other words, the intelligibility of an action depends on the narrative continuities in an agent's life. Yet the ability to narrate my life depends on having narratives available that make my peculiar life fit within narratives of a community that direct me toward an end that is not of my own making. The intelligibility of my life, therefore, depends on the stock of descriptions at a particular time, place, and culture. I am, at best, no more than a co-author of my life.

2. MacIntyre, "How Moral Agents became Ghosts," 295.

It is MacIntyre's contention that in modernity, particularly in that peculiar form of modernity called liberalism, the stock of descriptions has become inadequate for our ability to act in a manner that can be intelligible to others as well to ourselves. His critique of liberalism, as he puts it in *After Virtue*, "derives from a judgment that the best type of human life, that in which the tradition of the virtues is most adequately embodied, is lived by those engaged in constructing and sustaining forms of community directed towards the shared achievement of those common goods without which the ultimate human good cannot be achieved. Liberal political societies are characteristically committed to denying any place for a determinative conception of the human good in their public discourse, let alone allowing that their common life should be grounded in such a conception."

MacIntyre's critique of modernity is hardly wholesale rejection. *Ethics and Politics* ends with a fascinating defense of the virtue of toleration and free speech. From MacIntyre's perspective, the presumption that one might be capable of standing somewhere to reject modernity is the kind of peculiarly modern attitude his work is meant to disabuse. MacIntyre, moreover, understands that there is no past to which we might return. He notes that we are all "inescapably inhabitants of advanced modernity, bearing its social and cultural marks." Accordingly, he acknowledges that his understanding of the tradition of the virtues and the consequences for modernity of the rejection of that tradition is one that is only possible on this side of modernity.

Yet MacIntyre thinks we can only gain some understanding of the moral character of modernity from the standpoint of a different tradition—in particular, the tradition of the virtues represented by Aristotle. Given his early Marxism as well as the influence of Collingwood and Wittgenstein, it should not be surprising that MacIntyre grew to find in Aristotle's account of the virtues and practical reason an understanding of the conditions necessary for our actions to be intelligible. Aristotle provided MacIntyre with an account of why our actions require a conception of an end as well as the social and political conditions necessary to sustain a life formed by the virtues constitutive of that end, which is simply lacking in modern moral practice and theory.

MacIntyre notes that when he wrote *After Virtue* he was already an Aristotelian but not yet a Thomist. His Thomism came when he became convinced that in some respects Aquinas was a better Aristotelian than Aristotle. Indeed, MacIntyre reports, he learned that his attempt to provide an account of the human good in social terms was inadequate without a metaphysical grounding. As he argues in later works, such as *Dependent Rational Animals*, "It is only because human beings have an end toward which they are directed by reason of their specific nature that practices, traditions, and the like are able to function as they do."

Some have wondered how MacIntyre's old emphasis on the historical character of all enquiry can be consistent with his new emphasis on the necessity of a metaphysical grounding to sustain our endeavor to know. MacIntyre responds to these worries in a chapter in *The Task of Philosophy*, where he argues that first principles are not simply given before our engagement in a mode of inquiry. Rather, as Aristotle argued, through the activity necessary to achieve a perfected science, thought "gives expression to the adequacy of the mind to its object."

MacIntyre understands himself to be a metaphysical realist. Truth is the relation of an adequated mind to its object, but MacIntyre insists that the activity of enquiry is the necessary condition for the discovery of first principles. This is the metaphysical expression of his understanding of action—or, perhaps better put, his defense of first principles helps us see how his account of action has been metaphysical from the beginning. Thus his agreement with Thomas Aquinas, against Aristotle, that the proper object of human knowledge is not essence *qua* essence. Because we only know essences through effects, for MacIntyre there is no place to begin but in the middle.

MacIntyre's position is, I think, similar to his characterization of Rosenzweig's in *Edith Stein*: "We do not begin with some adequate grasp of the concepts of knowledge and truth and in the light of these pass judgment on whether or not we know something of God or whether or not it is true God exists, but rather it is from our encounters with God—and with the world and with human beings—that we learn what it is to have knowledge of what truth is."[3] Accordingly, MacIntyre's work is by necessity a continuing exploration of the adequacy and inadequacy of our conceptual resources.

Thus, with his realism comes an empiricism, which shapes his account of how we learn the precepts of natural law. Just as metaphysical first principles are discovered in a mode of enquiry, so the precepts of

---

3. MacIntyre, *Edith Stein*, 173.

natural law are those "presupposed in any situation in which learning and enquiry between rational individuals about their individual and common goods can be advanced and by any relationship in which individuals can conduct themselves with rational integrity." This observation from *Ethics and Politics* makes clear his view that a natural morality is forged by people over time through trial and error. He calls attention to Thomas Aquinas' contention that play and delight taken in play are necessary for exchanges and interchanges of human life, and he concludes, "the common good requires, and hence the natural law requires, the making of jokes and the staging and enjoyment of entertainment."

Such an account of natural law is subversive, because the way of life necessary for the discovery of natural law challenges "the persecutory activities of centralizing powers." Those in power seldom display a sense of humor—the correlative to the humility derived from the recognition that we know what is required of us fundamentally by our failure to live according to the precepts of the natural law. So, too, the virtues are equally subversive in capitalist social orders. For MacIntyre, the practices necessary for training in practical reason through which we acquire the ability to act intelligibly requires the systematic growth of human potential by acquired excellence that cannot help but challenge the character of modern moral practice and theory.

Conservatives who think they have found an ally in MacIntyre fail to attend to his understanding of the kind of politics necessary to sustain the virtues. He makes clear that his problem with most forms of contemporary conservatism is that conservatives mirror the fundamental characteristics of liberalism. The conservative commitment to a way of life structured by a free market results in an individualism, and in particular a moral psychology, that is as antithetical to the tradition of the virtues as liberalism. Conservatives and liberals, moreover, both try to employ the power of the modern state to support their positions in a manner alien to MacIntyre's understanding of the social practices necessary for the common good.

Those that fear MacIntyre's position might commit him to some form of confessional theological position should be comforted by his adamant declaration that his metaphysical position, his account of natural law, as well as his understanding of practical reason and the virtues are secular. By *secular*, I take him to mean that his argument that some overall good is necessary for our actions to be intelligible does not entail any theological convictions that are not available to anyone. In his important chapter called "Aquinas on Practical Rationality and Justice" in *Whose Justice? Which Rationality?*, MacIntyre does acknowledge that Thomas Aquinas' account of practical reason has a "theological dimension," because it requires knowledge of God. But he appeals to Thomas himself for evidence that such knowledge does not require revelation.

I find MacIntyre's implied distinction between nature and grace a serious problem, but it is understandable, given his commitment to maintaining a strong distinction between philosophy and theology. That MacIntyre is intent on a division between philosophy and theology—a division I think unknown to Thomas Aquinas—confirms his claim that he works within the conditions of modernity.

These theological questions, however, are seldom raised by MacIntyre's critics. His critics, at least his conservative critics, are usually more concerned with whether his position entails some form of relativism. They think his view that standards of truth and of rational justification in the contexts of diverse practices and inquiries means he has little defense against relativism. So, too, his view that standards of truth will vary from one time and place to another, as well as his denial that there are available to any rational agent standards of truth sufficient to resolve fundamental moral, scientific, and metaphysical disputes in a definitive way.

He has on numerous occasions responded to the charge. MacIntyre certainly holds that it is undeniable that many culturally embodied systems of thought and action exist with their own standards of excellence. Moreover adherents of these systems come to conclusions that are incompatible with other systems. Advocates of these alternative modes may from time to time judge the standpoint of the other party to be unsound. If this is what is meant by relativism, then MacIntyre is a relativist. But he distances himself from the kind of relativism that draws the further mistaken conclusion that, absent modes of reasoning that can resolve conflicts in principle, the contending parties must alter their own modes of justification and reject all substantive conceptions of truth.

Crucial for MacIntyre is the historical fact that one tradition of inquiry can put another tradition into an epistemological crisis. (For his account of such crises, see the chapter in *The Tasks of Philosophy*, "Epistemological Crisis and Dramatic Narrative.") Advocates of one tradition learn how to think in terms of another tradition—and then they learn to identify the unresolved issues characteristic of the other tradition. Through such acts of the imagination, adherents of a tradition "may be able to conclude that it is only from the standpoint of their tradition that the difficulties of that rival tradition can be understood and overcome."

In an extraordinary essay, "Colors, Cultures, and Practices" in *The Tasks of Philosophy*, MacIntyre draws explicitly on Wittgenstein's arguments against a private language to argue that our judgments of color are socially established standards. Accordingly, it is a necessary condition for skillful use of the vocabulary of color to master a socially established language. He then provides a fascinating account of how painters such as Hals and Turner discovered through the practice of their painting color discriminations that established standards of excellence which make impossible relativistic judgments.

I do not expect that this account of MacIntyre's rejection of relativism will still the worries of those who think his historicism is simply incompatible with his Thomism. For those so disposed to think MacIntyre inconsistent, I commend "Truth as a Good: A Reflection on *Fides et Ratio*," in *The Tasks of Philosophy*. There, he defends the encyclical's view that the task of philosophy is the articulation and pursuit of answers to questions posed by human beings, whatever their culture. It is the "characteristic of human beings," MacIntyre writes, "that by our nature we desire to know and to understand, that we cannot but reflect upon the meaning of our lives, upon suffering, and upon death, and in so doing attempt to pursue our good, making our own the tasks of rational enquiry and the achievement of truth."

When we begin by asking what makes an action intelligible, we cannot avoid God—at least if MacIntyre is right. Like Thomas Aquinas, MacIntyre thinks every human being has a natural desire for happiness "which is achieved only in union with God, integral to which is a recognition of God as the truth and of all truth is from God, so that the progress through truths to the truth is itself one part of the ascent of mind and heart to God." MacIntyre's critique of modernity, therefore, is but a footnote to his constructive attempt to help us recover the resources constitutive of our ability to act intelligibly.

Put differently, MacIntyre's fundamental problem with liberalism is the kind of people it produces. It would be a mistake, however, to conclude from MacIntyre's worries about liberalism that he thinks any hope of recovering the tradition of the virtues is doomed. The subtitle of his 1999 book, *Dependent Rational Animals*, is *Why Human Beings Need the Virtues*, which makes clear that MacIntyre thinks that we are necessarily teleological beings who must learn to trust one another.

The "plain person" is the character MacIntyre has identified to display the unavoidability of the virtues. Plain persons are those characterized by everyday practices such as sustaining families, schools, and local forms of political community. They engage in trades and professions that have required them to learn skills constitutive of a craft. Such people are the readers he hopes his books may reach. Grounded as they are in concrete practices necessary to sustain a common life, they acquire the virtues that make them capable of recognizing the principles of natural law and why those principles call into question the legitimating modes of modernity.

MacIntyre has sought within the world we necessarily inhabit to help us recover resources that must exist to enable us to act intelligibly. From beginning to end, he has attempted to help us locate those forms of life that can sustain lives well lived. In *Tradition, Rationality, and Virtue*, Thomas D. D'Andrea quotes the preface MacIntyre wrote to the Polish edition of *After Virtue*:

> The flourishing of the virtues requires and in turn sustains a certain kind of community, necessarily a small-scale community, within which the goods of various practices are ordered, so that, as far as possible, regard for each finds its due place with the lives of each individual, or each household and in the life of the community at large. Because, implicitly or explicitly, it is always by reference to some conception of the overall and final human good that other goods are ordered, the life of every individual, household or community by its orderings gives expression, wittingly or unwittingly, to some conception of the human good. And it is when goods are ordered in terms of an adequate conception of human good that the virtues genuinely flourish. "Politics" is the Aristotelian name for the set of activities through which goods are ordered in the life of the community.

Where such communities exist—and they cannot help but exist—it may be possible for some to live lives they understand.

18

The Virtues of the *Summa Theologiae*

with SHERYL OVERMYER*

The Virtues Theologically Considered

For the past fifty years, Thomas' work on the moral life has featured prominently in the recovery of a "virtue ethics tradition" in moral philosophy and moral theology. Thomas' work in "virtue ethics" is canonical, and its significance might seem so obvious it need not be stated. Characterizing Thomas' ethics as a "virtue ethic," however, can be slightly misleading. To call it a virtue ethic may give the impression that his virtues lay entirely within the reach of philosophers. Do they?

Looking to the *Summa Theologiae*, Thomas' *Prima Secundae* is dominated by his discussion of the habits and virtues necessary for our becoming friends with God. His *Secunda Secundae* is, moreover, primarily determined by his account of the theological virtues of faith, hope, and love. Indeed, Thomas stops nothing short of identifying God himself as Charity itself. The *Prima Secundae* and *Secunda Secundae*

---

* Note to the reader: Much of what is written on Thomas and the virtues is written for either novices or masters. This essay is written for readers who are already familiar with Thomas' understanding of the virtues, but desire an overview of the whole. We, the authors, realize that many of the claims we make are contestable; however, for the aims of this essay we judged it "prudent" to focus instead on developing this fuller picture.

214

are his investigation into how Christ, Who is Charity, established the way of charity that through the exercise of the virtues we can become friends with God. Therefore, Thomas would have us see that a purely philosophical understanding of the virtues, which stops short of charity and of God, is itself imperfect. A more perfect and complete understanding of the virtues, which includes virtues of a specifically theological character, emerges in the *Prima Secundae* and *Secunda Secundae* of the *Summa Theologiae.*

Such an interpretation depends on reading these two parts in continuity with the *Summa's* other parts, the *Prima Pars* and the *Tertia Pars.* The *Summa* has a profound unity, argues Servais Pinckaers, because Thomas believes that the source of theology, our knowledge of God, comes to us through faith and the gift of wisdom.[1] Thomas' synthesis bears out his refusal to adopt the Philosopher's division between metaphysics and ethics. Rather Thomas believes that faith makes possible a unified life unavailable to reason alone. Therefore, the *Summa* is his attempt "to reproduce the very movement of Wisdom and the divine action in the work of creation—culminating in man, the image of God—and in the work of government, which leads all creatures back to God, their ultimate goal and happiness. Preeminently, man is so drawn, by means of his free will, since he is master of his actions and capable of enjoying God. This work, at once divine and human, cannot be achieved without Christ, who in his humanity has become for all the way to the Father."[2] Thomas' development of his understanding of the Trinity in the *Prima Pars* receives its further display through his analysis of human action, the passions, and the virtues in the *Secunda Pars.* In the *Tertia Pars,* Thomas develops his Christology and correlative account of the sacraments to show how we are incorporated into the life of charity through God's action on our behalf.

Thus, the structure of the *Summa* shows how Thomas, in Pinckaers' description, "reproduce[s] the very movement of Wisdom."[3] This movement gives shape to the *Prima Secundae,* where Thomas' overall theological project informs his account of how the virtues form the human subject. Our task, then, is to display its general shape as the context for

1. Pinckaers, *Sources of Christian Ethics,* 221.
2. Ibid.
3. Ibid.

Thomas' treatment of the virtues within that part. Then we fill out what it means for Thomas' virtues to be theological in character by looking to the general character of these virtues in the *Prima Secundae* and their more special character in the *Secunda Secundae*. We draw on the important distinction mentioned at the outset between imperfect and perfect to describe how Thomas understands the role of different kinds of virtues in bringing about our union with God. Using both the *Prima Secundae* and *Secunda Secundae*, we show how Thomas' understanding of the virtues is in service to his overall aim of showing how it is possible for us to find our way back to God. This is no philosopher's feat, for the virtues are possible only because God overcame our sin to first find a way back to us.

The Shape of the *Prima Secundae*

To understand Thomas' account of the virtues, it is crucial to place the virtues as a subject among subjects in the *Prima Secundae*. Thomas begins with a theology of beatitude and then investigates human actions in general as they bear on happiness (action, passions), the interior principles of human action that would bring us to God (virtues, gifts) with their contraries (vices), and the exterior principles that assist us in obtaining our end (law, grace). Granted, in some sense the virtues stand at the summit of the *Prima Secundae* in pointing to the powers that bring us into God's life. But the virtues are not understood in full without the rest of the *Prima Secundae*—not without the basic theological anthropology they draw upon and not without the exterior helps which make them possible. This set of interdependencies suggests that there is a theological cast to the virtues, even for virtues that would seem to fall comfortably within the philosopher's reach.

Thomas begins the *Prima Secundae* with the question of what constitutes our last end as human beings. He answers that our last end is happiness. For Aristotle and for Thomas, the virtues are not the means to happiness. Rather, the virtues are happiness' form. Thomas uses Augustine's felicitous phrase, "happiness is joy in truth," which means that it consists in knowledge and love to involve the faculties of our whole being (*ST* 1a2ae q3 a4).[4] In this happiness, human beings

4. All references to the *Summa Theologiae* will be given parenthetically in the text.

participate in God's very life through friendship with God. That God would have us participate in his life means we must receive from God the virtues that make life with God possible. Therefore the question of the relation between the virtues infused by God and the virtues we develop by our natural powers—which Thomas will name "infused" and "acquired" virtues—is already inherent in Thomas' account of happiness. Even creatures' graced happiness is limited, which Thomas signals by using the language of "imperfect" and "perfect." Happiness can be found in God alone because God's very Being is his operation; he alone enjoys no other than himself (*ST* 1a2ae q2 a4).

Thomas conceives of freedom so differently from subsequent thinkers that it is sometimes hard to grasp its significance. He thinks of freedom as "for" something rather than "from" something. Freedom is a freedom "for excellence."[5] Freedom takes root in our powers of reason and will, such that developing these powers toward their ultimate ends—the role of education itself—makes us fully free. The intellect and will are human powers that are intended to know and love God. The intellect and will in Thomas also contrast to modern interpretations that would have them as separate, sometimes competing forces. For Thomas they are interdependent: the will is a *moved* mover and the intellect or reason is rational *desire*. God causes these powers to be and sustains them in being, thus Thomas claims that God alone can move the will nonviolently (*ST* 1a2ae q9 a6). God makes us genuinely free by enhancing our movement toward perfection according to the principle of the "truth of life" which comprises all virtues (*ST* 2a2ae q109 a3 ad3).

Thomas specifies this account of our reason and will by providing an analysis of the voluntary. A free, voluntary act is one in which we do what we will. A voluntary act is right in being good. Such an act is still tethered to our ultimate happiness and—in terms of the structure of the *Prima Secundae*—it looks forward to its realization in the virtues. What makes an action a free, voluntary, human action is important for the virtues. Charles Pinches puts the matter thus: "We cannot act well without the virtues; but also we have the virtues *in order to act*. Acts are where the virtues and vices meet the world."[6]

---

5. Pinckaers, *Sources of Christian Ethics*, 354–78.
6. Pinches, *Theology and Action*, 109.

Thomas' emphasis on training is a correlate of the centrality of habit for his understanding of the significance of the virtues. So Thomas provides an extensive exploration of habits and passions. Pinckaers characterizes Thomas' treatise on the passions as remarkable and unique,[7] and he is right to do so. Unfortunately, Thomas' extended accounts of the passions—love, hatred, delight, pleasure, sorrow, hope, despair, and anger—may be for the most part ignored exactly because of their unique character. Yet the passions cannot be ignored if we are to understand the nature and character of the individual virtues and their relation to one another. The passions are the source and condition necessary to receive training through habituation so that we might acquire the virtues.

From Thomas' perspective, we are bodily creatures whose passions and desires can pull us in a number of different and often destructive directions. If we are to have lives worth living, our passions cry out for the ordering that comes through habituation. Habits are the stable and lasting dispositions that form our passions and actions, making it possible for us to perform actions that otherwise would not be in our power. Bonnie Kent points out that our English word "habit" is associated with routine performances that require little thought. In contrast, Thomas understood habits to be "a durable characteristic of the agent inclining to certain kinds of actions and emotional reactions, not the actions and reactions themselves."[8] Action qualified by "habit" has three distinctive features: readiness to do something; ease or facility in performing the action; and joy while doing it.

Following Aristotle, Thomas uses the general formula: by like acts, like habits are formed (*ST* 1a2ae q50 a1). Yet that formula betrays a complex understanding of the relation of agent to action that Thomas develops through a careful analysis of what makes an act a human act. Thomas is well aware that actions can be described in multiple ways, but for an action to be a human act and thus moral it must be in accord with the order of reason. Thomas notes that if the object of an act includes something in accord with reason, such as giving alms to mitigate a person's want, it will be a good act according to its species. If it includes an act such as appropriating property that belongs to another,

7. Pinckaers, *Sources of Christian Ethics*, 224.
8. Kent, "Habits and Virtues," 224.

that is stealing, then the act is evil. Some acts, such as picking up a straw or walking in a field, are indifferent acts (*ST* 1a2ae q18 a8).

Thomas also follows Aristotle in claiming that one acquires virtue by doing what the virtuous person does. "The just man justices," in Gerard Manley Hopkins' words, meaning that just acts issue from the just person. The habits that make us virtuous must be habits acquired by acting as a person of virtue acts. For us to become virtuous, our good acts must issue from good habits. The complex relationship between act and description entails that some acts cannot be done justly. Thomas draws on Aristotle to define virtue as that which makes its possessor good and its possessor's works good (*ST* 1a2ae q55 a3). Therefore if the virtues are acquired in the right manner, we cannot make bad use of them. Since the virtuous person is good, his or her works are good as well. To say it differently, what a person of virtue does is not different from what they are.

Sinful habits are no less habits, and some argue even more so than the habits that constitute the virtues. Vices run contrary to our intended nature and happiness. Even as they undermine nature, they may take such root that they become an expression of an almost second nature (*ST* 1a2ae q71 a2). They express and are constitutive of a divided self. The vices are disconnected, meaning that they are oriented toward scattered objects which cannot help but be at odds with one another. The vices are not always easy to identify, for even a virtue made bad use of will turn out to be a "semblance" of virtue and in fact vice (*ST* 1a2ae q55 a4). In this respect, the virtues are construed as powers that enable us to struggle against old sinful habits toward more full and unified participation in the triune life. For us to be fully taken up, much more than freedom from vice is needed.

Thomas also treats the external helps that are gifts in our journey back to God—law and grace. The role of the law is to be a rule or measure whereby we are encouraged to act or restrained from acting in a manner by which we are bound to our act (*ST* 1a2ae q90, a1). Even though Thomas develops his account of the law under the rubric of the exterior principles of moral action, he assumes the law is the product of reason by a community meant to aid us in gradually becoming virtuous (*ST* 1a2ae q96 a2). Although we are created to have a natural aptitude for virtue, the perfection of virtue must come through some kind of training we receive from another (*ST* 1a2ae q95 a1). The law is one of the aids for such training. Moreover, grace names for Thomas what such training looks like as well as how it comes about. Grace is a special movement of God that works in us nonviolently, enabling us for the movement that is virtue's perfect and perfecting activity. Our account here is a gesture toward the work in the *Secunda Secundae* and *Tertia Pars*.

The Virtues of the *Prima Secundae*

Our emphases on the theological character of Thomas' treatment of the virtues and on his comprehensive study of human action means that we cannot leave these behind as we turn to Thomas' study of the virtues. Indeed, Thomas develops his account of the moral and theological virtues with the same deliberate care he dedicates to his analysis of habits. His theological anthropology serves as the basis for providing a comprehensive account of the powers that are the subject of virtue: the intellect, the rational appetite, and the sense appetites.

Thomas begins by distinguishing between the intellectual, moral, and theological virtues. It will become clear, however, that those distinctions tend to blur as his arguments develop. Exploring the nature of intellectual virtue, he asserts that the virtue of prudence enjoys a place of preeminence in the good life. Prudence is the virtue by which we rightly reason about the means to get something done. It perfects the intellect by directing what we do to a good end. Moreover it matters not only what good we do, but also how the good is done. Prudence is crucial for making what we do be done in a manner that we acquire the virtue corresponding to the action (*ST* 1a2ae q57 a5).

Thomas eventually identifies the intellectual virtue of prudence as a virtue of the appetitive faculty as well. Virtues of the appetitive faculty are called moral virtues. Not every intellectual virtue is a moral virtue. For example, the virtues of the speculative intellect—wisdom, science, and understanding—are not moral virtues. These virtues deal with necessary things that cannot be other than they are. They are not moral virtues because exercise of a virtue of the speculative intellect does not depend on a virtuous disposition of the appetite as it does with, say, exercise of the virtue of prudence or justice (*ST* 1a2ae q57 a1; q58 a5). Yet Thomas' distinction between the intellectual virtues and the moral virtues is not a hard and fast one. Indeed, Cessario writes, "Christian theology contributes to a softening of the hard distinctions that classical philosophy established between two classes of virtues."[9] For example, Thomas points out that the virtue of art, that is, right reason about works to be made, can contribute to the moral formation of the craftsman because faithfulness to the craft is a form of justice (*ST* 1a2ae q57 a3 ad2). For Thomas, the intellectual virtues must properly interact with the moral virtues for the intellectual virtues to have ultimate significance.

Prudence, a virtue of the intellect and will, is the central moral virtue because it is also crucial for the proper formation of the passions. Prudence cannot be without the moral virtues because to act in a right manner, we need universal principles supplied by prudence and the particular principles that require the perfection of the passions by the appropriate virtues. The circular relation between prudence and the moral virtues indicates that growth in virtue is ongoing. The ends for which we act depend on who we have become (*ST* 1a2ae q59 a5).

Yet not every moral virtue is about the passions. Some are about operations. By "operations," Thomas means those activities that involve relations with others. Justice, friendship, and religion are operational virtues. Joy should accompany an act of justice. As such, it overflows into the sensitive appetites making justice a more perfect virtue because it causes in us the appropriate passion (*ST* 1a2ae q59 a5). Not every virtue entails the formation of the passions. Nonetheless, no virtue can be without the passions.

Thomas distinguishes the virtues in terms of our varied operations and passions. Justice is the general operative virtue that directs us to the common good. Thomas also names the virtues of religion, piety, and gratitude as further specifications of justice. Religion is the virtue that we owe God; piety is the virtue that names our debt to our parents or country; and gratitude is the debt we owe to benefactors (*ST* 1a2ae q60 a3). Later Thomas identifies patience as a central virtue to sustain justice because it excludes not only unjust revenge, but also inordinate sorrow, which is the source of hatred and anger. Patience is also required for whoever would be brave (*ST* 1a2ae q66 a4).

9. Cessario, *Moral Virtues*, 60.

Thomas draws on his analysis of the passions to distinguish the moral virtues of fortitude and temperance. Courage, or fortitude, is the habit necessary for the formation of the passions of fear and daring. It has to do with the irascible passions. And temperance is about the moderation of the affections of the soul that have to do with the desire and pleasures of food and sex. Temperance is the virtue correlative of the concupiscible passions. Thomas concludes that Aristotle is right in naming ten moral virtues, distinguished by their relation to the passions—fortitude, temperance, liberality, magnificence, magnanimity, philotemia, gentleness, friendship, truthfulness, and eutrapelia (pleasures of games); the eleventh moral virtue is about operations—justice.

Thomas was writing a commentary of Aristotle's *Nichomachean Ethics* at the time he was writing the Treatise on the Virtues in the *Summa*. No doubt he means to be faithful to Aristotle's account of the virtues, but, Pinckaers points out, by the time he has finished his account of the virtues in the *Summa* he names fifty-three virtues.[10] Even though the names of the virtues may be the same, his analysis distinguishes his understanding from Aristotle's understanding of their nature and content. After all, Thomas identifies our last end as the enjoyment of friendship with God, requiring that we have instilled in us some virtues that Aristotle could not have known.

Even before developing his account of the theological virtues, Thomas draws on Cicero's understanding of the four cardinal virtues in suggesting that all the moral virtues can be grouped under the principle virtues of fortitude, temperance, justice, and prudence. According to Thomas, these virtues are called cardinal virtues because they are the "hinge" (*cardo*) on which all the other virtues pivot. They are also called cardinal virtues because of the importance of the matters with which they deal: prudence concerns commands; justice involves due actions between equals; temperance concerns desires of pleasure; and courage pertains to that which sustains us when faced with the dangers associated with death (*ST* 1a2ae q61 a3).

The introduction of the cardinal virtues provides Thomas with the occasion to distinguish his understanding of the virtues from Augustine's. Augustine maintained that the four cardinal virtues were all aspects of love. Thomas' view that charity is the form of the vir-

---

10. Pinckaers, *Sources of Christian Ethics*, 227.

tues may seem to confirm Augustine's understanding of the virtues as forms of love, but in fact Thomas differs from Augustine on this matter. Thomas does so because his understanding of the importance of the habits for our being virtuous means each virtue has its own characteristic form of habituation that makes it distinct (*ST* 1a2ae q61 a4). One of the differences between Augustine and Thomas is Thomas' use of Aristotle's habits to describe the virtues. By using the logic of habits, Thomas maintains a focus on bodily knowledge that requires habituation and allows for the individuation of the virtues. How significant a difference this is between Augustine and Thomas is controversial. These issues can bring out shifting affinities as we turn to Thomas' writing on the theological virtues.

Thomas follows his treatment of the moral virtues with the theological virtues: faith, hope, and love. These three are additional sources of activity endowed by God to make us virtuous and direct us to himself (*ST* 1a2ae q62 a1 ad2). Thomas writes: "First, as regards the intellect, man receives certain supernatural principles, which are held by means of a Divine light: these are the articles of faith, about which is faith. Secondly, the will is directed to this end, both as to that end as something attainable—and this pertains to hope—and as to a certain spiritual union, whereby the will is, so to speak, transformed into that end—and this belongs to charity" (*ST* 1a2ae q62 a3). Charity signifies a love of God, a certain friendship with God. Such a friendship can be begun by grace in this life but awaits glory for its perfection. Friendship with God is impossible without faith and hope. Faith is necessary to sustain our belief that fellowship with God is our destiny. We must have hope that we will attain such a fellowship.

When Thomas turns to the significance of the theological virtues, he may well be drawn closer to Augustine's position. Thomas writes that we cannot have any virtue without the virtue of prudence, but we cannot have the virtue of prudence without charity. In Thomas' language, charity is the "form" of the virtues (*ST* 1a2ae q62 a4 et 2a2ae q23 a8). Notice he does not say, as Augustine does, that the virtues are but forms of love. Rather charity forms the virtues by giving each virtue its proper telos, which is nothing less than to make us friends of God. Charity forms the other virtues by directing "the acts of all the other virtues to our final end. Charity shapes all these acts and to this extent is said to be the form of the virtues" becoming the "strategy" of the moral virtues

(*ST* 2a2ae q23 a8).[11] Thus faith and hope must be formed by charity if these virtues are to be perfect (*ST* 1a2ae q65 a4–5). All the theological virtues are needed to attain that happiness that comes through union with God.

Thomas takes himself to be quoting Augustine when he writes that we have some virtues from God, Who "works in us without us" (*ST* 1a2ae q63 a2). God works in us by charity. This does not mean, however, that God works without affecting us. Charity is a virtue, a habit, which means our created faculties and powers are formed by God's grace. Such virtues are not in to our power to acquire. All the acquired virtues may be present in our nature inchoatively, but our nature is insufficient to be perfected without God's help. God bestows on us not only the theological virtues, but also other habits corresponding, in due proportion, to the theological virtues.

Thus Thomas does not stop with the theological virtues but complements them with versions of the "infused moral virtues" and the gifts of the Holy Spirit. Thomas creates this category of infused moral virtues because the theological virtues alone do not sufficiently order us in relation to the good works that are the means to our supernatural end. These other virtues help name the many virtues associated with particular actions by which one attains human flourishing[12] The acquired moral virtues differ in species from the infused moral virtues because they have a different object and end. For example, the acquired virtue of temperance requires that we consume food in a manner that the health of the body is not harmed; the infused virtue of temperance may require our body be chastised by the abstinence of food and drink. In like manner, the acquired moral virtues are to make us behave well in respect to human affairs; the infused moral virtues are directed toward a different end because the theological virtues concern our conduct with fellow citizens in the divine household (*ST* 1a2ae q63 a4).

Questions surrounding the relationship between the acquired moral virtues and the infused moral virtues are disputed among interpreters of Thomas. In his discussion of how the four cardinal virtues differ from one another, he suggests that the four virtues qualify one another by a "kind of overflow." Prudence "overflows" into the other

11. Wadell, *Primacy of Love*, 90.
12. Sherwin, *By Knowledge and By Love*, 171.

virtues, but it is equally necessary that each of the other virtues overflow onto prudence as well as onto the other virtues. For example, Thomas observes that those who can curb their desire for pleasures of touch, which is a hard thing to do, are more able to check daring in the face of death so as not to go too far. Thus temperance must be brave just as fortitude must be temperate (*ST* 1a2ae q61 a4). It is tempting to think Thomas may believe the theological virtues "overflow" in a manner that transforms the acquired moral virtues into the infused moral virtues. Indeed he does say that acquired and infused temperance both moderate desire for the pleasure of touch. However they do so for different reasons. Their respective acts are not the same (*ST* 1a2ae q63 a4). What is clear is that Thomas believes that the "love of God is unitive in as much as it draws man's affections from the many to the one; so that the virtues, which flow from the love of God, are connected together" (*ST* 1a2ae q73 a1). The perfection of virtues is named in the Gifts of the Holy Spirit.

Thomas inherits the thesis regarding the connection of the virtues from both philosophers and theologians. When considering whether to have one virtue means to have them all, Thomas begins his answer by distinguishing between the acquired and infused virtues. Ultimately, however, he comes to rely more on the distinction between perfect and imperfect virtues. The acquired virtues direct us well in terms of some particular end, but not to our last end and are thus imperfect on their own. The infused virtues, however, direct us to our ultimate end. Moreover, quoting Augustine, Thomas argues that a virtue cannot be perfect if it is isolated from the other virtues. The infused virtues alone are connected in a manner that makes us perfect. Some are tempted to read Augustine as saying that the acquired virtues are in fact glittering vices, and thus on this count Thomas is opposed to Augustine. Although it is in fact possible to distinguish their views, it is also important that Thomas qualifies his own appreciation of the acquired virtues without the infused. What Thomas implies might be put this way: only if the acquired virtues are accompanied by the infused will they enjoy that perfect unity forged by charity. Thomas' language of "imperfect" and "perfect" clarifies the extent to which charity is a perfect and perfecting work worked in us.

The shape of the *Summa* remains important. Over the course of the *Prima Secundae*, Thomas shifts from questions of how the moral and theological virtues form a life to describing how we are worked on from the outside, so to speak. The *Prima Secundae* is the project of a theologian who looks into the natural structure of the human being to trace the extensive reach of God's work through both internal and, importantly, external helps. Thomas will follow this through in the *Secunda Secundae* where the virtues clearly issue from a theology of grace.

The Virtues of the *Secunda Secundae*

Thomas develops his account of the Christian life as a journey back to God in the *Secunda Secundae* of the *Summa*. For Thomas we are *viatores*, "wayfarers," whose end is to enjoy God. The end is also the way—for charity constitutes our beginning, our way, and our end. The way of charity is the journey God's grace makes possible so that we might become God's friends. It is, therefore, crucial to remember that the virtues are not abstract qualities, but rather names for the diverse ways in which we must develop if we are to enjoy the eternal happiness for which we have been created.

Thomas begins the *Secunda Secundae* by revisiting the theological virtues of faith, hope, and charity. He follows them with extended analysis of the moral virtues. For each of these seven virtues, he treats the primary virtue and related virtues, the contrary vices and sins, the corresponding gift of the Holy Spirit, and the legal precepts that aid the cultivation of the virtues.

This arrangement can give the impression that Thomas thought that there is a sequential ordering for our reception of the virtues. By this reading, we first receive faith, then hope, and finally charity. Thomas' rich and complex account of the relation between the virtues, however, defies any such simple ordering of how the virtues are acquired or infused. Thomas says plainly that faith precedes hope, and hope precedes charity, yet charity is the "form" of faith, hope, and all the virtues. Thomas develops what it means for charity to be the form of the virtues throughout this part of the *Summa*.

This view of the *Secunda Secundae* may seem odd since much of the content of this part involves the kind of casuistry that later becomes associated with a type of moral theology not determined by an account of the virtues. The argument of a casuist reading is that Thomas' treatment of such matters—for example war, murder, theft, backbiting, fasting, and other issues—can be divorced from an ethic that is virtue-centered. Yet, as we shall see, only with the virtue of justice can actions be analyzed separate from agents. So the work he does in the *Secunda Secundae* presumes and develops his analysis of action in the *Prima Secundae*, that is, an "act" cannot be isolated from the virtues because the action must be done in a manner that makes the subject good and the work itself good (*ST* 2a2ae q17 a1). The virtues remain crucial; indeed, charity forms the very manner in which we act. That charity is the form of all the virtues means therefore *how we do what we do* makes all the difference for how *what we do* makes us virtuous.

The *Secunda Secundae* is perhaps best understood as Thomas' attempt to provide exercises to help us discern true from false virtue. For Thomas is well aware that if a virtue is not formed by charity, it threatens to merely appear to be a virtue—a "semblance." Although he treats the virtues in sequence, it should never be assumed that he thinks that the virtues can be isolated from one another if we are to increase in the habits that can make us friends with God. Faith, hope, and charity are names for the effects of God's grace working in us. They make possible the journey necessary to enjoy friendship with God.

Thomas begins the *Secunda Secundae* with the virtue that is necessary for the beginning of such a journey, that is, the virtue of faith. Faith is an ordering of the mind to God whereby eternal life is begun in us (*ST* 2a2ae q4 a1). Its object is truth and its subject is reason. Reason is not antithetical to faith; rather, the perfection of reason is faith. Faith, however, is not a purely intellectual activity—whatever that would mean—because faith proceeds from the intellect *and* will. These connections show how in faith our whole being is taken up into grace. Thus faith is not the achievement of an individual, but a gift handed on through a community by its practices, namely the Church and the Sacraments (*ST* 2a2ae q1 a9). Given the preeminence of baptism for the Christian life, Thomas surprises some by arguing that children of unbelievers ought not to be baptized against their parents' will (*ST* 2a2ae q10 a12). To do so would be against natural justice. This underscores the extent to which faith is not a violation or suspension of reason, but an extension of it.

The significance Thomas gives to the virtue of hope is easy to overlook because he devotes just two questions to that virtue (*ST* 2a2ae q17 et 18). Yet hope is the virtue that is crucial to sustain our journey back to God. "Eternal happiness," Thomas writes, "does not enter into the heart of man perfectly, i.e., so that it be possible for a wayfarer to know its nature and quality; yet, under the general notion of the perfect good, it is possible for it to be apprehended by man, and it is in this way that the movement of hope towards it arises" (*ST* 2a2ae q17 a2 ad1). Thomas does not think of the ultimate end as something that was a number of stages away. Rather, at any given stage, at any minute, the ultimate end is present. Hope is the virtue that sustains that presence.

Hope at once leads us to charity, but also presupposes charity. Charity precedes hope and makes it more perfect because we learn to hope in our friends (*ST* 2a2ae q17 a8). Later Thomas makes the connection of hope to magnanimity and thus to fortitude, for the mind must be strengthened for a strenuous task as it stretches to great things by desire (*ST* 2a2ae q128 a1 ad6). Again these connections suggest that although the virtues are rightly distinguished, they are one. For charity directs them to our true end of being united with God in friendship.

Thomas' account of the vices that are contrary to hope, the vices of despair and presumption, is particularly rich because the theological vices determine our relationship to God. These vices are an offensive turning against God—they are mortal sins. Despair is born of spiritual sloth and unchastity. It fails to live into the work of redemption already wrought on our behalf. Presumption claims redemption as pardon and glory without repentance or merits. We have been given the means to avoid these vices by the Holy Scriptures, which chronicle God's promises, and by God's saving activity (e.g., *ST* 3a q52).

The greatest of the theological virtues is charity. Charity is God's befriending us so that our self is extended by learning to love our neighbor, our enemies, and even ourselves. This work is not our own but God's, for it can be in us "neither naturally, nor through acquisition by the natural powers, but by the infusion of the Holy Ghost Who is the love of the Father and the Son and the participation of Whom in us is created charity" (*ST* 2a2ae q24 a2). Charity is literally the ground of our union with God, which shows again that Thomas' "ethics" cannot be separated from his theology. His account of the virtues is also an account of our deification.[13] Yet Thomas would not have us be more perfect than we are—even those made perfect by charity may progress. We can never cease to grow in charity because of the abundance of God's love (*ST* 2a2ae q24 a9).

Thomas uses the Aristotelian language of causality to explain the non-Aristotelian claim of charity's influence on all the other virtues. Thomas changes his use of this language, however, even within the same vocabulary, e.g., charity from quasi-formal cause to efficient cause.[14] Some suggest that Thomas even drops causality in favor of another analogy altogether, that of motion.[15] Thomas' language shifts as he displays how conceptualizing God's work resists an equivocal or univocal understanding of it.

Thomas is clear that charity affects both the interior and exterior expression of our actions. Almsgiving and fraternal correction are done virtuously if their acts elicit joy, peace, and mercy. The character of the interior expressions on the one hand and the exterior expressions on the other, however, are mutually informed and bound together by the virtue itself. In like manner, Thomas discusses the gifts of the Holy Spirit that correspond to each of the virtues—with respect to charity this is wisdom, with hope, fear, and with faith, knowledge and understanding.

Having prepared the way through his discussion of the theological virtues, next Thomas turns to the moral virtues. Thomas revisits the "mother" of the moral virtues, prudence. No moral virtue is without prudence, and it makes possible their being virtues at all (*ST* 2a2ae q51 a2). Although Thomas seems quite close to Aristotle when he describes prudence as right reason applied to action, he ventures beyond Aristotle by iterating from the *Prima Secundae* the distinction between false, imperfect, and perfect virtues to distinguish true prudence from its resemblances and contraries (*ST* 2a2ae q47 a13). He does so to prepare us for the argument he develops in the next article to the effect that prudence is in all who have grace. This prudence is "merely sufficient with regard to things necessary for salvation; and such diligence is given to all who have grace." But Thomas mentions yet another kind of prudence: "there is also another diligence which is more than sufficient, whereby a man

13. See A. N. Williams, *Ground of Union.*
14. Sherwin, *By Knowledge and By Love,* 192–203.
15. Schockenhoff, *Bonum Hominis,* 345.

is able to make provision both for himself and for others, not only in matters necessary for salvation, but also in all things relating to human life; and such diligence as this is not in all who have grace" (*ST* 2a2ae q47 a14). Such prudence is a "fuller prudence" in which, Josef Pieper writes, "the natural *and* the supernatural, the acquired *and* the given, are combined in a felicitous, in a literally 'graced' unity."[16] Pieper counsels against prioritizing natural and acquired prudence over supernatural and infused or vice versa. Fuller prudence is best.

Although Thomas distinguishes between acquired prudence, infused prudence, and at last "fuller" prudence, one should not assume that they name different functions. It is clear, for example, that "fuller prudence" names the cooperation of both acquired and infused prudence in the one work of charity. Thomas' account of our lives as Christians becomes increasingly complex, implying that the virtues are merely the beginning of God's work. The virtues in turn prepare us for the gifts bestowed by the Holy Spirit. The acquired virtues are not insignificant if we remember that Thomas' account of the different forms of prudence is his display of how God's goodness transforms every aspect of our lives and becomes that on which every virtue depends.

Thomas' discussion of justice is by far the longest part of the *Secunda Secundae*. Justice has its own proper object over and above the other virtues, though it like the other virtues makes us capable of doing just actions. That object is the right, which means that a just act may be and should be done without taking into account the way it is done by the agent (*ST* 2a2ae q57 a1). Thomas' discussion of justice, therefore, deals with what might be thought to be legal questions that can be and should be considered without reference to how those actions may or may not make the agent just. It would be a mistake, however, to draw the conclusion that he thought it sufficient to do the just thing without our being just.

From Thomas' perspective we are social beings by nature. So our social relations consist in activities that cannot help but be just or fail to be so. Justice renders each his or her due as dictated by divine or human reason and finds expression in external actions. Its basic forms are communicative (by which individuals are ordered to one another), distributive (by which the community is ordered to the individual), and legal

---

16. Pieper, *Prudence*, 31.

(by which the members are ordered to the whole). Thomas has a good deal to say regarding each of these. Yet modern interpreters often focus on his treatments of capital punishment and private property rather than what he says about such matters as backbiting, cheating, or usury. Such elisions are genuine losses. Couched in his treatment of injuring one's neighbor, for example, Thomas argues that in cases of necessity it is lawful for man to steal. That one can so act indicates that a person of virtue may at times act in a manner that may seem counterintuitive.

Some modern readers may be surprised to discover that Thomas treats the virtue of religion as annexed to justice. Religion is what we owe God even though it is never possible for us to render to God what is his due. The associated virtues of religion include but are not limited to prayer, adoration, worship, obedience, and truth. This again suggests that the infused moral and theological virtues are all needed to love God. Thomas makes clear that true justice is also charity in his treatment of the Incarnation and Passion as the ultimate signs of God's justice. Notably Thomas waits until the *Tertia Pars* to treat penitence, a virtue concerned with sin in light of uniting justice and charity and bound to a sacrament whose effect is restoration of all the virtues.

Thomas concludes his account of the virtues formed by charity by discussing fortitude and temperance. The significance of charity is perhaps nowhere more apparent than in his calling attention to martyrdom as the exemplification of fortitude. Thomas follows Aristotle treating fortitude as necessary for facing death, particularly death in battle. Unlike in Aristotle, martyrdom exemplifies *perfect* fortitude. The martyrs exhibit a fear "born of love" which elicits neither cowardice nor fearlessness but rather exemplifies the perfect surrender of a life that delights in the triune God (*ST* 2a2ae q124 a4 ad2). Such fortitude comes through the gift of the Holy Spirit that bestows the patience and perseverance characteristic of the martyrs.

We mentioned earlier that temperance is about the moderation of the affections of the soul that have to do with the desire and pleasures of food and sex. "Moderation" can give a misleading impression because a temperate person considers the needs of this life as well as the needs of the life to come (*ST* 2a2ae q141 a6). As a result, temperance may mean that some will abstain from food and sex so that the "mind may arise more freely to the contemplation of heavenly things" (*ST* 2a2ae q147 a1). Those perfected by temperance are thereby able to act with an ease that comes from being freed of earthly desires based in our prideful self-love (*ST* 2a2ae q153 a5). Even so, Thomas would not have us withdraw from human affairs without qualification. He insists that the burdens of this world are imposed upon us must be borne "because of the demand of charity" (*ST* 1a2ae q61 a5 ad3, quoting Augustine). All activity—whether concerning the needs of this life or the needs of the life to come—must be charitably construed. We should not be surprised that Thomas understands honesty as an integral aspect of temperance. Honesty forms us to see the beauty that comes from seeing ourselves and the seeing the world as God's good creation (*ST* 2a2ae q145 a2).

The architectonic of Thomas' treatment of the virtues in the *Prima Secundae* testifies to a life drawn more deeply into the life of God, a life more fully described in *Secunda Secundae*. The theological context provides ample room, indeed creates space, in the Christian life for the philosopher's acquired virtues. Such virtues would remain imperfect on their own, but in the wider theological context are open to being perfected. On the whole, Thomas' vision is genuinely integrative as it sets out the image for the virtues ordered in cooperation akin to a living, structured organism whose parts work together in concrete action just as members of our bodies must be coordinated for us to move about.[17] The virtues are, therefore, best understood "all of a piece; they are interrelated, and they progress as a harmonious whole."[18] We hope, therefore, that we have made it clear that Thomas' account of the virtues is the working out of his fundamental theological conviction that God is charity itself who has given himself so that we might be made perfect through the exercise of the virtues.

17. Pinckaers, *Sources of Christian Ethics*, 227.
18. Ibid.

19

"A Recall to Christian Life":
What Is Social about the Catholic Social Teachings

with JANA BENNETT

Locating the Tradition

Catholic Social Teaching is usually identified with the papal encyclicals and a few Vatican II documents, beginning with Leo XIII's great encyclical *Rerum Novarum* (1891) and climaxing in the encyclical of John Paul II, *Centesimus Annus* (1991). The "Encyclical tradition" was created by the practice of the popes who referred to past encyclicals in order to set the context for the new encyclical they promulgated. For example, forty years after *Rerum Novarum* Pius XI celebrated its promulgation by issuing *Quadragesimo Anno* (1931). After *Quadragesimo Anno* it was assumed that modern popes should issue encyclicals about "social issues," vaguely associated with economic and political developments. These encyclicals invariably would refer to past encyclicals and describe new economic and political developments that needed to be addressed. Often the encyclicals would develop new interpretations of past encyclicals or use different emphases that would open up new lines of analysis.

The list of documents concerning societal issues usually looks like this:[1]

- *Rerum Novarum*, "The Condition of Labor" (1891), Pope Leo XIII

- *Quadragesimo Anno*, "After Forty Years" (1931), Pope Pius XI

- *Mater et Magistra*, "Christianity and Social Progress" (1961), Pope John XXI

- *Pacem in Terris*, "Peace on Earth" (1963), Pope John XXIII

- *Gaudium et Spes*, "Pastoral Constitution on the Church in the Modern World" (1965), Second Vatican Council

- *Dignitatis Humanae*, "Declaration on Religious Freedom" (1961), Second Vatican Council

- *Populorum Progressio*, "On the Development of Peoples" (1967), Pope Paul VI

- *Octogesima Adveniens*, "A Call to Action on the Eightieth Anniversary of *Rerum novarum*" (1971), Pope Paul VI

- *Justitia in Mundo*, "Justice in the World" (1971), Roman Synod

- *Evangelii Nuntiandi*, "Evangelization in the Modern World"(1975), Pope Paul VI

- *Laborem Exercens*, "On Human Work" (1981), Pope John Paul II

- *Sollicitudo Rei Socialis*, "On Social Concern" (1987), Pope John Paul II

- *Centesimus Annus*, "On the Hundredth Anniversary of *Rerum novarum*" (1991), Pope John Paul II

Such lists vary from author to author.[2] By any reckoning is a remarkable series of documents that most people consider to constitute the teachings of the Roman Catholic Church on social questions.

---

1. Curran, *Catholic Social Teaching*, 7. In addition to the collections of encyclicals listed below, all encyclicals may be found at the Vatican Web site or in paper editions from various publishers. All subsequent references to encyclicals will be provided parenthetically in the text.

2. e.g., Walsh and Davies, *Proclaiming Justice and Peace*; Gremillion, *Gospel of Peace and Justice*.

Articles about Catholic social teaching usually comment on the individual encyclicals by comparing them with one another. Later encyclicals usually claim to be in agreement with past teachings of the popes, but even the most cursory reading of the encyclicals reveals significant differences about what is thought important as well as clear disagreements. Leo XIII was anything but a friend of democracy, at least the kind of democracy he identified with developments in France, but Vatican II's *Dignitatis Humanae* suggests that certain forms of democracy are not only compatible with Catholicism but in fact may be the kind of government Catholic Christians should support. Thus the usual storyline regarding the encyclicals is that they deal with political and economic matters and may be more or less useful depending on the hearers' context.

In the "Introduction" to their collection of the Social Encyclicals, David J. O'Brien and Thomas Shannon observe that though *Rerum Novarum* was an attempt to respond to the changing economic conditions and, in particular, the attraction of socialist labor unions for Catholic faithful, the encyclicals of Leo XIII and Pius XI had little effect in America. There were a few American Catholic reformers such as Monsignor John Ryan who used those encyclicals to convince Catholics they should be for social reform, but:

> Leo XIII and Pius XI were too rigid in their theology, too rooted in preindusterial and to some degree antidemocratic ideologies to be directly useful to Americans. With Pope Pius XII's endorsement of democracy and human rights, and especially with publication of Pope John XXIII's *Mater et Magistra* in 1961, that began to change.[3]

We have no reason to deny the differences between the encyclicals, but we think the story O'Brien and Shannon tell is misleading. Indeed we believe it is a mistake to restrict the Catholic social teaching to lists that include only encyclicals that treat of political and economic matters. This is because this definition of "social" detracts from the encyclicals' *theological* nature.

Our contention that the encyclicals need to be read theologically may seem odd given that the encyclicals, particularly the early ones, argue on natural law grounds. While we cannot adequately deal with

3. O'Brien, and Shannon, *Catholic Social Thought*, 1.

the questions surrounding the content and status of natural law in the encyclicals in this article, it is important to note that the encyclicals make use, in different ways, of natural law arguments that can give the impression that the popes assume that the arguments they make in the encyclicals can be defended without appeal to theological convictions. Such an assumption, as we suggest below, is a mistake because natural law makes sense only against a theological background.[4]

Leo XIII argues in *Rerum Novarum* that people have a right to private property on the basis of natural law. Leo here critiques how socialists transfer privately owned goods into common ownership because "they worsen the conditions for all wage-earners" (§4). Though this use of natural law may appear "conservative," in fact it allows Leo XIII to sound a theme that will continue through the encyclicals of John Paul II—that is, that "man is older than the state. Before any state came into existence, man had already received from nature the right to make provision for his life and livelihood" (§7). No theme more characterizes the papal encyclicals than, before all else, persons are to be protected from all schemes that would sacrifice some for the good of others. Thus the popes from Leo XIII through John Paul II explicitly argue that crucial for our ability to enter into common tasks for the discovery of the good in common, as well as the protection of human life, is the recognition that we are not our own creators. The recognition of the dignity of each person depends on recognition that God is the beginning and end of existence, and so from beginning to end, theological issues are the burning center of the popes' understanding of the challenge of modernity for the church.

The theological agenda of the encyclicals has sometimes been lost because it has not been recognized that the encyclicals represent the Church's attempt to come to terms with the political and social changes represented by the Enlightenment. For example, Pius IX writes that *Rerum Novarum* is the "Magna Carta" that should direct Christians' social activity. However, in his extremely important book, Michael Schuck argues that the encyclicals are not their own best interpreter. Without denying that *Rerum Novarum* represented a different mood in papal encyclicals, Schuck argues that Pius XI was wrong to say in *Quadragesimo Anno*, "Leo's Encyclical has proved itself the *Magna*

4. Hittinger, *First Grace*; Porter, *Natural and Divine Law*.

Charta upon which all Christian activity in the social field ought to be based, as on a foundation." Leo was wrong because *Rerum Novarum*, according to Schuck, is best interpreted in the context of the encyclicals written from 1740 to 1877, that is, the encyclicals that were written in response to the French Revolution and the rise of the Enlightenment. Schuck notes it is tempting to forget these earlier encyclicals, encyclicals such as *Mirari vos, Singulari Nos*, as well as the infamous *Syllabus of Errors*, because they seem embarrassing from a modern perspective.[5] Yet when the social encyclicals are read without this background we can easily miss that from the perspective of the popes nothing less than worship, and the morality that depends on right worship, was a stake in their confrontation with the forces unleashed by the French Revolution and the Enlightenment.

A better reading of *Rerum Novarum* makes use of the fact that Leo XIII was not only responding to the rise of socialism and the threat he thought that presented to the Church in Europe but was also emphasizing, quoting Aquinas, that "No man is entitled to manage things merely for himself, he must do so in the interest of all, so that he is ready to share them with others in case of necessity. This is why Paul writes to Timothy: 'As for the rich of this world, charge them to be liberal and generous'" (§20). Leo XIII saw a social order of different levels each serving the other in harmony. Of course there are inequalities, but the inequalities that exist do so for the achievement of the common good. Here as in other encyclicals, common good does not mean the greatest good for the greatest number nor does it mean the satisfaction of the interests of the majority. Rather the common good names the good that all people share in common achieved through their distinctive histories (*Pacem in Terris*, §55). The common good is not whatever people decide they want such a good to be, for the good is discovered, which means it is not the result of arbitrary willing. The "state" is therefore subordinate to and legitimated only if it serves such a good. In order for the society to be appropriately ordered, therefore, "the Church, with Jesus Christ for teacher and guide, seeks persistently for more than justice. She warns men that it is by keeping a more perfect rule that class becomes joined to class in the closest neighborliness and friendship.

---

5. Schuck, *That They May Be One*, 39.

We cannot understand the goods of this mortal life unless we have a clear vision of that other life of immortality" (*Rerum Novarum* §18).

"Immortality" is not a motif usually associated with "social teachings," but if the so-called social encyclicals are read abstracted from such theological claims then their coherence is lost. The primary social challenge according to the encyclicals is quite simply atheism. For example, consider this quote, one we think informs the perspective of all the encyclicals, from *Quadragesimo Anno*:

> The root and font of this defection in economic and social life from the Christian law, and of the consequent apostasy of great numbers of workers from the Catholic faith, are the disordered passions of the soul, the sad result of original sin which has so destroyed the wonderful harmony of many faculties that, easily led astray by his evil desires, he is strongly incited to prefer the passing goods of this world to the lasting goods of Heaven. Hence arises that unquenchable thirst for riches and temporal goods, which has at all times impelled men to break God's laws and trample upon the rights of their neighbors but which, on account of the present economic system of economic life, is laying far more numerous snares for human frailty (§132).

Catholic social teachings are misunderstood if they are presented primarily as this or that pope's attitude toward socialism or capitalism. Whatever the popes have to say about socialism or capitalism is framed by their theological analysis of what form social life should take before God.

However, our contention is not only that we must recognize the theological claims inherent in the social encyclical tradition but also that the social encyclical tradition is not limited to the political and economic sphere, precisely because of those theological claims. The popes never forget that they are first and foremost pastors obligated to remind their flock that God matters not only in so-called "religious" matters, but for how all of life—economic, political, *and familial*—is ordered toward life in God. It is no accident, for example, that in nearly every encyclical the family is addressed, even where the supposed main topic may be working conditions for the poor or political problems with communism and capitalism. We thus deeply disagree with Curran when he makes the seemingly innocuous observation that "the documents of Catholic social teaching deal primarily with social, economic, and political issues. Some topics—such as the family, the role of women, and the environment—are mentioned in these documents but are developed in greater detail in other papal and hierarchical writings. This book does not deal in depth with these issues precisely because they lie outside the scope of Catholic social teaching."[6] In contrast, we argue that Catholic social thought cannot be understood if the Church's stand on sexual ethics is relegated to the sphere of "moral theology."

Following a discussion on the "theopolitics" of the encyclicals, we will therefore conclude this essay with a discussion of some of the encyclicals dealing with family. We think these encyclicals are not solely (or perhaps even primarily) about the controversial issues of birth control and the nature of the family, but that they help us see that Catholic social teaching must be interpreted as the ongoing attempt by the Church to respond to the challenge of social orders built on the assumption that we can live as if God does not exist.

The Theopolitics of the Encyclicals

We do not deny that the encyclicals are determinative political and economic documents; but the economic and political judgments of the encyclicals are meant to reflect the presumption that the Church has wisdom about politics and economics available to the Church because of her theological convictions. This presumption is clearly at work from *Rerum Novarum* to *Centesimus Annus*.

Leo XIII's *Rerum Novarum* was motivated by his concern that Catholic workmen were joining socialist labor movements, yet he addressed his concern for Catholic workers by responding to industrial growth, the rise in poverty for many while a few possess great wealth, and a general decline in "morality" (§1.1–1.2). The recommendations in *Rerum Novarum* are often assumed to favor the rich against the poor because Leo XIII assumed it was in the "nature of things" that society was made up of different classes necessary for the achievement of the common good. "A community needs to have within it different capacities for action and a variety of services at its disposal; and men are most impelled to supply these by the differences of their condition" (§15). He opposed the socialist presumption that there was a natural "warfare"

6. Curran, *Catholic Social Teaching*, 15.

between the classes or that a classless society could be built. He thought the rich had a paternalistic responsibility to aid the lower classes, but maintained the right of property against any attempt to hold property in common.

Yet Leo XIII's assumption that economic relations were subject to moral judgment meant that he refused to accept the capitalist assumption that economic relations should not be regulated by any considerations apart from the market. In many ways, Leo XIII's views, like those of Marx, were so conservative that he represented a radical alternative to capitalist assumptions. Economic relations from his perspective had to be subject to politics. He drew on Aquinas to maintain that while there might be a right to property that certainly does not mean there is a corresponding right to use that property in a manner that ignores the needs of others (§20). Accordingly the state has a right to intervene to insure that "unpropertied men" are not left to the mercy of those with property (§33–34). Without denying that the scale of wages can be established by free agreement, Leo XIII nonetheless maintained that a just wage must be paid. A just wage was not determined by the market, but rather by the needs of "a temperate and well-behaved worker" who works to sustain his family (§44–45).

What might be called Leo XIII's theological politics and economics simply did not "fit" into the secular alternatives of his day. In *Quadragesimo Anno*, Pius XI rightly praised Leo XIII's letter observing that Leo "sought no help from either Liberalism or socialism" (§10), and suggesting that he had begun "a true Catholic social science" that was neither individualistic nor a form of collectivism (§46). Pius XI, even more than Leo XIII, emphasized the social character of ownership and the necessity of the worker to be paid a sufficient wage to support him and his family. Without denying the right of the state to intervene, Pius XI articulated the principle of "subsidiary function," that is, that the family, for example, should not have its function replaced by the state or other political agencies (§80). This allowed Pius XI to distinguish some forms of socialism acceptable to Catholic social teachings distinct from communism. Yet many criticized these encyclicals for not being sufficiently concrete in what the Catholic social option might be. The encyclicals seemed to suggest that the Popes were committed to some "third way" between socialism and liberalism, but it was by no means clear what such a third way actually looked like.

John XXIII's encyclical *Mater et Magistra* affirmed the basic principles of the previous encyclicals but called attention to the disparity in economic wealth of different countries. He was particularly concerned about the fate of agriculture being overwhelmed by industrial development (§125). Accordingly he emphasized the "solidarity of the human race," a solidarity anticipated by the Church, which is by divine right universal and capable of embracing all people (§178). Such solidarity depends on the recognition of the moral order, which has no existence except from God (§208). Nothing is more pernicious in the modern era than the "absurd attempt to reconstruct a solid and fruitful temporal order divorced from God, who is, in fact, the only foundation on which it can endure" (§217).

Mater et Magistra proved to herald John XXIII's very important encyclical, *Pacem in Terris*. In this encyclical John XXIII not only introduced a more robust language of "rights" than had been characteristic of the earlier encyclicals, but more importantly he addressed the status and interrelation of states. John XXIII's appeal to rights, like the earlier encyclicals, stressed that duties precedes rights (§28), but his appeal also makes concessions to liberalism that previous popes avoided. He argues that "the universal common good" requires that the needs of refugees be met, that there be a cessation of the arms race, and that the growing economic interdependence between states be just. Though criticized for being "unrealistic," at the very least John XXIII made questions of international relations and war part of the social encyclical agenda. In doing so, he observed that it was crucial that Christians not allow a separation between their faith and their practices.

Gaudium et Spes, or the *Pastoral Constitution on the Church and the Modern World*, written during the Second Vatican Council, was unique insofar as it began by addressing "humanity", not bishops or even all Christians. That this pastoral constitution addresses "humanity" does not mean, however, that the Council represents a "humanism" divorced from theological commitments. It does so on the presumption that "in her most benign Lord and master can be found the key, the focal point and the goal of man, as well as of all human history" (§10.1). To be sure, the encyclical claims in the depths of his conscience every man detects a law that holds him to obedience (§16), but that law is the source of human dignity found in the call to communion with God (§19). This wide-ranging encyclical addresses every issue from the family to world peace by situating those challenges in the wider problem of faith in God.

In 1967 Paul VI continued John XXIII's attempt to address the international situation in his encyclical *Populorum Progressio*. In this encyclical, Paul VI was particularly critical of wealthy nations for their lack of concern for poorer nations. He calls attention to the debt that poorer nations incur with no possibility of relief. As a result, market prices that are freely agreed upon turn out to be the most unfair (§58). In *Redemptor Hominis*, John Paul II continues Paul VI's defense of the poor by maintaining the unity of the human family on the basis of the way that has stood the test of centuries, that is, the way indicated by the way of Christ the Lord; as the Council teaches, "'by his incarnation, he, the son of God in a certain way *united himself with each man*.' The Church therefore sees its fundamental task in enabling that union to be brought about and renewed continually" (§13).

John Paul II's encyclicals are more christological and biblical than the earlier "social encyclicals," but we hope we have made clear that a theological center has been there from the beginning. With John Paul II, however, there is a theological analysis of social challenges confronting the Church that makes his encyclicals unique. For example, in *Dives in Misericordia* he observes that there is an increasing feeling in the world of being under threat. As he noted in *Redemptor Hominis*, no doubt the feeling of being under threat many people feel in our day derives from the prospect of a conflict found in the stockpile of nuclear weapons, but he thinks the threat is not to be only found in the means provided by military technology. The threat also comes from the dangers "produced by a materialistic society which—in spite of 'humanistic' declarations-accepts the primacy of things over persons" (§11). In such a world, any justice to be found will depend on the recovery of the Christian refusal to be satisfied with anything other than the truth.

This same kind of analysis is also characteristic of his encyclical *Laborem Exercens*, issued on the ninetieth anniversary of *Rerum Novarum*. John Paul II clearly tries to end speculation about the Church's "third way" by focusing on the character of work. This can be seen as a strategy similar to the emphasis on the "just wage" in the earlier encyclicals, but in *Laborem Exercens* the just wage is given a wider meaning by John Paul II insisting that any society is to be judged by the quality of work that makes possible human flourishing. Accordingly the problem with communism or capitalism is the economization of work that assumes human labor primarily has an economic purpose (§13.2). So it is not merely a question of the remuneration for work, but whether work is "marked by the fundamental truth that man, created in the image of God, shares by his work in the activity of the creator and that, within the limits of his own human capabilities, man in a sense continues to develop that activity and perfects it as he advances further and further in the discovery of the resources and values contained in the whole of creation" (§25.1).

In 1987, John Paul II celebrated the twentieth anniversary of *Populorum Progressio* by issuing *Sollicitudo Rei Socialis* in which he addressed questions of development between nations. Particularly noteworthy in this encyclical is his use of the word "solidarity." He used this word to signal his support for the solidarity movement in Poland that finally led to the 1989 revolution. In this encyclical, which criticizes the arms race as well as the tension between East and West, John Paul II sounds the theme that what is needed is a civilization based on love if we are to meet the challenges of our day. Such a civilization is one in which we must see each person as the image of God, "called to share in the truth and the good which is God himself. In other words, true development must be based on the love of God and neighbour, and must help to promote the relationships between individuals and society" (§33.7). Such love is the basis for solidarity which helps us see the "other" not just as some kind of instrument, but as on "on a par with ourselves in the banquet of life to which all are equally invited by God" (§39.4). Accordingly John Paul II uses the language favored by liberation theology to suggest that Christians should have "a preference for the poor" in how they think and act about social life.

Perhaps the climax of John Paul II's encyclicals is *Centesimus Annus*, which was issued to celebrate the one hundredth anniversary of *Rerum Novarum*. John Paul begins by noting that *Rerum Novarum* had been preceded by other encyclicals dealing with teachings involving politics. He calls particular attention to *Libertas Praestantissimum* and the claim that the "bond between human freedom and truth, so that freedom which refused to be bound to the truth would fall into arbitrariness and end up submitting itself to the vilest passions to the point of self-destruction" (§4.4). That is the context, John Paul II suggests, that is crucial for interpreting *Rerum Novarum*. Moreover it is the connection between freedom and truth that is the hallmark not only of *Centesimus Annus*, but all of John Paul II's encyclicals.

The spirit of truth can be found in John Paul II's acknowledgement that the socialists got some things right (§12.2) but failed to see that without God there can be no human dignity. Yet in that respect the socialists were but creatures of the "rationalism of the Enlightenment, which views human and social reality in a mechanistic way" (§13.3). John Paul II equally criticizes the same kind of atheism that also characterizes the consumer cultures of the West. He gives a very qualified approval to "capitalism," if by capitalism is meant an economic system that recognizes the positive role of business and the market under the rule of law, but he remains a vigorous critic of consumer societies believing they are but the manifestations of atheistic materialism (§42.1).

The heart of *Centesimus Annus* is John Paul II's celebration of the year 1989 in which Eastern Europe threw off the shackles of communism. According to the pope what is "worthy of emphasis is the fact that the fall of this kind of 'bloc' or empire was accomplished almost everywhere by means of peaceful protest, using only the weapons of truth and justice" (§23.1). John Paul II is not unaware that many may find his call for a "civilization of love" to be naive, but he believes it was love, a truthful love, that triumphed in 1989. That triumph, moreover, testifies to the encyclical tradition emphasis that at the heart of so-called social problems is the question of faith in God.

We hope this review has sustained our contention that the intelligibility of the "social encyclical" tradition depends on the theological claims that are necessary to understand the political and economic perspectives taken in the social encyclicals. It should also be apparent that the social encyclicals' understanding of what should and should not be done turns on what preserves and does not preserve the flourishing of families. Therefore we will fail to understand the tradition of the social encyclicals if they are divorced from the Church's teachings about marriage, children, sex and other such topics. It is to those matters we now turn.

Family and Its Theological Significance in the Social Encyclicals

Most of the papal encyclicals, whether or not they deal ostensibly with "Church and state" as their primary topic, treat the family in relation to the Church and the state. Where this happens, it is not simply a minor referent; rather, its inclusion indicates that "social" is much broader than Charles Curran and other commentators believe. Although encyclicals such as *Humanae Vitae* are often seen as unrelated to the social encyclicals because they deal with "sexual ethics" rather than labor, socialism, capitalism, or the just wage, they should be included in the line-up of encyclicals precisely because of the way family is construed as political and seen as constitutive of justice. Moreover, the theological significance of the encyclicals is missed when these documents are not seen as part of the Catholic social tradition. There are numerous encyclicals we could treat in this section; here we shall discuss *Casti Connubii*, *Humanae Vitae*, and *Evangelium Vitae*.

In *Casti Connubii*, Pius XI puts a decidedly Thomistic flavor on the Church's understanding of marriage. In his introduction, he places marriage in the context of the new law and the sacramental grace that comes from Christ's redemption. Because he begins with Christ, Pius's concern is the great number of people who are "forgetful of that divine work of redemption" (§3). Marriage is also a human act (and therefore a moral act), and not solely a divine institution. Pius lays this out by noting the necessity of the will and particularly of "free consent" in order for a marriage to be valid (§6). Furthermore, paralleling Thomas on moral acts *vis-à-vis* animals, he says that marriage is "entirely different both from the union of animals entered into by the blind instinct of nature alone . . . and also from the haphazard unions of men, which are far removed from all true and honorable unions of the will and enjoy none of the rights of family life" (§7). Marriage may thus be subject to human law in the case of legitimate authority but such authority can never overtake the fact that God divinely ordained the institution of marriage.

Having established that entering into marriage connotes a human and moral activity, Pius continues by laying out the blessings obtained in such marriages and then addressing the virtues and vices related to these blessings. The blessings of a marriage are, predictably, the three ends that have been numbered by the church for centuries: "offspring, conjugal faith, and the sacrament" (§10). Pius's paragraphs on these blessings assume that the justice of Christ rather than justice offered by the state is necessary for rightly understanding the interrelationships of these blessings. For instance, on the blessing of conjugal faith, following Augustine, Pius suggests that the chastity lived out in the life of a husband and wife

> must have, as its primary purpose that man and wife help each other day by day in forming and perfecting themselves in the interior life so that through their partnership in life they may advance ever more and more in virtue, and above all that they may grow in true love toward God and their neighbor. (§23)

The conjugal faith expressed by a couple expresses, in part, the ordering and the justice that God's law requires, and it is not clear that this justice is at all related to the state's justice. Significantly, Pius ends his section on the blessings of marriage by suggesting that

> since it is a law of divine Providence in the supernatural order that men do not reap the full fruit of the Sacraments which they receive after acquiring the use of reason unless they cooperate with grace, the grace of matrimony will remain for the most part an unused talent hidden in the field unless the parties exercise these supernatural powers and cultivate and develop the seeds of grace they have received (§41).

The true justice of marriage and family is a grace that must be recognized and received from God. Following his section on blessings of marriage, Pius discusses the problems and vices relating to the goods of marriage, especially resulting from modernity and the rise in scientific discovery. This section therefore deals directly with the "social issues" that many contemporary theologians such as Curran see as more strictly belonging to the "social" encyclicals as opposed to the "sexual ethics" encyclicals. It is significant that a discussion of such issues comes only after Pius has first rigorously situated the place of marriage with respect to Christ's new law, but the importance of the connection is clear. For example, one key point Pius makes in this section is the relation of eugenics to the state. Pius is emphatic that "the family is more sacred than the State"; therefore, the state cannot require certain people to be sterilized or otherwise forbid their marriages. Here, the state is clearly at odds with the Church and the family; as we will see below, Pius's understanding of family/state relations is quite distinct from that found in *Gaudium et Spes*. In enumerating the corresponding vices (primarily adultery and divorce) for the sacrament of marriage, Pius again emphasizes the origins of marriage in the Church and de-emphasizes the idea that "matrimony belongs entirely to the profane and purely civil sphere" (§79). Pius also quotes Leo XIII's encyclical *Arcanum* in this section, in which Leo notes a connection between the destruction of the family and the ruin of the state. Aside from this brief interlude, which is mostly directed against communism rather than the state "as such," Pius does not wholeheartedly embrace a relationship between the Church and the state and in fact seems to be writing against his predecessor's encyclicals *Arcanum* and *Rerum Novarum* in terms of their placement of the state in relation to the family.

At the end of the encyclical Pius has a rather stern word for the state, reiterating its responsibility in economic matters and implying that the laws of the state (as seen in his example of the conflict between the civil government of Italy and the Holy See with respect to marriage laws) are best made when copied from canon law. Although Pius gives a nod to the "supreme authority of the state" in this paragraph, it seems nevertheless clear that he sees the state conceding its supposed authority on these matters to the Church (§126). When we connect this to what he says earlier, that "the best instruction given by the Church . . . will not alone suffice to bring about once more conformity of marriage to the law of God . . . a steadfast determination of the will [is needed] on the part of husband and wife . . ." it seems he is positing that the family, when seen in right relationship to Christ and the Church, is its own justice. Here we recall Pius's principle of "subsidiary function" which we noted above: that the family should not have its function replaced by the state or other political agencies. Elsewhere in *Quadragesimo Anno*, Pius writes, "Just freedom of action must, of course, be left both to individual citizens and to families, yet only on condition that the common good be preserved and wrong to any individual be abolished" (§25). Pius suggests in this whole section that the state can help the family provide justice (and indeed, through various laws enumerated in §28, it does so) and thus relationships between the family and the state are forged. However, because he insists on the family's great integrity precisely because it has been created and redeemed by God, the state and the family also experience significant distance from each other.

Indeed, on Pius's terms, we might well wonder if the state is needed at all. In §94, for instance (just following his quotes of Leo and *Arcanum*), Pius reminds his readers of the "firmly established principle . . . that whatever things have deviated from their right order, cannot be brought back to that original state which is in harmony with their nature except by a return to the divine plan." All that is necessary is our return to and reconciliation with God; the state may possibly but not necessarily be a means toward our end in God. Any justice achieved, any work done for the good of humanity, is work that may only truly be done with an eschatological view toward God and God's creation of us.

Humanae Vitae, the famously controversial document that is seemingly "about" birth control, may best be seen in line with *Casti Connubii* because it supports the view of the family taken by Pius XI and therefore other social issues. Its issuance was shocking for many moral theologians at the time because conciliar documents written only five years before, such as *Gaudium et Spes*, might be interpreted more favorably with respect to birth control and fertility (e.g. §50.2). Many in the Church assumed that subsequent Church documents on fertility would follow in the vein of *Gaudium et Spes*, especially since Pope John XXIII had established a commission to study these issues. However, Pope Paul VI wrote decisively against the commission's report and against such hopes. The storms of protest surrounding *Humanae Vitae* have yet to die down; indeed, in American Catholic circles, this document has likely been more influential than any other Church document, papal or otherwise, for moral theology.

The document begins similarly to *Casti Connubii*. Paul VI notes the institution of marriage in creation and connects it to the institution of sacramental marriage as conceived by Christ and the Church. Then he moves to consideration that marriage is not solely about divine will but also about human will in response to God. On this point, Martin Rhonheimer argues that many theologians have made a mistake by focusing on §14, which discusses unlawful methods of birth control (the biologistic section of the encyclical), and skipping over §16, which relates the procreative blessing of marriage to virtues of chastity and justice or, in other words, abstinence. Thus procreation clearly involves human beings' natural functions but must also be seen in relation to the institution of marriage in the Church, which is associated with the virtues of justice and chastity. Abstinence is therefore not part of a "method" of birth control but rather part of the virtue of chastity, and is thus a theological matter for Rhonheimer.[7]

---

7. Rhonheimer, *Natural* Law, 113ff.

By showing marriage in relation to virtues and as instituted by God, Paul VI has set the scene for marriage and related issues such as birth control to be inextricably connected to other, supposedly more "social" issues. On this point David Matzko McCarthy argues:

> This second section [in *Humanae Vitae*] discusses Paul VI's critique of modern accounts of economic development, which ironically do not advance but rather diminish human life since they block a full theological understanding of human flourishing. It is not merely coincidental that reductionist proposals for economic progress depend upon contraceptive technology as a means for advancement, for the upward mobility of citizens, and for the development of nations. To this degree, HV's opposition to artificial birth control parallels Paul VI's arguments in documents such as *Populorum Progressio* and *Octogesima Adveniens*. The teaching on contraception is a social teaching, and the social teaching is founded on theological claims about human solidarity and upon the continuity between our natural and supernatural, or eschatological fulfillment.[8]

Paul VI takes a strong stance against economic systems that support contraception because large families are barriers to economic advancement but which also assume that productivity and progress happen best when people turn away from so-called domestic affairs and turn toward producing wealth as autonomous individuals.

As with *Casti Connubii*, *Humanae Vitae* is best seen in terms of its description of our last end in God because both documents argue that when we recognize our God-given nature we best see how we fulfill our human destiny in God. Conversely, the modern political state and economics reduce human activity to choices, such as how to control births, that are best for "me" but do not also lay bare the fact that these choices already subsume us into a worldview in which we must reject some of what makes us human. In fact, the exclusion of the familial encyclicals from social encyclical lists does precisely what our contemporary global economy would want us to do: separate family and marriage from social issues because family and marriage are matters of choice that should have little to do with the social ills of our time whereas considerations of poverty and the just wage help society and especially the individual.

8. McCarthy, "Procreation," 700.

John Paul II's encyclical *Evangelium Vitae* deals precisely with this supposed distinction between the family and the social. As he writes,

> ... broad sectors of public opinion justify certain crimes against life in the name of the rights of individual freedom, and on this basis they claim not only exemption from punishment but even authorization by the State, ... In such a cultural and legislative situation, the serious demographic, social and family problems which weigh upon many of the world's peoples and which require responsible and effective attention from national and international bodies, are left open to false and deceptive solutions, opposed to the truth and the good of persons and nations. (§4)

John Paul II is very clear that the family and what are deemed as "social issues" are intertwined and neither one should be disposed as a matter of individual choice.

Evangelium Vitae is the encyclical from which we have two often-used phrases: "Culture of Death" and "Culture of Life." John Paul II here discusses abortion and birth control directly but throughout refers to the many other ways in which we, particularly in richer countries, try to assume control over life and death by pretending that these are matters of individual choice. For instance, he references the great injustices of poverty, malnutrition, ecological imbalance, drug use, and the like that are perpetuated in and by our culture even as we, as individuals, seek control over our experience of life and death (§10). "All this is aggravated," moreover,

> by a cultural climate which fails to perceive any meaning or value in suffering, but rather considers suffering the epitome of evil, to be eliminated at all costs. This is especially the case in the absence of a religious outlook which could help to provide a positive understanding of the mystery of suffering. (§13–15)

Where many might view the Church's stance against birth control and abortion as a blatant lack of concern for the world's over-population, and resultant overuse of global resources, poverty and malnutrition, the pope addresses these same problems by turning the blame squarely on those who reject the theological question of what it means to be human. It is not the Church, he says, but rather the Culture of Death, with its love of avoidance of suffering and its preference for inalienable rights and autonomy, that perpetuates the problems the human global community faces.

Conclusions

When we view *Casti Connubii, Humanae Vitae, Evangelium Vitae* and other supposedly non-social encyclicals as being in the same tradition as the "social" encyclicals, we see that Catholic social teaching, particularly as found in papal and conciliar encyclicals, demonstrates some of the best theological argumentation found concerning the Christian life. For instance, in *Rerum Novarum*, often described as a social encyclical concerned with just wages, the family also comes into the discussion. It is seen as a social unit older than the state, which is one important means by which Leo XIII argues against socialism. Socialism is problematic for Leo because it "dissolves the bonds of family life" and thus causes injustice (*Rerum Novarum*, §26). He also writes that "no human law can take away the original natural right of a man to marry or in any way impose limits on the principal purpose of marriage ordained by God's authority from the beginning" (§10). Still, for Leo, "the family is a true society equally with the state and, like the state, it possesses its own source of government, with the authority of the father." Such views are in tension with the positions taken in *Casti Connubii* and *Humanae Vitae*, which suggest that the family is not a society equal to the state, but surpassing the state. While Leo clearly puts forth a similar understanding of natural law that makes sense only in connection to our creation in and by God (as opposed to modern understandings of natural law), his view of family does not take into account Christ's new law in the way that *Casti Connubii* and *Humanae Vitae* do. These two later documents restore a theological understanding of Christian marriage and family as grounded in God; in their accounts, therefore, marriage and family are not merely elements whose brokenness demonstrates the destructiveness of socialism or any other governmental structure. Marriage and family enable us to see the character the God we worship and of our world as one created and endowed by God.

Similarly, *Gaudium et Spes* may be seen both as evaluating previous documents and being theologically critiqued in subsequent documents. This Vatican II document suggests that "man's social nature makes it evident that the progress of the human person and the advance of society itself hinge on one another. For the beginning, the subject and the goal of all social institutions is and must be the human person" (§25). The human person must be able to attain certain necessary items in order to live a properly human life; among these are "the right to choose of state of life freely [celibacy or marriage] and to found a family. . . ." (§26.1). Thus *Gaudium et Spes* seems to differ from *Rerum Novarum* just to the extent that in the latter marriage is understood as an elemental and more primitive institution that shows the destructiveness of the state. *Gaudium et Spes*, however, acknowledges that family and state are more complexly related, which means no account of the good of the human person is adequate in which that good is not first and foremost God. *Humanae Vitae* stands in tension with *Gaudium et Spes* just to the extent that *Humanae Vitae* reasserts the theology necessary for an understanding of "the human person." But this can only be shown if, as we argue, the "social encyclical" list is made much broader and examined much more deeply for the theological arguments running throughout.

Questions about gender roles, which necessarily arise in discussions of families, also come up in this tradition of argumentation. Feminist scholars as well as sociologists often discuss the ways in which women's "traditional" roles of wife, stay-at-home mother, and child-rearer support a hierarchical and oppressive family structure for women. As Lisa Cahill describes, "For women, marriage and family are dangerous, at least as traditionally practiced."[9] However, in the past few decades the Church has come to understand that the family is the "domestic Church" (*Familiaris Consortio* §21) and that it has a vocation to be a "community of disciples" concerned with economic and social justice.[10] On Cahill's view, this move toward an understanding of family as a community in relationship to the Church represents "a social and relational appreciation of marriage, now informed by more egalitarian and personalist insights."[11] Cahill rightly sees this discussion of the family as theological in nature; for her, the family is a "*topos*"

9. Cahill, *Sex, Gender, and Christian* Ethics, 198.

10. Ibid., 210.

11. Ibid., 209.

in Christian history and theology that has been recovered and reinterpreted in recent years.

The theological points the encyclical tradition makes about the family and women are not limited to questions of family in relation to Christian discipleship and relationships between men and women. Nor should the letters pertaining to women be read primarily as reactions to feminist theory or as defenses of patriarchal understandings of family. Rather, the primary question is how descriptions of "family" and "woman" faithfully give theological witness. For instance, in *Casti Connubii*, Pius XI believes that the right ordering of the couple toward also means "subjection of wife to husband," which "may vary according to the different conditions of persons, place, and time. . . . But the structure of the family and its fundamental law, established and confirmed by God, must always and everywhere be maintained intact" (§28). Paul VI's apostolic letter *Octagesima Adveniens* might be seen as taking a similar attitude where he speaks against women's "false equality which would deny the distinctions laid down by the Creator himself and which would be in contradiction with woman's proper role. . . ." (§13). Paul VI certainly has in mind the rise of feminist critique in the 1960s and 70s but his purpose in the letter is not to deal with this primarily. His is a response to particular historical circumstances, but the history is inscribed within the context of the gospel of Christ. In both Pius's and Paul's letters, the popes make clear the relationship between God's nature as Creator of all and the nature of people and families. The issue for both these popes is that atheism is not only a problem as a "belief" that is somehow psychologically internalized (which is often the way we think about atheism) but atheism is also concretely lived out in familial structures and in daily patterns of life.

In contradistinction to the popes mentioned above, John Paul II suggests a somewhat different reading of the Pauline passages about subjection of women to men and also a different theological argument. He follows Ephesians 5 in yoking the created dignity of marriage, in which, in their love for one another, man and woman become "one flesh," to the call for "*mutual subjection out of reverence for Christ*' (cf. Eph 5:21). This is especially true because the husband is called the 'head' of the wife *as* Christ is the head of the Church; he is so in order to give 'himself up for her' (Eph 5:25), and giving himself up for her means giving up even his own life . . . in the relationship between Christ and the Church the subjection is only on the part of the Church, in the relationship between husband and wife the 'subjection' is not one-sided but mutual" (*Mulieris Dignitatem*, §24). Admittedly, many contemporary feminists would find as much fault in John Paul II's statements as with claims made in the earlier encyclicals because the ideas of submission and subjection are present and potentially unhelpful for women who have been subjected to patriarchal authority and have thereby been oppressed. Nonetheless, here the pope offers a different reading of the relationship between gender and family than his predecessors. *Mulieris Dignitatem* provides some theological responses to feminist concerns by means of Christ's life and work. The question of who "woman" is, is first put into the context of the history of salvation and the mystery of the incarnation, of a woman bearing God's son (§3). "Woman" is first a theological matter; contemporary political questions of women's rights are continually read in this light.

In addition to women's roles, we could mention the environment, the nature of the family, the state, and the just wage, which all have theological import and continue to be assessed in the encyclicals and other documents. An artificial delineation of what counts as a social encyclical only detracts from the nature of the encyclicals and causes problems in reading them. What counts as social is also theological; that the popes and the councils have written encyclicals that intertwine all these matters makes this point clear. Our lives are beset on all sides by atheism and the popes have offered numerous counter-proposals.

20

Methodist Theological Ethics

with D. STEPHEN LONG

Why Methodists Cannot Distinguish between Theology and Ethics

In *Practical Divinity: Theology in the Wesleyan Tradition*, Tommy Langford suggest that an essential clue for appreciating Wesley's theological vision is the selection of materials he put in the *Christian Library*. The *Christian Library* was the fifty-volume theological resource Wesley published from 1749 through 1755. He described the books as "Extracts from the Abridgements of the Choicest Pieces of Practical Divinity." Langford observes that this is a perfect description of Wesley's understanding of theology—that is, theology is never an end in itself but should serve the interest of transformed living. Accordingly theology is in service to essential Christian practices, which means that theology is first and foremost to be preached, sung, and lived.[1] Wesleyan theology is not abstract speculation but joyful contemplation and obedience, manifest in the conjoining of happiness and holiness.

---

1. Langford, *Practical Divinity*, 20–21.

Perhaps one of the most striking implications of Wesley's theology is his insistence that there is an essential connection between happiness and holiness. Methodism defied the modern presumption that you must choose between being happy and being sanctified. Wesley was well aware that his refusal to separate happiness and holiness would put him at odds with much of his society, but one of the reasons he was so successful was his ability to describe how empty lives could be in which the desire to be happy was separated from holiness.

For example, in his "An Earnest Appeal to Men of Reason and Religion," Wesley observed that one of the most important questions you can ask anyone is "Are you happy?" He then describes the kind of life many lead, which they think confirms they are happy. But it leads only to boredom:

> You eat, and drink, and sleep, and dress, and dance, and sit down to play. You are carried abroad. You are at the masquerade, the theatre, the opera house, the park, the levee, the drawing-room. What do you do there? Why, sometimes you talk; sometimes you look, at one another. And what are you to do tomorrow, the next day, the next week, the next year? You are to eat, drink, and sleep, and dance, and play again. Are you, can you, or any reasonable man be satisfied with this? You are not. It is not possible you should. But what else can you do? You would have something better to employ your time; but you know not where to find it on earth. And, indeed, it is obvious that the earth, as it is now constituted, even with the help of all European arts, does not afford sufficient employment to take up half the waking hours of its inhabitants. What then can you do? How can you employ the time that lies so heavy upon your hands? This very thing which you seek declare we unto you. The thing you want is the religion we preach. That alone leaves no time upon our hands. It fills up all the blank spaces of life.[2]

Holiness makes us happy because it gives us something to do. Accordingly for Wesley there can be no separation between theology and ethics. For such a separation suggests a Christianity that has accommodated itself to the world in "beliefs" separated from how we live. It is, therefore, not surprising that many theologians in the Methodist tradition do their theology as "ethics" or, perhaps more accurately, as "theological ethics." But, as Langford suggests, perhaps the best descrip-

2. Wesley, *Works* 8:18–19.

tion we have for the way Methodists do theology is what Wesley called "practical divinity."

That Methodism is so constituted does not mean it is unique when compared with other ecclesial bodies. In fact, the question—"Are you happy?"—is a common question in much of the Christian and philosophical tradition. Methodists also share with other Christians common resources that enable the ethical life: Scripture, sacraments, the moral theological tradition, conciliar doctrinal commitments, as well as the communion of saints ancient and contemporary. Yet within this larger common treasury, it is not surprising that the sermons of John Wesley have proved to be a crucial resource for insuring that no strong distinction can be made between theology and ethics. Wesley's sermons, like most theology prior to modernity, are traditioned reflections on Scripture. For the refusal to divorce holiness and happiness is a refusal required by Scripture.

If Methodists have a distinct charism to contribute to the church, it is less the content of its theological ethic and more the form by which Methodists pursue this common end of happiness and holiness, as well as the expectation of its embodiment in the time between the times. In order to develop this understanding of a Methodist theological ethics, we will present three interrelated characteristics. First we will display Wesley's understanding of the content of a good life—that is, the relation between happiness and holiness—by directing attention to what the Methodist tradition calls this life of beatitude. Such a life is often identified as "the religion of the heart," but that phrase, so often used to separate theology from ethics, we hope to show must be understood in the light of the Sermon on the Mount.

Secondly, we will spell out the ecclesial presumption necessarily implied by the refusal to separate happiness and holiness. Every ethic, as MacIntyre has argued, entails a sociology. For Methodists, the sociology necessary that holiness not be separated from happiness is the church—a church, moreover, that must be separated from the world so that the world might be served. Finally, we will explore why Methodists have rightly refused to turn holiness into an ideal never to be realized. Wesley's understanding of perfect love we believe offers the means to help all Christians understand why growth is ongoing for Christians who would be holy and happy.

Religion of the Heart

Mr. Wesley stated, "The sum of all true religion is laid down in eight particulars." Those eight particulars he identifies with the beatitudes Jesus annunciated in the Sermon on the Mount in Matthew. Wesley referred to the first six of these—poverty of spirit, mournfulness, meekness, righteousness, mercy, and purity of heart—as "the religion of the heart."[3] The seventh, "peacemaking," expresses the Christian's outward embodiment of the six. Those who best exemplify the religion of the heart and its external witness will embody the eighth, "persecution for righteousness' sake." These "eight particulars" define the "sum of true religion" for Wesley and for the Methodist tradition.

Wesley's focus on the beatitudes for the depiction of the Christian life is, of course, not unique. Saints Augustine and Aquinas developed a very similar understanding of the Christian life in their reflections on the Sermon. Dietrich Bonhoeffer, Martin Luther King Jr., Dorothy Day, and Oscar Romero not only reflected on the Beatitudes in a similar fashion, they actually embodied this religion of the heart, which meant three of them received the eighth beatitude as well.

Methodist theological ethics, therefore, has no monopoly on, nor does it have any stake in claiming to be alone, the "religion of the heart." Servais Pinckaers, a contemporary Roman Catholic moral theologian, traces this kind of theological ethics in much of Christian tradition. He claims that Thomas Aquinas' monumental *Summa Theologiae*, which was vastly influential for the moral life from the Middle Ages on, was primarily a "listening to the Lord teaching on the mountain" in the company of the church fathers, doctors, and philosophers. For in this teaching we find "the answer to the question of happiness."[4]

We are not suggesting that Wesley drew directly on Aquinas to inform his account of the Christian life, but rather that Wesley stood in the central stream of the Christian tradition, refusing to separate happiness from holiness. Wesley rightly thought that all great philosophers and theologians maintained that the end of the moral life is happiness. For example, Aristotle claimed that happiness is our true end, which is rightly sought for its own sake rather than a means to something else.

---

3. Wesley, *Works*, 1:517.
4. Pinckaers, "Sources of the Ethics of St. Thomas Aquinas," 24, 28.

The Christian tradition built on and radically converted this basic Aristotelian notion. Such a conversion was necessary because only God is rightly sought for no other end than himself. Aristotle presumed everything was given an end for which it naturally had the means to achieve it. The virtues were the natural excellences one could achieve by rightly ordering the passions in order to achieve that end, which would bring happiness.

Yet for the Christian tradition, the end that would bring happiness was friendship with God, something Aristotle would have found impossible. This end could not be an achievement for we do not have the means intrinsic to such an end. Something more is needed. For this reason the Christian tradition found not only that the virtues were important for the moral life, but that the virtues themselves come to us as gifts. These gifts, the beatitudes and theological virtues, are given to us through the work of the Holy Spirit mediated through Word and Sacrament. For Wesley this meant happiness and holiness were inseparable through the one work of the Spirit.

Wesley's account of the beatitudes, therefore, locates him in the great catholic tradition of the virtues as crucial for the formation of a holy people. The virtues are habits that form our passions and direct our desires and actions toward their true end, the goodness of God. Christian tradition does not dispense with the natural virtues for the human ethical life, but it does resituate them. We cultivate virtues within the context of communities that form our character. Because only the church participates in Christ's divinity as one of the threefold forms of his body (along with his historical body and the Eucharist), it is necessary for the perfection of the ethical life. The church takes up the natural, everyday ordinary passions associated with family, economics, and politics and converts and perfects them by ordering them to their true end in God. The result is a holiness that bears witness to God's renewal of creation.

It is not surprising that this understanding of the role of the virtues in the Christian life has found resonance in Methodism. Wesley founded the Methodist societies that offered the resources necessary for people to acquire the virtues necessary for a happy and holy life. Originally they were small ecumenical communities within the church held together by three general rules: do good, avoid harm, and attend upon the ordinances of God. The first two rules are the primary precepts of the natural law tradition. The third shows how Wesley read that tradition in terms of the Word and Sacrament, which are the primary ordinances of God. They give us the resources necessary to live out this law. By themselves, the precepts "do good" and "avoid evil" are so purely formal that they are of little to no help. The Word and Sacraments specify the good to be achieved and any evil to be avoided. For this reason, the law is not an end in itself. It directs our actions to virtuous ends. The purpose of the law is the religion of the heart. The sacraments are the means that assist us in the journey.

The "religion of the heart" is Wesley's phrase to describe the life made possible by Jesus' death and resurrection. So there can be no separation of doctrine and life. As we suggested at the beginning, Methodist theological ethics brings those two modes of discourse—"theology" and "ethics"—into such a close identity that one cannot be decisively distinguished from the other. To understand and embody the good, we must know God. Ethics cannot be known or done well without theology. Theology cannot be done or known well without its performance in everyday life.

As a result Methodist theological ethics has never developed elaborate accounts of natural law or common grace that seek to explain ethics outside of specific theological doctrines. Nor does it fit well the modern political and moral theology that rejected revelatory doctrinal claims for a morality grounded in reason alone.[5] These developments were just coming into focus when Wesley came to the end of his life. But he recognized what was at stake—the notion that the first and second tables of the Law (Ten Commandments), the love of God and the love of neighbor, could be divided. In 1789, toward the end of his life, Wesley wrote,

> Thus almost all men of letters, both in England, France and Germany, yea, and all the civilized countries of Europe, extol "humanity" to the skies as the very essence of religion. To this great triumvirate, Rousseau, Voltaire and David Hume, have contributed all their labours, sparing no pains to establish a re-

5. So many have charted this history that a list of works that illustrate this point would be voluminous. Nonetheless Lilla's *Stillborn God* succinctly traces these developments in Rousseau and Kant. See especially 118–31 and 132–62. Lilla also notes the role "natural law" played in these developments. See 71. Charles Taylor makes a similar argument in *A Secular Age*.

ligion which should stand on its own foundation, independent of any revelation whatever, yea, not supposing even the being of a God. So leaving him, if he has any being, to himself, they have found out both a religion and a happiness which have no relation at all to God, nor any dependence upon him. It is no wonder that this religion should grow fashionable, and spread far and wide in the world. But call it "humanity", "virtue", "morality" or what you please, it is neither better nor worse than atheism. Men hereby willfully and designedly put asunder what God has joined, the duties of the first and the second table. It is separating the love of our neighbour from the love of God. It is a plausible way of thrusting God out of the world he has made.[6]

It is not surprising, given Wesley's critique of this modern development, that Methodist theological ethics found resonances with two twentieth-century theological movements from vastly different ecclesial homes: the Reformed theology of Karl Barth and the Catholic theology of Henri de Lubac. Both can help us identify what Wesley and the Methodist tradition recognized. The virtue of "liberality," which could also be understood as a genuine humanism or a generosity toward others, seems consistently to be abandoned when shorn of its theological particularity in christological and Trinitarian claims, as it inevitably does in procedural liberalism. Barth saw this in his former teacher Adolf von Harnack's politics where "culture" became a source of its own independent of Christology. De Lubac saw it in the politics of a neoscholastic like Garigou-Lagrange's defense of Vichy France based on "nature" as an autonomous source.[7] It may seem counter-intuitive for those of us taught that morality and theology should be divorced for the sake of humanism, but a Methodist ethics at its best recognizes the inextricable link between its particular doctrines of God and the shape of the moral life.

Methodist theological ethics, in conformity with previous moral theologies in the Christian tradition, brings together the two great mountains in the biblical narrative in order to give shape to the moral life. First, the law is given to Moses on Mount Sinai as he gazes upon the glory of God. Then, without abrogating that law, Jesus looks down from

---

6. *Works*, 4:69.

7. De Lubac's *Drama of Atheist Humanism* and well as Barth's correspondence with Harnack nicely explains the issues involved.

the mountain and pronounces blessedness upon all who embody its meaning. In so doing, he radiates the glory of God (a glory he also demonstrated on a mountain in his transfiguration). These two mountains merge into one as Jesus' beatitudes "fulfill," that is complete or perfect, the law. The law is not an end in itself,[8] but rather the law points forward to its figural fulfillment in Christ who alone recognizes its meaning and offers the eschatological judgment: "blessed are you when . . . ." Gazing upon the vision directs our will and intellect to the knowledge and desires of God. Theology and morality are united. This is the religion of the heart.

Means for the Pursuit of the Religion of the Heart

This "religion of the heart" should not be misunderstood as only an inward, pious disposition, which it can be, and has been, so misunderstood by Methodists. The blessed life Jesus announces in the beatitudes is not a private, interior possession of individuals but a communal form of life that will be displayed socially and politically. In the Sermon on the Mount, Jesus shows us the goal of the Christian life. This is the form of life he will bless on the Last Day. But between the times it is the great joy that Christ has made it possible for some to become the earnest of the kingdom to come.

The life of such a people will include three elements. First, they will recognize that only One Person ever lived this blessed way of life by his own agency. Jesus is the only one who embodied the fullness of righteousness found in the beatitudes. As often happens in a world in rebellion against God and God's goodness, such a perfect performance ended in his persecution even unto death. Thus, as we suggested above, some who fully embody the first seven beatitudes will often receive the "gift" of the eighth. The church is built on the blood of the martyrs.

Second, we must seek to embody his righteousness in our own life. This is what it means to confess "the Lord is our righteousness." It means more than a purely external imputation of righteousness; it also entails an inherent sanctifying righteousness. Third, we should honor those who embody these ways of life and hold them up as examples to be emulated, recognizing that such a righteousness must be socially

8. Nor was it to be this in Judaism as midrash itself demonstrates.

enacted. Holiness is not a heroic ethic for individuals. To be made holy is difficult and demanding because our lives are made vulnerable to others. Such a people become witnesses so that the world might see the kind of life God would have all people live.

Just as the doctrines of the church are the communal norms for how we should think and teach, so the beatitudes and gifts are the communal norms for how we should live. Whenever and wherever we find the fruits of peaceableness, righteousness, mercy, etc. we should recognize a proper performance of the grace of the Holy Spirit. We should not be surprised then, or dismiss it as the politicization of our doctrinal standards, when we discover that our Methodist doctrines speak about matters of war and economics.

For instance, Article XVI of the United Methodist Church states that we believe war and bloodshed are contrary to the gospel and spirit of Jesus. This is not a private judgment; it is a public confession that reminds us that the religion of the heart requires a political embodiment in how we think about matters like participation in war, economics, family life, and the government. We cannot assess how we should live in these important social institutions without keeping our vision on the way of life Christ announces as blessed. This vision must be the focus of the Christian life and the source of our evangelistic witness to the world.

This is why Wesley said, "Christianity is essentially a social religion." By that he did not mean that we should be involved in some vague thing called "social justice." Much good may be done in the name of justice, but too often calls for justice do not capture the rich character of the Methodist tradition's understanding of Christianity's essential social character. For Methodists, to live out the beatitudes means we must live in a community in which people have learned to be accountable to one another in their daily life. Such accountability means that we will also have to learn, as Matthew 18 indicates, what it means to live as a reconciled people. Only a justice shaped by the practice of reconciliation makes it possible for Christians to be a people of peace in a world of violence. We are called to witness to this peaceableness even while we wait upon it.

For instance, in reference to the beatitude of peacemaking, John Wesley "bemoaned" the violence Christians perpetrated on other Christians. He wrote,

> Yea, what is most dreadful, most to be lamented of all, these Christian churches!—churches ("Tell it not in Gath" but alas, how can we hide it, either from Jews, Turks, or pagans?) that hear the name of Christ, "the Prince of Peace," and wage continual war with each other. . . . O God! How long? Shall thy promise fail? Fear it not, ye little flock. Against hope believe in hope. It is your Father's good pleasure yet to renew the face of the earth. Surely all these things shall come to an end, and the inhabitants of the earth shall learn righteousness. "Nation shall not lift up sword against nation, neither shall they know war any more," . . . They shall all be without spot or blemish, loving one another, even as Christ hath loved us. Be thou part of the first-fruits if the harvest is not yet.[9]

Methodist ethics takes to heart this call to be "first fruits." Even though the face of the earth is not yet renewed, we are called to witness to its reality. This makes Christianity "social." This emphasis on a holiness that witnesses to the renewed creation gives Methodist ethics resonances with the work of the Anabaptist tradition. As Albert Outler noted, Wesley's ecclesiology is a potentially unstable blend of Anabaptist and Anglican or Catholic doctrines of the church. Like the Anabaptists, "holiness" and witness characterizes the church more so than its offices. Like the Catholics, Wesley still "unselfconsciously" assumed that the sacraments, and to some extent an episcopal order, gave the church its common identity across time and space.[10]

It is not surprising, given this understanding of the beatitudes, that some theologians in the Methodist tradition have been influenced by the Anabaptist theologian John Howard Yoder. For Yoder emphasized

---

9. *Works*, 1:507–9.

10. Outler writes, "One is bound to be impressed by Wesley's wholly unselfconscious assumption that, even after all he had done that would inevitably lead to separation, he was, and always had been, a devoted and loyal Anglican. He speaks quite naturally of 'our [Anglican] liturgy,' as when he cites the eucharistic prayer 'for the whole state of Christ's church militant here on earth.' . . . However, his final conclusions are neither Anglican, Lutheran, nor Calvinist. The essence of the church, for Wesley, need not be sought in its visible institutions, not even some invisible *numerus electorum*. The church as Body of Christ is the company of all true believers, 'holy' because its members are themselves holy. This is, therefore, an unstable blend of Anglican and Anabaptist ecclesiologies; it is also one of Wesley's most daring syntheses. Its outworking in the subsequent histories of Methodist and Anglican ecclesiology have yet to be probed as deeply as they deserve, which is also to say that its ecumenical significance has yet to be fully appreciated" (Outler, "An Introductory Comment," *Works*, 3:45–46).

the relationship between eschatology, ethics, and holiness. Christians engage in politics and ethics based not on the desire to find the right "handle" on history to insure it goes in the direction we think it should. Rather Yoder argues that we are called to faithfulness and patience to the Lamb who was slain and yet was victorious. Yoder, commenting on John's visions in *Revelation*, says,

> "The lamb that was slain is worthy to receive power!" John is here saying, not as an inscrutable paradox but as a meaningful affirmation, that the cross and not the sword, suffering and not brute power determines the meaning of history. The key to the obedience of God's people is not their effectiveness but their patience. The triumph of the right is assured not by the might that comes to the aid of the right, which is of course the justification of the use of violence and other kinds of power in every human conflict. The triumph of the right, although it is assured, is sure because of the power of the resurrection and not because of any calculation of causes and effects, nor because of the inherently greater strength of the good guys. The relationship between the obedience of God's people and the triumph of God's cause is not a relationship between cause and effect but one of cross and resurrection.[11]

Yoder's understanding of the relationship between ethics and eschatology nicely frames Wesley's understanding of the kind of life we must live as a holy people. It is no surprise so many Methodists draw on Yoder's work to help make sense of our calling as Christians in the Methodist tradition. For example, Yoder wrote an important essay originally titled, "Peace without Eschatology?" Much of Christian ethics from early to mid-twentieth century assumed that ethics replaced eschatology. Yoder challenged this displacement, arguing that only if we have a robust eschatology can Christian ethics make sense.

According to Yoder, to live eschatologically is to live in the light of "a hope which, defying present frustration, defines a present position in terms of the yet unseen goal which gives it meaning."[12] This is why "witness" is so important both to the Holiness and Anabaptist traditions—that is, we believe we can take the time to be faithful to what Jesus gives us in the Sermon on the Mount because we know that the present age does not constrain and define all our ethical options. We witness to what is coming because it already came: "Christ has did, Christ is risen, Christ will come again." Eschatological earnestness defines Methodist ethics. For this reason our ethics need not be reactive. It does not begin with evil and asks how we avoid it. It begins with the fullness of the gift received in Word and Sacrament and asks how we embody and bear witness to it.

The Embodiment of Sanctification and Perfection

While Methodism was still a movement and not yet a church, the only requirement for admission was "a desire to flee from the wrath to come and to be saved from sins." To flee from eschatological judgment is to acknowledge that God intends to restore creation consistent with Jesus' work in Scripture. The greatest ethical failure would be to reject or neglect that restoration. The role of the Methodist movement was to assist persons living into the life God intended, which was to flee from eschatological judgment by avoiding evil, doing good, and being attentive to what God gave us for this purpose.

The "General Rules" of the United Methodist Church were developed to help Methodists lead lives of accountability to one another. Membership vows assume these rules to this day. Under each of these general rules were a number of other rules Methodists were expected to abide. This could appear to be a contradiction. If the only requirement for membership in Methodism was a desire to flee from eschatological judgment and be saved from sin, why were the Methodists given so many rules to which they were held accountable? The answer is found in the understanding of what it means to "be saved from sin." As the United Methodist Discipline still states, "wherever this is really fixed in the soul, it will be shown by its fruits." This is why the "religion of the heart" cannot be understand as a private, interior disposition about which no one can discern or make judgments. A Methodist theological ethic assumes that the good to be done and the evil avoided will always have an external shape. It can be indicated by the manner of life of the Methodist people.

That Methodists expect the Christian life will of necessity be given an external shape provides its tradition with both its temptation and its promise. Its temptation is the tendency toward a moralistic legalism.

For instance, Methodists for long periods of their history did not drink. This violated one of the general rules that stated that Methodists should do no harm through "drunkenness: buying or selling spirituous liquors, or drinking them, unless in cases of extreme necessity." Drunkenness is not, of course, a vice Methodists alone opposed. It made the list of the "seven deadly vices" throughout Christian tradition, usually under the larger vice of gluttony, something the early Methodists particularly eschewed. It is also a social matter. Alcohol and drug abuse have grave social consequences. Methodist clergy were required to take vows against all drinking of alcohol throughout much of the twentieth century. But the Methodist opposition to alcohol was so strident and moralistic that they were even responsible for breaking the common Christian tradition of using wine for the Eucharist in favor of grape juice. (Welch was a Methodist.) Methodists turned an important social issue into a personal code of conduct that lost its social significance. Eucharists with wonder bread and grape juice show that Methodism succumbed to the temptation to be moralistic. The fact that in many Methodist churches and seminaries you can proclaim just about any kind of Christology available, but the use of wine for the Eucharist is impermissible, shows that Methodism still falls prey to legalism.

During the same time that Methodists were convinced a necessary external fruit of salvation would be prohibition from alcohol, we did not feel the same moral compunction in overturning another one of our General Rules: the prohibition against slaveholding. As we look back on our history, we can see that our attempts to identify the necessary fruit of salvation fell far short. Methodist theological ethics boldly asks and answers, "What does the religion of the heart look like in ordinary life?" We often got, and surely still get, those answers wrong. When we do we quickly become moralistic and legalistic. This occurs on one hand when Methodists turn the shape of the Christian life into a private piety. It happens on the other hand when we turn it into a proceduralism that will supposedly insures fairness through rigorous laws of interest group representation. Methodist theological ethics are tempted by "methodism."[13]

13. "Methodism" is the assumption that we must first have a method, or correct procedure, to justify our knowledge before we can legitimately hold it. See Abraham's *Crossing the Threshold*, 33. Abraham critiques "methodism" in favor of a particularism that does not work on the assumption that we can only claim knowledge if we have

Perhaps it would be easier and safer for a Methodist theological ethics to avoid altogether the effort to identify the shape of the Christian moral life? We could follow some Christian traditions who are much more sober about the ability either to identify or embody the shape of a blessed, happy good life in the time between the times. Who could know what it looks like? We could emphasize the importance of the Christian as *simul justus et peccator* and develop a theological ethics based on a dialectic, where every account of a righteous life must also stand under its negation by its inevitable participation in evil.

Yet Methodists have rightly refused this option. We have done so because, as we have emphasized, Methodism stands in the great catholic tradition that refuses to separate holiness and happiness. We pray and sing: "Finish, then, thy new creation; / pure and spotless let us be. / Let us see thy great salvation / perfectly restored in thee; / changed from glory into glory, / till in heaven we take our place, / till we cast our crows before thee, / lost in wonder, love, and praise."[14] Notice that the prayer to finish and perfect the new creation comes before we take our place in heaven.

Charles Wesley's hymn significantly suggests the eschatological position we identified above that is at the heart of Wesley's (and Yoder's) understanding of the Christian life. The new creation is not something that simply takes place in heaven at the end of time; it begins with Jesus' victory. He is the perfect performance of what it means to be human in time. Because we can now participate in his life, we do not know what is possible or impossible. Perfection of the new creation even in a small way is open because of Christ's work. The creation is not something inevitably marred with sin such that it must be destroyed. Christ vindicates it, and in that vindication new possibilities emerge, even the possibility of perfection. This is why Methodists are asked at ordination, "Do you expect to be made perfect in love in this lifetime?" Forensic notions of justification that only emphasize imputation cannot sustain

---

a method to verify it first. He thinks this is the problem with much of our modern accounts of knowledge. His critique of "methodism" concerns knowledge, not the Methodist church. But when "method" becomes defined by this account of how we understand, then "methodism" tempts Methodism. Our preoccupation with the right structure as the way to fix problems may be a sign that we have fallen prey to this temptation. Discipline becomes defined by "method" rather than holiness and happiness.

14. From Charles Wesley's hymn, "Love Divine, All Loves Excelling."

this theological ethic. As Wesley put it, we cannot claim the Lord is our righteousness if he, through the Holy Spirit, cannot then produce in us our own righteousness.

The Methodist understanding of sanctification and the call to holiness must refuse to forego the identification and embodiment of the Christian life in this lifetime because of its call to perfection. We do not expect to see it completely until Christ's return. Nor can we assume we have arrived. As Wesley put it, "Yea, and when we have attained a measure of perfect love, when God has circumcised our heart, and enabled you to love him with all your heart and with all your soul, think not of resting there. That is impossible. You cannot stand still; you must either rise or fall; rise higher or fall lower. Therefore the voice of God to the children of Israel, to the children of God, is, 'Go forward!'"[15]

But we have anticipations of the life we will share with God. The Christian therefore can bear witness to God's gift that sanctifies us into God's own perfection. Wesley saw this clearly exemplified in the beatitudes. Yet what is crucial to sustain his understanding of Christian holiness is that the call to perfection is never separated from its christological home that makes it intelligible. When such a separation occurs, as has sometimes happened, the call to perfection and holiness can degenerate into various versions of humanistic and sentimental progressivism.

We believe that Wesley has been and can continue to be a resource to help Methodists and all Christians recognize that anytime a strong distinction between theology and ethics occurs something has gone wrong. Wesley's insistence that holiness and happiness were but two sides of the same coin rightly indicates that Christian theology is an exercise in practical divinity. Whether a discipline exists or does not exist called theological ethics is not of great importance. What is important is that Christians at this time and this place discover—a discovery Wesley makes possible—that to be a Christian is to be made a participant in the very life of God.

---

15. Cited in Hauerwas, *Sanctify Them in the Truth*, 124. Hauerwas goes on to note that one of the weaknesses in Wesley and by implication the Methodist tradition is that this progress is presented as "stages" easily identifiable. See also 128.

21

Friendship and Freedom:
Reflections on Bonhoeffer's "The Friend"

Bonhoeffer and Bethge

Edwin Robertson reports that when *Letters and Papers from Prison* was published in 1953 it was not known that Bethge was the friend who received the letters. Nor was it known who was the subject of the poem "The Friend." However in 1957 Bethge was speaking at a student conference in New Hampshire where one of the participants asked him who the recipient of letters and poem might be because "it must be a homosexual partnership." "Bethge replied immediately, 'No, we were fairly normal!' and he went on to show that there was no such sexual relationship."[1]

I suppose we should not be surprised that an American assumed a poem as intense and intimate as "The Friend" must indicate a sexual relation. Such an assumption betrays the impoverished understanding of friendship characteristic of America in the 1950s and even more prevalent in our current context. However it is certainly true that the friendship between Bonhoeffer and Bethge was, as any real friendship must be, unusual depending as it did on their ability to negotiate their very different backgrounds and personalities.

1. Robertson, *Dietrich Bonhoeffer's Prison Poems*, 89–90. I will use Roberson's translation of "The Friend."

"The Friend" not only witnesses to the intensity of Bonhoeffer's friendship with Bethge, but Bonhoeffer's friendship obviously was equally important for Bethge. *Dietrich Bonhoeffer: A Biography* is surely a testimony to this extraordinary friendship.[2] In his lovely book, *Daring, Trusting Spirit: Bonhoeffer's Friend Eberhard Bethge*, John de Gruchy observes that Bonhoeffer and Bethge seldom expressed in public their deep feelings about anything, much less their friendship.[3] Indeed Bethge says he refrained from becoming involved in debates surrounding Bonhoeffer's theology because his "friendship (with Bonhoeffer) was of an intimacy which makes it impossible for me to enter the debate about him. I have quite deliberately kept out of that."[4] Bonhoeffer's poem, therefore, at once celebrates without betraying their friendship.

Bonhoeffer wrote "The Friend" as a birthday present to Bethge. Bonhoeffer had first sent Bethge "Stations on the Road to Freedom" for his birthday, but he later wrote and sent him "The Friend." When he received "Stations on the Road to Freedom," Bethge wrote Bonhoeffer observing,

> You can't give anything more personal than a poem. And you could hardly give me greater joy. There is no greater self-sacrifice, no better way of signifying an otherwise unattainable nearness than in a poem. And it is probably *the* form, because it makes visible the inwardness that is bound up and held in check within it. Unlimited surrender of the spirit awakens anxiety in the receiver. But this restrained surrender seems to me to be the highest degree of friendship and understanding. And as a result there is something very cheering and stimulating about it. Its touch is steadier and more far-reaching than that of a letter. Many thanks.[5]

2. Bethge, *Dietrich Bonhoeffer*.

3. De Gruchy, *Daring, Trusting Spirit*, 63.

4. As quoted in ibid., 114.

5. Bonhoeffer, *Letters and Papers From Prison*, 395. The relation between "Stations on the Road to Freedom" and "The Friend" is a subject in itself. Particularly important, given Bonhoeffer's stress on the relation between freedom and friendship in "The Friend," is his understanding of the relation of freedom and death in "Stations on the Road to Freedom." If, as he suggests in "Stations," it is only "through discipline may a man learn to be free," the discipline necessary to freedom is dying. Later in "Miscellaneous Thoughts," Bonhoeffer will observe "Death is the supreme festival on the road to freedom" (376). The freedom that makes friendship possible as well as friendship being the necessary form freedom takes is that gained through learning to die.

The poetry Bonhoeffer wrote in the last year of his life, as Geffrey Kelly and Burton Nelson suggest, no doubt reflects Bonhoeffer's sense of loss at being separated from those he so desperately loved.[6] In his letter to Bethge of June 5, 1944, Bonhoeffer says he would be behaving like "a shy boy" if he hid from Bethge that he has begun to write poetry. Bonhoeffer would soon acknowledge that "I'm certainly no poet!," but I do not think it was his lack of talent for poetry that made him hesitant to reveal he was writing poetry. Rather it was his sense that poetry, as Bethge suggested, made visible an inwardness that Bonhoeffer found difficult. Indeed Bonhoeffer noted he had not even told Maria he was writing poetry because he was unsure whether it "wouldn't frighten her more than please her." Which means, I believe, that the intimacy his poem "The Friend" displays is a commentary on all his poems.[7]

"The Friend" is not only the poem that illumines Bonhoeffer's other poems, but "The Friend" cannot be read well separate from *Letters and Papers from Prison*, and *Letters and Papers From Prison* is better read in the light of the poem. *Letters and Papers from Prison* was made possible by Bonhoeffer's and Bethge's friendship, but the book is also a testimony to and constitution of that friendship. Therefore to appreciate the poem it helps to catch glimpses into how Bonhoeffer and Bethge understood their friendship. I do not, however, want to give the impression that the poem is an *explanation* of their friendship. For I assume that one of the tasks of poetry is to teach why "explanations" are not all that interesting. However, a few remarks about Bonhoeffer and Bethge are important.

From an external perspective Bethge and Bonhoeffer were unlikely friends. Bethge described himself as a "country boy" in contrast to the cultured world from which Bonhoeffer came.[8] Bethge had not had Bonhoeffer's education nor did Bethge understand himself to be an intellectual, or at least Bethge did not pretend he ever desired to be a German professor. Bethge was first and foremost a pastor, which no

6. Kelly and Nelson, *Cost of Moral Leadership*, 236. As I will suggest below, Bonhoeffer's turn to poetry also involved his increasing conviction that he would be killed. That is why the poems often reflect his understanding of the relation of freedom and death.

7. Bonhoeffer's June 5, 1944, letter is on page 319 in *Letters and Papers From Prison* and his comment that he is no poet is on page 372.

8. De Gruchy, *Daring, Trusting Spirit*, x.

doubt was one of the reasons Bonhoeffer admired him. Bethge's commitment to the church no doubt was one of the reasons Bonhoeffer found him such a kindred spirit at Finkenwalde, but also important was their common love of music.

Bonhoffer captures the sheer enjoyment they seem to have taken in their early relationship in the lines of the poem:

> Playful, at first,
> on the far journeys of the spirit,
> into wonderful,
> distant realms,
> which in the haze of the mourning sun
> glitter like gold;
> but in the heat of the day
> encompassed;
> while in the stirrings of the night,
> lit only by the lamp,
> like hidden private treasures,
> they beckon the seeker.

Yet it would be a mistake to assume that Bonhoffer's and Bethge's friendship was always easy. Bethge admired Bonhoeffer, but he did not stand in awe of him. In one of his letters to Bethge, Bonhoeffer reports that the soldier who supervised Bethge's visits to Bonhoeffer in prison was amazed that Bethge did not flatter Bonhoeffer.[9] Neither Bethge nor Bonhoeffer would have befriended anyone who only told them what they wanted to hear. For example, Bethge, though he liked the poem "The Friend" very much, suggested that "lovely" in the line, "the lovely cornflower to bloom" could be omitted because "at that point you suddenly move from a continuous view point into a value judgment."[10]

It is not, therefore, surprising that in a letter dated November 18, 1943, Bonhoeffer writes to Bethge concerning his wish to discuss with Bethge a story he is writing about a middle-class family. Bonhoeffer observes that this is a subject that he and Bethge had often talked about, which makes him feel how much he misses their conversations. Bonhoeffer says, "I may often have originated our ideas, but the clarifi-

---

9. Bonhoeffer, *Letter and Papers From Prison*, 315.

10. Ibid., 396.

cation of them was completely on your side. I only learnt in conversation with you whether an idea was any good or not. . . . Your comments on details are so much better than mine."[11] In a later letter Bonhoeffer even tells Bethge that he lives in a daily spiritual exchange with him. "I can't read a book or write a paragraph without talking to you about it or write a paragraph without talking with you about it."[12]

Bonhoeffer quite simply trusted and depended on Bethge in a manner different than anyone else in his life including Maria. The kind of doubts Bonhoeffer explores in the poem "Who Am I?" he hopes someday he might share with Maria, but he cannot expect her yet to be ready for him to speak so directly.[13] According to Bonhoeffer, Bethge was the only person who knew "how often *accidie*, *tristitia*, with all its menacing consequences, has lain in wait for me."[14] Bonhoeffer knew that Bethge was in many ways a much more attractive person than he was. Bonhoeffer, for example, observed he did not know anyone who did not like Bethge, but many people did not like him. He acknowledges that he is not particularly concerned about this, because "whereever I find enemies I also find friends, and that satisfies me. But the reason is probably that you are by nature open and modest, whereas I am reticent and rather demanding . . ."[15]

The Poem

The inspiration and language for writing "The Friend" came directly from Bethge. Bonhoeffer had written Bethge on November 18, 1943, observing that it is not easy to resolve the conflict between marriage and friendship, but the marriage of Eberhard and Renate, a marriage Bonhoeffer celebrated and for which he wrote a wedding

11. Ibid., 130.

12. Ibid., 223.

13. Ibid., 370.

14. Ibid., 129.

15. Ibid., 189. Bonhoeffer could not only be demanding, he was quite capable of jealously. De Gruchy reports tension that developed concerning a trip that Bonhoeffer had planned with Bethge to Switzerland. Bethge invited Gerhard Vibrans and Bethge's brother to come with them, which irritated Bonhoeffer. Bethge clearly confronted Bonhoeffer, leading Bonhoeffer to apologize to Vibrans. De Gruchy, *Daring, Trusting Spirit*, 30–35.

sermon,[16] Bonhoeffer implied would be spared this problem because of Bonhoeffer's imprisonment.[17] Bethge, however, responds challenging Bonhoeffer's claim that friendship, next to marriage, should be considered one of the stable aspects of life. Bethge observes:

> But that is not the case, at least as far as the recognition and consideration of others is concerned. Marriage is recognized outwardly—regardless of whether the relationship between the couple is stable or not—each person, in this case the whole family, must take into account and finds it the right thing that much should and must be undertaken for it. Friendship—no matter how exclusive and how all-embracing it may be—has no *necessitas*. . . . Friendship is completely determined by its content and only in this way does it have its existence.[18]

Bonhoeffer responded agreeing, in contrast to marriage and kinship, that friendship depends entirely on its own inherent quality making friendship hard to classify sociologically. Bonhoeffer speculates that perhaps friendship can be regarded as a subheading of culture and education, but that may not be much help because, in contrast to work, state, and the church, each of which has a divine mandate, it is not clear where culture and education are to be classified. Culture and education do not belong to the sphere of obedience, but to freedom, which surrounds the three spheres of the mandates. But it is freedom that makes a good father, citizen, or worker a Christian. Therefore:

> Just because friendship belongs to this sphere of freedom ("of the Christian man"?!), it must be confidently defended against all the disapproving frowns of "ethical" existences, though without claiming for it the *necessitas* of a divine decree, but only the

16. Bonhoeffer, *Letters and Papers From Prison*, 41–47.

17. Ibid., 131. In a Christmas Eve letter he wrote to Renate and Eberhard just prior to Eberhard being sent to Italy, Bonhoeffer tried to prepare them for their separation. Bonhoeffer addresses Renate, observing that "so far, Eberhard and I have exchanged all the experiences that have been important to us, and this has been a great help to us; now you, Renate, will have some part in this. You must try to forget your 'uncle' and think more of your husband's friend" (176). We do not know what Renate must have thought about her uncle's offer to share Eberhard with her. Bonhoeffer does continue, noting that nothing can make up for the absence of someone we love and we should not try to find a substitute. Moreover, it is nonsense to say God can fill the gap separation creates. God wants us to keep it empty because the emptiness helps keep alive the communion we have enjoyed with one another.

18. Bonhoeffer, *Letters and Papers From Prison*, 181.

> *necessitas* of *freedom*. I believe that within the sphere of this free-
> dom friendship is by far the rarest and most priceless treasure,
> for where else does it survive in this world of ours, dominated as
> it is by the *three other* mandates? It cannot be compared with the
> treasures of the mandates, for in relation to them it is *sui generis*;
> it belongs to them as the cornflower belongs to the cornfield.[19]

"Cornflower belongs to the cornfield" becomes the major image
Bonhoeffer uses in his poem "The Friend." Though the poem is written
to celebrate his friendship with Bethge, the poem becomes the occasion
to explore the relation of friendship and the mandates. As early as 1932
Bonhoeffer had challenged the assumption that the "orders of creation"
could be considered revelations of the divine commandments, but good
Lutheran that he was the mandates remained givens, to be sure givens that are to be christologically disciplined, that give form to our life
together.[20] In *Performing the Faith: Bonhoeffer and the Practice of Non-
Violence*, I suggest that Bonhoeffer's attempt to rethink the mandates
remained incomplete, but that he never quite made up his mind about
the status of the mandates is exactly what gives life as well as makes his
poem "The Friend" so interesting.[21]

Bonhoeffer begins the poem reminding us that the mandates are
literally grounded in the ground.

> Not from the hard ground,
> where blood and race and binding oath
> are sacred and powerful;
> where the very earth itself
> keeps guard and defends
> the consecrated orders of creation

19. Ibid., 193.

20. Bonhoeffer's attack on the orders of creation being used to justify a nation going to war can be found in his July 26, 1932, address to the Youth Peace Conference in
Czechoslovakia in Bonhoeffer, *A Testament to Freedom*, 103–7.

21. Hauerwas, *Performing the Faith*, 48–54. I find it odd that Bonhoeffer, at least
as far as I know, never explored the relationship between the mandates and the powers. I am tempted to say he did not because as Yoder suggests in *Politics of Jesus*, the
church in the age of Constantine looked to other resources to construct a social ethic
(134–36). Yet how the mandates express God's fallen but good creation could have
provided Bonhoeffer with a way to think through the perversions of the mandates
as well as their christological *telos*. For a critique of my critique of Bonhoeffer on the
mandates, see Brock, "Bonhoeffer and the Bible," 28–29.

against the madness and frenzy of disorder;

not from the hard ground of the earth,

but freely chosen and desired,

the longing of the spirit,

which neither duty nor law requires,

the friend will offer to the friend.

The mandates are not arbitrary, but rather they are constitutive of our very ability to live life together. The state and work are rooted in the ground, but so is marriage. In a letter to Maria dated August 12, 1943, Bonhoeffer says

> When I think about the situation of the world, the complete darkness over our personal fate and my present imprisonment, then I believe that our union can only be a sign of God's grace and kindness, which calls us to faith. We would be blind if we did not see it. Jeremiah says at the moment of his people's great need "still one shall buy houses and acres in this land" as a sign of trust in the future. This is where faith belongs. May God give it to us daily. And I do not mean that faith which flees the world, but the one that endures the world and which loves and remains true to the world in spite of all the suffering which it contains for us. Our marriage shall be a yes to God's earth; it shall strengthen our courage to act and accomplish something on earth. I fear Christians who stand with only one leg upon earth also stand with only one leg in heaven.[22]

I have no doubt that Maria loved Bonhoeffer, but it is nonetheless remarkable that she was not offended by his suggestion that their marriage was equivalent to Jeremiah's purchase of land in the face of the exile. That purchase as well as Bonhoeffer's engagement was, of course, a gesture of hope against hopelessness, but even Maria would

---

22. Bonhoeffer, *Letters and Papers From Prison*, 415. Earthly beauty was extremely important to Bonhoeffer. For example in a letter to Bethge dated March 24, 1944, Bonhoeffer comments on Bethge's observation about the "rarity of landscape painting in the South." Bonhoeffer calls attention to Brueghel, Velasquez, and the French impressionists, noting, "There we have a beauty that is neither classical nor demonic, but simply earthly, though it has its own proper place. For myself, I must say that it's the only kind of beauty that really appeals to me. I would include the Magdeburg virgins and the Naumburg sculptures" (*Letters and Papers From Prison*, 239). The attraction of the beauty of the "natural" is clearly present in "Who Am I" in the line, "yearning for colors, for flowers, for the voices of birds."

have wanted Bonhoeffer to regard her as something more than the occasion of a prophetic sign-act. Maria makes clear that she knew well Bonhoeffer's love, observing that he "had the ability to convert his annoyance at the limitations of our relationship, and the misunderstandings that resulted from them, into a hopeful and eager expectation and challenge. He was able to transform the fumblings and erratic emotions of a young girl into the assured certainty that this was an addition and a source of strength to his own life."[23]

Bonhoeffer's understanding of marriage as a mandate is developed in his wedding sermon for Eberhard and Renate. "Marriage," he observed, "is more than your love for each other" because marriage is a "post of responsibility" toward the world and mankind. Accordingly it is not love that will sustain their marriage, but marriage that sustains their love making marriage indissoluble. There is a given relationship between husband and wife requiring that the wife be subject to the husband and the husband is to love the wife. By divine ordinance, wife honors the husband when he properly performs his office to represent to the world that as Christ was head of the church so the husband is head of his family.[24]

Bonhoeffer's account of marriage and the family may betray his class presuppositions, but far more important is how his account of marriage and the family is grounded in the ground.[25] Marriage, like the

23. Von Wedemeyer-Weller, "The Other Letters from Prison," in Bonhoeffer, *Letters and Papers From Prison*, 412.

24. Bonhoeffer, *Letters and Papers From Prison*, 43–46.

25. Bonhoeffer could be quite insightful about his family. For example, in the same letter to Bethge on August 14, 1944, in which he observed that "in the long run human relationships are the most important thing in life" he reflected on his family. He notes that Bethge strives to live up to the highest demands, noting how much depends on the demands we make on ourselves. He then observes, "I've found it one of the most potent educative factors in our family that we had so many hindrances to overcome (in connection with relevance, clarity, naturalness, tact, simplicity, etc.) before we could express ourselves properly. I think you found it so with us at first. It often takes a long time to clear such hurdles, and one is apt to feel that one could have achieved success with greater ease and at less cost of these obstacles could have been avoided . . . But one can never go back behind what one has worked out for oneself. That may be inconvenient for others and even for oneself sometimes, but those are the inconveniences of education" (*Letters and Papers From Prison*, 386–87). Yet he also regrets that Maria and he are not on the same "wavelength" about literary matters, regretting her reading habits. He observes "I would very much like my wife to be as much of the same mind as possible in such questions. But I think it's only a matter of time. I don't like it

field of corn, is given life by the realm of freedom in which friendship flourishes, making possible the transformation of the mandates by the gospel. No one planted or watered the "lovely cornflower" but it comes to life bringing life to those that have sacrificed their life's blood "beside the field of daily bread."

Such a growth by necessity is unplanned and defenseless, trusting its very beauty to make its existence possible. The fruit and the flower are alike beautiful:

> Whether the fruit serves the flower
> or the flower the fruit only—
> who knows?
> Yet both are given to us.
> Costly, rare blooms—
> Sprung from the freedom of the playful,
> brave, and trusting spirit
> in a happy hour—
> such is the friend to the friend.

So the mandates make friendship possible, but without friendship the mandates threaten not to be life-giving.

The spirit, Bonhoeffer tells us, will move a man to "great, serene, audacious thoughts of heart and mind," making him look the world in the face, "with clear eyes and open countenance." Then, in lines which I think give expression to Bonhoeffer's sense of isolation. Bonhoeffer says

> then action is joined to the spirit
> —by which it stands or falls—
> from this action,
> sound and strong,
> the work grows,
> giving content to thought and meaning
> to the life of the man;
> then the active, lonely man
> longs for
> the befriending, understanding spirit of another.

---

when husbands and wives have different opinions. They must stand together like an impregnable bulwark. Don't you think so? Or is that another aspect of my 'tyrannical' nature that you know so well?" (*Letters and Papers From Prison*, 148).

Loneliness was surely Bonhoeffer's fate as he confronted and opposed the Nazis. Bethge befriended Bonhoeffer, but he seems to have done so in a manner that acknowledged the necessary loneliness that Bonhoeffer (and he) must endure.[26] Their loneliness, however, was bounded by the discovery of common judgments that made a history possible. Bonhoeffer, in a letter to Bethge dated February 4, 1944, his birthday, recalls that for eight years he had celebrated this day with Bethge. He reminisces:

> Eight years ago we were sitting at the fireside together. You had given me as a present the D major violin concerto, and we listened to it together; then I had to tell you a little about Harnack and past times; for some reason or other you enjoyed that very much, and afterwards we decided definitely to go to Sweden. A year later you gave me the September Bible and a lovely inscription and your name at the top. There followed Schlonwitz and Sigurdshof, and we had the company of a good many people who are no longer with us. The singing at the door, the prayer at the service that you undertook that day, the Claudius hymn, for which I'm indebted to Gerhard—all those things are delightful recollections that are proof against the horrible atmosphere of this place. I hope confidently that we shall be together again for you next birthday, and perhaps—who knows?—even for Easter. Then we shall get back to what is really our life's work; we shall have ample work that we shall enjoy, and what we have expe-

26. An analysis of Bonhoeffer's understanding of the relation between shame, solitude, and loneliness needs to be made. In *Sanctorum Communio*, he distinguished solitude from loneliness, associating the former with "divine wrath." Accordingly he observed that "Solitude is an ethical category, and being under God's wrath is worse than the misery of loneliness" (*Sanctorum Communio*, 285). He continues to explore these relations in *Creation and Fall*, in his profound meditations on Adam's loneliness. He observes, "The first person is alone. Christ was alone; we also are alone. But everyone is alone in his own way. Adam is alone in anticipation of the other person, of community. Christ is alone because he alone loves the other person, because Christ is the way by which the human race has returned to its Creator" (96). Bonhoeffer saw quite well that we are only alone with another, which means every relation necessarily creates a form of loneliness. This leads him in the *Ethics* to say, "Even the most intimate community must not obliterate the secret of the disunited human being" (305). He notes that shame is produced by being revealed in words that expose one to another, meaning our most personal joys and pains we keep "from being revealed in words. Accordingly shame can truly be overcome" by being put to shame through the forgiveness of sin, which means through the restoration of community with God and human beings. This takes place in confession before God and before another human being" (306).

rienced in the meantime will not have been in vain. We shall probably always be grateful to each other for having been able to go through this present time as we're now doing. I know you're thinking of me today, and if our thoughts include not only the past, but also the hope of a future lived with common purpose, even though in a changed circumstance, then indeed I'm very happy.[27]

A long passage, but one essential to understand the "befriending" that Bonhoeffer's poem describes. Bethge's and Bonhoeffer's friendship, as any significant friendship must be, was constituted by contingencies. That is why friendship, and in particular the friendship between Bonhoeffer and Bethge, can only be captured by a story to be told, re-told, and revised. In the same letter to Bethge, Bonhoeffer wishes that Bethge might meet someone who has more in common with him, but observes, "I think that we, who have become more exacting than most people with regard to friendship, have more difficulty in finding what we miss and are looking for. In this respect, too, it isn't a simple matter to find a 'substitute.'"[28] Of course a substitute is not possible, because no one else has shared their history. What can be hoped for rather is that such a friendship opens the friends to new friendships that their history requires.

The next lines of the poem might suggest that Bonhoeffer understood his friendship with Bethge as an escape from the political struggle:

> Like a clear, fresh flow of water,
> in which the spirit cleanses itself from the dust of day,
> cooled from the burning heat,
> strengthened in the hour of tiredness—
> like a fortress, to which after the dangers of battle
> the spirit retires
> to find safety and, comfort and strength—
> such is the friend to the friend.

No doubt Bonhoeffer's and Bethge's friendship was a zone of safety, comfort, and strength, but I think it would be a mistake to read Bonhoeffer's understanding of friendship as an escape from the political. Rather, as the first lines of the poem suggest, friendship is that which saves the

27. Bonhoeffer, *Letters and Papers From Prison*, 207–8.
28. Ibid., 208.

mandates from their potential to be repressive. Such an interpretation I believe is justified by the stanza of the poem in which friendship becomes the necessary condition for the trust that saves us from cynicism and despair. In the "Prologue: After Ten Years," placed at the beginning to *Letters and Papers From Prison*, Bonhoeffer observed that one of the characteristics of their time was the experience of betrayal. "The air that we breathe is so polluted by mistrust that it almost chokes us."[29]

Yet where mistrust has been broken through Bonhoeffer notes that a confidence is discovered otherwise unimagined. Without trust life is impoverished.[30] Indeed without trust life is impossible. To trust requires that we put our lives, our very understanding of ourselves, into the hands of others. Accordingly our duty is to foster and strengthen trust when possible because trust is "one of the greatest, rarest and happiest blessing of our life in community, though it can emerge only on the dark background of a necessary mistrust. We have learnt never to trust a scoundrel an inch, but to give ourselves to the trustworthy without reserve."[31]

It is not surprising, therefore, in his "Thoughts on the Day of the Baptism of Dietrich Wilhelm Rudiger Bethge," Bonhoeffer observed that the presumption of modernity—that is, that people could make their way in life with reason and justice—has failed. Believing that no enemies existed, those who prided themselves on their ability to be rational found themselves in a war they did not want but for which they must now risk losing all they hold dear. They thus learned that the world is controlled by forces against which reason can do nothing. In contrast, Dietrich Bethge will "know that you have enemies and friends, and you know what they can mean in you life. You are learning very early in life ways (which we did not know) of fighting an enemy, and also the value of unreserved trust in a friend."[32]

Trust, the trust made possible by friendship, is for Bonhoeffer not a retreat into the private, but rather an alternative politics to the privatization of the self and friendship that is the natural breeding ground for totalitarian politics. Friendship is not a safe-haven from the struggle,

29. Ibid., 11.
30. Ibid., 29.
31. Ibid., 12.
32. Ibid., 298.

but rather the source of the truthfulness necessary to challenge the despair produced by the betrayal of trust.

> And the spirit wants to trust,
> trust unconditionally.
> Disgusted by the worm,
> hidden in the shadows of the good,
> nourishing itself on envy, scandal and suspicion,
> and the poisonous tongues of a nest of vipers,
> who fear and hate and vilify
> the secret of the free mind,
> and of the sincere heart.
> The spirit longs to cleanse itself
> from all hypocrisy
> and trust itself to the other spirit
> totally open,
> bound to that spirit, freely and in truth.

Bonhoeffer's love of the Psalms clearly shapes these lines of the poem. We were made to trust in God, but the very trust in which we were created becomes the source of distrust creating a world that flourishes on envy and scandal. Such a world cannot escape violence, because "there can only be a community of peace when it does not rest on lies and injustice."[33] "The Friend" is certainly a celebration of Bonhoeffer's and Bethge's friendship, but the poem also provides Bonhoeffer with the opportunity to claim the significance of friendship, and the trust friendship requires as well as makes possible, for a political alternative to the terror that was Germany.

Bonhoeffer refuses to hide, however, the difficulty friendship can create. The friend befriended gives praise and thanks, finds

> joy and strength
> in the other spirit.
> Even under severe pressure
> and strong rebuke
> he willingly submits.

33. Bonhoeffer, *No Rusty Swords*, 168. For my account of the significance of Bonhoeffer's understanding of the political significance of truthfulness see *Performing the Faith*, 55–72.

Not by command, nor by alien laws and doctrines,

but by good and earnest counsel,

which liberates,

the mature man seeks

from the true friend.

Far or near

in success and in failure,

the one recognizes in the other

the true helper

towards freedom

and humanity.

This is the *necessitas* of *freedom* Bonhoeffer had named in response to Bethge's suggestion that friendship has no *necessitas*. This is the *sui generis* character of friendship that makes the "cornflower belong to the cornfield." Bonhoeffer had learned to trust Bethge to tell him the truth, but he knew he was not one that always received the truth gladly. We should not, therefore, read it as an empty gesture that Bonhoeffer writes to Bethge on November 18, 1943, to express his gratitude that Bethge "bore with such patience and tolerance all the things with which I have sometimes made life hard for you. I ask you for forgiveness, and yet I know that we have shared spiritually, although not physically, in the gift of confession, absolution, and communion, and that we may be quite happy and easy in our minds about it. But I did just want to tell you this."[34]

Poetry is the Political

Does Bonhoeffer the poet say in his poetry what he was not able to say more directly? I see no reason to ask or to answer such a question. I have, however, tried to suggest that in this poem, "The Friend," Bonhoeffer explored how friendship, as Aristotle suggested, is the test case for any politic. In his reply to Bethge's claim that friendship has its own *necessitas*, Bonhoeffer observed,

Our "Protestant" (not Lutheran) Prussian world has been so dominated by the four mandates that the sphere of freedom has

34. Bonhoeffer, *Letters and Papers From Prison*, 193.

receded into the background. I wonder whether it is possible (it almost seems so today) to regain the idea of the church as providing an understanding of freedom (art, education, friendship, play), so that Kierkegaard's "aesthetic existence" would be re-established within it? I really think that is so, and it would mean that we should recover a link with the Middle Ages. Who is there, for instance, in our times, who can devote himself with an easy mind to music, friendship, games, or happiness? Surely not the "ethical" man, but only the Christian.[35]

"The Friend" is Bonhoeffer's attempt not only to say, but to enact in a world of terror, that God's church exists, making friendship possible. "The Friend" is Bonhoeffer's prayer thanking God for Bethge's friendship, but the poem is also his alternative politic.

35. Ibid., 193.

APPENDIX

Learning to See Red Wheelbarrows:
On Vision and Relativism

so much depends
upon

a red wheel
barrow

glazed with rain
water

beside the white
chickens

—WILLIAM CARLOS WILLIAMS

There are several strategies that one can take in responding to criticism. Perhaps one of the most successful is to thank the critic for bringing to light issues that you had overlooked: giving you a chance to address them will make your position that much stronger. There are several variations of the strategy: (1) the critic has raised some very interesting issues that I have dealt with elsewhere or have developed in my forthcoming publication; (2) the critic has certainly caught me in some unhappy expressions or found minor inconsistencies in my position, but with small qualification my substantive points all remain correct; (3) the critics' arguments are important but I can incorporate them into a larger synthesis. These strategies are designed to make both critic and criticized feel good, and it is assumed this is an example of how serious intellectual exchange should take place.

I have detailed the strategy because I want to make clear that it is not the one I'm following in this response.[1] As far as I am concerned, I do not need to give anything away to my critic. He has badly misread and misunderstood me—and his own position, as far as I can make sense of it, exemplifies some of the problems I have been criticizing. The mistakes in interpretation could have been corrected if he had taken the time to read some of my other work, but since he failed to understand the essay to which he has directed his criticism, I suspect that further reading would serve no useful purpose.

In one respect however I appreciate his criticism, for the way I have been misunderstood may exhibit the tendency among others who read my work. They may, like my critic, assume that my agenda is that of most contemporary philosophical ethicists—namely, an attempt to avoid relativism by providing an account of the "foundation of morality." Much of modern moral philosophy, for both philosophical and social reasons, involves a Kantian-inspired attempt to establish the objectivity of moral knowledge. The strategy has been to show that the "institution of morality" or "the moral point of view" is rooted in rationality itself and is thus independent of other forms of human activity such as politics, etiquette, religion or custom. Anyone who tries to suggest there may be other ways to conceive moral rationality and objectivity cannot help but appear from the Kantian perspective to be relativistic.[2]

My concerns however are theological, and in spite of my appreciation for some aspects of the Kantian program (I normally prefer Kant to his followers), I think it fails to provide sufficient intellectual tools to show how Christian convictions should function to direct our lives. Indeed, when one begins by assuming that there must be something like a "concept of morality" or a "foundation of morality," one artificially creates the problem of how such a "concept" or "foundation" is or

1. However, I cannot pass up this opportunity to call attention to my book *Truthfulness and Tragedy: Further Investigations in Christian Ethics*, which I hope everyone will buy and read. I think the argument there is relevant to some of the issues raised here.

2. For a fuller development of the issues raised in this paragraph, see Burrell and Hauerwas, "From System to Story." This essay also appears in Hauerwas, *Truthfulness and Tragedy*.

is not related to those "nonmoral" convictions that form our lives. The ahistorical and abstract nature of modern ethical theory is a witness to the theory's commitment to free the moral life from our contingent starting points in the hopes of securing moral certainty. Such a request is illusory as it ends not only by distorting the nature of Christian convictions, but also by failing to provide the moral skills necessary to negotiate the many claims and powers that inextricably constitutive our lives.

Thus I am accused of "arguing that some kind of total vision of life is a necessary condition for morality." But the only time I've ever used the phrase "total vision of life" is in the Murdoch quote and it is clear that she is not using it with the meaning or force that Professor Robbins ascribes to it. Indeed, closer attention to her work or to mine would make clear that the isolation of the phrase as indicating the moral need for some completely coherent worldview or "philosophy of life" runs counter to hers and to my understanding of moral existence. Secondly, I have never argued that a "total vision of life" is a "necessary condition" for morality, as indeed I do not think that "morality" needs or requires a "necessary condition" or foundation. While I do not think that "morality" is a "completely equivocal" term, neither do I think that there is a conception of morality that underlies all its manifold uses. Rather, there are many uses of the term "morality" whose family resemblances can be spelled out, but not in the way that encourages us to assume that we have the basis for a "theory of morality."

Moreover, use of the metaphor "vision" is not an attempt to find a functional equivalent to the Kantian notion of rationality for ethics, but I have rather used it as a way to direct attention away from ethical theories that make decisions about quandaries central to the moral life. To stress the importance of vision does not imply we need a "total vision of life," but that the moral life is much more a matter of learning the skill to see accurately what Aristotle called "ultimate particulars"—e.g., red wheelbarrows, kestrels, suicide, murder, lying, and so on.[3]

In that respect I have stressed as strongly as I can that we must be trained to see something since we cannot simply see by looking. In order to be able to see our vision must be trained by our ability to say. For unless we are able to say what we see, we lack the perduring dis-

---

3. For example, see my treatment of moral notions in *Vision and Virtue*, 11–29.

positions necessary to be able to describe particulars accurately. We're tempted to try to substitute "total vision of life" for the slow and painful acquisition of the virtues necessary to sustain the particularity and otherness of what confronts us. But this only leaves us more unable to see, as any "total vision of life" gives us the illusion that the other can be known within frameworks that render them safe,[4] and that we can know the others without mediation. But the relation between "seeing" and "saying" makes clear that our seeing inextricably depends on others, as what we see is known partly by how it can be shared. Put in different terms, the use of the language of "vision" is my attempt to reformulate Aristotle's *phronesis* and Aquinas' "prudence" in a manner that illustrates how inadequate it is to understand those concepts as "points of decision."

Furthermore, the skill required to see involves the virtues, since our vision is dependent on our character; for without the virtues, practical reason is little more than what Aristotle characterized as "cleverness."[5] I do not think, however, that any one set of virtues or hierarchy of virtues is sufficient to detail the form of life commensurate with Christian convictions. There is an order to the virtues but the order is more that of a particular narrative than of a "total vision of life." Indeed my analysis of the significance of character for the moral life is an attempt to account for moral continuity in a manner that avoids the assumption that such continuity can only be grounded in a "single unified orientation or theme"[6] or in "rationality" itself.

While vision is schooled by language and virtue, our ability to see is finally related to a community in which language and virtue alike

---

4. Those familiar with the philosophical essays and novels of Ms. Murdoch will recognize how much I owe to her for these points. For a further development, see Hauerwas, *Vision and Virtue*. It is hard for me to understand how Professor Robbins was able to ignore entirely Ms. Murdoch's and my analysis of how "total visions of life," whether in the form of metaphysics, *Weltungschauung*, or personal fantasy, can distort our ability to see. In this respect, my account of ethics is, like Aristotle's, anti-metaphysical (on this point, see Gadamer, *Truth and* Method, 278–79). However, unlike many contemporary philosophical ethicists, I do not assume that this means that ethics most thereby be "autonomous."

5. Aristotle, *Nicomachean Ethics* 1144a24–36.

6. For those interested, there is an extended analysis of moral agents with pluralistic or chaotic life plans, for which Mr. Robbins alleges I cannot account, in *Character and the Christian Life*, 117–28.

are nourished and sustained; for finally seeing must always involve the seeing of others, not as we want others to be, but as they are. But such a seeing is painful in the measure that it requires us to break with convention and our new neurotic self-infatuation, both of which only reinforce our inveterate tendency to self-deception.[7] To see, therefore, requires others to stand over against us to say how we have got it wrong. Such "over againstness" is not gained only through argument, though it is important, but also through tradition and liturgy. Indeed, the very nature of moral argument is correlative to the kind of narratives that form the particular traditions, institutions, and liturgies of communities.

Put in this manner it should be clear that there is nothing about my use of vision that invites an orgy of subjectivistic claims about an individual's own perception. Nor is there any lessening of the importance of the need to be able to give reasons for what we do or refrain from doing. I am not satisfied, however, with the way the distinction between objectivity and subjectivity functions in relation to moral reasons, behavior, and argument. All important moral convictions are objective exactly because they exact such a subjective price—that is, they are necessarily self-involving. Because of this I try to avoid objective–subjective language and instead speak of the demand for truthfulness.

Moreover, most modern forms of moral philosophy simply failed to concern themselves with learning how the agent comes to "be" and "see." Such a claim needs to be modified in two respects. Certainly there are many moral philosophers that such a charge does not indict such as Murdoch, Hampshire, Anscombe, MacIntyre, Toulmin, and Williams. It should be clear that I have learned many of my criticisms of contemporary moral philosophy from them.

There are other ethical theories, such as Hare's, in which the agent has an important place. But if a person is going to be a *moral* agent in such accounts, he or she is involved only to the extent that the agent's perspective can be expressed in the language of "the moral point of view." It is not the virtues of courage, faithfulness, or honesty that form moral agents. For agents to be moral agents, these virtues, while perhaps helpful, can be understood only in terms of the "moral point of view"—a point of view that necessarily must be impersonal. In other words, in order to be moral, the agent of contemporary moral

7. For an extended analysis of self-deception, see Burrell and Hauerwas "From System to Story."

philosophy is necessarily alienated from his or her convictions about themselves and the world.[8] Such convictions may be psychologically interesting but they are only contingently related to "morality" as the latter is fundamentally a form of "rationality."

I think some sense can be made out of these accounts of "morality" if they are freed from the theory that grips them. For there is an aspect of our moral activity that good societies exhibit, namely, that certain things should be required of all people irrespective of why they do what they do. The reason I found Strawson's distinction between lower and higher morality helpful is that it embodies more this sense of "morality"—better than the more theory-laden forms, which tend to associate basic morality with the "institution of morality."

However, I would not deny that the distinction between basic and higher morality can be misleading, as my own qualifications of the distinction suggest. Perhaps a more fruitful way of developing this point is MacIntyre's argument that all societies necessarily involve virtues like truthfulness, justice, and courage. Various societies will embody or acknowledge these goods in different ways, but this only witnesses to their unavoidability. However these ever-present virtues are never sufficient to constitute a morality—an actual form of life that is sufficient to guide our lives and set the boundaries of moral argument.[9] For these virtues require display through narratives that form a culture's sense of what is important and significant.

It is simply absurd therefore to claim that the difference between a Christian and a polytheistic society would not constitute a difference in the form of their morality. Only a studied blindness brought on by uncritical adherence to a theory would encourage one to claim that. Of course, some of the things people do in a Christian society and a polytheistic society might look the same and they might even discover areas of agreement for cooperation, but this is not a sufficient basis to claim that they share the same "morality." Such a claim could be sustained only if what people do is abstractly and artificially divorced from why they do what they do, i.e., what kind of agents they think themselves to be in doing what they do. For example, though both Christians and

8. Cf. B. Williams, *Morality*, for a more detailed exposition and analysis of this point.

9. Cf. MacIntyre, "How Virtues Become Vices"; and Hauerwas, *Character and the Christian Life.*

polytheists may have a "respect for the idea of law" (although I doubt they would mean the same thing by that), the reasons for that respect would make a difference in the agents that would defeat any attempt to claim that they are really sharing the same "morality."

Of course, my critic may well claim that even if this argument is correct I have lost the war by winning the battle, as this only shows that I cannot, as he argues, avoid a vicious relativism. However, I think it is clear from the above that there's nothing in my analysis of the significance of vision to suggest that persons are accountable "only for what their vision calls for of them." Moreover, it is important to note that Professor Robbins's own understanding of morality cannot defeat a morally sophisticated Charles Manson. For as Hare himself has demonstrated, the universalizability requirement, the purpose of which is to rule out first-person justifications, cannot defeat the moral fanatic.[10] There is no reason to think that Charles Manson with the aid of even a mediocre graduate student in philosophical ethics could not learn to state his position in a morally unassailable manner for those committed to the validity of some account of the "moral point of view" along the lines Professor Robbins suggests.

As I suggested at the beginning, I do not think there is nor does there need to be a moral argument against the moral skeptic or relativist. Rather, following the suggestion of Bernard Williams, I am content to challenge the relativist or skeptic to try to live out the implications of his or her position. After all, Aristotle reminded us that practical arguments may be best in practical discipline. It is a hard and demanding task to be a consistent relativist, as Williams argues such folk must school themselves to be free of care or regret.[11] I am willing to entertain the possibility that there may be such among us, but I do not think we will understand much about the nature of morality if we assume that such people have made a logical rather than a human mistake.[12]

10. Hare, *Freedom and Reason*, 157–85.

11. B. Williams, *Morality*, 10–11.

12. For a similar argument, see Ryle, "On Forgetting," who argues that to appreciate the difference between right and wrong does not require in the first instance an intellectual skill, but "and inculcated caring, the habit of taking certain sort of things seriously" (156). If we are asked why is it we should care, the only responses is to point out that in fact we do care and that it is hard to see how we can be people without caring.

The principle of universalizability as *the* hallmark of moral rationality is simply not up to doing the work that some moral philosophers and theologians wish it to do. For some, I suspect the principle has been adopted with such fervor for other than theoretical reasons as it provides the means for alienated Christians who find themselves with degrees in theology to be able to claim to be ethicists without being theologians. But the more serious issue is that the concentration on this aspect of moral reflection has failed to supply us with the categories that we need to assess properly what it means to have a Charles Manson in our midst. For the problem Manson raises is not the problem of skepticism or relativism but the problem of evil and its power.

In that respect I have tried to suggest that we must recover the narrative character of moral rationality—for the truthfulness appropriate to our moral behavior is the truthfulness that comes from being formed by true stories. In Gadamer's language, we must recognize the indispensability of tradition and authority for moral truthfulness.[13] While it is impossible to state the conditions of truthfulness separate from their narrative context, I have argued that any narrative that can rightly commend our allegiance must: (1) have the power to release us from destructive alternatives; (2) provide ways of seeing through concurrent distortions; (3) give us room to keep us from having to resort to violence; and (4) embody a sense of the tragic that enables us to see how meaning can transcend power.[14]

Such criteria do not provide grounds for claiming that only one narrative tradition is true as opposed to all others. However, they at least establish a basis for saying how one tradition might inform another both of its limits and possibilities. In this respect, my position involves what McClendon and Smith have happily called "soft-perspectivism."[15]

I have not been able to say anything about those matters that I take to be central to my work, namely, my understanding of the convictions that form and give direction to Christian existence. I think this is unfortunate because I agree with Bernard Williams that most of the problems of Christian ethics have little to do with issues raised by the problematic claims of morality's inescapable purity, "but from religion's

13. Gadamer, *Truth and Method*, 243–53.

14. For a fuller analysis of these, see Burrell and Hauerwas, "From System to Story."

15. McClendon and Smith, *Convictions*, 6–7.

being incurably unintelligible."[16] If my work has a center, it has been the attempt to show that, if we are to see the world accurately, the claims of religious folk at least deserve attention as intelligible and significant. I have no doubt that I have made some mistakes along the way, but I will be satisfied if my work has at least helped direct our attention to the right set of problems.

16. B. Williams, *Morality,* 78.

Bibliography

Abraham, William. *Crossing the Threshold of Divine Revelation*. Grand Rapids: Eerdmans, 2006.

Agamben, Giorgio. *Remnants of Auschwitz: The Witness and the Archive*. Translated by Daniel Heller-Roazen. New York: Zone, 2002.

Angel-Ajane, Asale. "Expert Witness." In *Engaged Observers: Anthropology, Advocacy, and Activism*, edited by Victoria Sanford and Asale Angel-Ajane, 76–92. New Brunswick, NJ: Rutgers University Press, 2006.

Anidjar, Gil. *Semites: Race, Religion, Literature*. Stanford, CA: Stanford University Press, 2008.

Aquinas, Thomas. *On Evil*. Translated by Richard Regan. Oxford: Oxford University Press, 2003.

———. *Summa Theologica*. Translated by Fathers of the English Dominican Province. Allen, TX: Christian Classics, 1981.

Asad, Talal. *Formations of the Secular: Christianity, Islam, Modernity*. Stanford, CA: Stanford University Press, 2003.

———. *Genealogies of Religion: Discipline and Reasons of Power in Christianity and Islam*. Baltimore: Johns Hopkins University Press, 1993.

Augustine. *The City of God*. Translated by Henry Bettenson. New York: Penguin, 1997.

———. *Confessions*. Translated with an introduction by R. S. Pine-Coffin. Baltimore: Penguin, 1961.

———. *Confessions and Enchiridion*. Translated and edited by Albert Outler. Philadelphia: Westminster, 1955.

Ayres, Lewis. *Nicaea and Its Legacy: An Approach to Fourth-Century Trinitarian Theology*. New York: Oxford University Press, 2004.

Badiou, Alain. *Saint Paul: The Foundation of Universalism*. Translated by Ray Brassier. Stanford, CA: Stanford University Press, 2003.

Barber, Daniel. "Epistemological Violence, Christianity, and the Secular." In *The New Yoder*, edited by Peter Dula and Chris K. Huebner, 271–93. Eugene, OR: Cascade, 2010.

Barrois, Georges, translator. *The Fathers Speak: St. Basil the Great, St. Gregory of Nazianzus, St. Gregory of Nyssa*. Crestwood, NY: St. Vladimir's Seminary Press, 1986.

Barth, Karl. *Church Dogmatics*. Vol. III/3, *The Doctrine of Creation*. Translated by Geoffrey W. Bromiley and R. J. Ehrlich. Edinburgh: T. & T. Clark, 1960.

———. *Church Dogmatics*. Vol. IV/1. Translated by Geoffrey W. Bromiley. New York: Scribner's Sons, 1956.

Becker, Ernest. *The Structure of Evil*. New York: George Braziller, 1968.

Bethge, Eberhard. *Dietrich Bonhoeffer: A Biography*. Rev. ed. Translated by Eric Mosbacher. Minneapolis: Fortress, 2000.

Bialecki, Jon, Naomi Haynes, and Joel Robbins. "The Anthropology of Christianity." *Religion Compass* 2 (2008) 1139–58

Bockmuehl, Marcus. *Jewish Law in Gentile Churches: Halakhah and the Beginning of Christian Public Ethics*. Edinburgh: T. & T. Clark, 2000.

———. *Seeing the Word: Refocusing New Testament Study*. Grand Rapids: Baker, 2006.

Bonhoeffer, Dietrich. *Creation and Fall*. Translated by Douglas Bax. Minneapolis: Fortress, 1997.

———. *Dietrich Bonhoeffer's Prison Poems*. Translated and edited by Edwin Robertson. Grand Rapids: Zondervan, 2005.

———. *Letters and Papers From Prison*. Edited by Eberhard Bethge. New York: Touchstone, 1997.

———. *No Rusty Swords*. Translated by John Bowden. Edited and introduced by Edwin Robertson. New York: Harper & Row, 1956.

———. *Sanctorum Communio: A Theological Study of the Sociology of the Church*. Translated by Reinhardt Krauss and Nancy Lukens. Minneapolis: Fortress, 1998.

———. *A Testament to Freedom: The Essential Writings of Dietrich Bonhoeffer*. Edited by Geffrey Kelly and F. Burton Nelson. San Francisco: HarperSanFransciso, 1990.

Boyarin, Daniel. "Neither Greek nor Jew." *Bookforum* April/May 2006. Online: http://www.bookforum.com/archive/apr_06/boyarin.html.

Brock, Brian. "Bonhoeffer and the Bible in Christian Ethics: Psalm 119, the Mandates, and Ethics as a 'May.'" *Studies in Christian Ethics* 18:3 (2005) 28–29.

Burrell, David, and Stanley Hauerwas, "From System to Story: An Alternative Pattern for Rationality in Ethics." In *Knowledge, Value and a Belief*, vol. 2, edited by H. Tristam Engelhardt and Faniel Callahan, 111–52. Hastings-on-Husdon: Institute of Society, Ethics, and the Life Sciences.

———. "Self-Deception and Autobiography: Theological and Ethical Teflection on Speer's *Inside the Third Reich*." *Journal of Religious Ethics* 2 (1974) 99–118.

Cahill, Lisa Sowell. *Sex, Gender and Christian Ethics*. Cambridge: Cambridge University Press, 1996.

Cannell, Fanella. *The Anthropology of Christianity*. Durham, NC: Duke University Press, 2006.

Carter, Warren. *Matthew and the Margins: A Sociopolitical and Religious Reading*. Maryknoll, NY: Orbis, 2003.

Cavanaugh, William T. *Theopolitical Imagination: Discovering the Liturgy as a Political Act in an Age of Global Consumerism*. London: T. & T. Clark, 2002.

Cavell, Stanley. *The Claim of Reason: Wittgenstein, Skepticism, Morality, and Tragedy*. Oxford: Oxford University Press, 1999.

———. "Forward." In *Life and Words: Violence and the Descent into the Ordinary*, by Veena Das, ix–xiv. Berkeley: University of California Press, 2007.

———. *Little Did I Know: Excerpts from Memory*. Stanford, CA: Stanford University Press, 2010.

Chouraqui, Andre. "The Psalms." *Liturgy O.C.S.O.* 29 (1995) 119–20.

Churchill, John. "Wonder and the End of Explanation: Wittgenstein and Religious Sensibility." *Philosophical Investigations* 17 (1994) 388–416.

Coleman, Simon. *The Globalisation of Charismatic Christianity: Spreading the Gospel of Prosperity* Cambridge: Cambridge University Press, 2000.

Collier, Charles Mayo. "A Nonviolent Augustinianism?: History and Politics in the Theologies of St. Augustine and John Howard Yoder." PhD diss., Duke University, 2008.

Conzelmann, Hans. *Acts of the Apostles*. Philadelphia: Fortress, 1987.

———. *Theology of St. Luke*. New York: Harper and Row, 1961.

Curran, Charles. *Catholic Social Teaching: 1891-Present: A Historical, Theological and Ethical Analysis*. Washington, DC: Georgetown University Press, 2002.

Dallaire, Roméo. *Shake Hands with the Devil: The Failure of Humanity in Rwanda*. New York: Carol & Graf, 2004.

Das, Veena. "Trauma and Testimony: Implications for Political Community." *Anthropological Theory* 3 (2003) 293–307

Davidson, Arnold I. "Spiritual Exercises and Ancient Philosophy: An Introduction to Pierre Hadot." *Critical Inquiry* 16 (Spring 1990) 475–82.

Davis, Ellen, and Richard Hays, editors. *The Art of Reading Scripture*. Grand Rapids: Eerdmans, 2003.

Dawson, David. *Christian Figural Reading and the Fashioning of Identity*. Berkeley: University of California Press, 2002.

DeHart, Paul. *The Trial of the Witnesses: The Rise and Decline of Postliberal Theology*. Challenges in Contemporary Theology. Oxford: Blackwell, 2006.

Delbanco, Andrew. *The Death of Satan: How Americans Have Lost the Sense of Evil*. New York: Farrar, Straus, and Giroux, 1995.

Diefenthaler, Jon. *H. Richard Niebuhr: A Lifetime of Reflections on the Church and the World*. Macon, GA: Mercer University Press, 1986.

Dodaro, Robert. *Christ and the Just Society in the Thought of Augustine*. Cambridge: Cambridge University Press, 2004.

Dumm, Thomas. *Loneliness as a Way of Life*. Cambridge, MA: Harvard University Press, 2008.

Eagleton, Terry. *After Theory*. New York: Basic, 2003.

Edwards, James. *The Plain Sense of Things: The Fate of Religion in an Age of Normal Nihilism*. University Park: Pennsylvania State University Press, 1997.

Engelke, Matthew. *A Problem of Presence: Beyond Scripture in an African Church*. Berkeley: University of California Press, 2007.

Evans, G. R. *Augustine on Evil*. Cambridge: Cambridge University Press, 1994.

Fairlie, Henry. *The Seven Deadly Sins Today*. Notre Dame, IN: University of Notre Dame Press, 1978.

Farrer, Austin. *Love Almighty and Ills Unlimited*. London: Collins, 1966.

Fassin, Didier. "The Humanitarian Politics of Testimony: Subjectification Through Trauma in the Israeli-Palestinian Conflict." *Cultural Anthropology* 23 (2008) 531–58

Fassin, Didier, and Richard Rechtman. *The Empire of Trauma: An Inquiry into the Condition of Victimhood*. Princeton, NJ: Princeton University Press, 2009.

Frei, Hans. "H. Richard Niebuhr on History, Church, and Nation." In *The Legacy of H. Richard Niebuhr*, edited by Ronald Thieman, 1–23. Minneapolis: Fortress, 1991.

———. "Niebuhr's Theological Background." In *Faith and Ethics: The Theology of H. Richard Niebuhr*, edited by Paul Ramsey, 9–118. New York: Harper, 1957.

———. *Theology and Narrative*. Edited by George Hunsinger and William Placher. New York: Oxford University Press, 1993.

Gadamer, Hans-Georg. *Truth and Method*. Translation edited by Garrett Barden and John Cumming. New York: Seabury, 1975.

Gaita, Raimond. *A Common Humanity: Thinking about Love and Truth and Justice*. London: Routledge, 2000.

———. *Good and Evil: An Absolute Conception*. London: MacMillan, 1991.

———. *The Philosopher's Dog*. London: Routledge, 2002.

———. *Romulus, My Father*. London: Headline Review, 1999.

Glover, Jonathan. *Humanity: A Moral History of the Twentieth Century*. New Haven, CT: Yale University Press, 2000.

Greene, Graham. *The Power and the Glory*. Introduction by John Updike. New York: Penguin, 1990.

Greer, Rowan. *Fear of Freedom: A Study of Miracles in the Roman Imperial Church* University Park: Pennsylvania State University Press, 1989.

Gregory, Eric. *Politics and the Order of Love: An Augustinian Ethic of Democratic Citizenship*. Chicago: University of Chicago Press, 2008.

Gremillion, Joseph, editor. *The Gospel of Peace and Justice: Catholic Social Teaching Since Pope John*. Maryknoll, NY: Orbis, 1976.

Griffiths, Paul. *Intellectual Appetite: A Theological Grammar*. Washington, DC: Catholic University Press, 2009.

Gruchy, John de. *Daring, Trusting Spirit: Bonhoeffer's Friend Eberhard Bethge*. Minneapolis: Fortress, 2005.

Gustafson, James. "Preface: An Appreciative Interpretation" In *Christ and Culture*, xiii–xxxv. San Francisco: HarperSanFrancisco, 2001.

Hacking, Ian. *The Taming of Chance*. Cambridge: Cambridge University Press, 1990.

Hadot, Pierre. "Forms of Life and Forms of Discourse in Ancient Philosophy." In *Philosophy as a Way of Life*, by Pierre Hadot, translated by Michael Chase, 49–70. Oxford: Blackwell, 1995.

———. *The Present Alone Is Our Happiness: Conversations with Jeannie Carlier and Arnold I. Davidson*. Translated by Marc Djaballah. Stanford, CA: Stanford University Press, 2009.

———. "Wittgenstein, philosophe du langage II." *Critique* 150 (1959) 973.

Hanby, Michael. *Augustine and Modernity*. Radical Orthodoxy. London: Routledge, 2003.

Hansen, Ron. *Exiles*. New York: Farrar, Straus, and Giroux, 2008.

Harding, Susan. "Representing Fundamentalism: The Problem of the Repugnant Cultural Other." *Social Research* 58 (1991) 373–93.

Hare, R. M. *Freedom and Reason*. New York: Galaxy, 1965.

Harink, Douglas. *Paul among the Postliberals: Pauline Theology beyond Christendom and Modernity*. Grand Rapids: Brazos, 2003.

Hauerwas, Stanley. *Against the Nations: War and Survival in a Liberal Society*. Notre Dame, IN: University of Notre Dame Press, 1992.

———. *A Better Hope: Resources for a Church Confronting Capitalism, Democracy, and Postmodernity*. Grand Rapids: Brazos, 2000.

———. *Character and the Christian Life: A Study in Theological Ethics*. San Antonio: University of Trinity Press, 1975.

———. *Cross-Shattered Christ: Meditations on the Seven Last Words*. Grand Rapids: Brazos, 2004.

———. *Dispatches from the Front: Theological Engagements with the Secular*. Durham, NC: Duke University Press, 1994.

———. *Hannah's Child: A Theologians Memoir*. Grand Rapids: Eerdmans, 2010.

———. *Matthew: A Theological Commentary on the Bible*. Grand Rapids: Brazos, 2006.

———. *Naming the Silences: God, Medicine, and the Problem of Suffering*. Grand Rapids: Eerdmans, 1990.

———. "Natural Law, Tragedy, and Theological Ethics." *American Journal of Jurisprudence* 20 (1975) 1–19.

———. *The Peaceable Kingdom: A Primer in Christian Ethics*. Notre Dame, IN: University of Notre Dame Press, 1983.

———. *Performing the Faith: Bonhoeffer and the Practice of Nonviolence*. Grand Rapids: Brazos, 2004.

———. *Sanctify Them in the Truth: Holiness Exemplified*. Nashville: Abingdon, 1998.

———. *The State of the University: Academic Knowledges and the Knowledge of God*. Oxford: Blackwell, 2007.

———. *Suffering Presence: Theological Reflections on Medicine, the Mentally Handicapped, and the Church*. Notre Dame, IN: University of Notre Dame Press, 1986.

———. *Truthfulness and Tragedy: Further Investigations into Christian Ethics*. Notre Dame, IN: University of Notre Dame Press, 1977.

———. *Vision and Virtue: Essays in Christian Ethical Reflection*. South Bend, IN: Fides, 1974.

———. *With the Grain of the Universe: The Church's Witness and Natural Theology*. Grand Rapids: Brazos, 2001.

Hauerwas, Stanley, and Romand Coles. *Christianity, Democracy, and the Radical Ordinary: Conversations between a Radical Democrat and a Christian*. Theopolitical Visions. Eugene, OR: Cascade, 2008.

Hays, Richard. *The Conversion of the Imagination: Paul as Interpreter of Israel's Scripture*. Grand Rapids: Eerdmans, 2005.

———. *The Moral Vision of the New Testament: Community, Cross, New Creation; A Contemporary Introduction to New Testament Ethics*. San Francisco: Harper Collins, 1996.

———. "Reading Scripture in the Light of the Resurrection." In *The Art of Reading Scripture*, edited by Ellen Davis and Richard Hays, 216–38. Grand Rapids: Eerdmans, 2003.

———. "Turning the World Upside Down: Israel's Scripture in Luke-Acts." Lecture delivered at the MacLaurin Institute, Minnesota, April 12, 2007. Online: http://www.marshillstudents.net/mp3_group.php?type=MacLaurin+Campus+Lectures.

Hittinger, Russell. *The First Grace: Rediscovering the Natural Law in a Post-Christian World*. Wilmington, DE: ISI, 2003.

———. "Social Roles and Ruling Virtues in Catholic Social Doctrine." *Annales Theologici* 16 (2002) 295–318.

Hollenbach, David. *Claims in Conflict: Retrieving and Renewing the Catholic Human Rights Tradition*. New York: Paulist, 1999.

Hovey, Craig. *To Share in the Body: A Theology of Martyrdom for Today's Church*.Grand Rapids: Brazos, 2008.

Howard, Thomas. *Protestant Theology and the Making of the Modern German University*. New York: Oxford University Press, 2006.

Howell, Brian. "The Repugnant Cultural Other Speaks Back: Christian Identity as Ethnographic Standpoint." *Anthropological Theory* 7:4 (2007) 371–91.

Huebner, Chris K. *A Precarious Peace: Yoderian Explorations on Theology, Knowledge, and Identity*. Scottdale, PA: Herald, 2006.

Jenson, Robert. "Nihilism: Sin, Death, and the Devil." *Newsletter: Report from the Center for Catholic and Evangelical Theology* (Summer 1998) 4.

Johnson, Kelly. *The Fear of Beggars: Stewardship and Poverty in Christian Ethics*. Eerdmans Ekklesia. Grand Rapids: Eerdmans, 2007.

Johnson, Luke Timothy. *The Writings of the New Testament: An Interpretation*. Minneapolis: Fortress, 1999.

Kant, Immanuel. *Religion within the Limits of Reason Alone*. Translated by Theodore Greene and Hoyt Hudson. New York: Harper, 1960.

Kaplan, Benjamin J. *Divided by Faith: Religious Conflict and the Practice of Toleration in Early Modern Europe*. Cambridge, MA: Harvard University Press, 2007.

Keane, Webb. *Christian Moderns: Freedom and Fetish in the Mission Encounter*. Berkeley, CA: University of California Press, 2007.

Kelly, Geffrey, and Burton Nelson. *The Cost of Moral Leadership: The Spirituality of Dietrich Bonhoeffer*. Grand Rapids: Eerdmans, 2003.

Kenney, John Peter. *The Mysticism of Saint Augustine: Reading the Confessions*.New York: Routledge, 2005.

Kent, Bonnie. "Habits and Virtues." In *Aquinas's Summa Theologiae: Critical Essays*, edited by Brian Davies, 223–45. New York: Rowan & Littlefield, 2006.

Kerr, Fergus. *"Work on Oneself": Wittgenstein's Philosophical Psychology*. Washington, DC: Catholic University of America Press: 2008.

Kleinberg, Aviad. *Seven Deadly Sins: A Very Partial List*. Cambridge, MA: Harvard University Press, 2008.

Koonz, Claudia. *The Nazi Conscience* Cambridge, MA: Harvard University Press, 2003.

Langford, Thomas. *Practical Divinity: Theology in the Wesleyan Tradition*. Nashville: Abingdon, 1983.

Langland, William. *Piers Plowman*. Translated by George Economou. Philadelphia: University of Pennsylvania Press, 1996.

Leveson, Jon D. *The Hebrew Bible, the Old Testament, and Historical Criticism*. Louisville: Westminster John Knox, 1993.

Lilla, Mark. *The Stillborn God: Religion, Politics and the Modern West*. New York: Vintage, 2008.

Lindbeck, George, *The Church in a Postliberal Age*. Grand Rapids: Eerdmans, 2003.

Lischer, Richard. *The End of Words: The Language of Reconciliation in a Culture of Violence*. Grand Rapids: Eerdmans, 2005.

Lubac, Henri de. *The Drama of Atheist Humanism*. San Francisco: Ignatius, 1995.

Lugg, Andrew. *Wittgenstein's Investigations, 1–133: A Guide and Interpretation*. London: Routledge, 2000.

Luther, Martin. *Faith and Freedom: An Invitation to the Writings of Martin Luther*. Edited by John Thornton and Susan Varenne. New York: Vintage, 2002.

MacIntyre, Alasdair. *Dependent Rational Animals: Why Human Beings Need the Virtues.* Chicago: Open Court, 1999.

———. *Edith Stein: A Philosophical Prologue, 1913–1922.* Lanham, MD: Rowman & Littlefield, 2006.

———. "How Moral Agents Became Ghosts, or, Why the History of Ethics Diverged from that of the Philosophy of Mind. *Synthese* 53 (1982) 295–312.

———. "How Virtues Become Vices: Values, Medicine and Social Context." In *Evaluation and Explanation in the Biological* Sciences, edited by H. Tristam Englehardt and Stuart Spicker, 97–111. Dordrecht: Reidel, 1975.

———. *Whose Justice? Which Rationality?* Notre Dame, IN: University of Notre Dame Press, 1988.

Mahmood, Saba. "Secularism, Hermeneutics, and Empire: The Politics of Islamic Reformation." *Public Culture* 18 (2006) 323–47

Mandeville, Bernard. *The Fable of the Bees and Other Writings.* Edited by E. J. Hundrert. Indianapolis: Hackett, 1997.

Mariniello, Silvrestra. "*St. Paul*: The Unmade Movie." *Cinémas: Journal of Film Studies* 9:2–3 (1999) 67–84

Maritain, Jacques. *St. Thomas Aquinas and the Problem of Evil.* Milwaukee: Marquette University Press, 1942.

Mastnak, Tomaz. *Crusading Peace: Christendom, the Muslim World, and Western Political Order.* Berkeley: University of California Press, 2002.

Mathewes, Charles. *Evil and the Augustinian Tradition.* Cambridge: Cambridge University Press, 2001.

May, William. *A Catalogue of Sins: A Contemporary Examination of Christian Conscience.* New York: Holt, Rinehart, and Winston, 1967.

McCabe, Herbert. *God Matters.* Springfield, IL: Templegate, 1991.

———. *Law, Love, and Language.* London: Continuum, 2003.

McCarthy, David Matzko. "Procreation, the Development of Peoples, and the Final Destiny of Humanity." *Communio* 26 (1999) 698–721.

McClendon, James, and James Smith. *Convictions: Diffusing Religious Relativism.* Notre Dame, IN: University of Notre Dame Press, 1975.

McCloskey, Deirdre. "Avarice, Prudence, and the Bourgeois Virtues." In *Having: Property and Possession in Religious and Social Life,* edited by William Schweiker and Charles Mathewes 312–36. Grand Rapids: Eerdmans, 2004.

Menand, Louis. *The Metaphysical Club: A Story of Ideas in America.* New York: Farrar, Straus, and Giroux, 2001.

Milbank, John. *The Suspended Middle: Henri de Lubac and the Debate Concerning the Supernatural.* Grand Rapids: Eerdmans, 2005.

———. *Theology and Social Theory: Beyond Secular Reason.* Oxford: Blackwell, 1990.

Mosès, Stéphane. *The Angel of History: Rosenzweig, Benjamin, Scholem.* Stanford, CA: Stanford University Press, 2009.

Murdoch, Iris. *The Sovereignty of Good.* New York: Shocken, 1971.

Neiman, Susan. *Evil in Modern Thought: An Alternative History of Philosophy.* Princeton, NJ: Princeton University Press, 2002.

Newhauser, Richard. "*Avaritia* and *Paupertas*: On the Place of the Early Franciscans in the History of Avarice." In *In the Garden of Evil: The Vices and Culture in the Middle Ages,* edited by Richard Newhauser, 324–48. Toronto: Pontifical Institute of Medieval Studies, 2005.

Bibliography

————. *The Early History of Greed: The Sin of Avarice in Early Medieval Thought and Literature*.Cambridge: Cambridge University Press, 2000.

Niebuhr, H. Richard. "Back to Benedict?" *Christian Century* 42 (July 2, 1925) 860–61.

————. *Christ and Culture*. With a new Preface by James Gustafson. San Francisco: HarperSanFrancisco, 2001.

————. *The Church against the World*. With Wilhelm Pauck and Francis Miller. New York: Willett Clark, 1935.

————. *Ernst Troeltsch's Philosophy of Religion*. New Haven, CT: Yale University Press, 1924.

————. *Faith on Earth: An Inquiry into the Structure of Human Faith*. Edited by Richard Reinhold Niebuhr. New Haven, CT: Yale University Press, 1989.

————. "The Grace of Doing Nothing." In *War in the Twentieth Century*, edited by Richard Miller, 6–11. Louisville: Westminster John Knox 1992.

————. "Introduction." In *The Religious Situation*, by Paul Tillich, translated by H. Richard Niebuhr. New York: Meridian, 1956.

————. *The Kingdom of God in America*. New York: Harper, 1959.

————. *The Meaning of Revelation*. New York: Harper, 1970.

————. *The Purpose of the Church and Its Ministry*. New York: Harper, 1956.

————. *Radical Monotheism and Western Culture, with Supplementary Essays*. Louisville: Westminster John Knox, 1993.

————. "Richard Niebuhr on History, Church, and Nation." In *The Legacy of H. Richard Niebuhr*, edited by Ronald Thiemann, 1–24. Minneapolis: Fortress, 1991.

————. *The Responsible Self: An Essay in Christian Moral Philosophy*. New York: Harper, 1978.

————. *The Social Sources of Denominationalism*. New York: New American Library, 1972.

————. *Theology, History, and Culture*. Edited by William Stacy Johnson. New Haven, CT: Yale University Press, 1996.

————. "War as Crucifixion." In *War in the Twentieth Century*, edited by Richard Miller, 63–70. Louisville: Westminster John Knox, 1992.

————. "War as the Judgment of God." In *War in the Twentieth Century*, edited by Richard Miller, 47–55. Louisville: Westminster John Knox, 1992.

O'Brien, David J., and Thomas Shannon. *Catholic Social Thought: The Documentary Heritage*. Maryknoll, NY: Orbis, 1992.

Ochs, Peter. "Morning Prayer as Redemptive Thinking." In *Liturgy, Time, and the Politics of Redemption*, edited by Randi Rashkover and C. C. Pecknold, 50–90. Grand Rapids: Eerdmans, 2006.

————. "Philosophic Warrants for Scriptural Reasoning." *Modern Theology* 22 (2005) 465–82.

Outler, Albert. "An Introductory Comment." In *The Works of John Wesley*, 3:45–46. Grand Rapids: Baker, 1978.

Parker, David. *The Self in Moral Space: Life Narrative and the Good*. Ithaca, NY: Cornell University Press, 2007.

Pecknold, C. C., and David Ford, editors. *The Promise of Scriptural Reasoning*. Directions in Modern Theology. Malden, MA: Blackwell, 2006.

Pieper, Josef. *Prudence*. Translated by R. and C. Winston. New York: Pantheon, 1959.

Pinches, Charles. *Theology and Action: After Theory in Christian Ethics*. Grand Rapids: Eerdmans, 2002.

Pinckaers, Servais. *Sources of Christian Ethics.* Translated by Mary Thomas Noble. Washington, DC: Catholic University of American Press, 1995.

———. "The Sources of the Ethics of St. Thomas Aquinas." In *The Ethics of Aquinas*, edited by Stephen J. Pope, 17–29. Washington, DC: Georgetown University Press, 2002.

"Pledge follows Bush to Church; Chaplain Adds Salute to Liturgy." *The Washington Times*, July 8, 2002.

Porter, Jean. *Natural and Law: Proclaiming the Tradition for Christian Ethics.* Grand Rapids: Eerdmans, 1999.

Power, Samantha. "A Hero of Our Time." *New York Review of Books*, November 18, 2004, 8–11.

Putnam, Hillary. *Jewish Philosophy as a Guide to Life: Rosenzweig, Buber, Levinas, Wittgenstein.* Bloomington, IN: Indiana University Press, 2004.

Putnam, Hillary. *Renewing Philosophy.* Cambridge, MA: Harvard University Press, 1992.

Ramsey, Paul. *The Just War: Force and Political Responsibility.* Foreword by Stanley Hauerwas. New York: Rowan & Littlefield, 2002.

———. *The Patient as Person: Explorations in Medical Ethics.* New Haven, CT: Yale University Press, 1970.

Reichberg, Gregory. "Beyond Privation: Moral Evil in Aquinas' *De Malvo.*" *Review of Metaphysics* 55 (2002) 751–84.

Reinders, Hans. *Receiving the Gift of Friendship: Profound Disability, Theological Anthropology, and Ethics.* Grand Rapids: Eerdmans, 2008.

Reno, R. R. "Apostolic Legitimacy and Apostolic Vitality." In *The Center for Catholic and Evangelical Theology Report*, Fall 2006, 6.

———. *Genesis.* Brazos Theological Commentary on the Bible. Grand Rapids: Brazos, 2010.

———. "Series Preface." In *Matthew: A Theological Commentary on the Bible*, by Stanley Hauerwas. Grand Rapids: Brazos, 2006.

Rhonheimer, Martin. *Natural Law and Practical Reason: A Thomist View of Moral Autonomy.* New York: Fordham University Press, 2000.

Rhonheimer, Martin. *The Perspective of the Acting Person: Essays in the Renewal of Thomistic Moral Philosophy.* Edited with an introduction by William F. Murphey Jr. Washington, DC: Catholic University of America Press, 2008.

Robbins, Joel. "Anthropology and Theology: An Awkward Relationship?" *Anthropological Quarterly* 79 (2006) 286–94.

———. "What Is a Christian? Notes Toward an Anthropology of Christianity." *Religion* 33:3 (2004) 191–99.

Rogers, Eugene. "How the Virtues of an Interpreter Presuppose and Perfect Hermeneutics: The Case of Thomas Aquinas." *Journal of Religion* 76 (1996) 64–81.

Rosenzweig, Franz. *Understanding the Sick and the Healthy: A View of World, Man, and God.* Translated by Nahum Glatzer. Cambridge, MA: Harvard University Press, 1999.

Rosner, Brian. *Greed and Idolatry: The Origin and Meaning of a Pauline Metaphor.* Grand Rapids: Eerdmans, 2007.

Rowe, C. Kavin. *Early Narrative Christology: The Lord in the Gospel of Luke.* Berlin: Walter de Gruyter, 2006.

Bibliography

Rowell, Geoffrey, Rowan Williams, and Kevin Stevenson. *Love's Redeeming Work: The Anglican Quest for Holiness*. Oxford: Oxford University Press, 2001.

Rubenstein, Mary-Jane. *Strange Wonder: The Closure of Metaphysics and the Opening of Awe*. New York: Columbia University Press, 2009.

Ryle, Gilbert. "On Forgetting the Difference between Right and Wrong." In *Essays in Moral Philosophy*, edited by A. I. Melden, 147–59. Seattle: University of Washington Press, 1958.

Santner, Eric L. *On the Psychotheology of Everyday Life: Reflections on Freud and Rosenzweig*. Chicago: University of Chicago Press, 2001.

Scheper-Hughes, Nancy. *Death without Weeping: The Violence of Everyday Life in Brazil*. Berkeley: University of California Press, 1992.

Schockenhoff, Eberhard. *Bonum Hominis: Die anthropologischen und theologischen Grundlagen der Tungendethik des Thomas von Aquin*. Mainz: Matthias-Grunewald, 1987.

Schuck, Michael. *That They Be One: The Social Teaching of the Papal Encyclicals, 1740–1989*. Washington, DC: Georgetown University Press, 1991.

Schweiker, William. "Comment." *Journal of Religious Ethics* 34:4 (2006).

———. "Reconsidering Greed." In *Having: Property and Possession in Religious and Social Life*, edited by William Schweiker and Charles Mathewes, 249–311. Grand Rapids: Eerdmans, 2004.

Sebald, W. G. *Austerlitz*. Translated by Anthea Bell. New York: Random House, 2001.

Sherwin, Michael, O.P. *By Knowledge and By Love: Charity and Knowledge in the Moral Theology of St. Thomas Aquinas* Washington, DC: Catholic University of America Press, 2005.

Smith, Daniel. "A Life of Pure Immanence: Deleuze's Critique et Clinique Project." In *Essays Critical and Clinical*, by Gilles Deleuze, translated by Daniel W. Smith and Michael A. Greco, xi–liii. Minneapolis: University of Minnesota Press, 1997.

Straw, Carole. "Gregory, Cassian, and the Cardinal Vices." In *In the Garden of Evil: The Vices and Culture in the Middle Ages*, 35–58. Toronto: Pontifical Institute of Medieval Studies, 2005.

Surin, Kenneth. *Theology and the Problem of Evil*. Oxford: Blackwell, 1986.

Taylor, Charles. *A Secular Age*. Cambridge, MA: Harvard University Press, 2007.

———. *Sources of the Self: The Making of Modern Identity*. Cambridge, MA: Harvard University Press, 1989.

———. *Varieties of Religion Today: William James Revisited*. Cambridge, MA: Harvard University Press, 2002.

Tilley, Terrence. *The Evils of Theodicy*. 1991. Reprint, Eugene, OR: Wipf & Stock, 2000.

Troeltsch, Ernst. *The Absoluteness of Christianity and the History of Religions*. Translated by David Reid. Louisville: Westminster John Knox, 2005.

Vanhoozer, Kevin. *The Drama of Doctrine: A Canonical-Linguistic Approach to Christian Theology*. Louisville: Westminster John Knox, 2005.

Vanier, Jean. *From Brokenness to Community* New York: Paulist, 1992.

———. *Made for Happiness: Discovering the Meaning of Life with Aristotle*. Translated by Kathryn Spink. London: Darton Longman & Todd, 2001.

Wadell, Paul J. *The Primacy of Love: An Introduction to the Ethics of Thomas Aquinas*. New York: Paulist, 1992.

Wallis, Jim. *Rediscovering Values: On Wall Street, Main Street, and Your Street*. New York: Simon & Schuster, 2010.

Walsh, Michael, and Brian Davies, editors. *Proclaiming Justice and Peace: Papal Documents from Rerum Novarum through Centesimus Annus.* Rev. ed. Eugene, OR: Wipf & Stock, 2001.

Webb, Lance. *Conquering the Seven Deadly Sins.* New York: Abingdon, 1955.

Wedemeyer-Weller, Maria von. "The Other Letters from Prison." In *Letters and Papers From Prison,* edited by Eberhard Bethge, 412. New York: Touchstone, 1997.

Weinberg, Steven. "Without God." *The New York Review* LV:14 (September 25, 2008) 76.

Wells, Samuel. *God's Companions: Reimaging Christian Ethics.* Oxford: Blackwell, 2006.

Werpehowski, William. *American Protestant Ethics and the Legacy of H. Richard Niebuhr.* Washington, DC: Georgetown University Press, 2002.

Wesley, John. *The Works of John Wesley.* 7 vols. Grand Rapids: Baker, 1978.

Wetzel, James. *Augustine and the Limits of Virtue.* Cambridge: Cambridge University Press, 1992.

———. "Labored Knowledge: Hauerwas on Augustine on Evil." Paper presented at "Speak No Evil: Moral Judgment in the Modern Age," in response to Stanley Hauerwas's paper, "Seeing Darkness, Hearing Silence: Augustine's Account of Evil," Duke University, Durham, NC, January 27–29, 2005.

Whitfield, Joshua. *Pilgrim Holiness: Martyrdom as Descriptive Witness.* Eugene, OR: Cascade, 2008.

Williams, A. N. *The Ground of Union: Deification in Aquinas and Palamas.* New York: Oxford University Press, 1999.

Williams, Bernard. *Morality: An Introduction to Ethics.* New York: Harper, 1972.

———. *Problems of the Self.* Cambridge: Cambridge University Press, 1973.

Williams, Rowan. *Christ on Trial: How the Gospel Unsettles Our Judgment.* Grand Rapids: Eerdmans, 2000.

———. "Politics and the Soul: A Reading of the *City of God.*" *Milltown Studies* 19:20 (1987) 55–72.

———. *Resurrection: Interpreting the Easter Gospel.* Cleveland: Pilgrim, 2004.

Willimon, William, and Stanley Hauerwas. *The Truth about God: The Ten Commandments and the Christian Life* Nashville: Abingdon, 1999.

Wittgenstein, Ludwig. *Culture and Value.* Translated by Peter Winch. Edited by G. H. von Wright. Chicago: University of Chicago Press, 1980.

———. *Philosophical Investigations.* Translated by G. E. M. Anscombe, P. M. S. Hacker, and Joachim Schulte. Oxford: Wiley-Blackwell, 2009.

Wright, John. *Telling God's Story: Narrative Preaching for Christian Formation.* Downers Grove, IL: InterVarsity, 2007.

Yoder, John Howard. *Christian Attitudes to War, Peace, and Revolution.* Edited by Theodore J. Koontz and Andy Alexis-Baker. Grand Rapids: Brazos, 2009.

———. "How H. Richard Niebuhr Reasoned: A Critique of *Christ and Culture.*" In *Authentic Transformation: A New Vision of Christ and Culture,* edited by Glen Stassen, D. M. Yeager, and John Howard Yoder, 31–89. Nashville: Abingdon: 1996.

———. *The Original Revolutios.* Scottdale, PA: Herald, 2003

———. *The Politics of Jesus: Vicit Agnus Noster.* 2nd ed. Grand Rapids: Eerdmans, 1995.

———. *The Royal Priesthood: Essays Ecclesiological and Ecumenical.* Edited by Michael G. Cartwright. Grand Rapids: Eerdmans, 1994.

———. *Preface to Theology: Christology and Theological Method.* Introduction by Stanley Hauerwas and Alex Sider. Grand Rapids: Brazos, 2002.

Index

317

Index

Lightning Source UK Ltd.
Milton Keynes UK
UKHW010717270223
417728UK00002B/324